Social Protest and Policy Change

Social Protest and Policy Change

*Ecology, Antinuclear, and Peace
Movements in Comparative Perspective*

Marco Giugni

ROWMAN & LITTLEFIELD PUBLISHERS, INC.
Lanham • Boulder • New York • Toronto • Oxford

ROWMAN & LITTLEFIELD PUBLISHERS, INC.

Published in the United States of America
by Rowman & Littlefield Publishers, Inc.
A wholly owned subsidary of The Rowman & Littlefield Publishing Group, Inc.
4501 Forbes Boulevard, Suite 200, Lanham, MD 20706
www.rowmanlittlefield.com

P.O. Box 317, Oxford OX2 9RU, UK

British Library Cataloguing in Publication Information Available

Library of Congress Cataloging-in-Publication Data

Giugni, Marco.
    Social protest and policy change : ecology, antinuclear, and peace movements
in comparative perspective / Marco Giugni.
        p.   cm.
    Includes bibliographical references (p.   ) and index.
    ISBN 0-7425-1826-4 (cloth : alk. paper) — ISBN 0-7425-1827-2 (pbk. : alk. paper)
        1. Social movements—Case studies.   2. Social policy—Case studies.   3. Antinuclear
movement—Cross-cultural studies.   4. Green movement—Cross-cultural studies.
5. Peace movements—Cross-cultural studies.   I. Title.

HM881.G53   2004
303.48'4—dc22   2003025314

Printed in the United States of America

⊗™ The paper used in this publication meets the minimum requirements of American
National Standard for Information Sciences—Permanence of Paper for Printed Library
Materials, ANSI/NISO Z39.48-1992.

For Claudia

Contents

Figures and Tables

Figures

Tables

Preface

When I began my journey into the outcomes of social movements, the so-called *new social movements* seemed at the time to have lost much of their mobilizing capacity across the Western world, which is curious considering that they have been one of the driving forces in contentious politics during the past three decades. In particular, ecology, antinuclear, and peace movements had seemed to decline: for the ecology movement, it had found its way into the political institutions; for the antinuclear movement, it had largely lost its main target and hence its raison d'être; and for the peace movement, it was no longer able to mobilize the popular masses as it did in the recent past. In other words, these three movements seemed to have come full circle, and they seemed to have completed an entire cycle of contention, one that began in the early 1970s and ended, as I erroneously thought at that time, in the early 1990s. This pushed me to inquire into the outcomes of that cycle of contention and in particular into the impact of those movements on public policy. After all, they each wanted to produce changes in existing policy with regard to their respective positions on environmental, nuclear, and military matters, although this is only one side of a broader range of goals, which includes social and cultural change as well. The alleged end of their "life cycle" seemed an apt time to conduct such an inquiry.

The new social movements, however, have resurrected much of the strength and popularity that they once enjoyed in the 1970s and 1980s. This can be seen not only in the revival of environmental and peace protests in various countries, including the United States, Italy, and Switzerland, but also in the emergence of a collective actor in the form of a movement that gathers these as well as others types of claims—namely, the so-called antiglobalization movement, which has entered the public space during the past few years. Furthermore, the protests against U.S. intervention in Iraq in 2002 have shown the strong potential of the peace movement. This revival and new shape of the new social movements gave me further stimulus to do research on the policy impact of ecology, antinuclear, and peace movements.

To do so, I took advantage of crucial external help. First of all, the research for this book would not have been possible without the financial support provided by the Swiss National Science Foundation through an advanced researcher fellowship that allowed me to spend three years abroad. The Schmidheiny Foundation (Geneva) also financed my research, which allowed me to update the dataset in the later stages of the project. In addition to the crucial financial support provided by these two institutions—and also by the University of Geneva, where I was based when I was not conducting field work abroad (and where I am currently based)—many people made my work easier. They are too numerous to be thanked individually, not least because my research has spanned over several years, but they all gave me valuable comments, criticisms, suggestions, and information that have proved crucial for achieving my study successfully. A big thanks, therefore, goes to all of them. Nevertheless, some people deserve special mention, starting with those who hosted me in their respective institutions during my stays in the United States and Italy and who are mentioned here in "order of appearance": Charles Tilly, who allowed me to use the material and intellectual resources of the Center for Studies of Social Change at the New School for Social Research (New York); Louise Tilly, who did the same when I went back to New York about two years later to complete my research on the case of the United States; Doug McAdam, who made my brief stay at the University of Arizona, Tucson, rich intellectually and even more joyful than the beautiful landscapes of the Sonora Desert had already made; and Donatella della Porta, who allowed me to conduct research at the University of Florence, a privileged standing point from both an intellectual and a culinary point of view.

A special thanks goes to Florence Passy, a colleague, friend, and still many other things, who has played a special role at various stages of this project. Not only did we discuss at length most of the materials included in this volume, but the book's main argument was formed directly as a result of these intense and fruitful discussions. In that sense, she almost is a coauthor. In addition, her continuous support and encouragement have proved decisive to achieving this project.

My warmest gratitude, however, goes perhaps to the thousands of people who have participated in the activities of the three movements that form the object of this study and that occurred during the three decades covered by this volume. Although I tried to avoid a normative position on the issues addressed in this book, and in spite of my apparently pessimistic conclusions, I do think that movements make a crucial contribution to a better world. The results of their challenges are not always easy to see, but they are certainly worth the effort, if only because they provide a model and example for the next generations of people who are not satisfied with how things are going.

Before we move on to the subject matter, allow me to dedicate this book to my contentious sister Claudia, who saw her brother struggle with the topic of social movement outcomes for several years but who was not lucky enough to be here to see the end product of that struggle.

CHAPTER ONE

Introduction

Although social movement activists spend much of their time and energy trying to change the world, and although we think that social movements matter, our theoretical and empirical knowledge in this field is still relatively poor. We must pay more attention to the impact of protest activities than has been done in the past. Therefore, this book is largely devoted to the analysis of the consequences of social movements, although it also examines mobilization and repertoires of contention. Specifically, it focuses on the impact of social movements on public policy as a way to ascertain their political consequences. In other words, what is at stake here is their role for social and political change. It is undeniable that social movements are a major feature of contemporary societies. This was true in the past and will arguably be true in the future, for ordinary people will always engage in claim making with the aim of asserting their underrepresented interests and identities. Such centrality of movements is reflected in the growing community of scholars studying them. Scholarly accounts of political contention, popular struggles, and social movements have multiplied, especially during the last three decades, forming a body of literature that has improved our knowledge of this social phenomenon. For example, today we have a better idea of where movements originate, under what conditions they emerge, and how they transform over time. Charles Tilly is undoubtedly among those who have done the most to lead us to that point. His work on the origins of popular struggles and on the historical transformations of action repertoires in France and Britain (Tilly 1986, 1995) stands as a landmark in this respect. But many other authors have provided important contributions as well. In particular, resource mobilization theories and political process approaches have shown that social movements can flourish to the extent that they can mobilize an important pool of resources (McCarthy and Zald 1977; Zald and McCarthy 1987) and to the extent that political opportunities exist to form a movement (Kriesi et al. 1995; McAdam 1982; McAdam, McCarthy, and Zald

1

1996; McAdam, Tarrow, and Tilly 2001; Tarrow 1998; Tilly 1978). We also have well-documented studies of the people who take part in social movements—that is, about the sociopsychological and microsociological determinants of individual participation (Klandermans 1997; McAdam 1988a).[1] All these efforts have dramatically increased our level of knowledge.

It is easy to find the jarring sound in this concert. Resource mobilization theory and the political process approach have also pointed out that social movements are rational collective efforts aimed at changing the current state of affairs, especially the decisions and policies of political elites. However, we still have little systematic understanding of the consequences of social movements. This in itself would give us enough reasons to pay careful attention to this aspect. But studying the consequences of social movements is important because people engage in collective action precisely—though not exclusively—with the aim of producing changes in the outside world, in particular political decisions and public policies. In general, people pursue their political goals in a limited number of ways: by voting on representatives in parliament or by voting on legislative matters directly (where direct democratic procedures are available); by charging organizations to lobby on their behalf; by expressing their interests, needs, and will in public opinion polls; and by participating in movement activities. While such actions are far from being the only means of effecting change, social movements constitute one such means, and we therefore must study this aspect carefully and thoroughly. Finally, it is likely that the protest activities carried out by social movements often do have important effects. This, at least, is what one might conclude from observing specific cases. Let us mention two significant examples. First, few of us would deny that the democracy movements that shook Eastern Europe in 1989 played a role in bringing about a new world order. Mass actions and street demonstrations in Czechoslovakia, East Germany, Hungary, Poland, and Romania are often considered as having significantly contributed to the fall of the Communist regimes in those countries and, with the popular mobilizations in the Baltic Republics later on, the collapse of the Soviet Union in 1991. Also having a strong impact, but on a much more specific level, was the boycott called by the environmental organization Greenpeace in the summer of 1995 against plans by the Dutch oil company Shell to destroy the Brent Spar offshore oil rig located in the North Sea, after it became unusable. The call for a boycott of Shell products worldwide was taken seriously by consumers, and the company's sales went down considerably in the days following the appeal. Worried by the fall of sales and the bad public image it was receiving, the oil company retracted its decision, to the joy of Greenpeace and environmental activists alike.

Of course, forcing political authorities to change their decisions and policies, though fundamental, is not the only goal of social movements. Activists often also aim to change the attitudes and mentalities of the general public. This is all the more true for the so-called new social movements, which put a strong emphasis on the individual responsibility vis-à-vis the environmental protection, the dangers of "technological progress," and the creation of a peaceful world. In addition, forcing policy change is far from being the movements' only impact. The range of their effects goes far beyond their explicit demands. It is possible that "the major effects of social movements will have little or nothing to do with the public claims their leaders make" (Tilly 1999, 270). Participating in protest activities can lead as well to increased repression (della Porta 1999), to changes in personal biographies or life-course patterns (McAdam 1989, 1999), to the spread of models of action by imitation or some other diffusion process (McAdam and Rucht 1993; Strang and Soule 1998), to the expansion of the repertoire of the legitimate forms of political participation (Tarrow 1989, 1993), to increased media attention (Gamson 1998), to alteration in social or political institutions (Clemens 1998; Kriesi and Wisler 1999; Moore 1999), and so forth. In brief, social movements inevitably have a series of consequences, some of which are direct outcomes of their stated goals and claims; and others, indirect and often unforeseen effects of their actions aimed at forcing policy change or modifying the public opinion. Although this book examines how a movement affects public opinion, the main focus is on how a movement affects public policy.

Two Debates about the Impact of Social Movements

It would be unfair to state that scholars have paid only scant attention to the consequences of social movements. Although various authors have pointed out that this aspect has largely been neglected (Berkowitz 1974; Gurr 1980; Marx and Wood 1975; McAdam, McCarthy, and Zald 1988; Tarrow 1993), the field is not as empty as these observers have maintained; yet, most of the existing work was aimed at answering one or both of two basic questions, and, as oversimplifying this might be, it has dealt with two related but nevertheless distinct debates: the disruption–moderation debate and the internal–external debate. In chapter 2, I discuss in more detail both of these two research axes, as well as other work on the outcomes and consequences of social movements. However, here I anticipate parts of this discussion to situate from the outset the present study within the extant literature and especially to see how it attempts to draw from previous studies and fill certain gaps.

A major line of inquiry in previous work has looked at the effects of disruptive and violent protest behavior, and it has opened a debate in the literature about whether the use of disruptive tactics by social movements is more likely to bring about policy change than the use of moderate tactics. A fairly large number of studies, most of them carried during the 1970s, has focused specifically on the effectiveness of violence. Gamson's *Strategy of Social Protest* (1990), which more than a quarter of a century later remains the most systematic attempt to inquire into the effects of social movements, pays much attention to this aspect.[2] One of the major findings of his study is that the use of violence and, more generally, disruptive tactics is often correlated with success. Other authors share this view about the effectiveness of disruptive movement tactics (McAdam 1983; Mirowsky and Ross 1981; Steedly and Foley 1979; Tarrow 1998; Tilly, Tilly, and Tilly 1975), a result that clearly counters pluralists' claim that moderation in politics is more effective than disruption (Dahl 1961, 1967). However, a number of studies have shown that the use of violence does not pay off and sometimes is even detrimental to the movement (Schumaker 1975; Snyder and Kelly 1976; Taft and Ross 1969).

Gamson's pathbreaking work suggests that groups who challenge successfully tend to be more bureaucratized and centralized and that they tend to escape factionalism. Here we enter the second debate and the question of which is more likely to bring about successful change, particularly policy change: the movements' internal characteristics (and hence the tactics they use) or their external context. In other words, are movement-controlled variables (or, rather, certain aspects of their larger environment) responsible for their success? In this respect, researchers have been looking specifically at the impact of various organizational variables on public policy. However, once again, it is difficult to discern consistent results. For example, most of the reanalyses of Gamson's data support his findings as to the crucial role of organizational, group-controlled variables (Frey, Dietz, and Kalof 1992; Mirowsky and Ross 1981; Steedly and Foley 1979). However, a number of studies stress the importance of external support for movements to be effective (Burstein, Einwohner, and Hollander 1995; Lipsky 1968, 1970). More generally, the political environment is often seen as playing a crucial role in the dynamics that lead social movements to produce policy changes (Barkan 1984; Goldstone 1980a; Jenkins and Perrow 1977; McAdam 1982, 1983; Piven and Cloward 1979, 1993; Schumaker 1975). In this context, more recent work has underscored that movement outcomes are strongly dependent on existing political opportunity structures (Kriesi et al. 1995, ch. 9; Kitschelt 1986; Tarrow 1998), in particular state capacities and political alliances.

In sum, the controversy is between authors who think of social movements as being capable of provoking social and political change without external support and those who consider the institutional context to be a necessary condition. On the one hand, movements are seen as weak and lacking indigenous resources to have an impact on their own. On the other hand, they are considered to have enough resources and disruptive potential to make things move; however, some critics claim that this is true only insofar as political opportunity structures are favorable. In the end, this opposition might be more apparent than real, as both the effectiveness of disruptive tactics and the impact of movement-controlled variables may depend on the context of protest (Kowalewski and Schumaker 1981; Amenta, Carruthers, and Zylan 1992). It has been suggested that research should therefore take into account not only movement strategies but also structural constraints (Frey, Dietz, and Kalof 1992). Therefore, this book tries to ascertain the role of movement organization and activities within the context of changing political opportunity structures, to which I add another crucial yet often neglected factor, that is, public opinion.

Political Opportunity Structures

Recent studies of social movements have stressed that political opportunity structures both constrain and enable a movement's mobilization (Kriesi et al. 1995; McAdam, McCarthy, and Zald 1996; Tarrow 1998). Inspired by the seminal work of Charles Tilly on the historical transformation of actions repertoires (1978, 1986, 1995), scholars have accumulated knowledge and evidence about the impact of the larger institutional environment on contentious collective action. As I mentioned earlier, most studies have focused on a movement's emergence and its changing form, while very little research has been done on how political opportunity structures influence social movement outcomes.

A variety of aspects and dimensions of political opportunity structures have been put forward that may affect the mobilization of social movements.[3] Two dimensions of political opportunities are particularly relevant for the study of their outcomes. Forming the first aspect are the structure of the state and the formal (as well as the informal) arrangements that govern the decision-making process in a given country. Public policy is the output of a decisional process that takes place among state actors. This process—hence, its output—is influenced by the capacity and effectiveness of the state in formulating and implementing policies. State capacity in turn depends on a series of structural factors, such as the degree of centralization of the state; the degree of separation between executive, legislative, and judiciary powers; and the coherence of the public administration. These aspects correspond to Kriesi and colleagues' (1995) characterization of the strength of the state, their first dimension of political opportunity structures. A political system in which decisions are taken quickly and effectively is more likely to respond positively to the claims raised by external challengers.

However, the capacity of the state is not sufficient for social movements to see their demands met. The authorities must also be willing to do so. Thus, the second relevant institutional factor that affects policy outcomes is formed by the configuration of power and the structure of political alliances. This is an aspect that was stressed most forcefully by Tarrow (1989, 1993, 1998), among others (della Porta 1996; della Porta and Rucht 1995; Kriesi et al. 1995). As Piven and Cloward (1979) have argued, social movements usually lack the power to force the authorities to meet their demands. In this sense, they are powerless (Jenkins and Perrow 1977). Apart from exceptional situations, only by establishing alliances with important institutional actors will they be in a position that allows them to influence the decision-making process. The role of political parties is crucial in this respect. For example, Kriesi and colleagues (1995) have argued that when a movement's major ally is in government, the chances are higher that the movement will see its demands met and hence obtain substantial gains. Similarly, when the configuration of power in the legislature is favorable to the movement, its chances of success increase. In addition, as Tarrow has pointed out (1993), political elites can take advantage from the presence of social movements in the public space and temporarily become their ally for electoral or opportunistic reasons. Both situations make movements more likely to contribute to policy change.

This book pays special attention to the role of political alliances as crucial resources and opportunities that facilitate the impact of social movements on public policy. One of its main arguments, more thoroughly addressed in chapter 5, is that protest actions and the movements' allies within the institutional arenas interact to place them in a better position to influence policy. In other words, protest and political alliances produce a joint effect that increases the chances that the movements have to reach their goals. A similar argument applies to public opinion.

Public Opinion

In addition to political opportunities, another factor likely to significantly affect the success chances of social movements is public opinion. The role of public opinion is often neglected in the study of the sources of policy change. Reviewing work on the determinants of public policy, Burstein (1998a) found that sociologists largely ignore the impact of public opinion; yet, he also remarked that authors who do look at the relationship between these two variables provide strong evidence of the existence of such an impact.[4] This finding has important implications for the study of the consequences of social movements. If public opinion is found to affect policy change, any assessment of the impact of protest activities should take this factor into account; otherwise we run the risk of specification errors. In other words, changes in policy on a given issue might stem from the stance of public opinion rather than from the mobilization of social movements. Furthermore, it is likely that one of the effects of social movements is precisely to increase public awareness about certain issues, hence influencing the stance of the general public vis-à-vis—for example—the state of the environment, the production of nuclear energy, or the spending for military purposes. Thus, the relationship between social movements and public opinion is more complex than a simple one-way causal pattern: they mutually influence each other.

To examine the role of public opinion for policy change is important also because it forces us to reflect on why and to what extent democratic governments are likely to respond to the preferences of citizens (Burstein 1998a, 1999). This brings us to the field of democratic theory. According to this theory, in representative democracies the power holders are responsive to the public opinion, mainly for electoral reasons. In a system based on electoral competition, political elites are sensitive to citizens' preferences because they aim to gain or preserve the power (Lohmann 1993). In this view, any shift in public opinion alerts the political elites, who adjust their behaviors and policies accordingly. As a consequence, public opinion should strongly affect public policy, particularly when political issues are seen as important by the general public. Thus, according to the theory of representative democracy, social movements should not have a direct impact on public policy, for political elites respond to the claims that are supported by the majority of citizens while tending to ignore particular interests of minority groups, such as social movements and interest groups (Krehbiel 1991; Lohmann 1993). By responding to minority demands, the power holders risk electoral failure, at least in the long run.

At the empirical level, I consider the effects social movements on public opinion—especially the role of the latter—in the relationship between protest and policy change. Specifically, I explore the possibility that the power holders do not automatically respond to shifts in public opinion. Social movements play a crucial role in that they provide decision makers with "signals" of the relevance of certain issues. That a strong public orientation is aligned forces the decision makers to meet a movement's demands, specifically, for electoral reasons. As I said, much like political alliances, public opinion may work as a powerful resource, increasing the political opportunities for social movements to influence public policy. When protest actions are combined with shifts in public opinion favorable to the movements, the actors' chances to obtain a substantial impact on policy should increase and thereby point to a joint effect of protest and public opinion.

Scope of the Study

Before I continue, let me clarify what a social movement is in the context of this study. For this book, I adopt a relational definition. Following Tilly (1994, 7), in this perspective "a social movement consists of *a sustained challenge to powerholders in the name of a population living under the jurisdiction of those powerholders by means of repeated public displays of that population's numbers, commitment, unity, and worthiness.*"[5] The interaction between challengers and political authorities—most often, state authorities—is therefore central to my view of social movements. Given this definition, it comes as natural to look at the changes that such interactions produce, or fail to produce. These changes can be of various kinds: political, social, cultural, and so forth. In this book, I narrow the explanandum by looking at legislative changes and the level of resources invested by the state in given policy areas—that is, public policy—during a given period. This choice places my study squarely into the mainstream of existing work on the consequences of social movements, which has mostly focused on the impact of movements on government policy or legislation (Amenta, Carruthers, and Zylan 1992; Banaszak 1996; Burstein 1998b, 1999; Burstein and Freudenburg 1978; Button 1978, 1989; Costain and Majstorovic 1994; Gelb 1989; Gelb and Palley 1987; Huberts 1989; MacDougal, Minicucci, and Myers 1995; Midttun and Rucht 1994; Nichols 1987; Tarrow 1993).[6]

Somewhat more systematically, we may delimit our explanandum from the point of view of the study of the consequences of social movements or, alternatively, from the point of view of the analysis of public policy. On the one hand, from the former vantage point, I look at movement outcomes, that is, those consequences of their activities that bear directly upon their claims. Furthermore, I focus on a specific set of outcomes. Burstein and colleagues (1995), elaborating on Schumaker's (1975) typology of responsiveness, distinguish six types of outcomes:

1. *access:* the "permeability" of the political system and the state authorities toward social movements and their claims;
2. *agenda:* the adding of an issue into governmental or public agenda;
3. *policy:* the adoption of desired legislation;
4. *output:* the enforcement and implementation of desired legislation;
5. *impact:* the substantial improvement of the existing situation; and
6. *structural outcomes:* the transformation of the social or political arrangements.[7]

My inquiry stops at the third type of outcome, with a strong emphasis put on policy outcomes. However, from the standpoint of the policy cycle, we may distinguish six different stages: agenda setting, policy formulation, policy legitimation, policy implementation, policy evaluation, and policy termination or change (Kraft and Vig

1994). Again, I do not go beyond the first two stages. In other words, what I am interested in is assessing the role of social movements in putting an issue into the political agenda and in bringing about policy change.

The scope of this study is limited in a number of other respects as well. Although my goal is to provide a systematic inquiry into the policy outcomes of social movements, "systematic" does not necessarily mean "all-embracing." Instead, I limit the scope of my inquiry in time and space as well as to its subject matter. To begin with, my study focuses on ecology, antinuclear, and peace movements. The rationale for this choice is threefold. First and foremost, although they have produced impressive levels of mobilization in recent decades, the effects of these movements have received surprisingly little attention from scholars (perhaps with the partial exception of the antinuclear movement). Much has been done to explain their emergence and development over time, much less to ascertain their impact. This would suffice to justify a study devoted to this aspect. However, not only might the readers object that the impact of other movements has been neglected, but they may also ask, why these movements and not other ones? The answer to this question leads me to the second reason of my choice of the object. These movements belong to the common family of the *new social movements* (Kriesi et al., 1995), and within this family, they have certain characteristics in common. In a way, they form a subfamily of movements that share issues and participants. In particular, ecology, antinuclear, and peace movements have the common goal of criticizing and fighting the risks brought by an increasing use of technology in society (Beck 1986), be it nuclear energy, nuclear arms, or other industrial technologies.[8]

The third reason for the selection of movements to be studied bears on one of the theoretical arguments of the book. In my study, I look at how social movements can produce social and political change. However, some changes are easier to produce than others. Schematically, we can distinguish two factors of variability from the impact of social movements. First, domestic policy is more easily influenced than foreign policy. External factors are involved in foreign policy that pose major constraints on the decisions of national authorities. Second, high-profile issues threaten the authorities to a greater extent than low-profile issues, for they strike the core interests of the state, although the threatening character of a political issue may vary from one country to the other (Duyvendak 1995; Kriesi et al. 1995). In brief, social movement outcomes depend on the type of issue targeted by the movements or, according to the concept I use in chapter 5, the viability of claims. The latter can be defined as the possibility for policy impact that is constrained by the combination of domestic–foreign policy and the high-profile–low-profile distinctions.

According to these two dimensions, our three movements have different possibilities for policy impact. The ecology movement, which addresses domestic policy and does not generally threaten the core interests of the state, has the highest chances to influence public policy. In contrast, the peace movement targets a policy area that is arguably the most difficult to change among those considered here. Since it addresses foreign policy and threatens the core interests of the state, the peace movement has a tough task in its attempts to bring about policy changes.

The antinuclear movement represents an intermediate case, insofar as it addresses domestic policy, but at the same time it raises a high-profile issue (nuclear energy or, more generally, the energy provision of the country). In sum, the viability of claims and the resulting chances to bring about policy changes should be the following: relatively high for the ecology movement, quite low for the antinuclear movement, and very low for the peace movement—hence, the choice of these three movements.

Not only is this book's subject matter narrowed to three specific movements, but the scope of this book is limited in space and time as well, which leads me to briefly discuss the comparative and historical approach adopted in the volume.

A Comparative and Historical Perspective

The general aim of this book is to study the interplay of social movements, political opportunity structures, and public opinion in contributing to produce policy change. It addresses this subject matter by comparing three movements across space and time. Indeed, what sets this book apart the most from previous studies is its comparative and historical perspective. This choice reflects the conviction that previous work on the consequences of social movements has often failed to acknowledge the role played by the political context and has not done justice to the dynamic nature of contention. I hope to be able to show that an approach that compares national situations while looking at the processes of mobilization can provide useful insights into the impact of social movements.

Many recent studies are informed by a comparative design to explain the extent, form, and content of political contention. As mentioned, this rapidly growing body of literature is inspired by the political process approach, and it centers the explanation on the concept of political opportunity structures (Brockett 1991; Costain 1992; della Porta 1995; Duyvendak 1995; Kitschelt 1986; Koopmans 1995; Kriesi et al. 1995; McAdam et al. 1996; Meyer 1993; Rucht 1994; Tarrow 1989, 1998; Tilly, Tilly, and Tilly 1975). Unfortunately, fewer efforts have been devoted to using comparisons to highlight the effects of movements. Most previous works are case studies, many of which have been made in the search for the variables most conducive to social movement outcomes, regardless of context, such as the organizational characteristics of movements or the levels of disruption. In contrast, one of the underlying assumptions of the present book is that the impact of social movements depends more on historical and contingent combinations and sequences of events than on general, invariant sets of factors; and only if we compare different contexts and situations will we be able to identify those combinations and disentangle those sequences. This is not to say, however, that case studies are useless; quite on the contrary, they can provide insightful results. They can in particular advance our knowledge about the mechanisms through which social movements produce their most relevant effects. Their value rests above all on their allowing us to examine in detail the processes that lead from protest to social and political change. However, case studies are most useful when one is interested in showing the consequences of particular movements rather than in looking for principles of variations of their effects as a result of different combinations of contextual and situational factors, which is the purpose of this book. In addition, only a comparative approach yields results that can be generalized beyond the specific case under study.

Ecology, antinuclear, and peace movements have emerged in virtually all Western countries (and in many non-Western countries, too). This book, however, focuses on three particular countries during a specific historical period: the United States, Italy, and Switzerland. These three countries have broadly comparable ecology, antinuclear, and peace movements, although the mobilization of these movements varies in its intensity. At the same time, these countries present different political opportunity structures as well as a different context for the impact of public opinion in the processes at hand. Specifically, the structure of political alliances for these movements within the arenas of institutionalized politics is quite different in the United States as compared to Italy and Switzerland. The American majority electoral system does not provide challengers with the same set of political opportunities that we find in proportional systems, such as the one in Italy (up to 1993), where parties co-opt large sectors of extraparliamentary opposition; or such as the one in Switzerland, where the main potential ally of the movements studied here, the Socialist Party, is in government (although it is in a minority and often ambivalent position within a grand ruling coalition; Kriesi et al. 1995).[9]

Within this comparative framework, I follow what Tilly (1984) has called *individualizing comparison*. My goal is not to provide a full-fledged comparison of the three countries (although I do try to be as systematic as I can in the presentation of data and in the description of each national situation). The focus of the book is on the case of the United States, and I use the other two countries mostly as a mirror to reflect the American situation and single out its peculiarities.

In addition to its specific geographical focus, the book is also limited to a specific period of time. As mentioned, the three movements studied belong to the family of new social movements. Although setting exact dates is always an artificial exercise that does not do justice to the complexity of social processes, we can say that this movement family has emerged in the Western world in the wake of the student and New Left protest cycle that peaked, at least symbolically, in 1968. My study starts when these movements began to mobilize important social sectors, in the early 1970s. At the other end, it stops when their mass mobilization entered a new phase of mobilization, in the late 1990s. Thus, my study focuses on a historical phase that comprises the rise, growth, and decline of a whole movement sector. To be more accurate, I look at the mobilization, and especially the impact, of ecology, antinuclear, and peace movements between 1975 and 1999 (1975–1995 for the impact).

From a theoretical point of view, to follow a historical and comparative perspective means to shift from the study of the determinants and causes of social movement outcomes to the conditions and circumstances of their occurrence, to the context-specific and time-specific conditions under which a given type of effect becomes possible. If social movements are conceived as rational political efforts aimed at producing social change, then the political conditions of certain changes become central to the analysis of social movement outcomes. Underlying this perspective is the idea that social change results from the interplay of social movement activities and other social forces and structures. Such perspective has been adopted, for example, in Burstein's (1998b) important work on equal employment opportunity legislation in the United States. Therefore, one should look at the circumstances that lead such interplay of actors and structures to produce certain changes at different levels: within the movement itself, in legislation, in the structure of the political system, in the society at large, and so forth. Here I try to resist the temptation of looking beyond changes in public policy; instead, I focus on this limited yet crucial dimension of social change and, more specifically, on the varying impact of social movements on policy changes as a function of variations in the structure of political opportunities— in particular, political alliances—and in the stance of public opinion on a given issue.

Data and Methods

The empirical analyses presented in this book rest on original data regarding the mobilization of ecology, antinuclear, and peace movements in the United States, Italy, and Switzerland. These data cover the period from 1975 to 1999 and have been gathered following a methodology that has now become widespread in research on social movements and contentious politics. This method is known among specialists in the field as *protest event analysis* (Kriesi et al. 1995; McAdam 1982; Rucht et al. 1998; Tarrow 1989; Tilly, Tilly, and Tilly 1975). Its goal is to measure movement mobilization, which consists of retrieving news of protest events systematically and longitudinally via a content analysis of a public source, most of the time newspapers. The events retrieved are coded following a structured scheme and then processed electronically, to be treated quantitatively. For each event found, a number of basic characteristics are coded, such as the place and time in which the event occurred, the form of the event (demonstration, blockade, violent action, etc.), its goal (preserve a natural reserve, stop the construction of a nuclear power plant, promote the peace, etc.), and the number of participants.

Generally speaking, a protest event is an action emanating from a social movement that aims to influence political decision making or sensitize public opinion. Unlike most previous studies of social movements (but see Kriesi et al. 1995), I adopt a broad definition of protest event, which includes not only unconventional actions (e.g., public demonstrations, occupations, blockades, violent demonstrations) but also more conventional actions that make use of institutional channels, such as juridical or political forms and media-oriented actions (in particular, public statements). Yet, despite the theoretical and methodological reasons mentioned in the following, my analyses generally comprise unconventional events.

Following a sampling procedure similar to that used by Kriesi and colleagues (1995), I coded protest events retrieved from one national newspaper for each country of the study. The three newspapers are the *New York Times*, for the United States; the *Corriere della Sera*, for Italy; and the *Neue Zürcher Zeitung*, for Switzerland. These papers were consulted because of their national scope and similar political orientation. All Sunday and Monday editions of the paper have been consulted for the period under consideration so as to cover events that occurred during the weekends.[10]

I chose to sample each data source basically for pragmatic reasons: it would simply be unreasonable, if not unfeasible, for a single researcher to retrieve data on protest events for three movements of three countries for a period covering a quarter of a century. In spite of this limitation, however, I think the sample provides quite a reliable empirical basis for the book, insofar as I am more interested in developments over time than I am in comparing absolute figures (see Koopmans 1998; Kriesi et al. 1995, appendix). This holds especially true for unconventional actions, whereas the distributions of conventional actions are more likely to be biased because they tend to be underrepresented in sample and hence less likely to reflect the actual occurrences. For this reason, the empirical analyses that go beyond simply describing developments over time are mainly restricted to unconventional actions. (I made this decision also because I am particularly interested in the relationship between public policy and unconventional protests, the latter of which are the most typical means of action of social movements.) Appendix A provides a comparison of the sample data, with continuous time data gathered for a short but significant period on the *New York Times*, as well as with additional information on the method of data retrieval and analysis.[11]

Protest events form the empirical basis of the book and are used throughout, both to show developments over time of the mobilization of the three movements and to study relationships between protest and public policy. In addition to protest event data, I gathered a wealth of information on other aspects central to my argument: social movement organization, public opinion, and public policy. All these data consist of annual figures covering either the period under study or a shorter period—such as in the case of public opinion, which lacked available data for some of the years.

Systematic information on movement organization comes from the *Encyclopedia of Organizations*, for the case of the United States; and from a questionnaire sent to a sample of major organizations of each movement, for Italy and Switzerland. I coded two types of information for each organization: the number of members and the amount of financial resources. This allowed me to measure the organizational strength and growth of the three movements under study. Data on movement organization provided the empirical basis for the analyses presented in chapter 6.

The most difficult task, as far as data collection is concerned, was probably to find reliable information on public opinion, especially since I am dealing with developments over a rather long period. This task was made easier in the United States by the presence of long-standing opinion poll institutes, such as Gallup and Harris. Drawing from these sources as well as from existing publications, I was able to reconstruct the state of American public opinion on matters dealt with by the three movements studied: environment, nuclear energy, and national security. Less-systematic information, however, is available for Italy and Switzerland. Data on public opinion are used above all in chapter 8.

A number of indicators of policy change in the areas touched by the three movements (environment, nuclear energy, and national security) have been gathered to measure public policy. Earlier work has measured policy outputs in terms of expenditures (e.g., Dye 1966; Hofferbert and Sharkansky 1971; Jacob and Vines 1971) or in terms of legislative activity or production. In spite of some problems that have been evoked by using expenditure data (Burstein and Freundenburg 1978; Hofferbert 1974), here we measure public policy basically through government spending. Drawing from official statistics, I include measures of government spending for the environment, nuclear energy production (a sort of functional equivalent of spending in this area), and national defense.

Finally, I took advantage of a great amount of previous studies on the three movements as well as documents provided by several movement organizations and interviews with key informants. This information is crucial, insofar as it puts the flesh around the backbone represented by the empirical analyses. This qualitative material provides necessary historical background, without which the quantitative analyses would remain quite abstract.

I utilize the materials gathered in two ways. First, I illustrate the development of the mobilization and organizational growth of the three movements under study as well as that of public opinion and public policy in the areas touched by the movements during the past three decades or so. Chapters 3 and 4 in particular are based on illustrating medium- to long-run trends. Second, I use the quantitative data selectively in the analyses of the relationship between social movements and public policy, as shown in chapters 5, 6, 7, and 8. This more explanatory aspect of my study is dealt with through time-series analysis, a longitudinal method that is particularly helpful to inquire into the impact of social movements on public policy. Unlike the descriptive overview of the mobilization of the three movements, these empirical analyses focus on a shorter period, namely, 1975 to 1995.

Outline of the Book

Figure 1.1 summarizes the general theoretical framework of the book. It outlines a simple model for the impact of social movements on public policy, whereby political opportunity structures, public opinion, and the type of issue at hand (viability of claims) form the three major factors that influence such impact.

Based on the example of ecology, antinuclear, and peace movements in the United States, Italy, and Switzerland, public policy at time t_1 is affected by the interaction at time t_0 of social movement actions; political opportunity structures stemming from the structure and arrangements of the state (in particular, the structure of political alliances); and the stance of the public opinion on a given issue. The type of issue, in

t_0

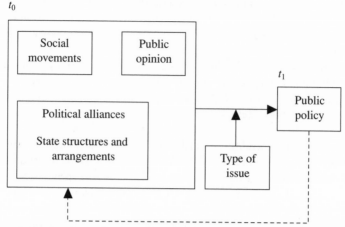

Figure 1.1. A Simple Model for the Impact of Social Movements on Public Policy.

turn, mediates the relationship between these factors and the changes in public policy, thereby accounting for variations in the impact of different movements.

The book divides into two parts. Part I has three chapters and addresses the book's subject matter from a theoretical and historical point of view. The general framework outlined in this introductory chapter, chapter 1, forms the backbone of the discussion provided in part II. Chapter 2 provides an overview of the extant literature on the outcomes and consequences of social movements. This chapter sets the stage for the discussion of the policy impact of ecology, antinuclear, and peace movements. It does so by reviewing previous work and by pointing to specific gaps in the literature. Specifically, I first deal in more detail with the two debates about the impact of social movements mentioned here—that is, the disruption–moderation debate and the internal–external debate. Then I discuss work that examines the movements' context, stressing the role of political opportunity structures and public opinion. Finally, I address some conceptual and methodological issues, particularly issues related to the definition of what is a movement's success or failure as compared to preferable notions, such as outcomes or consequences.

The next two chapters map the changes that have occurred in the mobilization of the three movements under study and in the state policies addressed by their protest activities. Chapter 3 provides a historical overview of the mobilization of peace, ecology, and antinuclear movements in the three countries under study, focusing on the 1975–1999 period. Knowing what the movements have been doing during that period (and what the main foci of their actions have been) is a necessary prerequisite to understanding their impact on policy. If we do not know how protest has unfolded over time, we will hardly be able to ascertain its effects. More generally, as Tilly (1999, 270) has put it, "only well-validated theories of social movement dynamics will give analysts a secure grip on social movement outcomes."

Chapter 4 looks at the other end of the process: public policy. It summarizes three decades of environmental, nuclear energy, and national security policies in the United States, Italy, and Switzerland. By comparing the two historical overviews, I try to draw some tentative conclusions on the relationship between social movements and policy change, all of which are summarized in the conclusion to part I.

Part II presents a more systematic empirical analysis of this relationship using the quantitative dataset described earlier. This part of the book is structured around a discussion of three explanations of the policy impact of social movements. These three explanations of social movement outcomes—the direct-effect model, the indirect-effect model, and the joint-effect model—are outlined in chapter 5. Arguing that the last best explains the policy impact of social movements, I try to show the promises of time-series analysis and the use of interactions for the study of the consequences of social movements. This chapter also presents the results of the empirical analyses concerning the direct-effect model. In particular, I focus on two dimensions of protest: the levels of mobilization and the forms of action.

Chapter 6 deals with the role of organization, an aspect that, as I said, has often been at the center of a debate among scholars (Gamson 1990; Piven and Cloward 1979). Are strong and organized movements more likely to provoke policy change than loose and spontaneous ones? Is organization or disruption more effective? These were the main terms of the debate, which I address from the longitudinal and comparative perspective adopted in this book.

Chapter 7 elaborates on the role of political alliances as an important external resource that may facilitate the impact of social movements on public policy. Here I draw from the literature on political opportunity structures to argue that the presence of institutional allies is crucial in understanding the policy impact of protest. I then apply this argument to the three movements under study. Specifically, I try to assess the explanatory power of the variant that stresses the role of political alliances with regard to both the indirect-effect and the joint-effect models of social movement outcomes.

Chapter 8 accomplishes a similar task, but it focuses on public opinion, the other external resource that I stress in this book. In this chapter, I first discuss the role of public opinion for policy change in general. Then I evaluate the explanatory power of the variant that underscores the role of public opinion, as seen through the indirect-effect and joint-effect models of movement outcomes. The chapter also discusses the broader implications of these findings for democratic theory. The conclusion to part II summarizes the main findings of the analyses shown in these three chapters. At the same time, it explores the possibility that, to have more chances at success, movements need the support of both political allies and public opinion.

In the concluding chapter, chapter 9, I briefly summarize the main arguments and findings of the book; I sketch some of its theoretical and policy implications; I point out some limitations of my study; and finally, I advance some suggestions for further research in light of the strengths and weaknesses of my study.

Notes

1. Most studies of the microsociological determinants of participation in social movements have stressed the role of the participants' previous embeddedness in social networks (e.g., Gould 1993, 1995; Fernandez and McAdam 1988; Kim and Bearman 1997; McAdam 1986, 1988b; McAdam and Paulsen 1993; Rosenthal et al. 1985; Snow, Zurcher, and Ekland-Olson 1980). Rationalist accounts of participation, on their part, have looked at individual-level factors, such as the perceived effectiveness of the individual action (e.g. Hardin 1982; Opp 1989; Sandler 1992).

2. The first edition of the book was published in 1975.

3. See McAdam (1996) for a synthetic discussion about the various dimensions of political opportunity structures.

4. Among the studies that have found a close relationship between public opinion and policy, we can mention Burstein (1998b), Costain and Majstorovic (1994), and Page and Shapiro (1983). I provide a more exhaustive list of references in chapter 6.

5. Emphasis in the original.

6. However, we still have rather few studies on the cultural impact of movements, although a considerable body of literature is needed on the individual-level consequences of participation in social movements and activism (for reviews, see McAdam 1989, 1999). On the cultural impact of movements in general, see, for example, Meyer and Whittier (1994), Diani (1997), Gamson (1998), Gamson and Wolfsfeld (1993).

7. In Gamson's (1990) terminology, the first type corresponds roughly to *acceptance*, the third type to *new advantages*. In Kitschelt's (1986) jargon, *access* means "procedural, policy substantial impact."

8. Other features have been mentioned that are common to the new social movements: a left-libertarian political and cultural orientation (della Porta 1995), a critical stance toward the bureaucratization of the modern society (Brand 1982), an emphasis on lifestyles and the quality of life (Raschke 1985), the centrality of individual and collective identities (Melucci 1989, 1996; Touraine 1978, 1984), and the belonging of the core participants to the sociocultural specialists' sector of the new middle class (Kriesi 1989, 1993). While ecology, antinuclear, and peace movements share all these features, the critique of the "risk society" is what most typically distinguishes them from other new social movements, such as the women's movement, the gay movement, the solidarity movement, and the squatters' movement.

9. In 1993, Italy shifted (partly) to a majority system but has had a proportional system throughout most of the period examined in this book.

10. Only the Monday edition has been retained in the case of Switzerland, for the Swiss paper does not have a Sunday edition.

11. Methodological discussions of protest event analysis can be found in, among others, Barranco and Wisler (1999), Danzger (1975), Franzosi (1987), McCarthy, McPhail, and Smith (1996), Mueller (1997), Olzak (1989), Rucht and Ohlemacher (1992), Snyder and Kelly (1977). See also various articles in Rucht, Koopmans, and Neidhart (1998).

PART I

HISTORICAL OVERVIEW

CHAPTER TWO

Was It Worth the Effort? The Outcomes and Consequences of Social Movements

If we trust our intuitions, the last big European cycle of protest caused such fundamental changes in the social and political structures that we are still wondering about the kind of world we are now living in. In the eyes of a neutral observer, the democracy movements that shook Eastern Europe in 1989 were clearly instrumental in bringing about the new order. Mass actions and street demonstrations in Czechoslovakia, East Germany, Hungary, Poland, and Romania have led to the fall of the Communist regimes in those countries and, with the subsequent popular mobilizations in the Baltic Republics, the collapse of the Soviet Union in 1991. That the movements must have played a significant role can be seen in the impressive growth of popular mobilizations in those countries. Take the example of East Germany. Oberschall (1996) reports an impressive increase in the number of participants in protests and demonstrations in Leipzig, where the key events took place during 1989. Whereas the celebration of the anniversary of Karl Liebknecht and Rosa Luxemburg on January 15 saw the presence of 150 to 200 participants, the protest marches from Nikolai Church to the city center, which took place every Monday from October 16 until Christmas, mobilized 110,000 to 450,000 people. Yet even the most relentless optimists would concede that, without major changes in the structures of power, protests and mass demonstrations would hardly have had such dramatic consequences. In fact, one can argue that in the absence of such changes the movements themselves would not take on such a big scale. What gave a big boost to the democracy movements in Eastern Europe, and thus helped change our world, were two major transformations in the state's structures: Mikhail Gorbachev's reforms and the cracks in the Communist states' alliance system. Movement mobilization and state breakdown combined in a complex way to bring about a revolutionary outcome.

Another example. During summer 1995, the Dutch oil company Shell announced plans to destroy the Brent Spar offshore oil rig located in the North Sea because it became unusable. This decision provoked the immediate reaction by outraged environmentalist groups, especially Greenpeace, which foresaw an ecological disaster and thus called for a boycott of Shell products worldwide. Many consumers took the boycott seriously, and the company's sales went down considerably in the days following the appeal. Particularly in Germany, drivers avoided Shell gas stations in favor of other companies. Worried by the fall of sales and the bad public image it was receiving, the oil company abandoned the project of destroying the oil rig, thus conceding a significant victory to Greenpeace and the environmental movement.

This example, however, is quite different from the previous one. For one thing, the events for the Shell protest were much more limited in time, space, and scope; in contrast, the revolutions in Eastern Europe lasted several months (indeed, a very short time for a revolution). In addition, whereas the revolutions involved thousands of participants and had dramatic social and political repercussions for the entire world, the Greenpeace boycott was called by a single organization and was successful within a few weeks; however, despite Greenpeace's success, it certainly did not alter the foundations of contemporary society. Another difference is that Greenpeace activists had seemingly expected, or at least hoped, that Shell would withdraw from its decision, whereas no one could have foreseen the fundamental changes brought about by the opposition to the Communist regimes. Despite these differences, the two examples collectively illustrate several problems and difficulties inherent to the study of the consequences of social movements. The principal difficulty is how to establish a causal relationship between a series of events that we can reasonably classify as social movement actions and an observed change in society—be it minor or fundamental, durable or temporary. Both our examples display social movement activities and were followed by changes that the movements had asked for, though the scope of those changes, in one case, went well beyond any possible anticipation. But the problem of causal attribution remains the same. Even for the apparently more obvious effect in the Shell case, we cannot a priori exclude the intervention of a third party (a member of the political elite, for example), which may have caused the withdrawal of Shell's decision. In addition, both the protest cycle for democracy and Greenpeace's call for a boycott might have had a series of long-term consequences that neither the populations of Eastern Europe nor Greenpeace activists had planned. As I hope will become clear by the end of this chapter, these methodological problems can only be resolved theoretically.

Social scientists often find difficulty in finding consensus on many aspects of their collective enterprise. Students of social movements are certainly no exception to this rule. They often disagree on the cause of protest, its development over time, its fate, and the methods of analysis. Yet they all seem to agree that the study of the effects of social movements has largely been neglected, and it has become common sense to acknowledge this state of affairs (e.g., Berkowitz 1974; Gurr 1980; Marx and Wood 1975; McAdam, McCarthy, and Zald 1988; Tarrow 1993). Such neglect is quite astonishing, for the ultimate end of movements is to bring about change. The field, however, is not as empty as several observers have maintained.[1] Nevertheless, we still lack systematic empirical analyses that would add to our knowledge of the conditions under which movements produce certain effects. A striking disparity, furthermore, exists between the large body of work on political and policy outcomes and the sporadic studies on the cultural and institutional effects of social movements. The following review reflects this state of affairs (for previous reviews, see Amenta et al. 1992; Burstein et al. 1995; Gurr 1980; Jenkins 1981; McAdam et al. 1988; Mirowsky and Ross 1981; Schumaker 1978). In doing so, I first address the two main axes of early research: the moderation–disruption axis and the organization–disorder axis. Second, I review work that has attempted to put movements and their outcomes in their larger social and political context. Third, I point to some logical as well as methodological problems of existing work that have prevented the cumulative gathering of systematic knowledge. In the end, I hope to be able to show that, despite the considerable amount of work on this topic, little systematic research has been done, especially with regard to comparisons across countries and across movements in singling out the conditions that facilitate certain types of impact, an approach that I view as one of the most promising avenues for future research.

The Power of Movements

Most research so far has focused on the intended effects of social movements. Early work has looked in particular at the impact of movement-controlled variables by attempting to single out the characteristics of movements that are most conducive to success or, more generally, that help certain outcomes to occur. In this respect, one can discern two closely interrelated lines of investigation. The first line concerns the impact, mostly on policy, of various organizational variables and has brought researchers to ask whether strongly organized movements are more successful than loosely organized movements. The second line of inquiry has looked at the effects of disruptive and violent protest behavior and has opened a debate in the literature about whether the use of disruptive tactics by social movements is more likely to lead to policy changes than use of moderate tactics. This debate has largely dealt with the effectiveness of violence. Let us briefly discuss each of these two aspects.

The Impact of Organization

Resource mobilization theory has dominated the study of social movements and contentious politics for at least three decades. It is therefore little surprising that research on movement outcomes has paid a lot of attention to the role of the organizational characteristics of movements. There is a fair amount of theoretical and empirical work that links various movement-controlled variables to their alleged impact. While early theoretical work has speculated about the link between government responsiveness and the nature of a movement's demands, organizational size and stability, leadership, and strategies (e.g., Etzioni 1970; Lipsky and Levi 1972), other authors have tried to show it empirically. Brill's finding (1971), based on a case study of rent strikes, is typical in this respect, namely, that success is not likely to be forthcoming if the movement leaders are not able to build an effective organization. Relevant work includes Shorter and Tilly's examination (1974) of the effect of organizational variables on the outcomes of strikes in France, Staggenborg's inquiry (1988) into the consequences of professionalization and formalization in the pro-choice movement, and Clemens's investigation (1993) of the impact of organizational repertoires on institutional change. We also have a substantial body of literature on the effects of lobbying strategies on governmental decisions and congressional action (e.g., Fowler and Shaiko 1987; Milbrath 1970; Metz 1986). However, these studies are more often concerned with interest-group politics than social movements tout court.

Important evidence about the relationship between various organizational variables and the success of social movements comes from Gamson's *Strategy of Social Protest* (1990), which after more than two decades remains perhaps the most systematic attempt to inquire into the impact and effectiveness of social movements. His comprehensive analysis of the careers of fifty-three American challenging groups active between 1800 and 1945 led him to conclude, first, that groups with single-issue demands were more successful than groups with multiple-issue demands. Second, the use of selective incentives was positively correlated with success. Third, as will be shown in more detail, the use of violence and disruptive tactics was associated with success, while being the recipient of violence made it more difficult. Fourth, and most important for the present purpose, successful groups tended to be more bureaucratized and centralized and tended to escape factionalism. Finally, he tested the role of context variables and found that time did not matter much, whereas political crises seemed to have an effect on the outcomes of the challenging groups examined.

Gamson's work has raised a number of criticisms, mostly regarding methodology (Goldstone 1980a; Gurr 1980; Snyder and Kelly 1976, Webb et al. 1983; Zelditch 1978) but also involving a series of reanalyses of his data, which the author appended to the book (Frey, Dietz, and Kalof 1992; Goldstone 1980a; Mirowsky and Ross 1981; Steedly and Foley 1979).[2] As in the case of the role of disruptive tactics, most of these works have confirmed Gamson's principal findings, at least in part. For example, Steedly and Foley (1979), using more sophisticated techniques, found group success related, in order of relative importance, to the nondisplacement nature of the goals, the number of alliances, the absence of factionalism, the specific and limited goals, and the willingness to use sanctions. Similarly, Mirowsky and Ross (1981), aiming at finding the locus of control over movement success, found protester-controlled factors more important than the support of third parties or the situation for a successful outcome. Of these protester-controlled factors, the organization and, above all, the beliefs and goals were seen as crucial for success. More recently, Frey, Dietz, and Kalof (1992) have pointed to the importance of avoiding displacement goals and group factionalism to obtain new advantages. Thus, Gamson's central argument, stressing internal variables and resource mobilization as determinants of group success, found further support. However, Piven and Cloward's thesis (1979) that movements have a chance to succeed to the extent that they avoid trying to build a strong organization brought a fundamental criticism to Gamson's stress on the effectiveness of organization, a criticism that has triggered a debate in both scholarly and general audience journals. In addition, Goldstone's reanalysis (1980a) of Gamson's data has cast serious doubts over his findings and has pointed to a perspective on social movement outcomes that takes into account their broader political context. Before I return to this aspect, I would like to discuss the second main axis of existing research: the impact of disruption.

The Effectiveness of Disruptive and Violent Protest

Overall, the use by social movements of disruptive tactics and violence seems to increase their potential for change. Several authors have argued that, contrary to the pluralist claim that moderation in politics is more effective than disruption, the use of force by social movements increases the chances that the participants reach their goals (Astin et al. 1975; McAdam 1983; Tarrow 1998; Tilly, Tilly, and Tilly 1975). Again, Gamson's study (1990) provides empirical evidence of the effectiveness of violence and the use of constraints. Gamson found that the challenging groups' use of violence and, more generally, their disruptive tactics were positively correlated to his two measures of success: the acceptance of challengers as legitimate claimants and the obtaining of new advantages for constituents. These findings are backed up by some of the aforementioned reanalyses of his data, in particular those by Mirowsky and Ross (1981) and Steedly and Foley (1979). Yet there is no consensus on this point nor on the implications of this for movements.

A great deal of evidence on the relationship between disruptive or violent movement tactics and their impact comes from two important strands of research: the study of strikes and the many analyses of the wave of urban riots that occurred in several American cities at the end of the sixties. Regarding strike activity, Taft and Ross (1969) found little evidence, based on their study of violent labor conflicts in the United States through 1968, that violence would help unions to reach their goals. Snyder and Kelly (1976) reached a similar conclusion as well. By analyzing quantitative data on strikes that occurred in Italy between 1878 and 1903, they were able to show that violent strikes were less successful than peaceful ones. These results contradict those obtained by Shorter and Tilly (1971), who found, in their study of strikes in France, a positive correlation between the use of violence and strike outcomes. Research on strike activity, however, has gone beyond the specific question of disruption or violence to examine broader issues related to the industrial conflict (Cohn 1993; Franzosi 1994; Shorter and Tilly 1974; Snyder and Kelly 1976).

The effectiveness of disruptive protest and movements has been analyzed thoroughly in the aftermath of the urban riots of the 1960s in the United States (for reviews, see Gurr 1980; Isaac and Kelly 1981; Piven and Cloward 1993). Rioting behavior and social movements are clearly not equivalent, though they are both instances of contentious politics, defined as "collective activity on the part of claimants—or those who claim to represent them—relying at least in part on noninstitutionalized forms of interaction with elites, opponents, or the state" (Tarrow 1996, 874). Social movements, though, may be defined as "sustained challenges to powerholders in the name of a disadvantaged population living under the jurisdiction or influence of those powerholders" (Tarrow 1996, 874; see also Tarrow 1998; Tilly 1984). However, studying riots can yield important insights on the effectiveness of disruption and violent protest by social movements. In addition, the American riots of the sixties have sparked the interest on the latter aspect among students of social movements. Some authors—including Hahn (1970), Mueller (1978), Isaac and Kelly (1981), Kelly and Snyder (1980), Sears and McConahay (1973)—have focused explicitly on the effects of violence. In general, the evidence gathered does not allow for a definitive answer to the question of whether rioting is beneficial or detrimental to the population involved. Kelly and Snyder (1980), for example, have suggested that there is no causal relationship between the frequency and severity of violence displayed in American cities during the 1960s and the distribution of black socioeconomic gains at the local level, either by income level or by employment and occupational changes. Feagin and Hahn (1973), in a monograph on ghetto riots, maintain that the latter led at best to limited reform and mostly to changes in police policies. Nevertheless, the authors do not provide systematic evidence for their argument. Berkowitz (1974), who has looked at socioeconomic changes at the neighborhood level brought about by ghetto riots between 1960 and 1970, found no differential improvement for riot tracts, arguing against a positive effect of the riots (see also Levitan, Johnston, and Taggart 1975). Even more pessimistically, Welch (1975) has shown that the riots led to an increase in urban expenditures for control and punishment of rioters, which is obviously much less in their favor. However, Colby's findings (1975) in a way contradict Welch's because Colby found that the riots had a positive influence on redistribution policy, though no influence on regulatory policy at the state level. Yet, Jennings (1979), also through a comparison of states but taking into account time as well, found some support for a positive correlation between the number of riots and the increase in recipients of Aid to Families with Dependent Children (AFDC).

Many studies of the urban riots in American cities are directly related to Piven and Cloward's well-known thesis (1993) about the regulating functions of public welfare (for reviews, see Piven and Cloward 1993; Trattner 1983). As it is known, these authors have provocatively argued that welfare systems serve two principal functions: to maintain a supply of low-wage labor and to restore order in periods of civil turmoil. According to this thesis, turmoil and disruptive actions do provoke policy change, though it can hardly be seen as success, for such concessions are usually withdrawn once the turmoil subsides. A series of studies carried out during the seventies and eighties have attempted to reexamine this thesis (e.g., Albritton 1979; Betz 1974; Colby 1982; Hicks and Swank 1983; Isaac and Kelly 1981; Jennings 1979, 1980, 1983; Schramm and Turbott 1983; Sharp and Maynard-Moody 1991). In addition, other authors have addressed Piven and Cloward's argument but have focused on the relief expansion of the thirties (e.g., Jenkins and Brents 1989; Kerbo and Shaffer 1992; see further Valocchi 1990). Again, though a great deal of the disagreement with Piven and Cloward's thesis hinges not so much on the results in themselves but rather their interpretation, in the whole it is difficult, out of this impressive amount of empirical work, to provide a clear-cut answer to the question of whether disruption can produce policy changes and, if so, what this means for the movements.

Such uncertainty of results calls for a conditional analysis that singles out the circumstances under which violence matters. This task has been accomplished by Button (1978), among others, in one of the most comprehensive empirical studies of the political impact of the 1960s riots. He has maintained that violence is conducive to political and social change under five general conditions:

1. when powerholders have enough public resources to meet the demands of the movement;
2. when violent actions and events are neither so frequent as to cause massive societal and political instability but are severe enough to be noticed and to represent a threat;
3. when a relevant share of power holders and the public are sympathetic to the goals of the movement and the violence is not so severe as to undermine this sympathy;
4. when the aims and demands of the movement are relatively limited, specific, and clear; and
5. when violence is adopted in combination with peaceful and conventional strategies. (Button 1978)

Button's approach has the advantage of avoiding the formulation of too simple a causal relationship between the use of violence and its outcomes. However, it seems so ecumenical as to run the risk of leading to trivial results. A more parsimonious argument in this respect has been put forth by Schumaker (1978), who has looked at the conditions under which disruptive tactics work. His results suggest that the use of constraints is more effective when the conflict is limited to the protest group and its target (i.e., when the scope of conflict is narrow). In contrast, when the public becomes involved in the conflict (i.e., when the scope of conflict is broad), the use of constraints tends to reduce the chances of a successful outcome. Other analyses based on the 1960s urban riots, however, suggest that militancy is generally not conducive to success (Schumaker 1975). Similarly, a study of official responses to sixty protest incidents that occurred in the Philippines, Malaysia, and Thailand between 1960 and 1977 has shown that the use of violent constraints (i.e., militancy), except when the group of protesters was large, had negative effects on the protest's outcomes because repression was more likely to occur (O'Keefe and Schumaker 1983).

Movement Outcomes in Context

As I have said, existing research seems to provide contrasting findings regarding the impact of several internal characteristics of social movements, such as the use of disruptive tactics and actions. Nevertheless, this contrast may well be more apparent than real. The puzzle may be solved once we acknowledge the crucial role of the broader political context in facilitating or constraining both the mobilization and the potential outcomes of movements. Strategies that work in a given context may simply be ineffective in other political settings and vice versa. Thus, more recent work has shifted away from the study of the effectiveness of disruption and the organizational characteristics of social movements and has moved toward the environmental conditions that channels their consequences. This has been done along two distinct directions. First, the role of public opinion in facilitating or preventing movements has been thoroughly investigated, particularly in the United States. A major turn in the study of movement outcomes, however, has also come from comparative analyses that attempt to link them to the movements' political context. Next, I briefly turn to these two avenues of research.

Public Opinion

Social movements—particularly when they express themselves through their most typical form of action, public demonstrations—address their message simultaneously to two distinct targets: the power holders and the general public. On the one hand, they press the political authorities in order to get recognized as well as to get their demands met, at least in part. On the other hand, they seek public support and try to sensitize the population to their cause. At the same time, the most common political targets of contemporary movements, local or national governments, pay particular attention to the public opinion and the fluctuations therein. All this makes a strong case for taking public opinion into account as an important external factor in the study of the outcomes of social movements. This has been done above all in the United States. Public opinion has entered the study of movement outcomes both as an explanatory variable and as an explanandum. In the former case, one examines how and to what extent movements produce changes in the perceptions people have of a given issue (e.g., Gusfield 1981; Lawson 1976; Oberschall 1973; Orfield 1975). However, while it seems rather obvious that protest activities raise the awareness of the population over certain political issues, changes in public opinion can also help movements to reach their goals by making decision makers more responsive to their demands. Hence, several authors have stressed the role of public opinion for legislative change, though the two factors do not necessarily add up to the impact of social movements (e.g., Burstein 1979a, 1979b, 1979c, 1985; Burstein and Freudenburg 1978; Costain and Majstorovic 1994; Page and Shapiro 1983; Weissberg 1976).

Paul Burstein is certainly among those who have paid most attention to this aspect. In his analysis of the struggle for equal employment opportunity in the United States, he shows how "equal employment opportunity legislation was adopted as the result of social changes that were manifested in public opinion, crystallized in the civil rights and women's movements, and transformed into public policy by political leaders" (Burstein 1985, 125), thus pointing to the interconnections of public opinion, movement activities, and congressional action in bringing about policy changes for discriminated groups. Similarly, Costain and Majstorovic (1994) have studied the multiple origins of women's rights legislation by stressing the same three sets of factors, arguing that there are several views of the relationship between public opinion and legislative action. They see four prevailing interpretations:

1. a public opinion interpretation, stating a direct relationship between public opinion and legislative change;
2. an interpretation that sees public opinion as filtering the impact of outside events on legislative action;
3. an elite behavior interpretation, according to which public opinion is affected by legislative elites; and

4. a social movement interpretation, whereby legislation results from the joint action of social movements, public opinion, and media coverage.

The fourth appears as the most plausible interpretation, for it not only takes into account movement actions and changes in public opinion, but it also acknowledges the fundamental role of the media for reporting movement mobilization and outcomes. The existing literature has largely neglected how the media covers, frames, and interprets social movements; however, with the analysis of the role of political opportunity structures for movement outcomes, the subject is a promising avenue for future research (e.g., Gamson and Wolfsfeld 1993).

Political Opportunity Structures

As our initial example about the fall of the Communist regimes of Eastern Europe illustrates, and as Goldstone's reanalysis (1980a) of Gamson's data made clear, the study of the outcomes of social movements cannot avoid taking into account the political context in which they are operating. On the basis of a series of methodological criticisms, Goldstone challenged both Gamson's main conclusions and his basic theoretical tenet. He found that the organizational and tactical characteristics had no effect on group success. The timing of success, he maintained, is independent of the challengers' organization and tactics. Most important, he suggested that the resource mobilization model be replaced by a model that stressed the crucial role of broad, systemwide national crises for the success of social movements. We have a name for it: the political process model. By looking at how external political factors affect protest behavior, this approach stresses the importance of the movements' larger environment and the eventual outcomes (e.g., Kitschelt 1986; Kriesi et al. 1995; McAdam 1982; Rochon and Mazmanian 1993; Tarrow 1998). This, I think, is a clear theoretical advance and a definite way to follow.

The central concept in the political process model is that of political opportunity structure. In spite of various conceptualizations, two aspects appear to be crucial for the understanding of the relation between social movements and their political environment: the system of alliances and oppositions, and the structure of the state. The importance of having powerful allies both within and outside the institutional arena has been stressed on several occasions. Early work has focused in particular on the context of social support and has conceived of alliances as a political resource that movements can use to become more successful, especially since movements were considered powerless challengers. One of the first systematic statements in this respect has been made by Lipsky (1968; see also Lipsky 1970; Lipsky and Olson 1977), who saw movements as strongly dependent on the activation of third parties to be successful in the long run. Schumaker (1975) arrived at a similar conclusion in his study of the responsiveness of political authorities to racial riots. However, third parties also include opponents, a factor that might influence the oversimplified relationship between movements and the state and either prevent or facilitate movements' outcomes; yet, few authors have looked at the role of opponents (e.g., Barkan 1984; Jasper and Poulsen 1993; McAdam 1982; Turk and Zucker 1984). This perspective would stipulate that the effectiveness of social movements depends on their capability to engage in bargaining activities with allies and opponents (Burstein, Einwohner, and Hollander 1995).

The importance of political resources and institutions for movement outcomes has also been stressed by Jenkins and Perrow (1977), who have suggested a link between changes in the political environment that offer social resources, on the one hand, and the rise and success of farm worker insurgents, on the other. The conducive environment in their study is represented by the government and by a coalition of liberal support organizations. They argue that the ultimate success of powerless insurgents is due to a combination of sustained outside support, the disunity of the political elites, and their tolerance, all of which provide the movement with crucial resources. Similarly, Piven and Cloward (1979) point to the important constraining role of institutions, which shapes opportunities for action, model its forms, and limit its impact. They maintain that protest is more likely to have a real impact when challengers have a central role in institutions and when powerful allies have a stake in those institutions. Specifically, they view the electoral–representative system as a major factor mediating the political impact of institutional disruptions.

In line with this emphasis on political institutions, more recent work has begun to follow what I see as the most promising avenue of research on the outcomes of social movements: first, to carry on cross-national comparisons of movements; and, second, to examine one or more instances and their array of various potential consequences in order to formulate plausible causal theories about the link between movement actions and those consequences. In so doing, one can assess the filtering role of the political context on movement outcomes. Following this perspective, Amenta, Carruthers, and Zylan (1992) have shown, for the case of early social policy in the United States, that the best explanation is the political mediation model, which places political opportunity structure as a mediating factor between social movements and their success. Their conclusion is that the state and the political party system ultimately determine whether social movements can win acceptance and new advantages.

Although attempts at comparing movement outcomes across countries are not new (e.g., Kitschelt 1986; Kowalewski and Schumaker 1981; Jasper 1990; Midttun and Rucht 1994; Rüdig 1990), there is still a huge void in the literature as opposed to case studies of single movements or countries. The most well-known of these cross-national studies is probably that of Kitschelt. In his influential comparison of the antinuclear movement in four Western democracies, he makes a strong case for the structural determinants of social movement outcomes, arguing that the success of the antinuclear movement is strongly dependent on political opportunity structures. A more recent contribution elaborates on Kitschelt's model to show the crucial role of political opportunities in shaping the outcomes of Western Europe's new social movements (Kriesi et al. 1995, ch. 9). Hopefully, other scholars will soon join these efforts and carry on comparative studies on the outcomes and consequences of social movements.

Success, Failure, Outcomes, Consequences

At this point, I need to clarify certain terms of our discussion. So far, we have seen that a first strand of research has inquired into the internal and organizational characteristics of social movements that may help them to bring about (policy) outcomes and hence become successful, whereas a second strand has tried to put the movements in their larger social and political environment, in particular by examining the role of public opinion and political opportunity structures as intervening factors mediating the movement–outcomes nexus. In doing so, scholars have relied on various typologies of outcomes. The most well-known is certainly the one proposed by Gamson (1990), who has defined *success* as a set of outcomes that fall into two basic clusters: first, the antagonists' acceptance of a challenging group, by their recognizing the group as a valid representative for a legitimate set of interests; second, the gain of new advantages by the group's beneficiary during the challenge and its aftermath. By combining these two dimensions, the author has defined four possible outcomes of a challenge: full response, preemption, co-optation, and collapse. Unfortunately, this typology is not fully exploited in the empirical analyses, which remain for the most part confined to the twofold distinction between acceptance and new advantages. I have elaborated on Gamson's main findings earlier. What matters here is to see how his simple typology has influenced much subsequent research. In some way, it has put some limits on research, for it brought the focus on the organizations instead of the broader cycles of protest, which may include various movements whose combined effect might be more important than the impact of a single challenging group (Tarrow 1998).

Several authors have adopted the distinction between acceptance and new advantages or have given a revised version of it. Among the former are obviously those who have reanalyzed Gamson's original data (Frey, Dietz, and Kalof 1992; Goldstone 1980a; Mirowsky and Ross 1981; Steedly and Foley 1979). Webb and several of his collaborators have built on Gamson's typology and work, but they used a different dataset (Webb et al. 1983). Amenta, Carruthers, and Zylan (1992), however, have defined three levels of success in an attempt to elaborate on Gamson's typology: co-optation, or the recognition from opponents or the state; gains in policies that aid the group; and the transformation of challengers into members of the polity. Within each type are various degrees of success. Here, however, we begin to see the dangers entailed in the use of the notions of success and failure. First, such a perspective assumes that social movements are homogeneous; hence, it tends to attribute success or failure to an entire movement (unless, however, one focuses on single organizations, as Gamson did). Yet, often there is little agreement among movement leaders and participants, even within a given organization, as to which goal must be pursued. Second, as it is not always uniformly evaluated by everyone, success raises the question of subjectivity. Movement participants and external observers may have different perceptions of what counts as success, and the same action may be judged as successful by some participants and as failed by others. Finally, the notion of success is problematic because it overstates the intention of participants. Once again, while social movements are rational efforts to bring about change, many of their consequences are unintended and often unrelated to their claims.

These ambiguities notwithstanding, a great many scholars have looked at the determinants of a movement's success or failure (e.g., Amenta, Carruthers, and Zylan 1992; Banaszak 1996; Brill 1971; Burstein, Einwohner, and Hollander 1995; Frey, Dietz, and Kalof 1992; Gamson 1990; Goldstone 1980a; Mirowsky and Ross 1981; Nichols 1987; Perrot 1987; Piven and Cloward 1979; Shorter and Tilly 1971; Steedly and Foley 1979). Therefore, most of the existing typologies are framed, explicitly or implicitly, in terms of success. Consider the following examples. First, Rochon and Mazmanian (1993) have added a third type of impact to Gamson's distinction, thus defining three arenas of movement success:

1. policy changes, or *new advantages*, in Gamson's terminology;
2. changes in the policy process, or Gamson's *acceptance*; and
3. changes in social values.

Drawing from the social problems literature and from the public policy literature, Schumaker (1975) has defined five criteria of government responsiveness to movement demands: access, agenda, policy, output, and impact. Rüdig (1990) has used it in his comprehensive study of the antinuclear movement worldwide. Burstein, Einwohner, and Hollander (1995) have also relied on this typology, pointing out correctly that it addresses several aspects of the political process that had previously been left out. However, they have added structural effects as a sixth type of government responsiveness, thus acknowledging that movement can provoke alterations in the institutional arrangements of society. Kitschelt (1986) has also stressed structural effects (i.e., a transformation of the political structures), in addition to procedural effects (Gamson's *acceptance*) and substantive effects (Gamson's *new advantages*). This typology allows for a link between the outcomes of social movements and their political context. In quite a similar way, Gurr (1980) had previously defined three types of outcomes of violent conflicts: effects on the group fate, policy changes, and societal or systemic effects. The advantage of this typology is that it makes a clear distinction between internal effects on the movement and external effects on policy or the larger society. Kriesi (1995a) added a further distinction to Kitschelt's typology by defining two types of substantive impact:

1. *reactive effects:* the prevention of "new disadvantages"; and
2. *proactive effects:* the introduction of "new advantages."

This distinction is relevant with regard to political opportunity structures: not only does it allow us to link social movement outcomes to the strength of the state, but it also has been used to investigate the outcomes of Western Europe's new social movements (Kriesi et al. 1995, ch. 9). Finally, Rucht (1992) acknowledges the need to distinguish between goal-related outcomes and broader consequences by classifying the effects of social movements according to two dimensions: internal or external, and intended or unintended.

Gurr's typology and Rochon and Mazmanian's typology present a further advantage: they acknowledge the possibility that different types of outcomes can be related to each other. This is an important point. Gurr, for example, has suggested that group changes and systemic changes can be seen as ultimate outcomes that take place through policy changes, which in turn are the proximate result of violent conflicts (Gurr 1980). Rochon and Mazmanian (1993) maintain that substantial gains may be more easily obtained once a challenging group has reached some degree of acceptance. Other authors have similarly explored how social movements can make a greater impact by pursuing goals in administrative agencies and courts once they have achieved policy responsiveness (e.g., Burstein 1985, 1991; Handler 1978; Sabatier 1975). A recent interesting variant has been proposed by Diani (1997), who claims that when movements are able to facilitate the emergence of new social networks, they will be more influential in processes of political and cultural change. Here we abandon the classificatory terrain to begin to reason in terms of relationships between variables. In other words, it is the beginning of a theory of movement outcomes. Unfortunately, very little research has been done to show how a certain type of impact can help to bring about another type. Here, however, we have another interesting avenue for future research.

Several authors have stressed the methodological problems that have been preventing social scientists from systematically analyzing the consequences of the presence and action of social movements, including the problem of causal attribution, the problem of time reference and effect stability, the problem of movement goal adaptation, the problem of interrelated effects, and the problem of unintended and perverse effects (Rucht 1992; see further Giugni 1994; Gurr 1980; Snyder and Kelly 1979). Although this is not the place to propose solutions to these and related methodological problems, it would perhaps help to point out a logical puzzle that lies uphill and the recognition of which would make the task of setting a research agenda easier. It has to do with the blurring of some fundamental distinctions between types of potential effects of movements. The majority of the existing studies deal with effects that are related to the movements' stated programs and conclusions. The Shell–Greenpeace case mentioned at the outset is an apt example: a declared goal by a challenging group is reached, allegedly as a result (at least in part) of the group's actions. But only under exceptional circumstances do movement actions have such an immediate and successful impact. Most of the time, movements promote their programs cumulatively over months and even years of claim-making (Tilly 1999). This makes the analysis much more complicated; yet, most research has focused on *outcomes* of social movements, which we may define as a special case of the more general set of their *consequences*: those that relate directly to the goals and ends of challengers.

Even more narrowly, work on outcomes has usually looked at the impact of movements on government policy or legislation (e.g., Amenta, Carruthers, and Zylan 1992; Banaszak 1996; Burstein 1979a, 1985; Burstein and Freudenburg 1978; Button 1978, 1989; Costain and Majstorovic 1994; Gelb 1989; Gelb and Palley 1987; Huberts 1989; MacDougal, Minicucci, and Myers 1995). Three (only partly correct) assumptions are perhaps at the origin of this strong focus on policy outcomes.

First, the view held by the political process approach is that social movements essentially target political authorities and institutions; hence, they are mainly aimed at provoking political change. While such definition covers a crucial aspect of the national social movement and is widely adopted in the literature (McAdam, McCarthy, and Zald 1996; Tarrow 1998; Tilly 1984), contemporary movements often address the larger public, aiming, for example, to change attitudes and opinions on a given matter. In addition, other authors have warned us about the dangers of restricting our attention to the political side of new social movements, as they have identity-related goals that do not necessarily require a political target (Melucci 1996). Second, and related to the first point, the eagerness to find the causes of a movement's success or failure is an attitude facilitated by the activist past of many scholars and by a sympathetic stand toward many contemporary movements. Third, there is a conviction that policy changes are more easily measured than cultural changes. The latter reason would explain why we still have rather few studies on the cultural aspects of movements, except for the individual-level consequences of participation in social movements and activism, on which there is a considerable body of literature (e.g., Abramowitz and Nassi 1981; Demerath et al. 1971; Fendrich 1974, 1977; Fendrich and Krauss 1978; Fendrich and Lovoy 1988; Fendrich and Tarleau 1973; Jennings 1987; Jennings and Niemi 1981; Meyer and Maidenberg 1970; Marwell, Aiken, and Demerath 1987; McAdam 1988a, 1989, 1999; Whalen and Flacks 1980). However, there is work on what may be seen as instances of the cultural impact of movements, such as their spillover effects from one movement to the other (Meyer and Whittier 1994), their capacity to generate social capitals (Diani 1997), their impact on the media (Gamson and Wolfsfeld 1993), and so forth; but these are rather sporadic in comparison to the huge amount of works on policy outcomes. Other authors, though, have looked at the cultural determinants of movement success as measured through policy or legislative change (e.g., Banaszak 1996), thus reversing the causal arrow.

Studying how social movements have their demands met is, of course, a legitimate endeavor that will help to improve our knowledge of the causal processes involved in social and political change. Yet, like all kinds of actions, the effects of social movements are often indirect, unintended, and sometimes even in contradiction to their goals (on the unintended consequences of social action, see Tilly 1996). Increased repression, for example, is often an immediate effect of protest (della Porta 1995). Tarrow (1989, 1993, 1998) goes precisely in this direction when he looks at the broad repercussions of cycles of protest, including cycles of reform. In his study of the Italian protest cycle of the sixties and seventies (Tarrow 1989), the author shows that this period of disorder has made a crucial impact and has had a positive legacy on Italian democracy by promoting reform, expanding the political arena, giving autonomy to Italian voters and, above all, by expanding the repertoire of the legitimate forms of political participation. By analyzing social movements at the macrolevel, Tarrow has established a link between two broad phenomena: the emergence, development, and decline of a cycle of protest, on the one hand, and political, institutional, and cultural changes, on the other hand, whereby the former plays a crucial role in bringing about the latter.

Empirical work that focuses explicitly on the unintended consequences of social movements is quite rare (e.g., Deng 1997); yet, as Charles Tilly (1999, 268) has put it, "this range of effects far surpasses the explicit demands made by activists in the course of social movements, and sometimes negates them. By any standard, 'success' and 'failure' hardly describe most of the effects." In addition, he maintains, third parties can act and produce changes in the zone of a movement's activities and interests. According to Tilly, the difficulties of analyzing the consequences of social movements arise precisely from this logical situation, which he has schematized as three overlapping circles. Analysts should take into consideration three sets of variables: all movement claims, all effects of movements actions, and all effects of outside events and actions. The overlapping of these three variables creates four situations that must be analytically distinguished. As figure 2.1 shows, what I define as outcomes—that is,

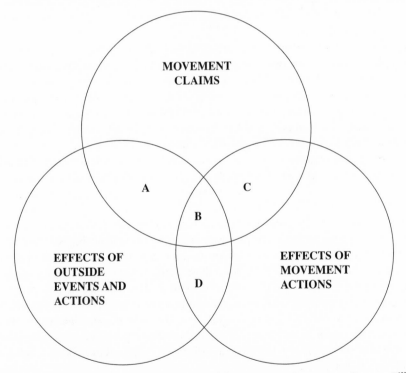

Figure 2.1. The Problem of Identifying Social Movement Outcomes. *Source*: Tilly **(1999).** A = Effects of movement actions that bear directly on movement claims. B = Joint effects of movement actions and outside influences that bear directly on movement claims. C = Effects of outside influences (but not of movement actions) that bear directly on movement claims. D = Joint effects of movement actions and outside influences that *don't* bear on movement claims.

the effects of movement actions that bear directly on movement claims—result from the overlapping of set 1 and set 2 mentioned above.

If the effects can be completely attributed to the movement's action, we can speak of success when the effects are positive, and failure when they are negative (intersection A), though the problem of the differential evaluation of success remains. But at least a part of the outcomes are produced as joint effects of movement actions and outside influences (intersection B). Furthermore, sometimes external events and actions may produce effects that satisfy movement claims (intersection C). Finally, we must take into account the possibility of joint effects of movement actions and outside influences that do not bear directly on movement claims—that is, unintended consequences. Once we have posed the fundamental logical problem (so nicely illustrated by Tilly), we will be in a better position to build causal theories about social movements, their success or failure, their outcomes, and the broader consequences of their actions.

Conclusion

As the review of the relevant literature reveals, much work on the impact of social movements and protest behavior has been done during the seventies. The spark was provided by the wave of student and antiwar protest as well as the riots that occurred in American cities during the sixties. The latter in particular incited American scholars to inquire not only into the causes but also into the consequences of violent political behavior. European scholars, however, have usually privileged the broad processes that have led to the emergence of the new social movements, hence paying only little attention to their repercussions on society, especially in empirical research. Subsequently, the interest in the effects of movements has some what waned. It has resurfaced recently, however. A collective volume (Giugni, McAdam, and Tilly, 1999), among other recently published works and ongoing studies, testifies to this renewed interest in the consequences of social movements, which stems less from the need to understand current practices in society, such as riot behavior in urban settings, than from the willingness to fill an important gap in the social movement literature. As such, it is less focused on those characteristics and features shown by the phenomena currently under way and more genuinely aimed at unveiling the processes and dynamics that allow movements to make an impact on different aspects of society. This alone gives us some reassurances that more attention will be paid in future to crucial consequences of social movements previously neglected. I am referring in particular to their potential for influencing processes of broader cultural and institutional change.

An agenda for future research should focus on the comparative study of the outcomes and consequences of social movements. Comparisons between different political contexts, different movements, and different periods will generate explanations regarding the causal dynamics involved in processes of social and political change. A promising way to do so is to adopt a historical comparative design aimed at analyzing concords and differences. Specifically, we would have much to gain from conducting in-depth comparisons of different national cases and different movements over a relatively long period, thereby comparing interactions that allow distinct movements to have a given type of consequences in different countries. By analyzing movement consequences following a comparative design, we will be able to avoid the formulation of invariant models, which serve the needs of social sciences so poorly (Tilly 1995). In addition, as Tilly (1999) has correctly put it, the study of the outcomes and consequences of social movements implies, and indeed requires, the analysis of movement interactions and dynamics. If we do not pay careful attention to such interactions and dynamics, the methodological problems I have pointed out will always render our analyses weak and our conclusions shaky. If we do not first clarify the dynamics that have led hundreds of thousands of people to challenge the Communist regimes in Eastern Europe, we will hardly be able to establish whether and how those protests were instrumental in the dramatic changes that occurred. Similarly, if we do not first shed light on the interactions among Greenpeace activists, political elites and institutions, public opinion, and Shell's leaders, we will find it difficult to attribute the company's decision not to destroy the Brent Spar oil rig to the environmentalists' outraged call for a boycott. After all, without interactions there are simply no outcomes or consequences.

Notes

Adapted and reprinted with permission from the *Annual Review of Sociology*, vol. 24, ©1998 by Annual Reviews (www.annualreviews.org). I tried to stay as close as possible to the original version to remain faithful to the ideas expressed in it. This explains certain minor, mainly formal, inconsistencies with other parts of the book and certain redundancies.

1. That I had to leave out a great many existing works, due to lack of space, is a clear indication that there is a large body of literature on movement consequences. It should also be noted that studies of social revolutions, insofar as the latter are the product of social movements or coalitions between movements and oppositional elites, may be considered as the most dramatic effect of movements. Again, for space reasons, I do not deal with this aspect.

2. These reanalyses have been included in the book's second edition (Gamson 1990).

CHAPTER THREE

A Brief History of Ecology, Antinuclear, and Peace Movements in Three Countries

A necessary step in the analysis of social movements and their the consequences consists in looking at how they have been acting. No study of the impact of movements can ignore the actions that are supposedly at the origin of those effects (Tilly 1999). That is the purpose of this chapter. I provide a brief historical overview of the mobilization by ecology, antinuclear, and peace movements in each of the three countries under study, focusing in particular on the past three decades, which have witnessed the rise of an important wave of protests on environmental, nuclear energy, and peace issues. Chapter 4 then gives an overview of the existing policies in the domains targeted by these movements: environmental protection, nuclear energy, and national security. In line with the stress on dynamic aspects given in this book, both chapters show developments over time. Of course, the descriptions of protest activities and state policies are quite sketchy. It is virtually impossible to go into the details of three social movements and three policy domains in three countries and, at the same time, remain within reasonable space. Therefore, I focus on the general trends and their most relevant aspects, in the hope of providing the ground for a preliminary assessment of the movements' impact, based on a comparison of the historical overviews presented in chapters 3 and 4.

The description of the mobilization of the three movements provided in this chapter is based on the protest event data collected for this study, and, using figures, I illustrate the patterns of development of protest over time.[1] Although the history of ecology, antinuclear, and peace movements is in part a common history due to partly overlapping issues, goals, and participants in multiorganizational fields, for the sake of clarity I present each movement separately, per country. In the final section of the chapter, I try to restore the historical interconnectedness of the movements by providing a comparative summary of their development with regard to their mobilization in the United States, Italy, and Switzerland.

A Brief History of Ecology, Antinuclear, and Peace Movements in the United States

The U.S. ecology, antinuclear, and peace movements share a historical characteristic: they all have been "early risers" (McAdam 1995a; Tarrow 1998), as compared to their homologous counterparts in other countries, such as those in Switzerland and, above all, those in Italy. In effect, what was probably the first "environmental" organization ever (at least at the national level) was the American Society for the Prevention of Cruelty to Animals, which was created in 1866. The first national conservation park, Yellowstone, opened in 1872. Similarly, the origins of pacifism conceived as an organized effort to promote the peace, also through political activities, are found in the Anglo-Saxon world. The New York Peace Society and the Massachusetts Peace Society were founded in 1815, while, on the other side of the Atlantic, the London Peace Society was created in 1816. As in the case of nature conservation, this early peace reformism had little to do with the ecology and peace movements of the mid- and late-twentieth century. They were movements of ideas led by a small number of intellectual elites, rather than popular movements involving thousands of middle-class citizens.

The new ecology and peace movements, too, have in a way started their cycle of protests in the United States before spreading to other Western countries.[2] Environmental concern took an upward swing during the 1960s, epitomized by Rachel Carson's (1962) alert against the danger of the use of pesticides; and by the end of the decade, it evolved into modern environmentalism, as witnessed by the huge impact of Earth Day in 1970. Similarly, the anti–Vietnam War protests that swept the American university campuses from 1965 to 1975 can be seen as the beginning of a new era of peace activism. Finally, although the first direct actions targeting projects of nuclear power plants occurred in Europe—most notably, in France, Germany, and Switzerland—significant antinuclear opposition in the form of expert dissent and legal actions started in the United States. In the following, I describe in more detail the mobilization of these three movements in the United States, in particular from the early 1970s onward. I do so with the help of figures 3.1a, 3.1b, and 3.1c, which show the development of these protest events per movement between 1975 and 1999. Two lines are shown in each figure: one for conventional actions (juridical, political, and media oriented) and one for unconventional actions (demonstrative, confrontational, and violent). The former, however, is only indicative, and in my comments I rely mainly on the latter.[3] These figures give us a raw indicator of the ebbs and flows in the mobilization of the three movements during the period under study. They serve as a canvas for the brief historical overview provided hereafter.

The U.S. Ecology Movement

During the 1960s, environmental concerns were put onto the public and political agendas in the United States.[4] At the same time, a new focus on pollution and the dangers of uncontrolled growth was added to the traditional conservationist issues. As Sale has put it (1993), a shift occurred from an earlier biocentric understanding to a newer anthropocentric understanding. If the 1960s witnessed a growing and

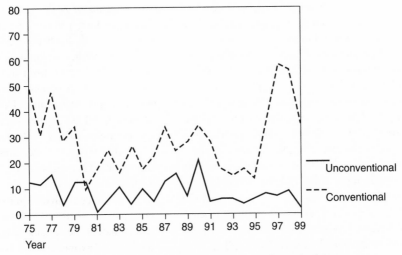

Figure 3.1a. Number of Ecology Protests in the United States.

widespread public concern about the state of the environment, it is only in 1970 that a truly national ecology movement took shape. At that time, a national mass movement in favor of environmental protection and related issues emerged. This can symbolically be dated even more precisely: April 22, 1970. That day, hundreds of thousands of Americans filled the streets of many cities to express their concern for the state of the environment.

The first Earth Day, with its reported twenty million participants (Dunlap and Gale 1972), was an impressive display of popular support for a common cause. In this sense, we can speak of the emergence of a social movement. However, we can also see an important distinguishing trait of the ecology movement as compared to antinuclear and peace movements: the highly consensual nature of the issues addressed. Especially when it comes to publicly demonstrated concern toward environmental problems, citizens and political elites become part of the same mass celebration. Earth Day symbolizes this alliance, as it was officially recognized across the country. In fact, the whole thing had been thought up by U.S. senator Gaylord Nelson.

The 1970s are often seen as a period of strong growth of the U.S. ecology movement. Although I do not have data at my disposal for the first half of the decade, there is little doubt that the first Earth Day spurred a series of activities that dramatically broadened the movement's base of support and produced an increase in its mobilization. Nevertheless, in spite of a certain general stability of unconventional mobilization over the whole period, figure 3.1a shows a declining trend—if any—from 1975 to 1981.

It thus seems that, after its emergence phase, the American ecology movement has experienced a decline during the years of the pro-environment Carter administration, at least as far as overt protest actions are concerned. However, during those years, the movement strengthened its organizational base through the multiplication of new organizations and the strengthening of old ones, in terms of both members and financial resources. Incidentally, this shows that action and organization do not necessarily go hand in hand. I return to this aspect more thoroughly in chapter 6.

In spite of some difficulties during the second half of the 1970s, environmental mobilization remained quite sustained, particularly at the local level, on the front of air and water pollution. For example, a strong and unusually disruptive protest occurred in 1977 on the occasion of the first flights of the supersonic airplane Concorde. This project encountered strong opposition in the New York area, where the inaugural trips took place, from local residents protesting against the noise and the pollution caused by the aircraft. Ironically, most demonstrations consisted of blocking the traffic around Kennedy International Airport with a long queue of cars. This can be seen as a typical example of the "NIMBY" approach ("Not in My Back Yard") that characterized much local environmental activity during the 1970s and 1980s, not only in the United States. It is an approach that might be labeled as narrow and self-interested but that has nevertheless contributed to create a pro-environment climate at the national level, particularly when it evolved into a "NIABY" approach ("Not in Anyone's Back Yard"; Freudenburg and Steinsapir 1992).

Local grassroots activism became more noteworthy during the 1980s, and at the same time, radical environmentalism spread across the country. Both developments were facilitated by the emergence of one of the most salient and enduring environmental issues in the United States: toxic and hazardous industrial wastes.[5] The problem of industrial wastes became a national issue starting in 1978. Before that year, it was a matter of sporadic, isolated instances of local protest (Szasz 1994), but in 1978 the story of Love Canal was suddenly brought to the attention of the national audience by intense media coverage.[6] Love Canal is an area of Niagara Falls, New York, where a chemical company had dumped toxic chemical waste decades before the American public became aware of it. The canal was covered up in 1952, and homes as well as a school were built in the following years. But during the 1970s, after heavy rains, the wastes resurfaced and alerted the residents about serious health problems caused by those substances. Starting from August 1978, the Love Canal and, more generally, the hazardous wastes were dramatized through intense and widespread media coverage, specifically through new stories carried by the major television networks. Media attention was particularly intense over the next two years, not only about Love Canal, but also concerning a number of other sites that, taken together, conveyed a sense that the toxic waste problem was a major one for the nation. At the same time, local protests and concern for this problem spread throughout the country.

The number of protest events increased in the 1980s, during an extremely unfavorable period for pro-environment supporters under the Reagan and first Bush Republican presidencies. In particular, what has been labeled the "Reagan Reaction" (Sale 1993) halted the progress of environmental policies and redistributed government resources toward the military sector. In fact, under the Reagan administration the level of mobilization remained rather stable; however, the movement itself divided not only into an increasingly professional mainstream sector but also into an increasingly radical grassroots sector. Only at the end of its mandate and during the Bush administration did the number of protest events rise again. Hardly a pro-environment advocate, Bush made the environment a centerpiece of his 1988 presidential campaign. Coupled with intense media reports on the dangers faced by the earth,[7] this probably helped to redirect the issue onto the national public agenda, although in the four years following election he remained quite ambivalent, to say the least, as to policies to protect the environment.

If the 1980s witnessed a slow but steady increase in the number of protest actions carried out by the ecology movement, the early 1990s are characterized by a sharp decline of mobilization, which then remained relatively low in a period apparently favorable to the movement. President Clinton's undoubtedly pro-environmental stance (to the extent that an American president can be so, given the various interests at stake) and the choice of Al Gore, a leading environmental advocate who has written a number of books on this topic, on the presidential ticket were a clear way of presenting the future administration during the campaign as one that would take this problem seriously. Indeed, the problem was taken seriously; when he took office, Clinton made environmental protection a major issue in his political agenda. This apparently discouraged the ecology movement from waging a high number of protest actions during the first years of his presidency.

Things, however, changed in the second half of the 1990s. Between 1996 and 1998, the U.S. ecology movement started again to mobilize in important ways. The number of unconventional protests increased at a slow but significant pace, yet the most striking aspect is the significant amount of conventional actions carried out during those years. While I cannot exclude certain coding problems,[8] this is something both unexpected and difficult to explain. It might partly be related to the debates that surrounded the Kyoto Protocol of the United Nations Framework Convention on Climate Change (UNFCCC), which was adopted in December 1997 and open for signature from March 1998 to March 1999.[9] This important event might have reinvigorated environmentalists in various parts of the world, and the following data on Italy and Switzerland show that the ecology movement indeed mobilized strongly in both countries during that period. The preeminently conventional mobilization could be due to the fact that this is quite a technical piece of environmental regulation, which ecology movement organizations have preferred to address through lobbying strategies and public statements aimed at influencing the states to ratify the convention and protocol. Yet, most of the events in the sample did not directly address the Kyoto Protocol; they were often local protests that may nevertheless have been spurred by the renewal of environmental concern in part due to the debate around the protocol.

The purpose of this book is not to explain the ebbs and flows of mobilization but to ascertain to what extent protest contributes to policy change; nevertheless, it is interesting to note that there seems to be a relationship between the presidency and the protest actions carried out by the ecology movement, especially if we focus on unconventional actions. The important exception to this rule is the large protest wave that occurred in the late 1990s, though it is one that mostly occurred through conventional actions. Apart from that, mobilization went up under Republican (and pro-business) presidents Reagan and George H. W. Bush, while it went down when Democratic (and pro-environment) presidents Carter and Clinton were in office. This confirms Kriesi and colleagues' argument (1995) about the impact of the configuration of power on social movements. According to them, when social movements' major potential ally within the institutional arenas shares government responsibilities, social movements have fewer political opportunities to act, which translates into lower levels of mobilization. In contrast, when the ally is in the opposition, it can openly support the movement, at least to the extent that it does not have a major electoral competitor within the same political camp. This theory was applied to Western Europe's new social movements, with the institutional ally being the Socialist Party. Here we have some evidence that this argument works in a totally different institutional context, such as in the United States: the ecology movements were less active when the Democratic Party—the movement's potential allies within the institutional political arena—was in power. One possible interpretation of this is that the U.S. ecology movement decreased its activity during the Democratic presidencies largely because environmental policies were undertaken; therefore, there was less "need" to act. I discuss this argument in more detail in chapter 7.

The U.S. Antinuclear Movement

The antinuclear movement and the ecology movement display both differences and similarities.[10] First, they share the underlying motive of their mobilization: a social critique of the risks and dangers of uncontrolled economic growth. In this respect, they can be seen as part of the same movement aimed at opposing a use of technology that overlooks its negative consequences for human beings and their environment. Second, they are different in at least two respects. Unlike environmental issues, antinuclear issues are relatively recent; in the United States, they originated in the "Atoms for Peace" initiative of the Eisenhower administration and, more concretely, in the Atomic Energy Act of 1954, which started the civilian use of nuclear power. Three years later, the first nuclear reactor to face public opposition was the Enrico Fermi fast-breeder plant in the Detroit area. The U.S. antinuclear movement was thus born, insofar as we include expert dissent and legal opposition in a social movement's range of activities. Also, environmental and nuclear energy issues differ as to their salience. The antinuclear issue is more high-profile, as it touches on one of the core interests of the state: the supply of energetic resources to the country (Duyvendak 1995; Kriesi et al. 1995). Furthermore, in countries that have a military nuclear industry, the civilian nuclear industry takes on its significance in relation to the former and hence becomes all the more salient. In contrast, most environmental issues are low profile; that is, they are more negotiable, and the state is more inclined to be "flexible" toward opposition to its policies in this domain. In other words, most environmental issues are more likely to bring to a consensus among political authorities and the civil society alike, whereas nuclear power is a more conflicting issue. This has important implications for the possibilities of the movements to be successful, insofar as the power holders are more or less likely to make concessions to them.

The pattern shown in figure 3.1b is clearly different than the one displayed by the ecology movement; here we observe a single big wave of protests that reached

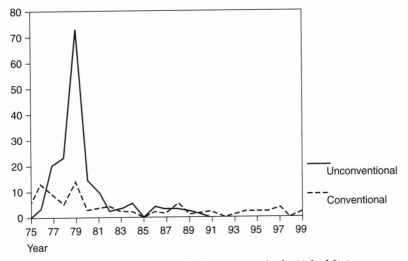

Figure 3.1b. Number of Antinuclear Protests in the United States.

its peak in 1979. Before this protest wave—between 1957 and 1973—opposition to nuclear power followed institutional channels. It was expressed above all through dissent by nuclear experts and through legal intervention by concerned citizens. Expert dissent arose first over low-level radiation and, later on, reactor safety (Joppke 1993). These were the early foci of the U.S. antinuclear movement. Legal intervention was facilitated by the formal openness of the nuclear licensing process in the United States. Citizen participation in hearings represented one of the main forms of action of the movement, also when more disruptive tactics were adopted after the energy crisis following the Arab oil embargo of 1973.

While citizen opposition was rather scant in the late 1950s and early 1960s, legal intervention increased dramatically starting from the second half of the 1960s, spurred by the rise of environmentalism and caught into a larger wave of student protest. For example, only 12 percent of all license applications reviewed in hearings held by the Atomic Energy Commission were contested by local groups between 1962 and 1966, as compared to 32 percent between 1967 and 1971, and 73 percent between 1970 and 1972 (Rolph 1979).

Things changed radically between 1975 and 1980. The opposition to the civilian use of nuclear power became increasingly politicized and national in scope, partly under the thrust of a number of national public-interest advocacy groups. During this phase, nuclear power captured media attention and spurred a real public debate. At the time, the antinuclear movements were using a repertoire of strategies, ranging from institutional tactics—such as lobbying, litigation, and petitions addressed to the Nuclear Regulatory Commission—to extra-institutional tactics, such as public campaigning and mass demonstrations. However, the main innovation of the 1970s was the use of disruptive strategies to halt the development of the nuclear energy industry. As in other countries, the mid-1970s have witnessed a series of direct actions and civil disobedience events by antinuclear activists, most of the time staged on the sites of planned nuclear power plants.

Given the high number of plants across the country,[11] it would be impossible to give an exhaustive overview of the protests targeting all these plants. However, five cases that captured national public attention deserve to be mentioned: Calvert Cliffs, Seabrook, Diablo Canyon, Shoreham, and Three Mile Island. Calvert Cliffs has an important place in the history of nuclear power in the United States because it represents one of the antinuclear movement's first successes, although the movement did not stop any plant but simply contributed to delay licensing and construction periods. In July 1971, the U.S. Appeals Court ruled that the National Environmental Policy Act was applicable to the nuclear licensing process, which caused a backlog of work and complicated the regulatory process. The *Calvert Cliffs Coordinating Committee v. Atomic Energy Commission* court rule was also instrumental in bringing about a reorganization of the country's nuclear policy, showing that the courts are an important part of the political opportunity structure and political process in the United States.

Seabrook station undoubtedly represents the most famous case of direct action by the antinuclear movement. Organized opposition to plans for a nuclear facility near the town of Seabrook, New Hampshire, goes back to the late 1960s, when the Seacoast Anti-Pollution League was formed. However, the protest reached national popularity when the Clamshell Alliance—a loosely organized group formed in 1976 that aimed to prevent construction of the plant mainly through nonviolent direct actions—made its first attempts to block the start of construction in August of the same year. These attempts led to 194 arrests. The largest mass occupation took place in April 1977 and ended up with 1,401 people arrested. This event served as a model for a number of similar alliances that were created around the country. However, this type of direct intervention, one based on civil disobedience, was short-lived and faded away as the momentum for antinuclear protests weakened. In addition, notwithstanding all the efforts made by the Clamshell Alliance, by the various other local oppositions, and by the firm rejection on the part of the governor of Massachusetts to participate in emerging planning procedures,[12] Seabrook station was built and it entered operation, although one unit was canceled in 1986. The major impact of opposition consisted in delaying the whole process for several years. In effect, only in 1990 was it granted an operating license, almost twenty years after the Public Service Company of New Hampshire had applied for approval of the Seabrook site for a nuclear power plant.

Although local opposition began in the early 1970s, the Diablo Canyon nuclear facility, located on the California coast near San Luis Obispo, was brought to the fore in the late 1970s due to strong direct intervention by antinuclear activists, in a way similar to the events in Seabrook. Opposition by means of direct action was led by the Abalone Alliance, a local group modeled on the Clamshell Alliance and sharing a similar history (Epstein 1991). Formed in 1977, the Abalone Alliance held a first blockade at Diablo Canyon on August 6 of the same year, when 47 people were arrested by the police; exactly one year later, a similar happening occurred, but with 487 arrests. Parallel to civil disobedience acts, a series of public rallies took place near the construction site. Probably the largest one was held on June 28, 1979, after the Three

Mile Island accident broke into public opinion and gave a short-lived but important boost to the U.S. antinuclear movement. In spite of intense and local opposition, using a wide range of tactics, the two Diablo Canyon reactors went into operation. Right after the operating licensing was granted by the Nuclear Regulatory Commission, the movement's largest and most dramatic occupation occurred in September 1981, a two-week event that led to 1,960 arrests; however, the event could only provoke a temporary shutdown of the plant, not its abandonment. Once the facility began operating, protests continued, although less dramatically than before.

The Shoreham case is interesting because, as in Seabrook, local authorities helped to delay licensing by refusing to participate in the setup of emergency evacuation plans. The latter became a high-priority issue after the accident at Three Mile Island, and the Nuclear Regulatory Commission required that local officeholders cooperate to provide a number of services needed in case of evacuation. Both Suffolk County and the state of New York (in particular the governor) have long been allied to the movement in trying to prevent the plant from being built.

Finally, Three Mile Island is well known due to the accident that shook the nation on March 28, 1979. Public reaction to this event is largely responsible for the peak of mobilization that we observe in figure 3.1b.[13] The American public reacted massively to the release of radioactive gases from the Three Mile Island nuclear plant, located near Harrisburg, Pennsylvania, and a series of mass demonstrations took place across the country in the following months. The largest one was held in New York in September and involved two hundred thousand people. Previously, in May, an antinuclear rally in Washington, D.C., was attended by sixty-five thousand participants. The Washington event was important also because, for the first time, the direct-action and public-interest sectors of the movement acted in coordination at the national level, hence overcoming existing divergences (Joppke 1993).

That the accident at Three Mile Island had such a huge impact on antinuclear protest is not an accident. Much of the merit has to be attributed to the movement's actions during the previous years, specifically the direct interventions at sites of prospective plants. Those actions brought the nuclear issue to the center of media attention and contributed to sensitizing the public opinion toward the dangers of nuclear energy. The number of American citizens opposing the construction of nuclear power plants was rapidly growing in the months preceding the accident. In addition, the mass media were ready to publicize and dramatize the accident, for the nuclear issue at that time was having high news value. These two related factors certainly provided fertile ground for the outraged reaction by concerned citizens. This shows, as Duyvendak and Koopmans have pointed out (1995), that "suddenly imposed grievances" do not automatically provoke mobilization but do so only to the extent that they are politically constructed. In the case of Three Mile Island, the political construction of the nuclear issue, to which previous actions by the movement have largely contributed, led to a intense outcry of concern. The absence of a strong structural base and the fact that the American nuclear industry was slowly disbanding, however, made this outcry short-lived, and soon the movement virtually disappeared from the public domain, moving to alternative issues such as radioactive wastes and emergency plans.

The former was integrated into the aforementioned issue of hazardous wastes, while other issues were rather technical and therefore less likely to lead to mass protest.

The U.S. Peace Movement

Among the three movements under study, the U.S. peace movement has the deeper historical tradition, has displayed the most intense mobilization, but at the same time was probably the least successful. Explaining why is one of the aims of this book. Here I outline the movement's historical trends to provide the ground for a preliminary assessment of its achievements and failures.[14]

In his survey of the American peace movement, Chatfield (1992) emphasizes six campaigns, three major and three minor, carried by the U.S. peace movement after World War II. The three major campaigns include the first campaign against nuclear arms (1955 to 1963), the anti–Vietnam War movement (1965 to 1975), and the second campaign against nuclear arms (1975 to 1987), which includes the more specific nuclear weapons freeze campaign (1979 to 1985). The three minor campaigns have targeted the antiballistic missile system (ABM), the B-1 bomber program, and the MX missile at different points between 1969 and 1979. To these, we must at least add the Central American peace movement of the 1980s and the protest against U.S. intervention in the Gulf War between 1990 and 1991. Before World War II, we could mention the emergency peace campaign of 1936 to 1937, which addressed the issue of neutrality and gathered the largest peace coalition to date (Kleidman 1993).

In spite of president Eisenhower's rhetoric of the "Atoms for Peace," in the mid-1950s, the nuclear arms race continued to be pursued during the Cold War years. The peace movement's participants have opposed this policy, what they call the "Atoms for War" policy, since the very beginning, and they have intensified their mobilization as the issue of nuclear arms sharpened between 1955 and 1956. A campaign for a test ban was launched, and two new organizations were created specifically to address this aspect: the Nonviolent Action against Nuclear Weapons, which later became the Committee for Nonviolent Action; and the National Committee for a Sane Nuclear Policy, which was at the core of the campaign and has been at the forefront of the antinuclear weapons struggle for decades. Between 1955 and 1963, direct actions, mass protests, and public appeals in the media combined in the attempt to force a comprehensive test ban and, more generally, to sensitize the political authorities and the larger public to the dangers of the nuclear arms race.[15]

The nuclear arms issue was put on the back burner by the American offensive in Vietnam. Needless to say, opposition to the Vietnam War represents the peak of the U.S. peace movement. Reconstituted around the nuclear arms issue and caught in a larger wave of student protests and civil rights protests, among others (McAdam 1995b), the peace movement staged impressive demonstrations during the period of American military involvement in Southeast Asia. The antiwar movement gained momentum starting from February 1965, when American troops began Operation Rolling Thunder in North Vietnam. That intervention set off a wave of protests that began with teach-ins in colleges but evolved into a range of activities, which lasted for about a decade and involved a broad coalition of congressional critics, liberal

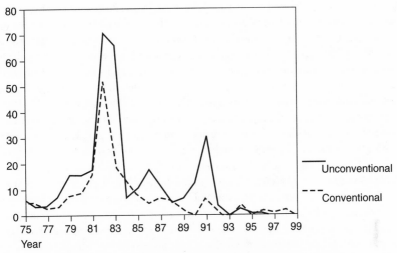

Figure 3.1c. Number of Peace Protests in the United States.

intellectuals, radical pacifists, New Left students, and, later, disillusioned war veterans. Among the young, a crucial role was played by the Students for a Democratic Society (Sale 1973), which radicalized the protest and brought it to university campuses but was a pulling force of the movement in general. Opposition escalated with the war, as witnessed by the increase in the number of events and the number of participants, as well as in the radicalization of the protest. From 1965 to 1971, capital and nationwide demonstrations multiplied, as did protests within university campuses.[16]

As figure 3.1c illustrates, the mobilization of the peace movement decreased after the end of the Vietnam War, but it began to rise again in the late 1970s, forming the first wave of contention, which is included in my data and represented by the second campaign against nuclear arms.

The Nuclear Weapons Freeze Campaign was the backbone of this protest wave. The idea of the freeze as an arms control proposal and a strategy for action was first proposed by peace activist Randall Forsberg in December 1979. It was asked that

> to improve national and international security, the United States and the Soviet Union should stop the nuclear arms race. Specifically, they should adopt a mutual freeze on the testing, production, and deployment of nuclear weapons and of missiles and new aircraft designed primarily to deliver nuclear weapons. This is an essential, verifiable first step toward lessening the risk of nuclear war and reducing the nuclear arsenals. (quoted in Meyer 1990, 160)

In the context of President Carter's military buildup (in spite of his announced goal of eliminating nuclear weapons) and in light of a series of world events that represented the ghost of the Cold War—in particular, the Soviet invasion of Afghanistan, the Nicaraguan revolution, and the Iranian militants' taking of American hostages in

Teheran—the proposal was immediately adopted by pacifists, and the movement gained momentum. In 1980, when Ronald Reagan won the presidential election and the Democrats lost control of the Senate, it soon became clear that his commitment to a military buildup and the strategy of nuclear deterrence would have provoked a vocal reaction by the peace movement. Protest took several forms, going from mass demonstrations to disruptive actions, such as those carried by the Plowshares Eight[17] (more rarely); to teach-ins at colleges and universities (151 on November 11, 1981, for example); to public education tactics, such as those adopted by the nonpartisan organization Ground Zero. As can be seen in figure 3.1c, 1982 represented the peak of peace mobilization. A number of important protest actions took place in that year, among others, the largest demonstration ever in U.S. history, when nearly one million people filled the street of New York City (June 12); nonviolent demonstrations at the Lawrence Livermore Laboratory, a major U.S. nuclear weapons facility, leading to over thirteen hundred arrests (June 21); a series of consultative referenda calling for a worldwide nuclear freeze, with the largest vote ever on a single referendum issue; and Ground Zero Week, a nationwide series of educational events that attracted broad media attention and involved informational programs in thirty cities, thirty college campuses, and more than one thousand high schools (Meyer 1990).

In the end, the freeze proposal was endorsed by no fewer than 12 state legislatures, 321 city councils, 10 labor unions, and even the UN General Assembly (Howlett and Zeitzer 1985). However, as the freeze issue gained ground and legitimacy within the institutional arenas, above all with the passing of nuclear freeze resolutions in both branches of Congress, the peace movement lost momentum, and by 1984 the impressive levels of mobilization displayed in the two preceding years were scaled down abruptly. The huge wave of protest against the nuclear arms race had successfully taken advantage of the broad public awareness toward the nuclear issue brought about by the mobilization of the antinuclear energy movement and by the accident at Three Mile Island; however, the movement declined as quickly as it had risen. The freeze campaign continued at the state and local level but lost its salience as a national political issue.

During the second half of the 1980s, the attention of peace activists shifted to the Reagan administration's foreign policy in Central America and its military spending. Although it did not reach the peaks of the nuclear freeze, as the figure shows, "the broader political battle over U.S. Central American policy in the 1980s, within which the peace movement was a major contender, was the most conspicuously protracted and volatile political struggle of the decade" (Smith 1996, xvii).[18] Opposition against Reagan's policies in Central America emerged in the early 1980s and went on all during his two presidential terms. However, this issue attracted far less attention in the media and was carried largely at the grassroots level.

The peace movement regained the media spotlight between 1990 and 1991, when thousands of American citizens protested their country's military intervention between Iraq and Kuwait after the former invaded the small emirate on August 2, 1990. The anti–Gulf War movement, which was intense but short-lived (like the war), developed along three phases (Peace 1991):

1. opposing U.S. military buildup in Saudi Arabia, from early August to early November 1990, following the Bush administration's change to an offensive strategy;
2. attempting to head off offensive U.S. military action, from early November 1990 to mid-January 1991, following the UN deadline for Iraq's withdrawal; and
3. calling for a cease-fire and negotiations, from mid-January to late February 1991.

The first major national demonstration, sponsored by the Coalition to Stop U.S. Intervention in the Middle East, gathered between 10,000 and 20,000 people in New York on October 10, 1990, but the protest soon escalated to reach much higher figures, especially once intervention began. For example, 50,000 people gathered in Washington and 100,000 in San Francisco, on January 19; one week later, during the National Campaign for Peace in the Middle East, between 100,000 and 250,000 people marched in the streets of the capital, while 100,000 did so in San Francisco (Peace 1991). At the same time, the protest became more disruptive. For example, the January 19 demonstration in San Francisco led to 1,000 arrests in civil disobedience actions; in the three weeks after the deadline, no fewer than 2,700 people were arrested, compared to 1,300 in the previous five months (Peace 1991).

After a cease-fire was called on February 28, 1991, the protest waned as quickly as it had risen. The peace movement has been quiescent since, at least as far as mobilization of national scope is concerned. Indeed, as we can see in figure 3.1c, the level of mobilization reached its historical minimum during the first years of the Clinton administration. The initial reluctance of the leadership to intervene with a strong hand in foreign policy, and its focus on internal politics, explains in part the latency of the movement in the 1990s. However, the United States did make a strong military move in 1999, when, under the banner of NATO, it intervened in the Serbian province of Kosovo to terminate Serbian oppression. Yet, unlike in other countries, such as Italy in particular, this intervention did not provoke a significant reaction by American pacifists.

A Brief History of Ecology, Antinuclear, and Peace Movements in Italy

Figures 3.2a, 3.2b, and 3.2c give us an overview of the mobilization (conventional and unconventional) by ecology, antinuclear, and peace movements in Italy between 1975 and 1999. If we compare these distributions to those referring to the United States, we observe not only a number of differences but also some similarities. First, while the U.S. ecology movement was already strong in the early 1970s, environmental protest in Italy became a truly national issue only after 1985. Second, while the U.S. antinuclear movement had significantly mobilized between 1976 and 1980, antinuclear protest in Italy was never quantitatively relevant; however, it was important from a qualitative point of view, and it peaked after the 1986 accident at Chernobyl.

Third, the mobilization by the peace movement displays a similar development in the two countries, with a large wave of antinuclear weapons protest in the early 1980s and a smaller peak during the Gulf War, but with a different behavior at the beginning and especially at the very end of the period under study.

The Italian Ecology Movement

As in most Western countries, there is a conservationist tradition of environmentalism in Italy, which was originally marked above all by the issue of nature preservation. Also similar to what occurred elsewhere, a political ecology sector developed in the late 1960s and early 1970s, following the rise and fall of antagonistic student movements. The history of the Italian ecology movement can be read in the light of the divisions and alliances between these two sectors, between moderate and radical organizations (Diani 1988, 1990; Donati 1995).[19]

Before 1968, environmental concerns remained restricted to intellectual and scientific elites; no real environmental movement was active at that time, although the Italian branch of the World Wildlife Fund was set up in 1966 and other conservationist organizations were formed some years earlier (Diani 1990).[20] Given the virtually nonexistent grassroots participation by citizens, in this phase we should speak of small public-interest lobbies rather than any major social movements (Diani 1990). Local protests began to emerge in the 1970s. Conditions for the expansion of environmental concern, however, were unfavorable, especially during a period in which class conflict and the political violence related to it were the most salient national issues. Therefore, in spite of growing local activities, we can hardly speak of environmental campaigns before 1976. Although concern about increasing pollution, especially in urban areas, arose during the first half of the 1970s, most protests were reactions to industrial accidents.

A particular feature of the Italian ecology movement lies in the initial difficulty of framing environmental issues outside the traditional class cleavage. The strength of this cleavage in Italy had at least three important consequences on environmentalism. First, unlike in the United States, the "ecological" literature of the 1960s and 1970s had only a limited impact on the general public, mainly because of the dominant framing of reality in terms of class struggle. This, with a lack of coordination that lasted well into the 1980s, delayed the nationalization of the movement. Second, a large part of the ecology movement emerged from the old Left, although this parenthood has lost its salience since. Thus, the first protests against pollution in living conditions arose within the labor movement, for example, in industrial places such as Castellanza, Porto Marghera, and Secondigliano in the early 1970s. Furthermore, the birth of the most important environmental organization—the League for the Environment— was sponsored by the ARCI (Associazione Ricreativa Culturale Italiana), the cultural and leisure time association that was run jointly by the Communist Party and the Socialist Party. Third, the salience of the class cleavage in the Italian society favored the emergence of a division between "green-greens" and "red-greens," which added up to the initial lack of coordination among environmental groups and helped to explain its difficulty to become a truly national movement.

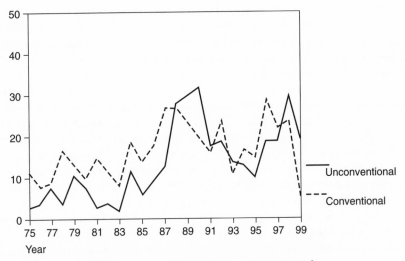

Figure 3.2a. Number of Ecology Protests in Italy.

The difficulty of the Italian ecology movement to reach a national scope is well testified to by the Seveso accident. On July 10, 1976, the Icmesa chemical factory, located in Seveso, a small town near Milan, released a large cloud of dioxin, a highly toxic gas. While the accident inspired the formation of new environmental groups and organizations, particularly at the local level, it had virtually no impact on public perceptions of environmental problems. In brief, the ecology movement failed in its attempt to transform the Seveso accident in a major national issue. This is confirmed by figure 3.2a, as the number of conventional protest events carried by the ecology movement in 1976 does not substantially differ from that of the previous year.

However, there was an increase in mobilization the year after, though it was not due to the industrial accident but rather to traditional issues, such as nature protection as well as animal rights. At the same time, protest activities by the ecology movement in various sectors were stimulated by the rise of overt opposition to nuclear energy during the second half of the 1970s. In a way, the conflict over nuclear energy gave rise to the environmental movement (Diani 1994). The rapprochement between environmental protection and the antinuclear struggle was facilitated by the active involvement in the latter of several major environmental organizations, such as Friends of the Earth, the League for the Environment, and the World Wildlife Fund. (I come back to the antinuclear movement in more detail in the following section.)

One major difference with the United States lies in the creation of a Green Party. Of course, the American two-party system prevents any minor party from entering the congressional arena and discourages any attempt at doing so, whereas the Italian multiparty and proportional system, which existed until 1993, provides small parties with more opportunities to emerge. The first example of the Green Party's running for office at the local level dates back to 1980, when ecology groups presented their candidates at city council elections in four cities (Diani 1989).[21] After several local groups held national conventions between 1984 and 1985, coordination efforts led to the participation of the Greens in the local administrative elections of May 1985, where about 150 lists polled 2.1 percent of the voters in the electoral districts where they competed. Two years later, after the formal constitution of the Italian Federation of Green Lists, in November 1986, participation in the June 1987 elections for the national parliament brought to the Greens 2.5 percent of the votes, thirteen representatives to the lower chamber (*Camera dei Deputati*) and two to the higher chamber (*Senato della Repubblica*). The results were confirmed in the following elections, and the Greens eventually became part of the coalition that ruled the country from 1996 to 2001. It is also worth noting that, in view of the elections for the European parliament in 1989, a second Green list saw the light, called Rainbow Greens, which was closer to small parties with environmental aims, such as the Radical Party and the Workers' Democracy.

The rise and formal constitution of the Green Party corresponds to the expansion of the mobilization of the ecology movement starting from 1983, which can be seen in figure 3.2a. The 1980s witnessed an explosion of environmental actions, which sped up after 1985 and which were probably facilitated by a process of unification among the movement's various components—a process started with the creation of the League for the Environment in 1980, as well as with Green Archipelago in 1981. Besides some rare large demonstrations, such as the one held in Rome in 1983 with thirty thousand participants, a variety of events and campaigns lie behind this rise of mobilization. First, a series of protests occurred in this period, particularly in 1984, that were organized by local grassroots groups and that addressed large chemical industries. Second, the League for the Environment launched a series of monitoring and denunciation campaigns, such as "Green Schooner" (1986) and "Green Train" (1988). More generally, the League for the Environment, which was the leading political ecology organization in Italy, has largely contributed to the increase in the number of events during the 1980s. Third and most notably, a number of national referenda were launched.[22] This implied a series of activities aimed at sustaining the movement. A major role in the referenda campaigns was played by the Radical Party, a small party of the New Left that has often promoted direct democratic campaigns on various themes, from divorce to abortion, from nuclear energy to environmental protection. Already at the beginning of the decade, demands for a referendum on restriction on hunting and one against vivisection experiments either were turned down by the Constitutional Court or had failed to reach the required number of signatures. In 1986, the most prominent environmental organizations jointly launched two national referenda: one on hunting and the other on nuclear energy. The latter, about which I discuss more in detail later, represents one of the greatest victories of the new social movements in Italy. Finally, two referenda, dealing with pesticides and hunting, were defeated in 1990.

Parallel to the increase in protest activities, there was an expansion at the organizational level. Starting from the early 1980s, which can be seen as a turning point for the Italian ecology movement (Diani 1990), established organizations underwent a growth in membership and resources while new grassroots groups were being formed as well (a point that I show systematically in chapter 6). Nevertheless, in spite of the impressive rise of environmental mobilization during the 1980s, national mass demonstrations have only rarely been organized.

After the strong expansion of the 1980s—like the one in the United States and, as we shall see, the one in Switzerland—the mobilization of the ecology movement diminished in the early 1990s but went up again in the second half of the decade, to peak again in 1998. Again, the debate around the Kyoto Protocol of 1997 might at least in part be responsible for this rise of environmental protest, which we observe in all three countries more or less in the same period.

The Italian Antinuclear Movement

As figure 3.2b makes clear, antinuclear opposition in Italy has witnessed two waves of contention: one in the late 1970s and another in the mid-1980s.[23] Following Diani (1994), we can distinguish four phases of the Italian antinuclear movement:

1. a long pre-movement phase characterized by a large consensus on nuclear policy and some elite dissent, from 1946 to 1975;
2. a first encounter addressing the National Energy Plans, from 1975 to 1981;
3. a transition phase, from 1981 to 1985; and
4. a second encounter marked by the Chernobyl accident, from 1985 to 1988.

Although it remained somewhat active at the local level, the movement virtually disappeared from the public domain after 1988, simply because its main target—nuclear power plants and nuclear energy production—dropped in focus.

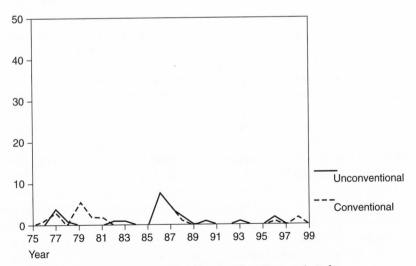

Figure 3.2b.   Number of Antinuclear Protests in Italy.

As in most countries, the development of nuclear energy in the 1950s and 1960s benefited from a consensus among the major political forces. The first three power plants, built between 1958 and 1961, began operating in the absence of significant opposition. It is only from 1975 onward that a true antinuclear movement took shape in Italy. In fact, in my sample, no events targeted nuclear energy in 1975. Before that, an antinuclear critique began to arise but was mostly confined to other business sectors—in particular, oil companies—as well as citizens and municipalities in affected areas. No public conflict was yet present; encounters occurred only in the lobbying and parliamentary arenas.

Things changed after the 1975 National Energy Plan, in which the government made strong commitments to nuclear energy. The Radical Party took up the nuclear issue and the League for Alternative Energy and Anti-Nuclear Opposition was formed in 1977. A few months later, this organization became the Italian section of Friends of the Earth. An explicit opposition at the national level developed; however, it must not make us forget that the Italian antinuclear movement was characterized by strong local opposition but weak national mobilization (Rüdig 1990), quite a surprising situation for a centralized country. At this point, the rising antinuclear movement was made of local groups, sectors of the New Left, and specific organizations dealing with energy and nuclear problems. Demonstrations, marches, and roadblocks were organized, such as those held at Montalto di Castro—the site of a planned power plant that has represented the major focus of antinuclear opposition and that was the only site-related nuclear conflict to attract broad national attention (Rüdig 1990)—in March and November 1976 as well as in August 1977; at Caorso in April 1977; and at Trino Vercellese at the end of the same year. Protest camps were held during the summers of 1977 and 1978. A few large national demonstrations also took place, such as the one held in Rome in May 1979 with fifty thousand participants. Of course, technical and legal tactics continued, but during this phase the antinuclear movement entered the public domain, thanks to mass actions. At the same time, concerned citizens staged protests against dumping nuclear wastes. However, the core of the movement's activities consisted of demonstrations held at the sites where future plants were to be built. In addition, during this phase was the first attempt to use the referendum as a means of stopping the growth of nuclear energy. A national referendum on siting procedures was proposed by Friends of the Earth in 1978 but was invalidated by the Constitutional Court in 1981 on legal matters.

As public attention shifted to the atomic weapons issue, and as public opinion was still largely favorable to the development of nuclear energy, this first wave of antinuclear protest came to an end in the early 1980s. It is worth noting that, unlike in the United States and Switzerland, during this phase no mass civil disobedience events could become the symbolic focus for the movement, at least for its radical flank. In the transition phase, between 1981 and 1985, antinuclear energy protest was quite limited. Once the mass campaigns were over and after the attempt to uphold the direct democratic means at the national level had failed, the movement tried to slow down the pace of siting and construction procedures, via administrative routes and by launching referenda locally. As the interests of antinuclear groups, citizens, and local political parties converged to set the preconditions for a halt to the nuclear program (Diani 1994), the movement took advantage of this phase of relative latency to reorganize by differentiating and institutionalizing its mobilization tactics at the local level. However, some large demonstrations did take place during the first half of the 1980s. Perhaps the most notable were held in Avetrana (1981) and Manduria (1985), two small towns located in the Puglia region. Yet, as figure 3.2b shows, the level of mobilization had its highest peak ever in 1986, during the second encounter phase, which is characterized by two crucial events: the Chernobyl accident and the national referenda on nuclear energy.

On April 28, 1986, the core of the nuclear power plant in Chernobyl, Ukraine, burned, releasing a vast cloud of radioactive gas. Having occurred not too long after a huge wave of protest against atomic weapons, this accident provoked an outburst of mobilization in various European countries. Similar to what happened after the accident at Three Mile Island in the United States, the number of protest events went up dramatically. In Italy, this increase was perhaps less dramatic than in other countries, but it nevertheless took place and, most important, had crucial consequences for the fate of the nuclear power industry in that country (Diani 1994). First, the nuclear conflict acquired national relevance. Second, the public opinion became massively antinuclear, although a trend in this direction was occurring well before the accident. As a result, both local and national mobilization strengthened, and, for a short but significant period, participation in mass demonstrations became higher; as in May 1986, when 150,000 to 200,000 people marched in Rome to protest against the nuclear program, and 50,000 showed up in Milan; or as in April 1987, when a demonstration drew 50,000 participants. Third, contrasts within and between parties as well as between state agencies became the object of public debate, and disagreements in the scientific community increased. In brief, there was a multiplication of conflict arenas. Fourth, the nuclear issue broadened, from a strictly environmental issue to one related to safety.

Yet the most significant effect of the Chernobyl accident for the Italian nuclear industry lies in the role it played in the antinuclear referendum campaign. The latter had been planned before the accident but was officially launched on May 9, 1986. Three referenda were proposed: one on siting procedures, one on financial incentives for towns willing to accept a nuclear power plant, and one on regulations concerning cooperation with foreign agencies on nuclear energy matters. About one million signatures were collected in less than two months (Diani 1994), a sufficiently large number to force a vote. During the campaign, all major parties joined the Radical Party and the Workers' Democracy, which were in the antinuclear camp. Given this rapid shift and only one year after the accident at Chernobyl, it is hardly surprising that all three referenda were largely successful.[24] Rarely has a referendum been so timely. Of course, although some local struggles remained active for some time, antinuclear mobilization almost disappeared after the vote. For example, in the months following the vote, the government proposed a new plant, decided to complete the plant at Montalto di Castro (but this decision was reversed few months later), and declared that the plant at Caorso would have started again. This kept antinuclear protest alive at the local level, particularly at Montalto di Castro. Yet the season of antinuclear protest was over, and activists turned to other polluting plants, above all coal plants, showing once more the interconnectedness of environmental and antinuclear issues.

The Italian Peace Movement

Judging from figure 3.2c, the development of the Italian peace movement over the last three decades resembles to a large extent that of its American homologue.[25] They both display a huge wave of contention in the early 1980s and a smaller one in 1991. Moreover, these protest waves addressed similar issues: respectively, nuclear weapons and the Gulf War. Yet important differences can be observed at the beginning and especially at the very end of the period under study. First, opposition to the Vietnam War in the late 1960s and early 1970 was much less intense and widespread in Italy, partly due to the weak salience of peace issues in this period of Italian history as compared to issues related to the industrial conflict. Second, while the U.S. peace movement was virtually absent from the public domain in the second half of the 1990s, the Italian one was still quite active in 1995 and especially in 1999 in relation to the intervention of NATO forces in Kosovo.

As in other European countries, pacifism in Italy goes back to protosocialism in the second half of the nineteenth century (Ilari 1994). The first peace mobilization was organized by the Committee for the Recall of Troops from Eritrea. In general, the early peace and antimilitarist activities were held in the context of the debates within the Socialist and Communist movements and between socialists and anarchists. From 1911 to 1912, protests took place against the War of Libya, including a not-so-successful general strike. Later on, an important role was played by the Communist Party. Moving from a strategy aimed at carrying an antimilitarist propaganda within

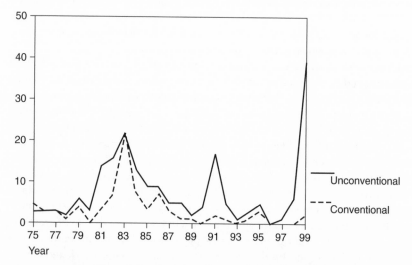

Figure 3.2c. Number of Peace Protests in Italy.

the army to the strong opposition against the Atlantic Pact (thus adding to a nationalistic opposition to the pact), the Communists participated in the international movement of the "partisans of peace," formed in 1947. The Communist Party held a "campaign for peace" in 1949, and it mobilized against the deployment of Jupiter missiles.

During the Cold War years, the Italian peace movement participated in the campaigns to promote a relaxing of the international climate. A widespread means of action during those years was the organization of "marches for peace," following the example of those held by the British Campaign for Nuclear Disarmament. The first such marches took place in 1961, bringing a small group of participants from Assisi to Perugia; another one was held in 1967, from Milan to Venice. From this year onward, they were organized by the radicals, who changed the name of "marches for peace" to "antimilitary marches." They took place every summer until 1976, but they never attracted a high number of participants. In general, during the Vietnam War years, the small Radical Party became hegemonic within Italian pacifism, thus smoothing its strong nationalist and anti-American characters and infusing it with a Progressive-Libertarian cultural model (Ilari 1994).

The Radical Party was also active on the front of the struggle for a civil service. Indeed, objection to the military service forms a relevant stream of the Italian peace movement. In Catholic countries such as Italy, the phenomenon of conscientious objection remained practically unknown until the second postwar period (Ilari 1994). Draft objection intensified in the 1960s and exploded after 1988. For example, the League for the Recognition of Conscientious Objection was formed in 1969.[26] Religious groups and organizations have traditionally been deeply involved in this issue, but libertarian and revolutionary streams were put into the debate as the New Left joined the struggle for a civil service.

Concerning the period I am most interested in, we can observe two important peaks of the Italian peace movement: a strong mass mobilization against the NATO decision to deploy nuclear weapons in the early 1980s, and an abrupt but short-lived opposition to the Gulf War, in 1991. By and large, the most important mobilization by the Italian peace movement was the one addressing the nuclear arms race. The ultimate cause of the mobilization followed a couple of years later: the so-called two-track decision, which was taken on December 12, 1979, by the foreign and defense ministers of the NATO alliance. The decision consisted of NATO's continuing negotiations for an agreement on medium-range nuclear weapons while modernizing the intermediate nuclear forces (INF), which deployed 572 Cruise and Pershing II missiles in five European countries. However, the issue at first did not spur opposition in Italy.[27] In fact, as we can see in figure 3.2c, there was a decline of mobilization in 1980. Only after the government, on August 7, 1981, announced its readiness to host the missiles on Italian soil did the peace movement react. On the European level, antinuclear weapons protests started on Easter 1981 with a large rally in Brussels (Rochon 1988). From that moment on and for at least two and a half years, one of the most impressive waves of contention took shape across Europe, with peaks in fall 1981, summer 1982, and fall 1983.

In Italy, the start of mobilization can be dated back to the demonstration that gathered thirty thousand people in Comiso, Sicily—the site destined to host the missiles—on October 11, 1981. Yet, the first demonstration comparable to those that were taking place in other parts of Europe at that time was held two weeks later, on October 24, in Rome. That day, an estimated crowd of 300,000 to 500,000 people voiced their opposition to nuclear weapons and their desire for a relaxing of the international climate. One week later, there were 100,000 in Milan. Other large demonstrations occurred in that turbulent end of 1981, including one with 200,000 participants, held in Florence on November 26. At the same time, that year saw the revival of the traditional Assisi–Perugia peace marches, freed from the patronizing shadow of the Radical Party and with a greatly increased number of participants.

The large protests of fall 1981 were held in the context of the approaching INF negotiations, which opened in Geneva on November 30. Yet protests continued at a sustained pace in 1982. The larger demonstrations occurred in Milan on April 18, and they were organized by the Communist Party and gathered 200,000 people; and on June 5, in Rome, on the occasion of Reagan's visit to Italy, 100,000 people marched in the streets of the capital. A few weeks earlier, a signature gathering project was launched, and it reached the considerable number of one million, which testifies to the widespread public concern at the time. In the meantime, the movement held activities on the site foreseen for the missiles, such as the demonstration organized by the Communist Party and attended by some 50,000 participants (April 5), the organization of the International Camp for Peace (July 27), and the Milano–Comiso march for peace (November 27–December 18).

The peak of mass mobilization was reached on October 22—the "peace world day"—when hundreds of thousands of citizens, including 500,000 in Rome, protested against nuclear arms and for their disarmament in various European cities. However, with the date for the beginning of deployment of the missiles approaching, the activities of the peace movement were increasingly focused on Comiso and eventually intensified around the base under construction. At the same time, the protest radicalized. A series of direct actions, sit-ins, civil disobedience acts, and blockades took place, which encouraged the police to clear the International Camp for Peace held in Comiso. Another camp was then built and hosted the International Meeting against the Cruise Missiles (July 1–September 30, 1983). During this year, the police intervened on several occasions and the camp eventually had to be removed; however, the protest in general moved to other bases that hosted nuclear weapons or vectors, such as Sigonella, Rimini Miramare, and Piacenza (Ilari 1994).

As figure 3.2c shows, this huge mobilization declined as rapidly as it rose, after the Italian government confirmed the arrival of the missiles on November 8, 1983. Similar to what happened to the U.S. nuclear freeze movement, antinuclear protest in the years following mainly took the form of debates and seminars, as well as the declaration of nuclear-free zones. The latter increased every year from 1981 to 1989, ultimately reaching almost eight hundred places (Ruzza 1997). As far as the peace movement itself is concerned, it lost vitality, and only its Catholic component underwent a significant but more subdued growth, which peaked in 1986 (Ruzza

1997) and contributed to the struggle for improving the civil service as well as reducing military spending. Also suffering a significant decline were the two other traditional actors of the peace movement: the Left and the nonviolent movement. Even the creation of the Association for Peace in 1988 could do little to revamp the movement.

The threat of U.S. intervention in Kuwait, in 1990, temporarily awakened the Italian peace movement from its lethargy; however, after the decline of antinuclear weapons mobilization, peace activities continued to be organized around such issues as civil service, military spending (for example, through fiscal objection), and arms exports. Yet mass mobilization resumed only with the Gulf War. This new wave of protest began a couple of months after Iraq invaded Kuwait, on August 2, 1990, and it sped up as the American ultimatum for military intervention approached. Large demonstrations took place, for example, on October 7, 1990 (100,000 participants in Assisi, which was the starting place of the traditional peace marches); January 12, 1991 (200,000 people in Rome); and January 26, 1991 (100,000 people again in Rome). Furthermore, a whole range of actions were held before and during the war. It is important to remark that peace mobilization in Italy was probably encouraged by the fact that the Italian army was involved in the conflict as part of the international military forces. Nevertheless, protests subsided quickly after the war ended.

Finally, even more so than the Gulf War, the military intervention in Kosovo rallied the Italian pacifists, who publicly expressed their outrage through an impressive series of demonstrative actions; after that, France's decision to resume nuclear tests in 1995 also remobilized the movement, but on a much smaller scale. Indeed, in terms of unconventional protest events, the year 1999 represents, at least in my sample, the historical peak of peace mobilization, even more than the large protest wave of the early 1980s, which to a large extent was also made of conventional actions. Large demonstrations, such as the one in Rome on April 24, 1999—which rallied up to two hundred thousand people—made clear that the peace movement was still alive in spite of phases of quiescence, which are typical of this movement (not only in Italy but also elsewhere in Europe).

A Brief History of Ecology, Antinuclear, and Peace Movements in Switzerland

Figures 3.3a, 3.3b, and 3.3c give us an overview of the mobilization (conventional and unconventional) by ecology, antinuclear, and peace movements in Switzerland between 1975 and 1999.[28] If we compare their overall development with those of the United States and Italy, we can again stress certain differences and similarities. First, like its American and Italian homologues, the Swiss ecology movement mobilized to a large extent through conventional forms of action. In addition, the period of strong expansion of environmental issues occurred later than in the United States but earlier than in Italy. Second, although it fluctuated more, the development of the Swiss antinuclear movement combines the characteristics of those in the other two countries, for it displays a large wave of contention in the 1970s (although it did not reach such a high level as in the United States) but also a revival in response to the Chernobyl accident, in 1986. Third, over the past three decades, the Swiss peace movement has mobilized in a way relatively similar to those in America and Italy, producing a large protest wave in the early 1980s (nuclear weapons) and in the early 1990s (Gulf War). At the same time, as compared to Italy, the level of mobilization was higher in 1995 and much lower in 1999.

The Swiss Ecology Movement

As in the United States and Italy, the modern Swiss ecology movement has its roots in earlier calls for the protection and preservation of the natural environment. From the organizational point of view, the first steps were made in the early nineteenth century. Later, the Swiss League for the Protection of Nature—which was established in 1909, in the context of a campaign aimed at financing the creation of a national park—is perhaps the first environmental organization to appear in Switzerland. Of course, at that time, it was still a matter of a relatively small group of social, intellectual, and scientific elites, who generally adopted lobbying as their main strategy. Although this stream of the movement and its strategies remain active today, the rise of new social movements has brought fresh air to the struggle for a better environment. Environmental issues expanded to include, in addition to nature protection, the prevention of air, water, and soil pollution, as well as all kinds of negative consequences of economic growth. At the same time, those issues became increasingly politicized.

As with the other two countries, I do not have data for the period before the one being examined, to show the movement's mobilization before that year. However, Kriesi and colleagues' work (1981) on mobilization processes in Switzerland indicates that environmental claims (defined broadly and in opposition to traditional Left and New Left claims) began to rise right after the turmoil of 1968, to peak in 1973. The level of mobilization remained quite high and then stable, up until the decade's end. As can be seen in figure 3.3a, the number of protest actions dealing with environmental issues took a sharp upward turn in the 1980s.

A first peak occurred in 1981, mostly due to the increase of events related to transportation issues and partly also to actions dealing with animal rights. A second abrupt increase in mobilization took place in 1986. Again, transportation issues are in part responsible for this growth, and claims regarding nature protection were also following an upward trend. However, during that year, a "suddenly imposed grievance" provoked a massive reaction by concerned citizens. In the night of November 1, a fire burned more than eight hundred tons of hazardous substances at the Sandoz chemical plant, which polluted the nearby Rhine River. Several protest demonstrations took place in the two weeks following the accident, making 1986 one of the heydays of the ecology movement in Switzerland; in fact, members of the parliament also intervened to avoid possible future accidents of this type.

Transportation issues have largely contributed to the movement's growth and sustained level of mobilization during the 1980s. Indeed, a typical characteristic of the Swiss ecology movement is the important share of actions targeting this policy area.

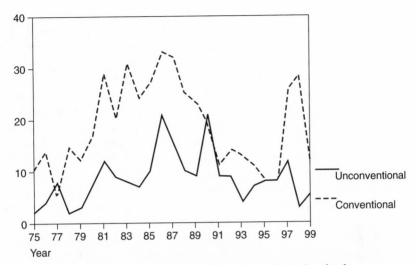

Figure 3.3a. Number of Ecology Protests in Switzerland.

About half of the protest events carried by the movement dealt with transportation issues (as compared to less than 20 percent in the United States and Italy). Among these, opposition against the buildup of the national highway system played a particularly significant role. For example, the high number of events found in 1981 are in part due to the reactions to the presentation of the results of the consultative commission charged to examine a certain number of road construction projects that were being contested. The government had appointed this commission under the pressures coming from within and outside the parliamentary arena. The results, presented on September 25, 1981, were largely in favor of all but one of the construction projects and were therefore largely unfavorable to the movement. Similarly, the rise of mobilization in 1990 is largely due to transportation issues.

The mobilization of the Swiss ecology movement around transportation issues has followed a pattern that we may call "institutional protest." In the first phase, from 1960 to 1968, protest was weak and illustrated by its predominant use of legal channels. The second phase, from 1968 to 1974, was characterized by a new awareness toward the threats posed by transportation to the environment, but protest still went mainly through institutional and procedural channels. The third phase, from 1974 to 1982, saw the beginning of the use of direct democratic procedures and a diversification of the forms of action. In the fourth phase, from 1982 to 1990, popular initiatives became a crucial means of action, and the protest reached national scope. Finally, in the fifth phase, from 1990 onward, the protest became relatively latent after the poor success of the initiatives. During the whole process, peripheral actors, including the ecology movement, became increasingly involved in the decisional process and acquired national relevance (Bassand et al. 1986).

The struggle against national highways highlights a second fundamental characteristic of the political action of the ecology movement in Switzerland: the use of direct democracy. Indeed, this was a general feature of the mobilization by social movements in this country and one that strongly shaped the political opportunities for the movements' mobilization and for their chances of success. The ecology movement was no exception and made a large use of popular initiatives to reach its goals. Indeed, if the level of mobilization of the ecology movement had remained high during the 1980s, it was due to the proliferation of popular initiatives (and, to a lesser extent, referenda), in particular those dealing with transportation issues. No fewer than eleven national initiatives were launched during the 1980s, and many more at the cantonal and communal levels. The most famous is perhaps the so-called four-leaf clover initiative, launched by the Swiss Association for Transport[29] in 1987 and opposing the construction of four highway projects that were among those favorably assessed by the aforementioned consultative commission. The initiative was rejected in a popular vote on April 1, 1990, thus resulting in a new failure of the ecology movement in using this means of action.[30]

The intense use of direct democracy reflects a more pragmatic way of mobilizing around environmental issues. As compared to the more ideological activism of the 1960s and 1970s, the 1980s and 1990s witnessed a more eclectic and pragmatic environmentalism, one aimed at problem solving rather than politicizing the issues. This new approach can be seen as a third stream of the ecology movement—after traditional nature protection and political ecology—not only in Switzerland, but more generally in Western societies (Rucht 1989). At the same time, however, the poor success of national initiatives probably contributed to the demobilization of the ecology movement in the 1990s. After the vote on the "four-leaf clover" initiative, the number of protest events declined, returning to the level of the late 1970s and hence giving us a picture of a large (and long) wave of mobilization that lasted from 1979 to 1991, as can be seen in figure 3.3a. Yet, as we will see in more detail in chapter 6, the movement's organizations continued to grow steadily.

Like Italy, Switzerland has witnessed the emergence of a Green Party, that is, of an institutionalized branch of the ecology movement. But the Swiss Greens emerged much earlier than their Italian counterparts. Given the decentralized political system, the opportunities for the emergence of new small parties were even higher in Switzerland than in Italy, although the system of concordance erects a cultural barrier to this openness because of its stabilizing effect on the configuration of power. Thus, the first Green Party was founded at the local level, in 1972: the Popular Movement for the Environment, in the city of Neuchâtel, in the country's French part (Ladner 1989). It came out of a local struggle against a planned motorway. In 1978 a Green Party was formed in the German part of the country at the cantonal level, namely, in the canton of Zürich. One year later, the Group for the Protection of the Environment in the canton of Vaud became one of the first Green Parties in a Western country to have a representative elected in the national parliament (Ladner 1989). In the years preceding the national elections of 1983, Green Parties appeared in various cantons. The attempt to bring them together resulted in the formation of two parties: the Federation of Swiss Green Parties, gathering the more moderate groups and later to become the Green Party of Switzerland; and the

Green Alternative of Switzerland, in which converged the more radical and alternative groups and which became the Green Alliance Switzerland. Both lists obtained impressive results at the 1987 national elections, gaining, respectively, 5.1 percent and 4.3 percent of the votes. Later on, environmentalists entered executive bodies at the local level.

Finally, it is important to stress that, like its Italian and American homologues (especially the latter)—and in contrast to the peace and antinuclear movements—the Swiss ecology movement largely acted through conventional means, such as lobbying, appeals, and public statements. Mass demonstrations are seldom used, usually only as a way of claim making and mostly at the local level. Thus, in my sample, I list only one large national demonstration: the one held in Bern on May 5, 1984, and attended by thirty thousand citizens concerned about the state of the Swiss forests. Mass participation occurred mainly through the signature of popular initiatives, referenda, or the less institutionally constraining petitions, much more rarely through direct participation in mass demonstrations. This characteristic became even more true in the late 1980s and in the 1990s, giving us a picture of an increasingly institutionalized ecology movement.

The Swiss Antinuclear Movement

If the story of the Swiss ecology movement is made of little popular mobilization and much institutional protest, the antinuclear movement tells us a story of both institutional and mass mobilization.[31] If we look at figure 3.3b, we can see that the Swiss antinuclear movement mobilized above all in the mid- to late 1970s (up to 1981), then again in the mid- and late 1980s, but entered a phase of latency in the 1990s. Yet, antinuclear activism had arisen earlier.

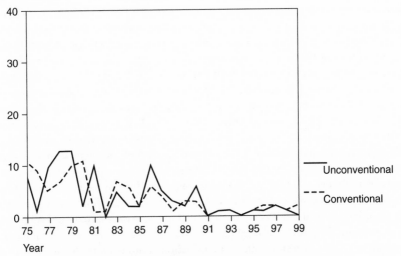

Figure 3.3b. Number of Antinuclear Protests in Switzerland.

As in most countries—including Italy and the United States—the early days of the nuclear industry could benefit from a favorable climate. Thus, in the 1960s, nuclear energy plans in Switzerland were adopted with virtually no opposition. After the parliament had promulgated the Nuclear Energy Act in 1959, the first three plants entered production between 1969 and 1972 without serious antinuclear mobilization. Protest started in the late 1960s, principally directed against what was to become the focal point of the Swiss antinuclear movement for the two decades to come: a planned nuclear power plant in Kaiseraugst, a small village not far from the city of Basel. The beginning of this opposition can be dated back to the creation in 1969 of a local group called Kaiseraugst Inhabitants for a Sane Habitat. From that moment onward, the history of the Swiss antinuclear movement can be divided in six phases.[32] In the first phase, from 1969 to 1973, the movement predominantly used the existing institutional opportunities and channels, focusing on Kaiseraugst. In the second phase, from 1973 to 1979, it shifted to direct action, reached its heyday, and acquired national scope in spite of a first internal division. The third phase, from 1979 to 1981, witnessed a new fragmentation of the movement but also a revival around the opposition to the nuclear plants planned in Kaiseraugst and Graben, followed by the beginning of a rapid demobilization. In the fourth phase, from 1981 to 1986, the movement continued its demobilization but was revived in 1983, in the midst of the wave of antinuclear weapons protest. During the fifth phase, from 1986 to 1990, the accident at Chernobyl brought the second important peak of antinuclear protests in Switzerland, which increased public awareness toward nuclear energy and favored the acceptance in 1990 of a popular initiative for a ten-year moratorium on the construction of new plants. Finally, the sixth phase was characterized not only by a new demobilization after the success of the initiative but also by a low level of mobilization.

The first antinuclear opposition went mainly through institutional means of action, such as political and juridical appeals. These forms became quite frequent in 1972 and 1973, targeting several plants or plant projects during this period. In addition, the first demonstrations were organized. The oil crisis produced a major change in the strategies of the antinuclear movement. The salience of the energy issue and the failure of conventional forms induced the movement to resort to direct action. It is in this context that a major occupation took place in 1975, in Kaiseraugst, after construction work had begun.[33] The occupation was organized by the Nonviolent Action Kaiseraugst and lasted about ten weeks, between April and June 1975. On that occasion, a large demonstration was organized, in which fifteen thousand people participated. Although it targeted a specific project, this action became the catalyst for the mass mobilization and was instrumental in making nuclear energy a national issue; following its mobilization, a number of other "nonviolent actions" were formed nationwide, and mass demonstrations became national in scope. The first demonstration was held in Bern on April 26, 1975, and it was attended by eighteen thousand people and supported by more than 170 associations and parties. From 1975 to 1979—and, to a lesser extent, up to 1981—a period of intense mobilization occurred for the Swiss antinuclear movement, in spite of the two movement crises that occurred around 1976 and 1980.

Gösgen, but above all Kaiseraugst, were the two principal targets of the movement. Not incidentally, given the overlapping in time with the nuclear weapons issue, the largest one was perhaps the so-called demonstration "of the following Saturday," which was held on the construction site in Kaiseraugst on October 31, 1981—that is, the first Saturday after the government had granted the construction permit (three days earlier).

As we can see in figure 3.3b, the year 1979 represented, as it did in the United States, the historical peak in the number of antinuclear protest events. That year, the first national initiative against nuclear installations, launched in 1975, was rejected by Swiss voters. In addition, 1979 was also the year of the accident at Three Mile Island, which had some repercussions on the Swiss antinuclear movement. In effect, most of the events in my sample for that year took place in the months after the disaster. Given its location, this accident naturally produced the strongest reaction in the United States, followed by Switzerland and Italy. The weak reaction in Italy, as compared to the two other countries, seems to confirm the idea mentioned earlier that such a "suddenly imposed grievance" must be politically constructed to give rise to mobilization. Both the American and the Swiss antinuclear movements were in the midst of an intense and politicized wave of contention when the accident occurred, whereas in Italy the nuclear issue in that period was on the back burner.

The movement and its main allies—the parties of the Left—also launched a number of popular initiatives, both at the national and at the cantonal level. Here we see once again that direct democracy offers major political opportunities for social movements in Switzerland, and the antinuclear movement, like other new social movements, made extensive use of these opportunities. The movement's moderate wing in particular was quite active on this front, while the radical wing was more inclined to adopt direct-action tactics. For example, three national initiatives were launched in 1980, two by the movement's moderate wing and one by its radical wing. The first initiative asked for a halt in the construction of new plants. The second one wanted a safer, cheaper, and environmentally sound energy policy. The third initiative asked for the prohibition on building new plants and to halt production by existing plants; that is, it wanted a total abandonment of nuclear energy. The two initiatives of the moderates were rejected in 1984, while the one by the radicals had been withdrawn in the meantime. These failures favored the movement's decline in the early 1980s.

In spite of a revival in 1983—the year the construction of a plant in Kaiseraugst was approved by the higher chamber (Council of States) and recommended by a committee from the lower chamber (National Council)—the second important peak of antinuclear protests occurred in 1986, provoked by the accident at Chernobyl. Before that day, the movement had continued its activities mainly through institutional means, but the accident revived the mobilization through mass demonstrations, though only for a short time. At the same time, it helped the launching of other popular initiatives at the national level in 1986 and 1987. Although the request for a ten-year moratorium on the construction of new plants was accepted in 1990 and thus brought a major success to the movement, it also caused the movement's demobilization in the following years. As usually is the case in Switzerland, what temporarily revived the mobilization was both the launching of the initiative and the current campaign of the popular vote.

After the successful vote, the level of mobilization of the Swiss antinuclear movement went down considerably; yet, antinuclear opponents did not completely fold their arms but instead revamped the conflict over nuclear waste disposal. During the heydays of the opposition against power plant projects, this issue had been somewhat put on the back burner; the moratorium, however, gave it some vigor. This conflict originated with the creation in 1972 of the National Cooperation for the Disposal of Nuclear Waste, a joint organization of the nuclear industry and the public authorities charged with building and operating nuclear waste repositories (Wälti 1995). A program was presented in 1978 that foresaw the start of storing low-level wastes by 1985 and high-level wastes after the turn of the century. A 1979 referendum asked for more citizen participation in the nuclear waste policy, but it was rejected in the popular vote. In 1982, a list of twenty potential sites for the storage of low-level wastes was issued, and, one year later, three sites were selected, one in each of the country's three major linguistic regions.[34] From that moment onward, strong local opposition arose in each of the three sites (Wälti 1993). This opposition, which presented some typical NIMBY features, became at times particularly disruptive, combining a mix of demonstrations, public petitions, direct actions, and so forth. Later on, a fourth site was selected.[35] Opposition arose there as well, but it was never as virulent as it was in the three other sites (Wälti 1995). Finally, in 1993—eight years later than the planned deadline—the last site was chosen, but the whole process was halted by a cantonal vote unfavorable to a nuclear waste repository.

The Swiss Peace Movement

Finally, if we look at figure 3.3c, we can see that the development of the Swiss peace movement during the last three decades resembles that of its homologues in Italy and the United States.[36] Specifically, it presents two large waves of contention in the early 1980s and early 1990s. Unlike the two other countries, however, Switzerland observed a high level of mobilization in 1995.

Although peace ideals and issues go back to nineteenth-century Switzerland, under the thrust of the Enlightenment, it was only on the eve of World War I that the Swiss peace movement showed the first true signs of mobilization. In 1905, the Antimilitary League was formed, with the aim of fighting the imperialistic drives that eventually led to World War I. At about the same period, the first wave of conscientious objection took place. In the late 1950s and early 1960s, Swiss pacifists joined the international campaign for international distension and against nuclear proliferation. They did so in basically two ways. The first way was common to all other countries: staging mass demonstrations and protests. The first Easter march, which would become a traditional occasion for addressing the peace issues usually organized by the Swiss Movement of Peace, was held in 1963 under the banner of "No to the bomb, yes to democracy." The second way was typically Swiss and consisted in exploiting the institutional opportunities offered by direct democracy. Although not the first to

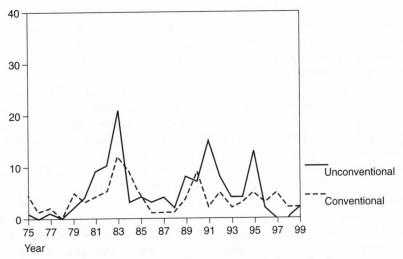

Figure 3.3c. Number of Peace Protests in Switzerland.

address military issues, two popular initiatives against atomic weapons were launched in 1958 with the help of the Socialist Party, the movement's principal ally.

The years of the student movement were characterized in Switzerland by intense peace movement activities. In the context of a renewed and more ideological engagement for peace—one featuring a strong anticapitalist and anti-imperialist discourse typical of 1968, which brought Swiss students to protest the Vietnam War—internal peace actions dealt in particular with three traditional issues: military spending, arms export, and the civil service. All three became the object of popular initiatives at some point, in addition to other forms of actions, such as mass demonstrations and public statements. In fact, two well-known initiatives aimed at reducing or limiting the budget of the Swiss army had been launched in the 1950s, though they had little success. Others would follow in the early 1980s and 1990s. Furthermore, an initiative targeting arms exports saw the light in 1969, after the discovery of an illegal traffic in weapons by the Bührle-Oerlikon, a major Swiss company. Finally, the first of a series of popular initiatives aimed at introducing the civil service in Switzerland was sent forth in 1970.

During the late 1970s, peace movement mobilization was low. It started to rise again in 1979, forming the beginning of the largest protest wave that has touched most Western European countries. Of course, since Switzerland is not a member of NATO, the country was not directly involved in the decision to station INF missiles in Europe. The Swiss government was not in a position of having to decide whether to host the missiles. Despite this lack of a substantial internal target, the peace movement mobilized massively to voice concern about the proliferation of nuclear weapons and to call for a relaxing of the international climate. The beginning of the protest wave can be dated with the launching of the "Swiss appeal for the peace, against the atomic death" by the Swiss Peace Movement on August 6, 1981, the anniversary of the

Hiroshima bomb. That day, the campaign against nuclear weapons entered the first of three phases. In the first phase, from August 1981 to April 1982, mass mobilization grew rapidly as peace protests crossed the entire European continent. One of the largest demonstrations in Switzerland was held in Bern on December 5, 1981, one week after the start of negotiations between the two superpowers. Nearly forty thousand people attended that event, quite a high number for Swiss standards. A series of further mass demonstrations, symbolic actions, discussion seminars, and other actions took place in the following months. A second large demonstration opened the second phase, from April 1982 to November 1983. It was held in the context of the traditional Easter march in the so-called triangle region around the city of Basel—where the borders of France, Germany, and Switzerland meet—and it gathered thirty thousand participants. During this period, similar to what happened in Italy, internal divisions emerged—or rather, reemerged—within the movement, above all the one between the religious-based Swiss Peace Council and the Communist-led Swiss Peace Movement. Parallel to a certain fragmentation of the movement, new claims emerged, mainly dealing with the Swiss army. In addition, parties tried to appropriate the nuclear weapons issue, a way of institutionalizing dissent, which proved effective in the case of the U.S. freeze movement (Meyer 1990, 1993). However, although one would have to wait until fall 1983 to see another large demonstration, the number of protest events continued to grow during that year. The third and final phase, November 1983 to December 1984, opened with what is probably the largest mass demonstration held by the new social movements in Switzerland, when perhaps fifty thousand people took part in the November 5, 1983, event in Bern, showing the support of a wide coalition of political forces. The approaching threat of the stationing of the missiles in five European countries brought new vigor to the movement; yet, this vigor soon became lost, as the substantial goal to impede the stationing of the missiles failed and the movement demobilized in the following years, reaching a very low level of mobilization between 1986 and 1987.

While the wave of antinuclear weapons protest follows a similar pattern in Italy and Switzerland, there is an important difference concerning the content of claims. While most of the Italian mobilization targeted nuclear weapons and international distension, other important issues were raised in Switzerland toward the end of the protest wave, showing that in general the Swiss peace movement typically addressed internal issues (Bein and Epple 1984). In effect, at least 57 percent of the events in 1983 dealt with issues other than nuclear arms. One of them dealt with the civil service, a traditional claim of the peace movement. The other was a new issue: the abolition of the Swiss army. More than 36 percent of the events in 1983 dealt with this issue. In fact, the Group for a Switzerland without an Army, formed in 1982, almost single-handedly carried the issue, as it became the leading peace issue in the 1980s and 1990s. This organization acted above all through popular initiatives, with the most famous being the one aimed at abolishing the army, an initiative formally launched in 1985 but rejected in 1989 by the Swiss population. However, more than one-third of the Swiss voted for the initiative, a surprising result given the central symbolic value attributed to the army in Switzerland.

The vote on the army initiative helps explain the length of the wave of contention that peaked in 1991. Reactions to U.S. intervention in the Persian Gulf are mainly responsible for this protest wave. Although the number of participants in the early 1990s never reached the number of those during the early 1980s, the Swiss peace movement mobilized on the Gulf War; yet, the early rise in 1989 is the result of the voting campaign on the army initiative. In addition, the intensity, height, and length of this protest wave are also due to the launching of five other popular initiatives between 1990 and 1992, which bore on such issues as the civil service, military structures, military spending, arms export, and the purchase by the government of new combat airplanes.

Clearly, direct democracy provided a crucial opportunity for social movements in Switzerland to make their claims. The peace movement fully exploited this opportunity. The first popular initiative dealing with military issues goes back to 1916. Since then, no fewer than twenty-three were launched at the national level. Among the areas targeted by popular initiatives were military spending (five times), atomic weapons (twice), arms export (twice), civil service (three times), military structures, and (of course) the army itself. Lower-level campaigns were obviously pointless, for the national security and the defense domains have always been exclusive of competence of the central government. In the light of this extensive use of direct democratic means, some have spoken of the Swiss peace movement as an "initiative movement" and warned about the institutionalizing effects of a too-intensive use of direct democracy by social movements (Epple 1988). In addition, only once was the movement successful in using this form of action. This, however, should not make us forget its positive vicarious effects on the general public and on the movement itself.

The last peak of mobilization by the peace movement was mostly due to a comeback of the nuclear issue. In 1995, the freshly elected French president Chirac decided to temporarily resume nuclear weapons testing. Once again, an international wave of contention occurred, led by a series of spectacular actions by Greenpeace in the Mururoa Atoll and mixing peace and environmental issues. The Swiss peace movement participated in this protest wave, with some demonstrations reaching a considerable number of participants. Once again, this mobilization was short-lived, not least because the resumption of testing was explicitly temporary. Finally, in sharp contrast to Italy, Swiss pacifists did not mobilize massively to protest against the military intervention by NATO forces in Kosovo. In Switzerland, as in the United States, this event did not seem to have been able to rally a rather demobilizing movement.

Comparative Summary

At this point, it is useful to summarize the main trends in the mobilization of ecology, antinuclear, and peace movements in the three countries under study, limited to unconventional actions and to the period that interests us the most, namely, 1975 to 1999. For the United States (figures 3.1a, 3.1b, and 3.1c), the period opens with a sustained but declining mobilization by the ecology movement; a virtually inactive antinuclear movement; and a similarly declining pattern for the peace movement, but at a lower level. The nuclear energy issue had not become a mobilizing issue yet, and protests against the Vietnam War had come to an end by that time. During the second half of the 1970s, ecology protests fluctuated but generally displayed a decreasing trend. Antinuclear protests began to increase rapidly, reaching their highest level in 1979, after the Three Mile Island incident. By 1980, however, the level of mobilization of the antinuclear movement dropped as quickly as it had risen. The first part of the 1980s was characterized by a huge wave of peace protest against nuclear weapons and proliferation, by the continuing decline of the antinuclear movement, and by a certain stability of ecology protests. The peace movement underwent an abrupt decline in 1984 and remained more discrete during the second half of the 1980s, in spite of a smaller peak in 1986. During the same period, the ecology movement began to increase its mobilization, which peaked in 1990. One year later, at the time of the Gulf War, the peace movement reached a second important peak as well. After that, both movements diminished their protest activities in the early 1990s: the peace movement nearly disappeared from the public domain, and antinuclear protests never recovered after having declined in the early 1980s. Finally, all three movements remained quite discrete in the second part of the 1990s, except perhaps for the ecology movement (but this holds especially if we include conventional actions as well).

In Italy (figures 3.2a, 3.2b, and 3.2c), we observe a similar pattern for the peace movement, but only if we exclude 1998 and above all 1999 from the comparison; otherwise, we see quite different trends for the other two movements. The level of mobilization of the ecology movement remained more or less stable during the late 1970s and early 1980s, with an increasing trend in the former and a decreasing one in the latter. Both the antinuclear and the peace movements were present in the public domain during the same period but were infrequently active, at least at the national level. Peace actions had an outburst between 1981 and 1983, as the nuclear weapons issue awakened old ghosts across Europe. When this wave of contention started to decline, the ecology movement began an upward trend, which characterized the second half of the 1980s. In the meantime, peace protests continued their downward trend, and antinuclear protests made a short-lived comeback in 1986 in response to the Chernobyl accident. The first part of the 1990s saw a demobilization of the ecology movement; a continued absence of the antinuclear movement; and a second large protest wave by the peace movement, this time against the Gulf War. Finally, in the second part of the 1990s, ecology protests increased again to a high level; antinuclear protests remained latent; and peace protests reached an unusually high peak in 1999, in relation to the intervention of NATO forces in Kosovo.

In Switzerland (figures 3.3a, 3.3b, and 3.3c), we observe a second half of the 1970s characterized by a fluctuating mobilization by the ecology and antinuclear movements, with the latter reaching its peak between 1978 and 1979. Although the peace movement remained relatively inactive, it joined the European protest wave of the early 1980s against nuclear missiles, and its mobilization reached its peak in 1983. Ecology protests started to increase in the early 1980s, but always among important ebbs and flows, including two peaks in 1986 and 1990. In the same period, antinuclear actions decreased and remained relatively low for some years; however, they underwent a second abrupt rise in response to the Chernobyl accident, in 1986. The peace movement demobilized after the protest wave of the early 1980s, but a second important wave of contention occurred at the time of the Gulf War, in 1991. Finally, in the 1990s, the ecology movement demobilized in the first part of the decade but then regained strength, especially if we include conventional actions; the antinuclear movement remained quite inactive; and the peace movement produced a third protest wave in 1995.

In my discussion, I stress overall trends in the levels of mobilization of the three movements, but I also hint at important country-specific variations in the content of their claims. Indeed, the focus and target of protest actions often differ from one country to the other. The most obvious and general variation is, of course, that among the three movements. As table 3.1 shows, the "ranking" of movements for the whole 1975–1999 period is the same in all three countries, with ecology movements having mobilized the most, and antinuclear movements the least; however, in Switzerland the difference between the latter and the peace movement is quite small. We also see that in Italy environmental claims are more important than other claims. Furthermore, the weakness of the Italian antinuclear movement is confirmed by this overall assessment. Finally, peace movement actions have played a greater role in the United States. In fact, their role would be even stronger if we took into account the years before 1975, owing to the enormous mobilization against the Vietnam War.

Significant differences exist within each movement as well. Table 3.2 shows a more detailed distribution of protest events, by issue field and by country for the 1975–1999 period. It confirms that the three movements had different thematic foci in each country.

First of all, concerning the ecology movement, the more traditional environmental issues—nature protection and animal rights—are much more often addressed in Italy. While animal rights are an equally important ecology issue, they are much more so in the United States than in Italy, where it largely remains framed in terms of conservation of the species. The higher share of traditional environmental issues in Italy might be a result of the still largely traditional cleavage structure, which not only leaves a narrower space for the mobilization by new social movements (Kriesi et al. 1995) but also seems to push these movements toward more traditional areas. In the United States, we observe a high proportion of other environmental events, suggesting that the ecology movement in this country often makes general and abstract claims

Table 3.1. Distribution of Protest Events by Movement and by Country, 1975–1999

	United States	Italy	Switzerland
Ecology movement	55.5	69.3	62.0
Antinuclear movement	14.8	5.1	17.9
Peace movement	29.7	25.6	20.1
Total	100%	100%	100%
N	(1,703)	(1,088)	(1,102)

Table 3.2. Distribution of Protest Events by Issue Field and by Country, 1975–1999 (percent)

	United States	Italy	Switzerland
Ecology Movement	**55.5**	**69.3**	**62.1**
Nature protection	9.2	23.5	13.2
Animal rights	9.9	18.4	5.1
Pollution	9.7	7.9	2.2
Transportation[a]	8.1	12.1	31.0
Energy[b]	3.0	1.3	4.1
Other ecology	15.6	6.1	6.5
Antinuclear Movement	**14.8**	**5.1**	**17.9**
Peace Movement	**29.9**	**25.7**	**20.1**
Nuclear weapons[c]	16.5	5.6	2.5
Military structures and spending	2.0	0.7	5.1
Civil service	1.8	1.7	2.6
Other peace[d]	9.6	17.7	9.9
Total	100%	100%	100%
N	(1,703)	(1,088)	(1,102)

[a]Includes noise.
[b]Excludes nuclear power.
[c]Includes international distension.
[d]Includes general and abstract goals.

rather than addressing specific problems. Finally, the data confirm the central place of transportation issues in Switzerland. Here, actions targeting pollution seem to be rather marginal, although environmental events in general certainly do include such actions in all three countries. Second, we observe the lower level of mobilization of the Italian antinuclear movement as compared to its American and Swiss counterparts. Third, while the nuclear weapons issue dominated the mobilization of the peace movement in the United States, it was less important in Italy and especially in Switzerland. This is hardly surprising: not only is the United States a nuclear power, but Italy agreed to station nuclear missiles on its soil, and Switzerland was never directly involved in such matters. The category of other peace events includes antiwar protests as well as abstract and general claims. If we add to this events pertaining to nuclear weapons, we can see to what extent the Italian and U.S. peace movements are externally oriented; however, the Swiss peace movement has largely addressed internal issues, such as the civil service and, above all, military structures and spending. Among the latter, a crucial role was played by the campaign for the abolition of the army, which has represented the leading peace issue all during the 1980s and 1990s.

To conclude, in this chapter I describe in some detail the development of the mobilization by ecology, antinuclear, and peace movements in the United States, Italy, and Switzerland. Although I briefly hint at previous epochs, I focus on the 1975–1999 period. Using the quantitative indicator of the number of protest events as a background, I show that although their mobilization displays both similarities and differences, it is predominantly characterized by important variations over time.

Furthermore, by looking more closely at the content of their mobilization, I show that variations also exist both among countries and over time as to the thematic foci and targets of the claims made by the three movements during this historical period. Next, I turn to the other end of the problem and give a brief historical overview of public policy on environmental, nuclear energy, and national security matters in the three countries under study.

Notes

1. To have a sense of the relative levels of mobilization for each movement, the figures are all set within the same scale per country. Of course, the scale varies from one country to the next, as we cannot compare directly the samples of protest events gathered from different newspapers, which probably have varying degrees of selectivity.

2. Of course, we cannot assume a priori that a process of international diffusion has been at work, which has spread the protest from the United States to Western Europe. This is rather something that should be demonstrated. For a review of work on diffusion in social movements, see Strang and Soule (1998).

3. As I hinted in the introductory chapter, the distribution of conventional actions is likely to be biased due to the underrepresentation of these types of events in the sample. I show them to have an indicative reference line against which to compare the development of unconventional actions (see appendix A for further information).

4. Useful historical accounts of the American ecology movement can be found in Caulfield (1989), Dunlap and Mertig (1992), Hays (1987), Kline (2000), Sale (1993), and Shabecoff (1993).

5. For accounts of protests and policies over toxic wastes, see Barnett (1994), Mazmanian and Morell (1992), and Szasz (1994).

6. For accounts of the Love Canal affair, see Brown (1979); Epstein, Brown, and Pope (1982); Fowlkes and Miller (1982); Freudenberg (1984); Gibbs (1982); and Levine (1982).

7. For example, in 1988, the magazine *Time* awarded its usual man-of-the-year issue to the "Planet of the Year."

8. The data for the 1975–1995 period and those for the 1996–1999 period were collected by two coders. In spite of the efforts I put into instructing coders, this might result in certain differences between them in the selectivity of retrieving protest events reports, which might partly bias the distributions. A similar potential bias, but one not necessarily concerning the same time slots, applies to the other distributions shown in this chapter. For more, see appendix A.

9. The Kyoto Convention, which preceded the protocol, was adopted in New York in May 1992 and was open to signature from June 1992 to June 1993, as well as in March 1994.

10. For historical accounts of the American antinuclear movement and citizen participation with regard to nuclear energy policy, see Freudenburg and Rosa (1984), Joppke (1993), and Price (1990). For significant case studies focused on local oppositions, see Bedford (1990), Ebbin and Kasper (1974), Nelkin (1971), and Stever (1980).

11. For example, the number of operating reactors equaled 111 in 1990.

12. Although the site of the planned nuclear facility is in New Hampshire, it is only a few miles from Massachusetts; therefore, the state's governor was involved in the process.

13. See Walsh (1988) on the mobilization around the accident at Three Mile Island.

14. For historical accounts of the American peace movement, see Chatfield (1992), DeBenedetti (1980), Kleidman (1993), and Wittner (1984). More specific accounts dealing

with particular aspects or periods also exist: on the Vietnam Era, DeBenedetti and Chatfield (1990), Halstead (1978), Heineman (1993), and Small (1988); on antinuclear bomb campaigns and, specifically, on the Committee for a Sane Nuclear Policy, Katz (1986); on the nuclear freeze, Garfinkle (1984), McCrae and Markle (1989), Meyer (1990), Solo (1988), and Waller (1987); on peace and justice campaigns, Peace (1991); on the Central American peace movement, Smith (1996); and for a sociological account of the movement in 1980s, one paying particular attention to its culture and organization, Lofland (1993). A more concise historical overview of the movement can be found in Howlett and Zeitzer (1985).

15. For example, on November 15, 1957, Sane ran a full-page ad in the *New York Times* stating that "we are facing a danger unlike any danger that has ever existed."

16. Two examples can give an idea of the scope of the antiwar movement. First, a national demonstration held in Washington on November 15, 1969, was attended by nearly 500,000 people. Second, between 200,000 and 500,000 people participated in another large demonstration, on November 24, once again in the streets of the capital.

17. A group of protesters who were arrested for entering a General Electric plant in Pennsylvania and beating nose cones for ICBM missiles with hammers.

18. As an indication of the breadth of the protest over this issue, Smith (1996, 387) mentions that the Directory of Central America Organizations, published in 1986, contains 1,061 organizations.

19. For historical accounts of the Italian ecology movement, see Biorcio and Lodi (1988), De Meo and Giovannini (1985), Diani (1990), Donati (1995), Farro (1991), and Fiore (1991). A particularly interesting perspective, one based on network analysis, is provided by Diani (1988, 1995).

20. For example, Italia Nostra was created in 1955 and the Federation Pro Natura in 1959.

21. Usmate, Mantova, Este, and Lugo di Romagna.

22. In Italy, a national referendum can only abrogate existing laws.

23. For a historical account of the Italian antinuclear movement, see Diani (1994) and Farro (1991, ch. 1). For my overview, I used the former above all.

24. The share of votes in favor of the referenda was 80.6 percent against current siting procedures, 79.9 percent against extra money incentives to local councils, and 71.8 percent against cooperation with foreign agencies (Diani 1994).

25. For a historical account of the Italian peace movement, see Ilari (1994). On the 1980s, see Battistelli and colleagues (1990) and Lodi (1984). On the 1980s and 1990s, see Ruzza (1997).

26. This organization was replaced in 1973 by the League of Conscientious Objectors.

27. Rochon (1988) provides a comparative analysis of the antinuclear weapons movement. Unfortunately, his study does not include Italy.

28. For historical accounts of the Swiss ecology movement, see Giugni (1995), Giugni and Passy (1997, ch. 5), and Zwicky (1993). On transportation issues, see Bassand and colleagues (1986) and Burnier (1985).

29. Later on, this organization changed its name to Swiss Association for Transport and Environment.

30. In the meantime, opposition to one of the four projects was abandoned, so the vote bore only on three projects.

31. For historical accounts of the Swiss antinuclear movement, see Giugni (1995), Giugni and Passy (1997, ch. 2), and Kriesi (1982). For more specific account on the case of Kaiseraugst, see Cudry (1988) and Schroeren (1977).

32. This division in phases slightly modifies those proposed in Giugni and Passy (1997) and Kriesi (1982).

33. A shorter occupation had already been held in Kaiseraugst in 1973. It was conceived as a test in view of a more important action that would have been necessary had the construction works begun.

34. The three selected sites (and their respective cantons) are Bauen (Uri), Mesocco (Graubünden), and Ollon (Vaud).

35. The fourth selected site is Wolfenschiessen (canton Nidwalden).

36. For historical accounts of the Swiss peace movement, see Bein and Epple (1984), Brassel and Tanner (1986), Giugni and Passy (1997, ch. 3), and Tanner (1988). Epple (1988) provides a challenging interpretation of the movement with regard to its usage of direct democracy.

~~~

CHAPTER FOUR

Environmental, Nuclear Energy, and National Security Policy in Three Countries

The mobilization by ecology, antinuclear, and peace movements is the starting point of the causal path that I am trying to follow in this book. Public policy—better: policy change—is the end point. In this chapter, I give an overview of the development of policy in the environmental protection, nuclear energy, and national security areas in each of the three countries under study, over the last three decades or so. This task is not unproblematic, as the assessment of the evolution of policy may differ according to the indicator considered. In this respect, policy change can be observed on at least two counts. Outlays are perhaps the most straightforward indicator of state action. Most work on policy change has measured policy outcomes in terms of expenditures (e.g., Dye 1966; Hofferbert and Sharkansky 1971; Jacob and Vines 1971). By looking only at expenditures, however, we miss the qualitative changes produced by certain important pieces of legislation. Thus, other studies of the policy impact of social movements conducted in a time-series perspective have focused on legislative activity or production. Burstein and Freudenburg (1978), for example, looked at the roll call votes received by bills and amendments related to the Vietnam War, voted by the U.S. Senate between 1963 and 1974. More recently, Costain and Majstorovic (1994) employed a coded measure of the percentage of bills passed by the U.S Congress that focused on gender.

While the quantitative analyses made in part II of this book use government expenditures and nuclear energy production as indicators of policy change, the follow- ing overview of environmental, nuclear energy, and national security policies takes into account both indicators. This allows us to trace a quantitative baseline, covering the period from 1975 to 1995, without missing the crucial qualitative shifts that occurred during this period.

Before I get to the point, some qualifications are in order. First of all, I do not deal with policy implementation or enforcement of legislation; rather, I am interested in the outputs of the policy-making process. In addition, my look at environmental, nuclear energy, and national security policies is limited to the general trends, as they can be observed not only in the development of spending for environmental protection and national defense but also in the amount of production of nuclear energy, including a number of crucial laws and amendments. It is virtually impossible to go into the details for each policy area in each country. Such enterprise goes far beyond the present purpose, which is more modest: to give an idea of how policy in the three areas addressed by ecology, antinuclear, and peace movements has evolved during the past three decades, to compare it with the development of the actions of the movements outlined in the previous chapter. Such a comparison is the object of the conclusion to part I.

Environmental, Nuclear Energy, and National Security Policy in the United States

Environmental Policy in the United States

Until the late 1960s, environmental policy in the United States[1] was above all focused on resource conservation and public land management, while the federal government played only a limited role in other areas (Kraft and Vig 1994). The establishment of a national parks system is fully in line with this first stream of state intervention to protect the natural environment. Government action aimed at preserving and managing the land in the public interest continues to be one of the main lines of intervention on behalf of the environment. The Wilderness Act of 1964 and the Land and Water Conservation Fund Act of 1964 are in this respect among the first major laws passed at the federal level.

State action, however, has expanded over the year to cover a much larger range of issues, beginning with industrial pollution and human waste. Early legislative efforts in these areas go back to the late nineteenth century, for example, with the Refuse Act of 1899, which required that a permit from the Army Corps of Engineers be obtained to dump refuse into navigable waters. Much more effective and consequential was a series of public laws that were enacted in the post–World War II period that aimed at fighting air and water pollution: the Water Pollution Control Act of 1948 and its 1956 amendments; the Air Pollution Control Act of 1955; the Clean Air Act of 1963; the Water Quality Act of 1965; and the Motor Vehicle Air Pollution Control Act of 1965 (Yandle 1989).

In spite of sometimes quite consequential early efforts, it is only starting from the late 1960s that an attempt at producing a comprehensive environmental policy was made in the United States. This goal was stated in the National Environmental Policy Act (NEPA) of 1969.

NEPA required environmental impact statements for all major federal action; implied implementation tasks by all federal agencies; and established the Council on Environmental Quality (CEQ), which was to advise the president and Congress on environmental matters. A series of legislative acts followed, particularly during the 1970s. All these laws can be seen as responding to five kinds of ecological problems:

1. the preservation and conservation of natural resources, including wildlife;
2. air and water pollution, as well as pollution from solid wastes;
3. toxic and hazardous wastes;
4. energy management; and
5. global climate change, biodiversity, and sustainable development.

Until recently, however, the last two areas received less attention than the first three. Energy issues have been characterized by policy gridlock (Kraft and Vig 1994). Also, global climate change, biodiversity, and sustainable development represent a new generation of ecological problems; therefore, still relatively little has been done in this regard. Furthermore, these problems are often handled at the supranational level, rather than the national.

In 1970, the Environmental Protection Agency (EPA) was established. While no fewer than twenty-seven federal agencies share regulatory responsibilities in matters concerning environmental and occupational health (Rosenbaum 1995), most policies are concentrated in the EPA as well as in the Departments of Interior and Agriculture (Kraft and Vig 1994).[2] However, the EPA is the principal institution responsible for the protection of the environment; specifically, it deals with air and water pollution, pesticides, radiation, solid waste, toxic and hazardous waste, and noise levels. In brief, the EPA is involved in the crucial environmental issues. In addition, this agency receives a large share of the federal budget to respond to ecological problems and threats. Indeed, looking at spending is an appropriate way to assess the path of public policy in favor of the environment. New legislation and the creation of permanent structures for handling ecological problems are only one part of the story. Another important part is represented by budget and expenditures. Figure 4.1 gives three measures of the development of spending for the environment between 1975 and 1995: the EPA budget, the spending for natural resources, and the total outlays.[3] As do all the other figures in this chapter, it divides into two parts: one showing developments in absolute terms (constant currencies), the other as percentages of total expenditures (or energy/electricity production, in the case of nuclear power).

All the distributions shown in figure 4.1 display a similar pattern, suggesting to divide the 1975–1995 period into three distinct phases. During the first phase, covering the second half of the 1970s, spending for the environment increased, or at least did not decline; in fact, the biggest rise took place in the first half of the decade, when outlays for natural resources and the environment more than doubled. Things went much worse in the 1980s, particularly during the first few years. The new situation is best summarized in the following statement by two leading students of environmental policy: "Virtually all environmental protection and resource policies enacted during the 1970s were reevaluated in light of the president's desire to reduce the scope of government regulation, shift responsibilities to the states, and rely more on the private sector" (Kraft and Vig 1994, 14). The issue's weakening salience, coupled with an increasing concern over the impact of environmental regulations on the economy, slowed the pace of public policy by the end of the Carter administration, although congressional commitment allowed for the enactment of

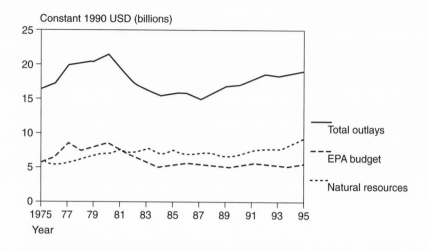

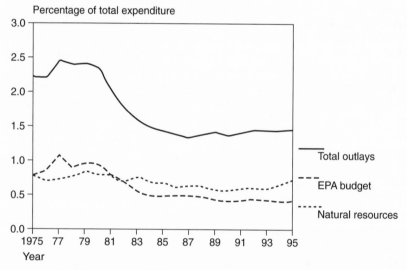

Figure 4.1. Spending for the Environment (USA, National).

crucial legislative pieces, most notably the Comprehensive Environmental Response, Compensation and Liability Act (CERCLA). However, as we can see in figure 4.1, available money to be invested in the management of natural resources and, above all, in the protection of the environment underwent a rapid decline during Reagan's first term.

The declining trend stopped around 1987. Starting from that year, total outlays began to rise again, although at a slow pace. The EPA's budget remained at best stable during the following years. Here we can see that George H. W. Bush's Republican administration and Clinton's Democratic first term do not differ much as to spending for environmental protection. Of course, one must consider that in periods of economic crisis it is more difficult to invest in certain areas; yet, the figure concerning the percentage of total expenditure shows that environmental protection did not have the right of priority under Clinton's administration, in spite of the strong pro-environmental image and campaign of the Clinton–Gore ticket. The most substantial increase in spending concerns natural resources, thus the less "threatening," less salient, and most consensual area of environmental policy.

The U.S. environmental policy was said to fail on the level of law enforcement and implementation, especially in the early 1980s, when massive cuts in environmental funding severely reduced the government's capacity to act in this field (Kraft and Vig 1994). This can be seen most clearly during the Reagan years, when legislative efforts continued at a fairly high level but when little money was available to implement the laws enacted. The domain of toxic wastes has been described as one of particularly inefficient policy implementation (Barnett 1994; Mazmanian and Morell 1992). Largely in response to public concern caused by the Love Canal affair in 1980, Congress passed CERCLA, a major piece of legislation that set out a cleanup program for hazardous waste sites and that defined a new liability scheme. Important laws on hazardous waste had been passed before,[4] but CERCLA stands out: one, for the large amount of money invested, from which it got the label of "Superfund"; and, two, because for the first time anyone who had contributed to the problem could be made to pay. The Superfund Amendments and Reauthorization Act (SARA) of 1986 increased the fund from $1.6 billion to $8.5 billion and introduced the community's right-to-know. Mazmanian and Morell (1992, xii) explain why they use the term *superfailure* to characterize America's first attempt at dealing with toxics, in spite of the large amount of money invested and in spite of the innovative liability scheme:

> Public pressures to act have been enormous; both Congress and state legislatures have responded admirably, passing numerous new laws. Yet the enactment of law after law in pursuit of toxics management has resulted in a nightmarish web of federal, state, and local regulations that seem to impede as much as facilitate the cleanup effort and to confuse further the picture. Litigation dominates over remediation.

In a federal system such as the United States, much public policy occurs at the local level. This is all the more true for environmental policy, which has a strong local dimension, even in more centralized states such as Italy. Thus, environmental responsibilities are not only distributed among the three branches of the state, the various executive agencies, and the many congressional committees and subcommittees but also among the fifty states and thousands of local governments. To have a crude picture of the efforts made at the local level, figure 4.2 shows the development of spending for natural resources in U.S. states from 1975 to 1995. The pattern is quite different from the national one.

In absolute terms, we observe a steady increase in spending virtually throughout the whole period. In fact, the biggest increase occurred in the early 1980s, precisely when major cuts were made at the national level. Perhaps the latter explains the former, as

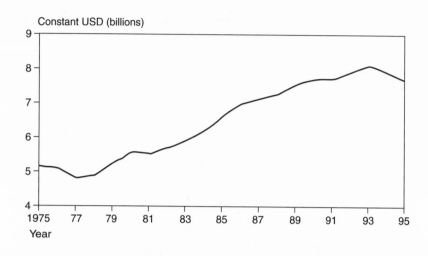

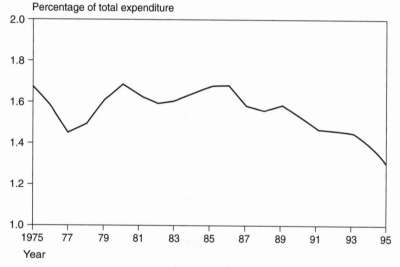

Figure 4.2. Spending for Natural Resources (USA, States).

state rulers felt the need to invest more money to protect the environment because they saw that the federal government was not doing enough. In terms of percentage of total expenditure, the picture is more negative: although differences from one year to the other are small, overall spending for natural resources in American states has decreased during the period under examination, particularly so in the late 1980s and in the 1990s. In sum, if we combine the development of spending both at the national and local level, we can conclude that the financial means used to protect the environment and preserve the natural resources in the United States have tended to diminish during the period under study.

Nuclear Energy Policy in the United States

The Atomic Energy Act of 1954 paved the way for the private development of nuclear power in the United States. This law allowed for the private ownership of nuclear reactors, and it provided for the lease of nuclear fuel from the government. The following year, the Atomic Energy Commission launched the Power Reactor Demonstration Program, aimed at encouraging and funding private reactors to produce electricity. The Price-Anderson Act of 1957 further spurred the new industry by almost completely underwriting liability for nuclear accidents, the burden of which was taken by the government. The Price-Anderson Act is also important from the perspective of social movements, for it opened public access to licensing hearings and thus created an important channel for the intervention of nuclear opponents. Supported by a wave of technological enthusiasm, first within the Atomic Energy Commission and later among private companies (particularly at Westinghouse and General Electric, the two giant electronic manufacturers), the first commercially competitive light water reactor was sold in 1963 (Jasper 1990).

The expansion of U.S. nuclear energy occurred through two waves of the so-called great bandwagon market (Jasper 1990). Between 1965 and 1967, the first wave of orders for commercial reactors occurred. A second, even larger wave took place between 1970 and 1973. These were the heydays of the American nuclear energy policy.

The oil crisis of 1973 to 1974 dramatically changed the rules of the game and set in motion a series of processes internal to the nuclear industry that, combined with the external challenges coming from the antinuclear movement, provoked the crisis of the U.S nuclear energy policy. In his comparative analysis of nuclear politics, Jasper (1990) points out three major consequences. First, media scrutiny over energy policy increased. Second, due to the dramatization and increased importance of energy issues, the emerging antinuclear movement became a visible force in policy discussions. Third, a cost–benefit frame became more influential, as the oil crisis encouraged more rational energy planning. On his part, President Nixon responded to the oil crisis with a speech he gave on November 7, 1973, in which he outlined Project Independence, a set of governmental initiatives—including a strong emphasis on nuclear power—aimed at giving the country energy independence by 1980.

A series of changes occurred in the U.S. nuclear energy regulation during the 1970s. These changes were largely, though indirectly, caused by the expansion of the antinuclear movement (Jasper 1990) and were aimed at strengthening nuclear energy policy; however, in the end, they had the opposite effect, the most important of which was the separation of the regulation of nuclear energy from its promotion, a combination of tasks that were until then carried by a single governmental agency, namely the Atomic Energy Commission (AEC). Two new agencies were then created in 1974 under the Energy Reorganization Act. Thus, the promotion of nuclear energy was entrusted to the Energy Research and Development Agency (ERDA), while the Nuclear Regulatory Commission (NRC) was charged with its regulation.[5] A second important reformist move took place in 1975 and 1976, in the direction of decentralizing the decisional structure in state agencies in charge of nuclear energy policy. Congress then reduced the powers of the Joint Committee on Atomic Energy (JCAE), which was dismantled in 1977, to be replaced by eight parliamentary commissions. Furthermore, several changes also occurred during the 1970s and 1980s in the form of formal concessions made to the antinuclear movement regarding thermal pollution and plant security matters. In this regard, the NRC—and, before it, the AEC—progressively tightened the construction standards for nuclear plants. The licensing procedure was also modified between 1970 and 1975, and public access to the regulatory process became more open during the 1970s. In addition, the progressive decentralization of U.S nuclear energy policy continued in the 1980s, as state legislation and public utility commissions eroded power from the federal government in nuclear energy matters, a process that was underway already since the late 1970s. As a result, during the 1980s, the control by states has never stopped increasing, while that by the federal administration has diminished.

All these regulatory changes—as well as others that took place during the first half of the 1970s—were made with the aim of accelerating the expansion of nuclear energy in the United States (Jasper 1990). They were carried at a time when major delays in the construction of power plants and the resulting increasing costs, which skyrocketed after the 1973–1974 oil crisis, began to endanger the country's nuclear energy policy. In addition, these reforms were made parallel to the strengthening of the antinuclear movement and to the rise of its mobilization, not only locally, but also nationally, and when antinuclear opposition was becoming heard both outside and inside Congress.

Besides the regulatory reforms that occurred at the institutional and administrative levels in the management of nuclear energy policy, we are most interested in substantive changes in policy from the perspective of social movement outcomes. While environmental policy can be measured by looking at government spending, actual energy production levels are a better indicator of government investment in the field of nuclear power. Figure 4.3 shows the development of nuclear energy production from 1975 to 1995 as expressed in thousands of gigawatt-hours (gWh) and in a percentage of total electricity production.

According to both indicators, we observe a steady increase in production—indeed, a remarkably regular one. In percentage terms, the share of electricity from nuclear power grew from less than 10 percent in 1975 to more than 20 percent in 1995. The increase was particularly persistent during the 1980s, after a small decline in the late 1970s.

However, if we take another indicator and look at the number of nuclear power plants instead of the amount of energy production, we have quite a different picture. Table 4.1 gives us this measure of policy change, distinguishing between operating units, units on order, construction permits, and total units.

On all counts, except for the number of operating plants, the nuclear power sector appears to have lost ground, at least from 1979 onward. The number of units in

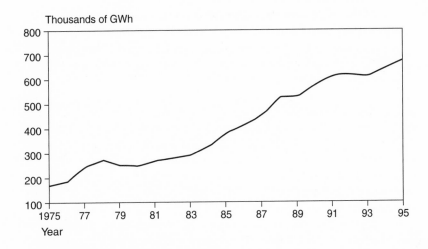

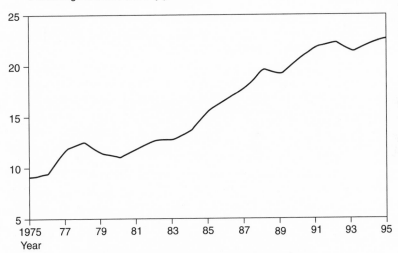

Figure 4.3. Nuclear Energy Production (USA).

operation, of course, has continued to grow in spite of a general decline of the sector due to the time frame needed to build a plant. In the end, however, operating nuclear plants have remained stable since 1987. Concerning the number of units on order, which is perhaps the best indicator, we observe a dramatic fall in 1978. In addition, parallel to the decrease in the number of reactors ordered, that of cancellations began to rise, starting from 1972 (Jasper 1990), reinforcing the picture of a progressively weakening American nuclear power industry. When we see that 231 plants were ordered through 1974 but only 15 the following year and none after 1978—and when we consider that they canceled orders for more than 100 plants between 1974 and 1982

Table 4.1. Nuclear Energy Production in the United States

Year	Operating Units	Units on Order	Construction Permits	Total Units
1975	54	14	69	213
1976	61	16	71	214
1977	65	13	78	209
1978	70	5	88	195
1979	68	3	90	185
1980	70	3	82	168
1981	74	2	76	163
1982	77	2	60	144
1983	80	2	53	138
1984	86	2	38	132
1985	95	2	30	130
1986	100	2	19	128
1987	107	2	14	127
1988	108	0	12	123
1989	110	0	10	121
1990	111	0	8	119
1991	111	0	8	119
1992	109	0	8	117
1993	109	0	7	116
1994	109	0	7	116
1995	109	0	6	116

(Campbell 1988)—we can speak of a real collapse of the nuclear sector. Interestingly, the fall of orders occurred before the 1979 accident at Three Mile Island, which is often considered as having caused the decline of the American nuclear industry. It seems instead that such decline preceded the accident, which simply accelerated this process and made it visible to the general public. Finally, a similar declining pattern can be observed in the development of construction permits and the total number of units.

In the end, the U.S. nuclear energy policy, as many observers have stressed (Campbell 1988; Jasper 1990; Tomain 1987), has been a remarkable instance of policy failure, in spite of an increase in the production of nuclear energy both in absolute terms and in relation to electricity production. Increasing regulatory, political, and economic uncertainty imposed a de facto moratorium after 1979 (Rüdig 1990), as orders for new reactors virtually stopped in 1978 and many of the planned ones were decommissioned. As Campbell (1988) has pointed out in his merciless analysis of the U.S. nuclear power industry, management weaknesses, skyrocketing costs, and financial crises largely contributed to the collapse of commercial nuclear energy policy. According to Jasper (1990), the causes of this failure go back to a time when the nuclear industry was flourishing:

The hidden weaknesses of the 1960s—utility financing, premature deployment, causal managerial attitudes, and hands-off regulation—began to have an effect in the early

1970s, and they overwhelmed nuclear deployment by the late 1970s. Yet nuclear energy was not widely seen as in trouble until the late 1970s. Only [Three Mile Island] in 1979 revealed clearly the nature of its problems. The hidden weaknesses contributed to nuclear energy's cost problems, which in turn caught the attention of cost-benefiters and contributed to the collapse of orders for nuclear plants. The technological enthusiasts who had controlled nuclear decisions at utilities and the government in the 1960s were blind to all weaknesses. The outsiders who became concerned with nuclear energy because of the antinuclear movement and the oil crisis were better equipped to see them. (Jasper 1990, 215–16)

In sum, Jasper concludes that the main reason for the policy failure was the high and unpredictable costs of building nuclear plants, a factor already exacerbated by increasing construction delays. One of my tasks in the following chapters is to ascertain whether the antinuclear movement played only a marginal role in this process or a more important one.

National Security Policy in the United States

The U.S. national security policy can be assessed by means of three indicators:

1. the development of government spending for military purposes;
2. the entering into or signing of international peace treaties, in particular with the former Soviet Union; and
3. the carrying of active or passive military interventions abroad.

Figure 4.4 shows the development over time of the U.S. defense budget. Three distinct patterns can be discerned, both in the absolute and relative figures.

First, during the second half of the 1970s, military spending declined, then remained quite stable. But apart from the decline, which was due to the end of the long and costly military involvement in Southeast Asia,[6] the defense budget has followed a pattern reflecting changes in presidency, although not always along partisan lines. During the Carter years, the level of expenditure remained relatively low, particularly in absolute terms. Things changed dramatically after Reagan was elected for his first presidential term. Paralleling—and largely provoking—a tightening of U.S.–Soviet relations, the new administration took a more bellicose posture and brought military spending to unprecedented high levels. Measured in constant dollars, military spending rose to nearly $320 billion in 1986, from less than $200 billion in 1979. In relative terms, the peak was reached in 1987, when the defense budget went close to 30 percent of total government expenditure.

The military buildup was mainly due to Reagan's strong reliance on nuclear arms as a way of asserting American superiority vis-à-vis the Soviet Union. It went on relentlessly, especially during his first term, in spite of emerging arms control advocates within the parliamentary arena. In fact, the peace movement succeeded in convincing members of Congress to act in favor of arms control. Thus, Senators Edward Kennedy and Mark Hatfield introduced in the Senate the Joint Resolution on Nuclear Weapons

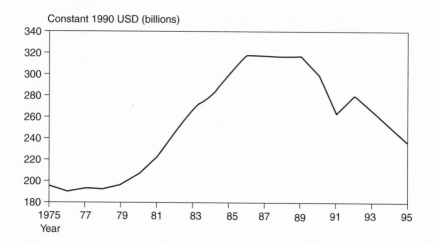

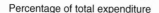

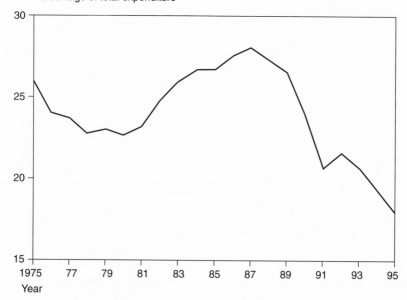

Figure 4.4. Military Spending (USA).

Freeze and Reductions.[7] An analogous resolution was proposed by Senators Henry Jackson and John Warner.[8] The Kennedy–Hatfield resolution made its way to the House of Representatives, where it was first defeated on August 5, 1982,[9] but eventually passed with several amendments on May 4, 1983.[10] However, this congressional action in favor of arms control did little to influence the administration to reduce its commitment to the arms race, let alone force it to engage in a nuclear freeze. Paradoxically, its major effect was to help dissipate the peace movement through processes of marginalization, depoliticization, and institutionalization (Meyer 1993).

Reagan's military buildup continued in his second term, in spite of his new rhetoric that pictured himself as an arms control advocate. Indeed, he proclaimed his landslide of historical proportions in the 1984 presidential election a mandate for arms control. A few months earlier, on March 23, 1983, he delivered what would come to be known as the "Star Wars" speech, in which he called for the creation of a ballistic missile defense system—the Strategic Defense Initiative (SDI)—which would have made nuclear weapons obsolete and allowed for a large reduction in the nuclear arsenals. Despite this new rhetoric, however, defense spending remained at high levels. Other factors would effect a changing international context and, in particular, the seizure of power by Mikhail Gorbachev in March 1985. Gorbachev's new deal in the Soviet Union forestalled Reagan and forced him not only to change his rhetoric but also to reduce his commitment to a national security policy inspired by Cold War standards. As can be seen in figure 4.4, military spending stopped its upward trend during Reagan's second term and began to decline even before Bush took office in 1989. Finally, after the fall of the Soviet Union, after the Warsaw Pact, and after the end of the Cold War, the U.S. defense budget went into a steady decline, with the only exception of a short-lived rise due to American involvement in the Gulf War. This decline occurred under Bush's Republican presidency as well as under Clinton's Democratic presidency.

The U.S. national security policy can also be judged on the basis of the United States' entering into or signing of international treaties. Most of such agreements deal with nuclear arms control—above all, strategic nuclear weapons. One of the first major international treaties in this regard is the Limited Test Ban Treaty, entered into by the United States, the Soviet Union, and Great Britain on August 5, 1963, which banned nuclear weapon tests in the atmosphere, in outer space, and under water. On January 27, 1967, sixty-two nations, including the United States and the Soviet Union, signed the Outer Space Treaty, which banned placement of weapons of mass destruction in Earth's orbit. On November 25, 1969—one week after the beginning of the Strategic Arms Limitation Talks (SALT), between the United States and the Soviet Union, the first such agreements of cooperation among the two countries at this level—President Nixon signed the Nuclear Nonproliferation Treaty, which was simultaneously ratified by the Soviet Union.[11] On February 11, 1971, the United States and the Soviet Union entered a treaty banning nuclear weapons from the ocean floor. On May 26, 1972, the SALT I agreements were signed in Moscow. They included two agreements: the first one, the Antiballistic Missile Treaty (ABM), limited construction of missile defenses to those around each national capital and to a single intercontinental ballistic missile (ICBM) site; the second one established a five-year freeze on existing ICBM deployments. On September 30, 1972, the United States and the Soviet Union entered into the Agreement to Reduce the Risk of Nuclear War Outbreak, with the aim of reaching control over accidental and unauthorized nuclear weapons use. On July 3, 1974, the two countries signed the Threshold Test Ban Treaty, which limited nuclear weapons tests to no more than 150 kilotons.[12] On June 18, 1979, the SALT II agreements were signed in Vienna, after more than six years of negotiations. They limited the United States and the Soviet Union to the same maximum number of long-range missiles and bombers. On April 7, 1987, after several years of secret negotiations, the United States, Canada, Britain, France, Italy, Japan, and West Germany agreed to control exports of missiles and other technology amenable to nuclear weapons use. On September 15, 1987, President Reagan and Soviet general secretary Gorbachev signed the Intermediate Nuclear Forces Treaty, which provided for the destruction of more than twelve hundred nuclear missiles and two thousand nuclear warheads. This was the first treaty between the two countries that actually reduced the size of their nuclear arsenals.[13] On June 1, 1990, President George H. W. Bush and Gorbachev agreed on a framework for reducing strategic nuclear weapons. On December 11, 1990, Bush signed two treaties with the Soviet Union limiting underground nuclear testing. Though its negotiations began in 1982, the Strategic Arms Reduction Treaty (START), which covered long-range nuclear weapons, was signed in Moscow on July 31, 1991. On September 27, 1991, Bush announced, among other moves, a rare unilateral reduction of U.S. nuclear weapons in Europe.

These are only the major agreements reached between the two great powers on arms control matters.[14] It is enough, however, to see that the clustering in time of international treaties reflects that of military spending. Most treaties were signed in the 1970s, whereas the 1980s are characterized by a relative lack of agreements aimed at controlling the arms race, particularly during the decade's first half.

Finally, due to the strong position of the country in the international system, the U.S. national security policy can be assessed in terms of military interventions abroad. Once again, we can see the strong impact of President Reagan on military matters. In particular, his policies in Central America spurred a series of protests during the 1980s. However, Democratic and Republican administrations do not behave in substantially different ways when it comes to foreign policy (Peterson 1994). Military interventions abroad are quite a constant in U.S. foreign policy, regardless of the party or the president in power. If the Reagan administration focused on Central America in the 1980s, Bush engaged the country in the Gulf War, and Clinton was at the forefront of the NATO intervention in Kosovo, only to mention the most famous cases. That these interventions were often justified in terms of restoring the peace does certainly not change their military nature, which spurred opposition by peace activists.

Environmental, Nuclear Energy, and National Security Policy in Italy

Environmental Policy in Italy

On the most general level, we can distinguish three phases in the development of Italy's environmental policy (Lewanski 1990), at least up to the 1990s. During the first phase, from the mid-1960s to the mid-1970s, environmental problems became publicly more visible, stimulating attempts to provide adequate responses. The normative tool kit, however, was largely inadequate, for it had been created for other purposes, such as public health or specific economic interests. At the same time, pollution control makes its way onto the political agenda; and the very term *pollution* appears for the first time, in the Maritime Fishing Act of 1965, thereby formalizing the beginning of a new way of framing environmental issues. In 1966, the Antismog Act went into effect, and it can be considered the first modern law for environmental protection in Italy. However, this law remained quite an isolated case, at least until the early 1970s, when rules were made for its actual application. Special laws were enacted for the Venice area, where there is the industrial concern of Porto Marghera. The second phase went from the mid-1970s to the mid-1980s and was characterized by the enlargement of the normative apparatus, which underwent a significant growth both in qualitative and quantitative terms. This phase opened with the Merli Act (Act 319/1976), on water pollution, and closed with the Galasso Act (Act 431/1985), on landscapes. In between, a series of laws and regulations were made on various aspects of environmental protection: drinkable waters, solid wastes, sea and coasts, biodegradability of detergents, and so forth. The third phase began with the creation of the Ministry of Environment, in 1986. This event opened up a new era in Italy's environmental policy making. From that point forward, policy responsibilities, which were previously spread over various ministries, were to be carried by a single institutional actor.[15] This facilitated the formulation and, above all, the implementation of specific policies aimed at protecting the environment. Although felt in the previous phase, the influence of the European Community increased and became a major vector of policy change in this area.

In sum, from a legislative point of view, Italy's environmental policy displayed, first, a growing trend that accelerated in the 1980s and, second, a delay of about ten years with respect not only to other countries, such as the United States, but also to the scope of the problems being dealt with (Lewanski 1990). Figure 4.5, which shows the development of spending for environmental protection by the Italian government, allows us to see whether a similar pattern can be observed regarding public funds.

Unfortunately, the period covered by the data is shorter than the twenty-year period used for the other policy areas. Information on spending for the environment in Italy starts only from 1986, with the creation of the Ministry of Environment.[16] The data show a clear increase in spending during the second half of the 1980s. Expenditures peaked in 1991, then fell in 1992 and 1993, only to start rising again in the final part of the period under study. Overall, this pattern confirms the important growth in state intervention for the environment during the late 1980s and a general rising trend from the mid-1980s onward.

As far as structural conditions are concerned, one crucial event was the creation of the Ministry of Environment, in 1986.[17] Another, less-important structure—the National Council for the Environment—was established during the same year. The largest ecology organizations are accorded an official status in both institutions, though only a consultative one. The setting up of a political–bureaucratic actor with real deci-sional power, such as the Ministry of Environment, meant a substantial improvement in the conditions for the regulation of environmental protection. At the same time, the

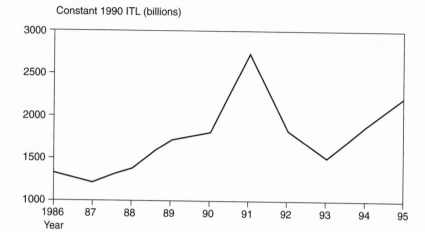

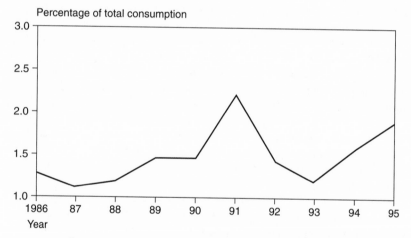

Figure 4.5. Spending for the Environment (Italy, National).

ministry promoted a large normative production, which contributed to the growth of activities aimed at protecting Italy's natural patrimony.

The 1990s saw the creation of further governmental structures. The National Agency for the Protection of the Environment (ANPA) was set up in 1994, although it started operations the following year. This governmental unit was set up after a referendum on environmental controls, which was launched by the ecology organization Friends of the Earth and voted on in April 1993. After this successful effort, the organization promoted and influenced the parliamentary event that led to the birth of ANPA.[18] ANPA has four basic tasks:

1. to provide the central administrations with technical–scientific support on environmental matters;

2. to orient and coordinate the environmental controls made by the regional agencies;
3. to gather and spread environmental information of national relevance;
4. to promote research and technological innovation.

The same law that concerned the reorganization of environmental controls and established ANPA also gave the regions the task of setting up Regional Agencies for the Protection of the Environment (ARPA). In fact, even in a centralized political system such as the one in Italy, the local level is crucial not only for the implementation of environmental policy but also for its formulation. Unfortunately, the data at our disposal for the local level is even more limited than those pertaining to the national level. Figure 4.6 shows the Italian regions' spending for the protection of the environment from 1986 to 1992.

A first aspect to be noticed is that the regions spent more than the central government did. In 1986, for example, they spent more than £2,600 billion, while spending at the national level hardly reached £1,500 billion. In general, there was an increase in spending, particularly between 1988 and 1991, paralleling the growth at the national level. In terms of percentage of total consumption, fluctuations are, of course, minimal at such low levels of spending. Yet we observe a slightly decreasing trend over the period considered. In other words, if we compare it to investments in other policy areas, spending for the environment by the Italian regions cannot be said to have increased during the second half of the 1980s and early 1990s.

Nuclear Energy Policy in Italy

Our overview of Italy's nuclear energy policy can be relatively brief for two simple reasons (which represent also its two main features). First, nuclear energy has always been a rather marginal policy area in this country. In spite of a strong dependency on imported energy sources, it has not played an important role in the Italian economy or in energy policies (Diani 1994). Second, it virtually ended after a referendum vote in 1987, as shown in figure 4.7, which shows the development of nuclear power production for the 1975–1995 period.

As in the United States, the beginnings of nuclear power in Italy go back to the years immediately following the end of World War II. Private companies jointly set up a research and experimentation group in 1946. The public sector intervened in the nuclear business a few years later, and research in this field was completely taken up by public agencies in 1960 as the National Council for Nuclear Energy (CNEN), which replaced the former National Council for Nuclear Research (CNRN). The first three plants were built in the late 1950s and early 1960s, and they began operations between 1962 and 1964, placing Italy quite in the vanguard of development in the nuclear sector. The project that would become the main target of the antinuclear movement, Montalto di Castro, was started in 1971 with the formal siting procedure; however, strong opposition, also against the other important target of the movement, Caorso, only took place in the second half of the 1970s.

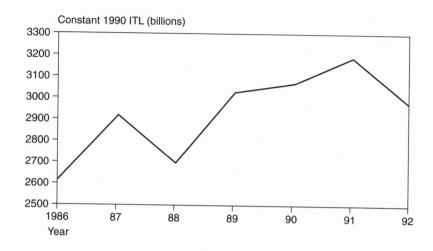

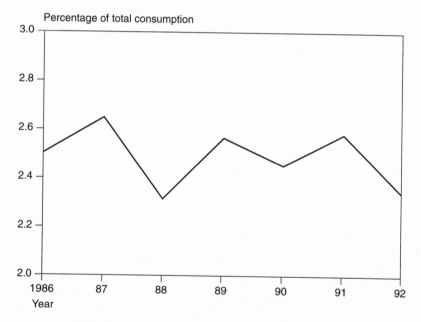

Figure 4.6. Spending for the Environment (Italy, Regions).

In spite of this early development and in spite of the boost received from the "Atoms for Peace" enthusiasm, nuclear energy remained secondary with respect to other sources. Already in the late 1960s, for example, the parliament gave priority to oil as a major energy source. The National Agency for Electric Energy (ENEL) was favoring oil, an option that was obviously supported by powerful oil companies; yet, much like the situations in other countries, the 1973–1974 energy crisis incited the

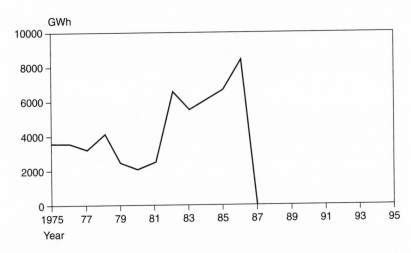

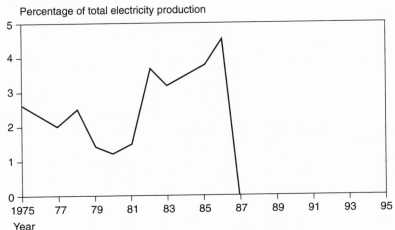

Figure 4.7. Nuclear Energy Production (Italy).

government to rely heavily on nuclear power. It is in this context that the first National Energy Plan (PEN) was passed, in 1975. For the first time, a crucial role was assigned to nuclear power, with plans for twenty additional plants. In the same year, concern about rapidly growing antinuclear opposition forced the government to introduce new regulations for the building of nuclear power plants: "The growing obstacles faced by the ENEL in building new plants pressed the government to change the rules of the game in 1975" (Diani 1994, 206). These changes, described in Act 393/1975, can be summarized in three points:

1. to keep the constraints over the use of money given by the government to local municipalities that would be ready to host an electric plant;

2. to reduce the power of local and regional authorities in the matter of communal planning and environmental protection; and
3. to centralize the zoning procedures by putting them under the control of the Industry Department.

Further regulatory changes were introduced later on with Act 8/1983, which modified the procedures for the zoning plans by introducing more flexible regulations for the use of public money given to local councils as a compensation for the risks of hosting a nuclear plant.

That Italian decision makers were not enthusiastic about nuclear power began to become clear when the parliament passed the second PEN, in 1977, which reduced nearly by half the total amount of planned nuclear capacity and the number of plants to be built. Further cuts were foreseen in the 1981 PEN. Most important, this revised version of the PEN in some way officially acknowledged the trend against nuclear power and was in favor of oil as well as alternative energy sources. Created to replace the CNEN, the Agency for Alternative Energy Sources (ENEA) marks this shift on the institutional level. However, the nuclear option was not yet abandoned, and all major parties and unions were still in favor of nuclear energy, although some cracks could now be seen in the pronuclear front.

As can be seen in figure 4.7, the production of nuclear energy took a strong upward turn during the 1980s. Unfortunately for those who were still confident in the promises of nuclear power, the antinuclear referendum came in the worst of times. The referendum campaign began on May 9, 1986, a few days after the accident at Chernobyl and the year after the 1985 PEN, which did not fundamentally change the provisions of the 1981 PEN. By the time the referendum was to be voted on, all major parties joined the antinuclear camp, and public opinion was clearly against nuclear energy. Even the leading Christian-Democratic Party supported the referendum, although probably for tactical reasons rather than because of a genuine and quite unlikely last-minute change of mind. With such a large consensus, the antinuclear referendum—more precisely, the three referenda—were accepted by a majority of voters.

In 1988, and in spite of the result of the referendum, the government proposed to build a new plant, to resume operation at Caorso, and to complete the plant in Montalto di Castro. The last decision created not only a division within the government, between the Christian-Democratic Party and the Socialist Party, but a political crisis as well. However, in August of the same year, this decision was reversed. With the abandoning of the Montalto di Castro plant, Italian energy policy took a further step away from nuclear power. This new stance can be seen in the 1988 PEN, which included a growing differentiation of energy sources and which gave priority to smaller plants.

National Security Policy in Italy

Generally speaking, the Italian defense system is considered efficient from a technical–administrative point of view but vulnerable in the strategic–operational sphere (Caligaris 1990). Specifically, it feels the effects of a number of limitations: the absence of a clear national demand for an efficient defense apparatus and a lack of coherent policy guidelines; a low political consensus on basic defense activities such as training; a low cultural interest toward broad defense issues both within and outside the system; and a political summit structure inadequate to its functions as a military summit structure and characterized by fragmentation and a lack of efficacy.

Italy's national security policy cannot be understood without reference to the country's belonging to NATO. If one browses through the various reports by the Ministry of Defense, it clearly appears that the Atlantic Treaty is a keystone of Italy's military and defense policies. It is on behalf of this loyalty toward NATO that the Italian government announced on August 7, 1981, its readiness to host cruise missiles. Even the Communist Party, while criticizing the latter decision, did not call into question the military alliance. In fact, what ultimately led to a consensus on national security issues was the Communist Party's acceptance of Italy's place within the Western bloc and within its system of political–military alliances in the mid-1970s. This loyalty to NATO also explains Italy's active involvement in the Gulf War.

However, I am more interested in the development of the Italian national security policy than I am in studying its characteristics. In this respect, of the three indicators considered in the case of the United States—military spending, international peace treaties, and military interventions abroad—only the first one applies to Italy. Figure 4.8 shows the development of spending for the national defense by the Italian government between 1975 and 1995.

In absolute terms, the pattern is not too different from that observed in the United States. In both countries, expenditures for military purposes have increased steadily during the 1980s. The growth began earlier, lasted longer, and was followed by a less-dramatic decrease in Italy; but the distribution over time is more or less the same. In percentage terms, however, we observe some important differences. Specifically, military spending in Italy has been more stable. Thus, we can speak of a relative stability of military spending by the Italian government during the two decades under examination: variation is less than 4 percent, as compared with about 10 percent in the United States. Expenditures have increased in the early 1980s but not as much as the absolute figures would suggest. Furthermore, apart from sporadic rises in 1979 and in 1994, spending went up substantially from 1981 to 1985. Both in absolute and relative terms, however, the most significant feature is the declining trend after 1989.

Quite significant, a new defense model was presented in November 1991. The fall of the Berlin Wall and the end of the United States–Soviet Union bipolar system led Italy, like many other countries, to revise its guidelines and priorities in this area. The new defense model proposed a series of reforms that can be summarized in five points (Bellucci 1994). First, operational missions of the armed forces were cut to three (from the five mentioned by the Italian White Book of 1985): presence and surveillance, the defense of external interests and the contribution to international security, and the integrated defense of the domestic spaces. This included the possibility of military intervention outside the national territory to defend national interests, constituting a clear break with previous policy. Second, the reform provided for a substantial reduction of armed forces. Third, new professional forces were to

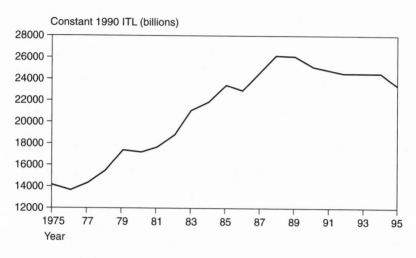

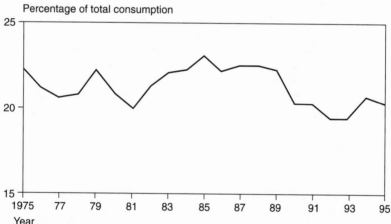

Figure 4.8. Military Spending (Italy).

be set up with external projection capacity to defend the national interests as well as to perform peacekeeping and enforcing actions. Fourth, the recruiting system was to become mixed, that is, draft and voluntary. Fifth, the new model provided for a reform of the military summits in the direction of an increased centralization of responsibilities.

Today, Italy's military and defense policies are moving, like those of other Western countries, toward increasing professionalization and toward a reduction of the role of the traditional draft system. In 1999, Prime Minister Massimo D'Alema announced plans to abolish the traditional draft-based army in favor of a smaller, professional-based army. This leads me to spend a few words on the issue of conscientious objection.

The problem of conscientious objection in Italy has been addressed, and partly solved, from early on. Already in the early 1970s, Act 772/1972 introduced the substitutive civil service. The implementation rules for this act were made only five years later, in 1977, and included the contract of the civil service to the voluntary sector. However, access to the civil service was contingent on the evaluation by the military authorities of the foundation of the objection. Furthermore, the latter excluded political motives, and the length of the service was one-third longer than the military service. In spite of the advance made in comparison to the previous period, this solution was criticized by peace activists. A number of decisions have subsequently modified this initial measure. An important role in this respect was played by the Constitutional Court.[19] The most important decision, taken in 1989, ruled that conscientious objectors could not be constitutionally required to serve a longer term. As a result, the number of objectors went up considerably in the following years (Ruzza 1997). In another decision taken in 1989, the Constitutional Court ruled out penal sanctions given to total objectors, that is, those objectors who were not admitted to the civil service. More recently, Act 772/1972 was replaced by Act 230/1998, which introduced new rules concerning conscientious objection. According to the new rules, apart from some exceptions, those citizens who do not accept the military draft can fulfill their obligations in the civil service.

Environmental, Nuclear Energy, and National Security Policy in Switzerland

Environmental Policy in Switzerland

As in other policy areas, the legislative process concerning environmental policy in Switzerland is characterized by its speed—or, more specifically, its lack thereof. Perhaps the best example is represented by the fifteen years that elapsed since the federal constitution was amended to protect the environment, in 1971; to the moment the Environmental Protection Act was passed, in 1983; and, finally, to the time the act came into force, in 1985. In spite of such slowness, Switzerland has in this field one of the most modern environmental legislative apparatuses among European countries, though a relatively new one (Knoepfel 1990). However, progress has been different in the eight traditional areas of environmental policy: waters, air, waste management and recycling, noise, soils, toxic substances, treatment of hazardous substances, and nature and landscape protection. The greatest improvements have been made in the treatment of wastes and hazardous substances, the poorest in the field of noise as well as in the field of nature and landscape protection; however, progress in the other areas stands somewhere in between (Benninghoff et al. 1999).

While the 1970s focused on water pollution, the 1980s focused not only on air pollution, noise, and soil but also on chemical substances (Knoepfel 1990). Policy instruments evolved from classical regulatory means, during the mid-1980s, to a more frequent use of cooperative and planning instruments. More specifically, we can distinguish four phases in the development of Swiss environmental policy (Benninghoff et al. 1999; Jänicke and Weidner 1997), not only at the national level, but also at the local.[20] The first phase, covering the period from 1960 to 1975, represents the beginnings of environmental policy action in Switzerland. As in other countries, among the first laws enacted were those relating to nature conservation. Within this period, an important one was the Nature and Homeland Protection Act of 1966. In this phase, state intervention was mostly limited to "firefighter exercises" featuring an emission-oriented strategy. Policy was aimed at improving the distribution of pollutants over time and in taking measures concerning particularly exposed sectors.

The landmark Ordinance on Waste Water Discharge of 1975 marked the beginning of a change of strategy and the entry into a second phase of Swiss environmental policy.[21] For the first time, general limitations on emissions were set regardless of the gravity of specific situations. The period from 1975 to 1986 was thus characterized by the introduction of "end-of-the-pipe" policies (Benninghoff et al. 1999). The two-step approach of Swiss environmental policy was thus developed. Legally inscribed with the Environmental Protection Act of 1983, this approach mandated that emissions of pollutants be limited in the whole country, independent of the seriousness of the specific situation. If an overwhelming aggravation of the situation occurred, in terms of emission standards, then new emission standards would further be set. This policy was first applied to water protection, then to air protection, and finally to waste management.

This policy was intensified during the third phase, from 1986 to 1992, during which several important ordinances were issued, such as the Ordinance on Environmentally Hazardous Substances (1986), the Ordinance on Soil Pollutants (1986), the Ordinance on Hazardous Wastes (1986), the Ordinance on Environmental Impact Assessment (1988), and the Ordinance on Waste Treatment (1990), to mention only a few examples (all of which were preceded by the Ordinance on Air Quality Control of 1985). During this phase, the industry became more aware of the opportunities given by the rise of environmental consciousness and policies, not only of the constraints posed by them. It was in this phase that the most important institutional actor was set up: the Swiss Agency for the Environment, Forests, and Landscape (SAEFL), which was created in 1989 by merging two former federal agencies, the Environmental Protection Agency and the Agency of Forestry and Landscape Protection.[22]

The fourth and final phase began in 1992 and was characterized by an environmental modernization. As in other countries, there was a change in the definition and conception of environmental policy. Under the influence of the Rio Conference of 1992 and subsequent international summits, the notion of sustainable development took on increasing importance. Furthermore, the various social and political actors become aware of the fact that environmental policy was much more than simply setting standards for pollutant emissions (Minsch et al. 1996).

While legislation concerning various aspects of environmental protection has been slow but nevertheless forthcoming, the financial means employed by the Swiss government in this policy area have undergone a declining trend, or at best have stagnated during the period considered here, depending on what we include under the label "environmental protection." This can be seen in figure 4.9, which shows the development of spending for the environment from 1975 to 1995.

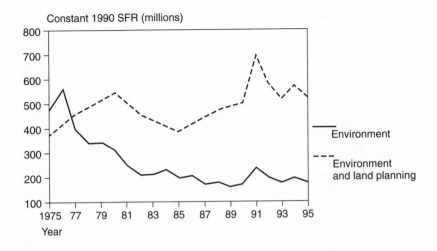

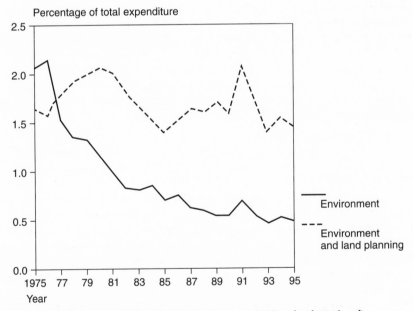

Figure 4.9. Spending for the Environment (Switzerland, National).

The figure gives two distributions, one regarding the environment in a strict sense (water protection, wastes, etc.) and one including land planning as well. This distinction is important not only because these two areas are often treated separately in scholarly accounts (e.g., Benninghoff et al. 1999) but also because the two distributions unfolded quite differently. As we can see in figure 4.9, environmental spending has decreased in both absolute and relative terms; but if we include land planning, we get a more positive picture. This means that expenditures devoted to land planning has tended to increase; yet, the early 1980s witnessed a general decline, regardless of which indicator we look at. Although this declining trend has stabilized somewhat since the mid-1980s, the overall trend remains on the wane.[23]

Although important legislative efforts have been made at the national level, environmental protection in Switzerland is largely a matter of regional and local policy communities. This can easily be seen by comparing figure 4.9 to figure 4.10, which shows the development of spending for the environment for all three administrative levels: federal, cantonal, and communal.

The mean value referring to environmental protection, in the strict sense of the term, for the whole period equals 2,294 million Swiss francs for all levels, against 255 million for the national level only. One reason for the diminishing expenditures by the federal government could have lain in a different distribution of resources between the national and the local level. This does not seem to be the case, however, as we observe a similar, though less pronounced, decrease in spending for all three administrative levels taken together. In 1995, the federal government, the cantons, and the communes spent more or less the same amount of money as in 1975 and much less in terms of percentage of total expenditure. Apart from a short-lived resumption from 1985 to 1988, the only notable exception is the growth of spending that includes land planning during the first part of the period considered. In general, however, we can conclude that spending for the environment in Switzerland has diminished from the late 1970s to the early 1990s, especially in relative terms and especially if we exclude land planning.

Nuclear Energy Policy in Switzerland

While the share of nuclear power over the total electricity production always remained below 5 percent in Italy, at some point it went beyond 40 percent in Switzerland, despite the country's small number of plants. This simple comparison clearly shows the weight given to nuclear energy by the Swiss authorities as compared to the Italians. As in the other European countries, the beginning of nuclear power in Switzerland goes back to the 1950s. More precisely, in 1957, a constitutional article on the peaceful use of nuclear energy was accepted. Two years later, the parliament approved the Nuclear Energy Act, which paved the way for the exploitation of this energy source. At the time, a widespread trust in economic growth and progress provided a fertile ground for the development of nuclear power, which was seen as the best way toward affluence. Furthermore, skepticism toward the military's use of the atom in a way gave more legitimacy to its civilian use.

The nuclear power industry moved from projects to reality in the late 1960s and early 1970s. In spite of plans for ten plants, to be completed by year 2000, only four were built. After a first reactor test, made in Lucens in 1968, the first nuclear power plant began operating in 1969, in Beznau. A second unit started operating there in 1971. Another plant was ready to function the following year in Mühleberg, and a

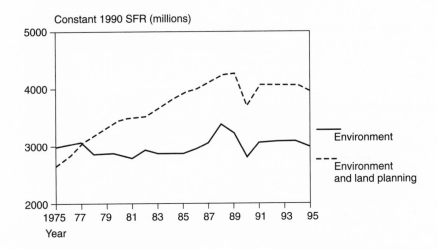

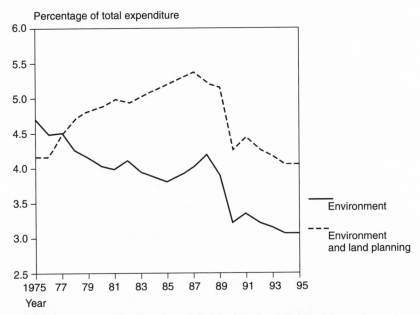

Figure 4.10. Spending for the Environment (Switzerland, All Levels).

further one began operations in 1979, in Gösgen. Finally, a plant in Leibstadt started commercial operations in 1984.

The specific contribution of the various plants to the amount of nuclear energy produced in Switzerland can be seen in figure 4.11, which gives us the development of production between 1975 and 1995, again in absolute and relative terms.

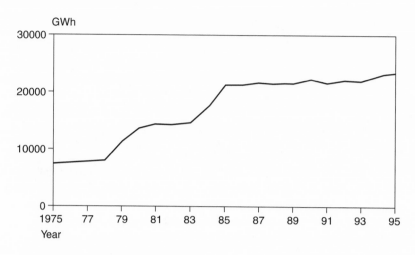

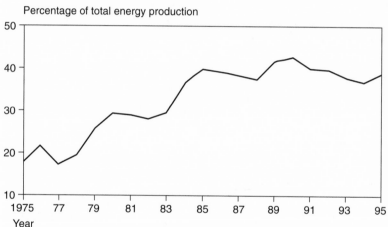

Figure 4.11. Nuclear Energy Production (Switzerland).

We observe similar development on both counts. Production underwent an important growth from the late 1970s to 1985. From that year onward, we observe a stagnation in the amount of nuclear energy. It is important to remark that the halt to the increasing trend occurred the very same year as the Chernobyl accident. As in Italy, this event could have played a significant role in stopping the growth of nuclear power. Specifically, it pressed the antinuclear movement to launch two antinuclear initiatives in 1986 and 1987. One of them, which called for a ten-year moratorium on the building of new plants, was accepted in September 1990. Unlike in Italy, where the vote on the antinuclear referendum took place shortly after the Chernobyl accident and hence could take advantage of the public concern about nuclear energy it raised, the Swiss moratorium initiative was voted on four years later. The accident, however, was instrumental in setting in motion the whole process, and it probably also influenced the vote, as antinuclear opponents could rely on exploiting that event during their campaign. The moratorium apparently did not affect the level of production, but it certainly constrained the possibilities for the Swiss government to increase the share of nuclear energy other than by improving the efficiency of existing units.

Beside production levels, the Swiss nuclear energy policy can be assessed by looking at some key governmental decisions. An important one was taken in 1978, when Swiss authorities proposed a partial revision of the Nuclear Energy Act that was virtually a counterproject to the 1976 antinuclear initiative. The revision, which was accepted against a popular referendum in 1979, proposed a democratization of the procedure for granting construction permits, as well as new criteria for accepting new plants. In brief, only those plants needed for the energy supply for the country were to be built. In practice, the authorities were pressed by the antinuclear movement to revise the decisional procedure for the construction and functioning of nuclear power plants.

With regard to the specific decisions taken by the political authorities in nuclear energy matters, the history of the Kaiseraugst project is worth mentioning in more detail, as it was to become the focal point of the antinuclear movement for several years. This example is also interesting because it shows the complex interplay of national, regional, and local decision-making levels in Switzerland. In 1966, the company Motor Columbus requested a siting license for a plant to be built in Kaiseraugst, a small village near Basel; in August 1969, local authorities gave the green light for the zoning plan. By 1972, however, the local authorities, with those of the nearby canton Basel-Stadt and with local antinuclear activists as well, came to oppose the project and thus engaged in a legal battle against the strongly pronuclear canton Aargau, which was to host the plant, and against a study consortium (Cudry 1988). The Federal Court, with an August 1973 decision, gave federal competencies the priority over local ones in matters of nuclear energy, which paved the way for the construction of the Kaiseraugst plants as well as those planned in Gösgen and Leibstadt.[24] A few months later, the local parliament of Kaiseraugst voted in favor of granting the construction permit for the plant, which spurred the movement to mobilize. In September 1979, the federal authorities opened a phase not only allowing appeals to be addressed against the project but also granting a typically Swiss consultation procedure, during which several cantons, communes, and various organizations were to be heard. In spite of strong opposition,[25] the government publicly declared in September 1981 that the plant was necessary, but they did not grant the statutory permit to lead the project further. In a quite ambivalent posture, the government tried to negotiate with the company a retreat of the project, and at the same time it stated its willingness to carry out the project. While the government continued its ambivalent attitude, in February 1983, the Council of States approved the construction of the plant, and a National Council's committee in charge of the case recommended it in September of the same year. In June 1985, the National Council decided to grant the statutory permit, but this decision was opposed by the governments of the cantons of Basel-Stadt and Basel-Land. In the search for a compromise, the government authorized in November 1987 the construction of a plant without a cooling tower, but once again this decision was opposed by the canton of Basel-Stadt, a canton flanked by two communes (Kaiseraugst and Liestal). The seemingly never-ending story came to a surprising end in 1988, when the pronuclear rights coalition launched two parliamentary motions in March asking to give up the project and when the Council of States confirmed in October of the same year the definitive abandoning of the project.

National Security Policy in Switzerland

Switzerland's national security policy is based on the principle of neutrality, which is one of the three pillars upon which the country is based (Kriesi 1995b).[26] The neutrality principle implies that Switzerland is not a member of international military agreements, most notably, NATO. Thus, while Italy's security policy is less related to the international context than that of the United States, due to a weaker military role, this interdependence is even smaller in the case of Switzerland. This marginal role in world politics is certainly also one of the reasons why the Swiss peace movement has traditionally mobilized around domestic issues (Bein and Epple 1984).

In spite of the neutrality principle and the willingness to remain out of military agreements, Switzerland's national security policy during the Cold War years was based on a strategic thinking largely borrowed from the United States. This can clearly be seen in Report 73 (Gabriel and Hedinger 1999), an official document outlining the general lines of Swiss security and national defense policies. While in the American context it was a matter of "deterrence," the term used in Switzerland was "dissuasion." If the United States were ready to determine a war's escalation in several steps, the Swiss report distinguished six strategic cases, going from a normal situation to a situation of occupation by a foreign country. This strategy, typical of the Cold War period, also included a nuclear component and gave an important place to civil protection.

As I said, the fall of the Berlin Wall and the end of the East–West bipolar system have provoked a fundamental shift in the general orientation of national security policies all over Europe. In Switzerland, this shift was further influenced by two significant domestic events (Gabriel and Hedinger 1999). First, the initiative for the abolition of the army, voted in November 1989, captured an unexpected amount of support, in spite of its overall failure. This led to a widespread and intense public debate over the role of the Swiss army in a changing international context. Second, at that time, the government was planning to buy a number of military airplanes for a large amount of money, a project that was strongly opposed by peace activists through a popular initiative launched in 1992 and rejected by voters the following year. However, Report 90 outlined a strategy only slightly different from that followed during the Cold War years (Gabriel and Hedinger 1999). Switzerland continued to dispose of a mass army and to follow a dissuasion strategy, only with reduced armed forces, a somewhat different structure, and a reorganized administration.[27] Finally, the international dimension of security policy, already present in Report 73, was further emphasized, and the concept of security policy itself was expanded.

Today, the Swiss government is proposing a further change of strategy based on the conclusion that the international context is changing rapidly. The new strategy, which can be read in the so-called Brunner Report, puts a greater emphasis on cooperation. Internally, collaboration between civil and military means will be increased. Externally, cooperation will be pursued through a strengthened collaboration with other states and international security organizations, as well as through a larger involvement in peacekeeping operations. Thus, during the period under study, the basic lines of Switzerland's national security policy have been transformed, though not in a fundamental way—indeed, owing to fundamental changes in the international context.

With regard to expenditures, figure 4.12, which shows the development of spending for national defense by the Swiss government between 1975 and 1995, clearly indicates a declining trend. If we look at the absolute level, we observe an increase in military spending, especially from the mid-1970s to the mid-1980s. In percentage terms, however, the share of money devoted to national defense stagnated until 1985 and has steadily decreased since. A modest resumption can be seen in the last two years of the period, but the general trend is clearly a declining one, starting from the mid-1980s.

Several changes that have occurred in the field of conscientious objection to military service should finally be mentioned. These changes, however, have remained largely cosmetic. Ending a long phase of stalemate after the first initiative for a civil service, which was launched in 1970, several reforms were introduced in the 1990s, starting from the so-called Barras project, a modification of the military penal code aimed at decriminalizing the status of conscientious objectors. In 1992, a constitutional amendment was accepted that paved the way for the creation of a civil service, which is described in the Civil Service Act of 1995. Yet, the Swiss version of the civil service is quite unsatisfactory from the point of view of peace activists, as one must prove to have a fundamental conscientious objection; furthermore, the length of the service is one-and-one-half times longer than the military service. However, it should also be noted that in 1999, in the context of a more recent reform of national security policy, the government proposed that the choice be given between military service and civil protection. This is, of course, a substantial step in the direction of those who are for a real civil service.

Comparative Summary

A brief comparative summary of the main trends in environmental, nuclear energy, and national security policies can help us make sense of the information provided in this chapter. For the sake of clarity, I focus mainly on the quantitative distributions. If we first look at the case of the United States, we observe two clear-cut and complementary patterns for environmental and military spending. As far as the former is concerned, spending slightly increased in the years of the Carter presidency. The dramatic cuts made by the Reagan administration brought outlays down to their lowest level. This declining trend began to reverse under Bush and became a slightly rising pattern during

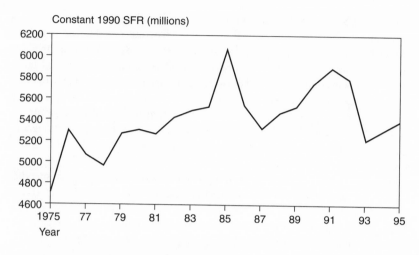

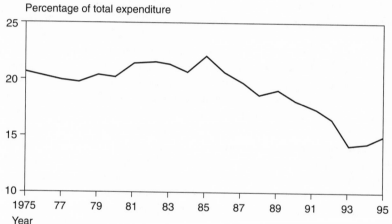

Figure 4.12. Military Spending (Switzerland).

Clinton's first term. As a whole and in percentage of total expenditures, however, spending for the environment was much higher in 1975 than it was in 1995. Only in the area of natural resources have investments remained more or less stable throughout the period, although this aspect of environmental policy scores somewhat worse at the state level, at least in relative terms. To that, we should add an intense legislative production all over the period under study. A similar pattern, but the other way around, can be observed for national security policy. In this case, the development of military spending shows a downward trend during the Carter administration, which is not surprising given the end of the Vietnam War in 1975. Then again, we observe a radical shift in the first half of the 1980s, this time an impressive rise produced by Reagan's bold military buildup. As we saw, Reagan's strategy changed in his second term, translating in a stabilization and even in the beginning a decrease in the amount of money devoted to national defense. Except for a short-lived rise due to the American intervention in the Persian Gulf, military spending has undergone a sharp decline since the late 1980s, which brought it to its lowest level in percentage terms. If we compare the distributions of environmental and military spending, we see that they both have followed shifts in the configuration of power. Specifically, when the White House was occupied by a Democratic president, spending for the environment tended to increase and for military purposes tended to decrease, and vice versa for a Republican president. This correlation would be almost perfect had not Republican president George H. W. Bush somewhat deviated from it. In contrast, nuclear energy policy has developed largely independent of the shifts in the configuration of power. For instance, nuclear capacity has increased steadily throughout the entire period, while the total number of units and construction permits has dramatically diminished, in particular and perhaps not accidentally, starting from 1979.

Turning to the case of Italy, it should be stressed in the first place that the data at my disposal are less reliable than that for the United States. In general, the distributions for Italy are more fluctuating, perhaps reflecting the higher instability of this country's political system. After the creation of the Ministry of Environment in 1986, environmental spending by the Italian government witnessed a substantial increase until 1991. It then receded the following two years and went up again in 1994 and 1995. Apart from the peak in 1991, which is hard to explain, the general trend is a rising one. The same can be said of the regional level but only as far as absolute figures are concerned, while in relative terms we observe a fluctuating and slightly declining development. Things are much simpler for nuclear energy policy. Here the 1987 referendum that led Italy to stop the production of nuclear power had a crucial impact. It must be noted that in the years preceding the referendum, production increased considerably, although always at low levels as compared to other countries. As regards the national security policy, two aspects can be stressed. First, in absolute terms, military spending increased steadily until 1989 and has slightly decreased since. In relative terms, however, the distribution is more stable over time, although we observe an important decline in the late 1980s and early 1990s. Second, in 1991, the government proposed a new defense model that modified the strategic and operational features of Italy's security policy.

In Switzerland, environmental spending witnessed a sharp decline until the late 1980s, where it has since remained more or less stable. However, if we include land planning in the measure of environmental policy, the amount of money spent in 1995 is not so different from that invested twenty years earlier. In addition, the downward trend is less pronounced if we consider all administrative levels: federal, cantonal, and communal. The picture remains nevertheless quite negative from the point of view of the environmental movement. The picture is also not so positive as regards nuclear energy policy. The production of nuclear power has followed a sort of stepwise increase, up to the mid-1980s. Starting from 1985, it stabilized under the effect of both the Chernobyl accident and the moratorium on new power plants. Finally, when we look at the absolute levels of the distribution of military spending, they first appear somewhat chaotic but much more clear when viewed in terms of percentage of total expenditure. In the latter case, we observe a stable development until 1985 and a subsequent decrease since, with the exception of the last two years of the period. In addition, in the early 1990s, the Swiss government proposed new strategic guidelines for the country's national security policy, though they are only slightly different from the previous ones; a more substantial change in strategy was proposed in the late 1990s.

Notes

1. The following overview of U.S. environmental policy is largely based on Kraft and Vig (1994), as well as Sale (1993).

2. To this fragmentation within the executive branch of the government, we must add the division of responsibilities among the executive, the legislative, and the judiciary branches, as well as that among dozens of congressional committees and subcommittees.

3. Totals include federal outlays for natural resources and the environment.

4. In particular, the Toxic Substances Control Act (TSCA) and the Resource Conservation and Recovery Act (RCRA) in 1976.

5. The NRC has executive, judicial, and legislative powers.

6. The Vietnam War officially ended in April 1975.

7. S. J. Res. 163, March 10, 1982.

8. S. J. Res. 177, March 30, 1982.

9. H. J. Res. 521.

10. H. J. Res. 13.

11. This treaty was approved by the United Nations Assembly in 1968 and took effect in 1970. It prohibited the nuclear nations from supplying nuclear weapons or nuclear weapons technology to nonnuclear states. Furthermore, it mandated that nonnuclear states remain nonnuclear and that the International Atomic Energy Agency's safeguards against weapons proliferation be accepted. The Nuclear Nonproliferation Act became law on March 10, 1978.

12. A similar treaty concerning peaceful test explosions is signed two years later.

13. The INF treaty was ratified by the Senate on May 27, and it was the first ratification of an arms control treaty since 1972.

14. See Burns (1992) for a more exhaustive chronology of events on nuclear matters.

15. This should not make us forget that environmental policy is typically a cross-sectional policy, in the sense that it implies that responsibilities be taken up by different actors and in different sectors.

16. Lewanski (1990, 285) mentions an increase in state spending for the environment from £1,418 billion in 1982 to £3,022 billion in 1988, which suggests a clear growth throughout the decade. The figure for the latter year, however, does not correspond to the one we have, which comes from official sources. In the analyses carried in part II of the book, I use estimates based on research and development spending for the 1975–1985 period.

17. A Ministry of Environment was set up in 1972, but without real power. In the Italian jargon, it was a "ministry without portfolio."

18. Witnessing the strict relationship between this agency and the organization that is at its origin, the former president of Friends of the Earth became its first president.

19. The Constitutional Court is the high court that must decide whether a legislative decision is in accordance with the constitution.

20. An important law enacted prior to these four phases is the Water Resources Protection Act, the first relating to the protection of water resources from pollution (1955).

21. In the Swiss political system, ordinances are an often-used policy instrument. They are issued by the government, a ministry, or an administration agency and are related to a more general law, such as the Environmental Protection Act, usually with the objective of specifying the implementation details of the law.

22. The Environmental Protection Agency replaced the former Water Protection Agency in 1972.

23. It should be noted that the peak observed in 1991 might be artificial due to a change in the calculation system.

24. The Federal Court has a status and functions similar to the Supreme Court in the United States.

25. About seven thousand appeals were addressed against the project.

26. Federalism and direct democracy are the other two pillars.

27. The administrative reorganization was later undertaken under the so-called Army 95 project.

CONCLUSION TO PART I

What tentative conclusions can we draw from comparing the historical overview of the mobilization of the three movements with that of the policies they targeted? Do we discern a relationship between the development during the past three decades of ecology, antinuclear, and peace protests and that of environmental, nuclear energy, and national security policies in the three countries under study? We can try to ascertain whether these two developments covariate by drawing a parallel between them. Unlike in the two previous chapters, here I take the movements instead of the countries as the main units of comparison and focus on the 1975–1995 period, which covers both protest and public policy.

The ecology movement was already quite active in the United States at the beginning of the period considered. In fact, its level of mobilization declined in the second half of the 1970s and then remained rather stable until the late 1980s, when the number of protest events increased somewhat; however, it fell to its lowest level in the 1990s. Spending by the U.S. government for environmental protection seems to have followed a development opposed to that of protest, in particular with a strong decline during the early 1980s. This might lead us to conclude that the ecology movement was instrumental in bringing about changes in environmental policy, at least as far as spending is concerned; yet, the reverse causal path is just as likely. Changes in environmental spending might have provoked a decline of the mobilization. Furthermore, both developments over time largely reflect shifts in the presidency. Protest went up when a Republican president was in power and down with a Democrat in the White House. Similarly, spending increased under Democratic presidencies and diminished under Republican ones.

In Italy, the ecology movement became a real force only in the second half of the 1980s, although it had not been completely absent from the public domain beforehand. Given the subsequent fall in the number of actions, it displays a wave of contention that peaks between 1988 and 1990. Unfortunately, the data concerning environmental spending in Italy cover only the period from 1986 onward. However, the available information shows that the rise of the ecology movement was paralleled by an expansion of the resources invested by the state to protect the environment. Again, the comparison of the two distributions suggests that protest and policy covary in a nonrandom way. Yet again, we cannot determine which causes what. The rise in spending after 1986 might be unrelated to the movement's mobilization, for in that year the Ministry of Environment was created, and the larger investment of money could as well be due to the growth of this governmental arm in its early years.

In Switzerland, too, the ecology movement displays a protest wave but a larger one that peaks some years earlier than in the Italian case. Yet the picture we draw from comparing the number of protest actions with the development of environmental spending is quite a negative one from the point of view of the ecology movement and its possibilities to influence public policy. In effect, in spite of a strong mobilization, environmental spending by the Swiss government has declined steadily throughout the period under study, especially during the second half of the 1970s. The situation is somewhat better when we include the regional and local levels, but the picture remains nevertheless negative. Thus, it would be difficult to speak of a positive impact of the ecology movement on environmental policy.

Things went apparently better for the antinuclear movement. Its mobilization in the United States displays a pattern quite different from that of the ecology movement, as most actions are concentrated in a short but intense wave of contention that peaks in 1979. After 1980 the movement virtually disappeared from the public space. At the same time, the production of nuclear energy continued to increase virtually undisturbed, except perhaps for a stop in the late 1970s. The accident at the Three Mile Island facility occurred in 1979, and it would be at least unfair not to take this event into account to explain the temporary halt of nuclear production. In addition, perhaps not incidentally, the number of construction permits for new plants began their downward trend precisely in that year. However, as many observers have remarked, the American nuclear power industry had entered a deep crisis already before the accident. The number of units on order, for example, diminished in 1977 and 1978. Thus, the situation here is quite puzzling.

The situation is also puzzling in Italy, where the antinuclear movement mobilized very little except for a short period between 1986 and 1987. The production of nuclear energy suddenly stopped in 1987 as a result of the referendum whose campaign certainly accounts for the rise of mobilization that took place the year before. Yet it is difficult to attribute this result to the movement's actions when we remember that few months earlier another significant nuclear accident occurred, this time in Chernobyl. Without this accident the outcome of the vote would probably have been different, for the support by all major parties would have been unlikely.

In Switzerland, too, the impact of the antinuclear action is debatable. First, the production of nuclear power did not increase after the moratorium was passed, in 1990. Furthermore, the movement seems to have been instrumental in impeding the construction of the Kaiseraugst power plant, back in the 1970s. Second, nuclear

Table I.1.   Implementation of Nuclear Programs, 1974–1988

	United States	Italy	Switzerland
Total nuclear capacity/under construction/ordered 1974	223,146	5,300	5,444
Total nuclear capacity 1988	95,273	0	2,852
% deviation	−57	−100	−48

Source: Rüdig (1990, table 6.4)

production was already on a stagnating trend before the moratorium. Again, it is not by accident that the shift occurred after the Chernobyl accident. In addition, the largest antinuclear mobilization took place in the 1970s, but this has not prevented the production level from continuing to rise until the mid-1980s, at least in general terms. Nevertheless, it is undeniable that the United States, Italy, and Switzerland have all failed to meet their plans regarding the production of nuclear power. We have a better sense of the difficulties—to say the least—encountered by the respective governments in making an effective nuclear energy policy when we compare the implementation of nuclear programs in the three countries, as shown in table I.1, which compares the nuclear capacity planned in 1974 with that actually available in 1988. In all three countries the governments were unable to reach the objective set fifteen years earlier. The worst result is that of Italy, as none of the nuclear capacity planned was reached due to the 1987 referendum. In the United States and Switzerland, about a half of it was not implemented; yet, once again, this does not necessarily mean that the antinuclear movement has caused these failures.

Concerning the peace movement, things do not seem to be clearer, and its impact is even more difficult to discern. In the United States, within the period under consideration—hence, without taking into account anti–Vietnam War protests—most of the mobilization occurred in two waves. A first, a large wave of contention took place between 1981 and 1984, addressed against the nuclear arms race. A second, smaller protest wave in 1991 opposed U.S. intervention in the Gulf War. Both were ineffective with respect to their immediate goal. The freeze movement waned, while spending for military purposes by the U.S. government continued to grow for some years. The Gulf War came to an end in a short time but certainly not due to the movement's pressure. Yet military spending did not only halt its rising trend but underwent a dramatic fall starting from the mid-1980s. Gorbachev's perestroïka changed the relations between the United States and the Soviet Union more dramatically than any other event before. The subsequent fall of the Berlin Wall only gave the final cut to the East–West opposition and to the logic of deterrence underlying it. Thus, here too, we find an external and, to some extent, contingent event that might well be at the origin of the outcome that one could consider a long-term impact of the peace movement.

The pattern of mobilization of the Italian peace movement is similar to its American counterpart. A phase of low mobilization was interrupted by a large wave of contention in the early 1980s; then activities went down again, followed by a revival in 1991 and another fall afterward. The two protest waves dealt with issues similar to those addressed by the peace movement in the United States: nuclear arms and military intervention in the Persian Gulf. Did the movement have an effect on Italy's national security policy? There is little evidence of this, at least in the short run. First of all, military spending increased during the first half of the 1980s, when mobilization was strong. Much like in the United States, spending began to be curbed when the international political climate became less tight, and it declined only after the fall of the Berlin Wall. Furthermore, one had to wait until the 1990s to see the government's proposing a new defense model.

The Swiss government was even slower in modifying the strategic guidelines for the country's national security policy. Switzerland has been reluctant to abandon the old model adopted in the Cold War years, which remained the basic framework well into the 1990s. Little changed after the largest wave of contention occurred, as in other Western European countries, at the beginning of the 1980s. Military spending by the Swiss government remained quite stable until 1985 when it began to decrease, to reach its lowest level in 1993. It is unlikely that this decline is due to the important mobilization that took place in the early 1980s. Similarly, the second protest wave, in the late 1980s and early 1990s, probably played only a minor role—if any— in the decrease of spending for military purposes. Again, the cooling down of the Eastern–Western divide and the fall of the Berlin Wall seem more plausible causes of this outcome. In addition, the peace movement was certainly able to mobilize a large sector of the society, also thanks to the presence of direct democracy; but it was seldom successful in terms of policy change.

Part I of the book is devoted to a comparison of long-term trends of protest and public policy. To conclude it, we can say, first, that we can observe to some extent a covariation between the development of the mobilization by ecology, antinuclear, and peace movements and that of environmental, nuclear energy, and national security policies. However, we cannot maintain that the former caused the latter. To move from covariation to causality, we need to study more closely and more systematically the relationship between protest and policy. In addition, we must inquire into the role of other aspects of the social and political environment that, alone or jointly with protest, may produce changes in public policy. These are the objectives of part II.

PART II

TIME-SERIES ANALYSIS

CHAPTER FIVE

✑

Toward a Joint-Effect Model of Social Movement Outcomes

In the first part of this book, I confront the historical development of the mobilization of ecology, antinuclear, and peace movements; and that of public policy in the areas addressed by them. However, doing so provides little evidence, if any, of any impact that the former makes on the latter. It is now time to study this relationship more systematically.

The chapters that form the second part of the book are entirely devoted to this systematic assessment of the impact that the three movements had on public policy. I make this assessment by addressing three models of social movement outcomes:

1. the *direct-effect model,* which maintains that movements can have a positive impact on policy, with their own forces and in the absence of external support;
2. the *indirect-effect model,* which sees movements as having an impact following a two-stage process, first by influencing certain aspects of their external environment—specifically, political alliances and public opinion—and then by allowing the effect of the latter to influence policy; and
3. the *joint-effect model,* which states that movement impact is forthcoming when political allies or public opinion (or both) intervene with movement mobilization.

I argue that this interpretation better reflects the reality of movement–policy interaction.

This chapter presents the three types of explanations and thus provides the ground for the empirical analyses that follow. After having laid out the main traits of these three explanations and after having briefly described the method I use to systematically study the relationships among protest, political alliances, public opinion, and public policy—via time-series analysis—I move on to the empirical analyses by looking at the direct effect of the three movements on policy. In doing so, I examine, but only for the case of the United States, the impact of less-visible movement strategies, such as lobbying. I then discuss indirect and joint effects in chapters 7 and 8, respectively.

Direct, Indirect, and Joint Effects of Social Movements

As we have seen in chapter 2, studies of social movement outcomes have long been framed along two main lines of inquiry and have attempted to give an answer to one of two basic questions: one, whether the use of disruptive tactics by social movements is more likely to bring about policy changes than moderate tactics; and, two, whether strongly organized movements are more successful than those loosely organized. This double and partly overlapping question of the effectiveness of disruption and organization has led scholars to focus on the internal characteristics of movements that are most likely to produce social and political change. At the same time, an intense debate emerges bearing on the question of whether movement-controlled variables or some aspects of their environment better account for their success. First, authors who stress the internal strength of protest groups as the most important determinant of effectiveness, hence pointing to the ability of movements to produce social and political change, implicitly establish a direct link between protest activities and the authorities' responsiveness—in other words, our direct-effect model of movement outcomes. Second, a number of scholars have stressed the importance of the political environment and the context of social support, thus suggesting that movement impact is mediated by exogenous variables.

As we saw in chapter 2 as well, two kinds of exogenous factors have usually been stressed. First, certain features of the political context, such as the political system and the party system, have been indicated as mediating the relationship between protest and outcomes (Amenta, Carruthers, and Zylan 1992). In particular, the existence of powerful allies within the institutional arenas strongly facilitates the impact of social movements (Jenkins and Perrow 1977; Kriesi et al. 1995, ch. 9; Tarrow 1993, 1998). Second, a lower but significant number of studies have pointed to the presence of a favorable public opinion as crucial for movements to reach their goals (Burstein 1985, 1999; Burstein and Freudenburg 1978; Costain and Majstorovic 1994). Both factors work in two ways, which are often blurred in the extant literature. In the first way political allies carry into the institutional arenas the issues addressed by social movements in the public space. They react to movement claims by incorporating them into their agenda. Once in the institutional arenas, the claims have better chances to translate into policy changes. In other words, social movements are more likely to succeed once their demands have gained access to the system (Rochon and Mazmanian 1993). Protest actions may similarly influence the public opinion, which in turn encourages the power holders to act for policy change (Costain and Majstorovic 1994). In both cases the impact of social movements is an indirect one, filtered by an intervening variable, either political alliances or public opinion—that is, our indirect-effect model of movement outcomes.

In this book, and more specifically in the next three chapters, I propose to explore the possibility that political allies and public opinion facilitate the impact of social movements simultaneously, namely through their joint action with protest activities—our joint-effect model of movement outcomes. According to this model, political alliances and public opinion represent crucial external resources for social movements and hence strengthen the weight of protest, thereby increasing the chances that protest forces the power holders to promote public policies that meet the movement's demands. In this perspective, we may expect the effects of protest on policy to be greater when both political alliances and public opinion form a favorable environment for policy changes to occur.

In addition, I suggest that the joint action of political alliances and public opinion is especially needed when movements address certain types of issues. Previous work has treated all kinds of movement claims as if they were equivalent, yet some demands are more difficult to meet than others. We need to take into account the varying viability of claims depending on the policy area and the issue at hand. First, certain policy areas are subject to international constraints that diminish the autonomy of the authorities with respect to their environment and that limit their margin for action. Foreign policy is a typical example (Meyer 1999). Second, mobilizations that address certain issues threaten the state to a larger extent than others, depending on how authorities and allies define the core tasks and interests of the state (Duyvendak 1995; Kriesi et al. 1995, ch. 4). To put it briefly, either the willingness or the capacity of power holders to meet movement demands (or both) is diminished in some situations. In both cases the ability of social movements to influence public policy should shrink.

Before I empirically address the direct-effect model in the remainder of this chapter and the indirect-effect and the joint-effect models in the next two chapters, I would like to elaborate a little further on the ideas underlying the joint-effect model.

Political Alliances, Public Opinion, and the Outcomes of Social Movements

Political Alliances

The political process approach to social movements has stressed the role of political opportunities for movement emergence, development, and outcomes (e.g., Kitschelt 1986; Kriesi et al. 1995; McAdam 1999; Tarrow 1998; Tilly 1978). One key variable in this respect is the configuration of power relations within the institutional arenas, in particular within the parliamentary arena (Kriesi et al. 1995). Changes in the configuration of power among parties modify the structure of political alliances, which are seen as a crucial resource for social movements to reach their goals (e.g., della Porta 1996; della Porta and Rucht 1995; Kriesi et al. 1995; Tarrow 1998). Kriesi and colleagues (1995) argue that political opportunity structures are more conducive to movement emergence when allies are not in the government. They show that the new social movements in France flourished when their major ally—the Socialist Party—was in the opposition. Once the Socialists seized power in 1981, the new social movements lost their main political support and underwent a rapid process of demobilization. In contrast, to obtain political responsiveness and substantial gains, challengers need allies who obtain power; thus, to represent an opportunity for social movements, allies must be in a position to reform policies, which becomes easier, for example, when they hold the majority in the parliament.

In an insightful article on the impact of the May 1968 university reforms in France, Tarrow (1993) points out that protest opened up a "window for reform." The student movement exerted a strong pressure on the political elites and thus was able to bring about substantial changes in university policies, but this success would have been impossible if the students had not been helped by institutional allies. One part of the elites supported the movement's claims and initiated a reform of the university system. State reformers, led by the French minister of education, endorsed the reform, taking advantage of the fact that conservative elites feared major troubles of the public order. A study by Amenta, Carruthers, and Zylan (1992) on the impact of the Townsend movement in the United States puts forward a similar argument, although in a somewhat different perspective. In an attempt to test various models of social movement formation and outcomes (economic, social, political opportunity, and political mediation), they find strong support for the claim that political opportunities mediate the relationship between social movements and their policy outcomes. They stress the role of the state and the party system in explaining why and how mobilization gains acceptance and produces benefits for the constituency, the two dimensions put forward by Gamson (1990) and used in a number of subsequent studies.

Tarrow (1993) and Amenta, Carruthers, and Zylan (1992) provide two authoritative examples of the first variant of the indirect-effect approach to social movement outcomes. This variant posits that the impact of social movements on public policy is largely contingent on a favorable intervention by political allies who are first willing to take up the movements' claims in the institutional arenas and, in a second stage, translate them into policy changes. The important point stressed by such authors as Amenta, Carruthers, and Zylan (1992); Jenkins and Perrow (1977); Lipsky (1968); Schumaker (1975, 1978); Tarrow (1993, 1998); and many others is that protest hardly translates directly into policy change. Social movements must be backed by insiders if they are to succeed in influencing public policy. What is lacking from these studies is the role of public opinion.

Public Opinion

Public opinion is another potentially crucial resource for social movements. Burstein (1998b) argues that when scholars find a direct effect of protest on policy, the direct effect diminishes or even disappears when they include the preferences of the public in their models. What often underlies studies that underscore the importance of public opinion for policy change is the theory of representative democracy (Burstein 1998b, 1999). According to democratic theory, power holders respond to public opinion basically for electoral reasons. In an electoral competition system, elites become sensitive to citizens' demands with the aim of maintaining power. This theory underscores the so-called tyranny of the majority. Taking into account the public's preferences does not mean to follow naively the democratic ideal of respecting the citizens' will; rather, it is an instrumental attitude by elected officials aimed at preserving their power (Lohmann 1993). The democratic struggle gives the ruled considerable power over their rulers (Burstein 1998b, 1999). Any shift in public opinion alerts the political elites, who then adjust their behavior accordingly. If this view is correct, changes in public opinion should be followed by corresponding changes in public policies (Burstein 1998b). A number of studies have stressed this close relationship between public opinion and policy, maintaining that, especially when an issue is felt as important or salient by the public, a clear and visible shift in the pubic opinion leads the authorities to modify their policies (see Burstein 1998b for a review).

Given its stress on mass preferences, the theory of representative democracy implies that neither social movements nor interest groups should have a direct effect on public policy.[1] In a well-functioning democracy, political elites would respond to claims that are supported by a majority of citizens and would not take into account particular interests of minority actors, such as social movements and interest groups (Krehbiel 1991; Lohmann 1993). If they respond to minority demands, elites run the risk of not being reelected. In brief, according to this view of democracy, which has an elitist bias and is opposed to the pluralist theories (e.g., Dahl 1961), the policy impact of social movements depends on the presence of a favorable public opinion.

Two noteworthy examples of this view were proposed by Burstein (1998a) as well as Costain and Majstorovic (1994). Burstein emphasizes the crucial role played by social movements and media coverage in shaping the public's preferences. His study shows that the civil rights movement and its media coverage together affected the people's awareness of the issue, and this in turn led Congress to act in favor of African Americans' rights. Costain and Majstorovic have put forward a nonrecursive model of policy change whereby public opinion both influences and is influenced by legislation. They illustrate their theory with time-series data on the American women's movement and show that the movement's mobilization heightened public awareness, which in turn influenced legislative production. The important point for my present purpose is that both studies suggest that the impact of social movements on policy is not a direct one but that it depends on the presence of a favorable public opinion.

A Joint-Effect Model of Social Movement Outcomes

Elaborating on the indirect-effect approach to social movement outcomes, I propose an alternative, though not necessarily competing, view based on the idea that social movements, political alliances, and public opinion interact to bring about policy change. In the theories discussed here, the impact of social movements on public policy occurs in two steps: first, movement claims affect either political allies or public opinion; then these two intervening factors translate movement claims into policy changes. According to my alternative view, political alliances and public opinion do provide movements with crucial resources for policy impact. However, I argue that, to force the power holders to engage in substantial policy reform, a movement must have the joint and simultaneous presence of mobilization and the presence of either a major political ally within the institutional arenas or a favorable public opinion, or both—thus, the joint-effect approach to social movement outcomes.

As far as political alliances are concerned, Tarrow's study of French university policy encourages me to follow this line of reasoning. At the time, protest offered a major incentive to reform the academic system by putting the French authorities under pressure. The student movement found crucial allies among progressive elites for reforming the system. But, in Tarrow's apt formulation (1993, 595), "the season for reforms, like the season of protest, was very short." Once the movement demobilized and once the fear of protest abated, the movement's allies no longer had the impetus to reform the system. Reformist elites lost their main allies—the movement—and reform was abandoned. This example suggests that policy change needs sustained action both within and outside the institutional arenas.

A similar reasoning can be applied to public opinion. As the agenda-building approach to social problems (Cobb and Elder 1972) has shown, a variety of factors may contribute to placing a political issue onto the public agenda and hence increase its visibility. Social movements and protest are among these factors. Burstein's work (1998a) on equal employment legislation shows that the civil rights movement greatly increased the salience of the issue in the public opinion, which in turn strongly influenced congressional activity. Without the joint effect of the movement and the public's growing concern, legislation would probably not have changed. Humans are serial processors of information (Jones 1994); that is, they have a limited capability to pay attention to many issues at the same time. Therefore, if the civil rights movement had not mobilized strongly during that period, public opinion could easily have shifted its attention to other issues.

Figure 5.1 summarizes the three models, which emphasize the importance of timing. The difference between an explanation in terms of joint effect and an explanation in terms of indirect effect lies precisely in that political allies and public opinion intervene simultaneously in the former model and following a two-step process in the latter model.

Now, two questions remain open. First, which is the more important resource for social movements and their affecting public policy: political alliances or public opinion? Second, is either of these two external resources a sufficient condition, or are they both necessary—and, if so, when? To answer these two questions, we need to introduce a further element: the viability of claims. By that, I mean a simple idea—namely, that some claims are more difficult to meet than others. This may occur for at least two reasons. First, with respect to certain issues or policies—for example, foreign policy, as opposed to domestic policy (Meyer 1999)—the authorities are less autonomous and have

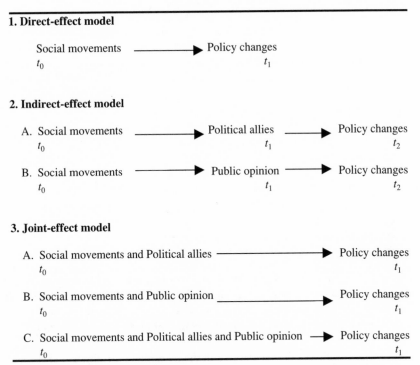

Figure 5.1. Three Models of Social Movement Outcomes.

a more limited margin for action. With foreign policy, international factors pose major constraints on the decisions of national authorities. Second, challenges that target certain issues or policies pose a more serious threat to the authorities than others, to the extent that they strike the core interests of the state. Kriesi and colleagues (1995) have called these issues, respectively, "high profile" and "low profile."[2] A number of reasons account for the more threatening character of certain issues or policies: the amount of material resources involved, the power at stake, the electoral relevance, and the extent to which the "national interest" is challenged (Duyvendak 1995; Kriesi et al. 1995, ch. 4).

Figure 5.2 maps the varying viability of claims as a combination of the threat and autonomy dimensions, or the high-profile/low-profile issues as opposed to the domestic/foreign policy. The three movements under study can be placed in different locations within this conceptual map.

The ecology movement should have the highest chances to influence public policy, for this movement mostly addresses "valence issues" (Dunlap 1989), upon which, at least in the United States, there is today a broad consensus.[3] In contrast, the peace movement targets a policy area that is arguably the most difficult to change among those considered here. The antinuclear movement is an intermediate case, insofar as it addresses a high-profile issue in a domestic policy area. Finally, the solidarity

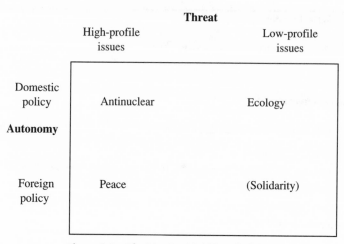

Figure 5.2. The Varying Viability of Claims.

movement, which is not part of my study, would be an example of a movement that partly mobilizes around low-profile foreign policies.[4] Thus, we can expect the ecology movement to be more likely to produce policy changes—or the degree of closedness of political opportunity structures—followed by the antinuclear movement and finally the peace movement.

As a result of the viability of claims and the possibilities for different challengers to influence public policy, I expect political allies and public opinion to become more important as we move from a domestic/low-profile to foreign/high-profile. In other words, the closer we get to the lower left-hand corner of figure 5.2, the more urgent the need for both political and public support. In this case, to increase their chances to influence public policy, social movements need not only a powerful ally within institutional arenas but also a favorable public opinion. In contrast, the closer we get to the upper right-hand corner, the higher the capacity of movements to influence public policy in the absence of such support.

In the remainder of this chapter and in the next three chapters, I test the explanatory power of the three general models of social movement outcomes presented so far: the direct-effect, the indirect-effect, and the joint-effect models. Before I present my findings, however, I need to say a few words on the method used in the empirical analyses.

A Method to Study the Impact of Social Movements on Public Policy

Although I provide more detailed information in appendix A, the analyses that follow require at least a brief discussion of the data and methods used. The data analyzed in this and the next three chapters consist of yearly time-series measuring for each of the three countries included in the study; for the organizational growth of ecology, antinuclear, and peace movements; for the shifts in their level of mobilization; and for the development of the structure of political alliances, trends in public opinion, and changes in public policy between 1975 and 1995.

Public policy—the dependent variable—is measured through the following indicators: for the ecology movement, state spending for environmental protection; for the antinuclear movement, the production of nuclear energy and the number of construction permits for new nuclear power plants; for the peace movement, state spending for national defense purposes. In addition, given that environmental policy has a strong local character, in the case of the two federal countries (the United States and Switzerland), I also look at spending at the local level (by, respectively, the states and the cantons).

The data come from a variety of primary and secondary sources. Data on the mobilization of the three movements, which I used in chapter 3 to depict the development of protest, were retrieved from primary newspaper sources. Part of the information on political alliances also derives from this source. The other kinds of data come from secondary sources, such as statistical yearbooks (political alliances, public policy) and existing surveys (public opinion). This is also true in chapter 6 for the data on the United States regarding organizational growth; for the data regarding Italy and Switzerland, a questionnaire was sent to respective organizations.

The data are analyzed by means of time-series analysis. I mention this method in the introductory chapter, but now it is time to discuss it in more detail. Time-series analysis is a longitudinal method that is particularly suited to capture the dynamic nature of social and political phenomena. This approach allows us to incorporate time into the explanation of the effects of protest activities on public policy. In spite of the obvious fact that political and decision-making processes are time dependent, only rarely has previous work analyzed the effects of social movements with respect to time (see Burstein and Freudenburg 1978; Costain and Majstorovic 1994; Giugni 2001; Giugni and Passy 1998). Yet, an approach that allows the researcher to capture the dynamic nature of movement outcomes has clear advantages over a static approach. Specifically, the chronological ordering of observations in time-series analysis yields a stronger case for causal inference than cross-sectional approaches (Janoski and Isaac 1994), especially if a temporal lag is introduced in the models. This is all the more important when one is studying the outcomes of protest, for establishing the causal relationship that links social movements to their alleged outcomes is one of the major obstacles that have hindered previous research in this field.

There are several, more or less sophisticated ways to conduct time-series analysis to explore relationships between variables of interest. Here I use the regression approach, which is a simple one based on the search for covariation between variables expressed as developments over time. I chose this method especially because I am interested in exploring covariation and causal patterns rather than predicting future evolutions of a given variable. In other words, I am interested in bivariate rather than univariate analyses, and regression techniques are particularly helpful to this purpose.[5]

The specific approach I follow to investigate the relationship between social movements and public policy has a number of methodological features that
need to be mentioned. The first one stems from longitudinal analysis, which
looks at relationships between variables measured as developments over time. As
I said, this way of studying the policy impact of social movements better reflects the dynamic nature of the political process in which movements participate. This allows us to ascertain the extent to which policy makers respond to
changes in movement mobilization or other aspects of the social and political
environment.

In addition to analyzing the relationships in which the independent variables
(e.g., movement mobilization) are measured as absolute levels, I push the analyses
even further in this direction by conducting the same analyses with variables expressed in terms of differences from one period to the other. In effect, one might
argue that social actors often react to the difference they perceive from a previous
situation or period rather than to the absolute levels. For example, members of parliament may adopt new legislation against pollution after they have observed and
made sense of a significant increase in public awareness of this issue or in popular
protests in favor of environmental protection. Reactions to changes in time could
thus be greater than reactions to absolute levels, which in the absence of a measure
for comparison cannot be easily evaluated. Therefore, a more exhaustive analysis
of the responsiveness of political authorities (in the form of formulating and implementing public policy) should also look at variations from one period to the
next. The results of these additional analyses are shown in the tables included in
appendix B.

A second methodological feature of my study follows straightforwardly from the
main theoretical argument that the interaction with political alliances and public
opinion should improve the likelihood that protest affects public policy (the joint-
effect model). To capture this aspect methodologically, I introduce in my analyses a
number of interactive terms among the covariates. This is done in testing the joint-
effect model in the next two chapters.

A third methodological feature—more technical, but important from a theoretical
point of view—is that all the regressions shown in the remainder of the book include
lagged variables, that is, independent variables measured at time t_0 and dependent
variables measured at time t_1. Again, this allows us to make a stronger case for causal
effects; specifically, I use a one-year lag. While the choice of the unit lag is to some
extent always arbitrary, I think that this is a reasonable choice to study policy change.
This holds true especially in the case of government spending, as it usually takes a year
before the administration can have an impact on budgets and, hence, policy. In addition, specific analysis has shown that most of the variables used in my analyses follow
an autoregressive process of order 1, which has led me to opt for a specification of time
series with a one-year lag.[6] Finally, protest event data do not allow for shorter lags
(especially regarding antinuclear and peace protests), owing to the small number of
events.

Table 5.1. Effect of Unconventional Mobilization on Public Policy in Three Countries, 1975–1995

Dependent Variables	Spending for Environmental Protection (National) (t_1)	Spending for Environmental Protection (Local) (t_1)	Nuclear Energy Production (t_1)	Number of Construction Permits (t_1)	Spending for Defense (t_1)
United States					
Unconventional mobilization (t_0)	.02	−.21	−.31	−.08	.45*
(D-W)	(1.92)	(1.91)	(1.97)	(2.15)	(1.88)
N	20	20	20	20	20
Italy					
Unconventional mobilization (t_0)	.23	—	−.49**	—	.25
(D-W)	(1.93)	—	(2.02)	—	(2.03)
N	20	—	20	—	20
Switzerland					
Unconventional mobilization (t_0)	.24	.45*	.51**	—	−.34
(D-W)	(2.13)	(1.98)	(1.91)	—	(1.90)
N	20	20	20	—	20

Note: Standardized regression coefficients (bivariate) generated with a generalized least-squared method of estimation (Prais-Winsten) assuming a first-order autoregressive process. Durbin-Watson test for serial correlation and number of observations (series length) are shown within parentheses. The independent variables include a one-year lag. The dependent variables are expressed in terms of annual percentage change.
$*p < .10; **p < .05; ***p < .01$.

Social Movement Actions and Public Policy: Direct Effect

With these methodological remarks in mind, we can now test the three interpretations of the outcomes of social movements outlined earlier, starting from the simplest and most straightforward: the direct-effect model. Table 5.1 presents, for each country, the results of bivariate regressions between the indicator of mobilization for the three movements (the number of unconventional protest events produced yearly by each movement) and the respective indicators of substantial changes in the policy domains targeted by the movements (expressed in terms of changes in annual percentage).

In interpreting the coefficients shown in this and the following similar tables (including those in the next chapters), we should pay attention to four related aspects. The first aspect, and for our purpose the most important, is the statistical significance, which indicates the presence or absence of a relationship between independent and dependent variables (for example, between the level of mobilization by the ecology movement and the state's budget for environmental protection). The second aspect is the value of the coefficient once we observe a statistically significant relationship, which indicates the strength of that relationship, that is, how much change on the dependent variable is produced by a change in the independent variable. The third aspect is the sign of the coefficient, which indicates whether the relationship is positive or negative, that is, whether a change in the independent variable makes the dependent variable increase or decrease. The fourth and final aspect, less directly related to the observed relationships, is the Durbin-Watson statistic, to check for the presence of serial correlation, which indicates that a change in the dependent variable is (partly) produced by a change in the lagged independent variable, that is, itself in the previous year.[7] Thus, this and the following tables show the value, sign, and level of significance of the regression coefficients (first row), the value of the Durbin-Watson statistic (second row), and the number of annual observations in the series (third row).

According to the findings, no direct effect can be observed in the case of the United States. The coefficient concerning the impact of unconventional mobilization on defense spending is statistically significant at the 10 percent level, but its positive sign suggests that higher levels of mobilizations are associated with increases in spending, which certainly does not mean the presence of an impact of the movement—if by impact we mean a change going in the direction of the movements' aims.

A strong effect of the antinuclear movement, in contrast, is found in Italy. This finding should be read with some care, however. If we look at the distribution over time of nuclear energy production in this country (see table 4.7 in chapter 4), we see that it went down to zero in 1987 as a result of the successful antinuclear referenda. Therefore, all the values in the series from 1987 to 1995 equal zero, and the resulting skewed distribution might artificially inflate the regression coefficient, especially because the series is so short. This methodological limitation prevents our completely trusting this finding and all the others based on the measure of changes in nuclear energy production in Italy.

The only real direct effect is the one concerning the ecology movement in Switzerland. More precisely, ecology protests seem to have had some impact on spending for environmental protection at the local level but not at the national level. This makes sense, as the federal structure of the Swiss state and the subsidiarity principle applied in various policy areas—according to which many state tasks are carried at the lowest administrative level possible—suggest that many policy efforts are made at this level.[8] In contrast, similar to the peace movement in the United States, the significant coefficient for the antinuclear movement has a positive sign and therefore does not indicate an impact of the movement.

In sum, these first analyses suggest that there is at best only little direct impact of protest on public policy. The only trustable effect that we observe is the one of the Swiss ecology movement on local environmental policy. All other coefficients are statistically insignificant, or they go in the direction opposite to the movements' goals (or they cannot be fully trusted due to methodological reasons).

In addition to analyses with the mobilization of the three movements measured as absolute numbers, I also explore the possibility that independent variables expressed in terms of annual differences might have a stronger impact (see table B5.1, in appendix B). Concerning the direct effect of protest activities on public policy, the results of these additional analyses yield no statistically significant coefficient, hence strengthening the general finding that ecology, antinuclear, and peace movements have had only little direct effect on targeted public policies in the three countries under study.[9] Does this general finding hold if we focus on more disruptive forms of actions? I try to answer this question in what follows.

The Impact of Disruption

One of the most compelling aspects of research on social movements concerns the effectiveness of disruption and violence. We saw in chapter 2 that a great many studies have addressed this question in scholarly work and found no definitive answer; however, the use of constraints often, but certainly not always, seems to pay off. Various studies, including Gamson's seminal work (1990), provides empirical evidence of the effectiveness of radical forms of action, a finding that seems to contradict the pluralist claim that moderation in politics is more effective than disruption. Yet, as on many other aspects of the study of contentious politics, there is no consensus on this point and even less so on its implications for social movements.

Far from aiming at providing a definitive answer to this important question, here I would like to ascertain empirically whether ecology, antinuclear, and peace movements in the three countries of my study were more successful when using disruptive or radical forms of action.

Before doing so, however, I would like briefly to discuss the forms of actions used by the three movements in their attempt to influence policy making. Table 5.2 shows the distribution of unconventional actions carried out by ecology, antinuclear, and peace movements in the three countries according to two main forms: peaceful (i.e., demonstrative and signature-collection campaigns) and disruptive (confrontational and violent).[10]

A few cursory comments will suffice for this static view of the forms of actions. If we first look at the aggregate distributions for the three movements (lower section), we can see that in all three countries these movements mobilize mostly through peaceful actions and only rarely make use of disruptive or radical forms. At the same time, however, they are more moderate in Switzerland than in the other two countries. This confirms previous analyses that have pointed to the openness of the political system for challengers in Switzerland and the consequent moderation of the action repertoire of social movements, as compared to other countries (Kriesi et al. 1995), including Italy and the United States. Italian movements seem to be more radical than American ones, especially if we look at the percentage of violent actions (which are shown within parentheses), a specific form of disruption. In this respect, movements—in particular, the antinuclear and peace movements—seem to be even more radical in Switzerland than in the United States, where most disruptive actions take the form of confrontational actions, such as, civil disobedience or illegal though peaceful demonstrations.

The distributions for the single movements, of course, do not differ substantially from the general pattern. All three movements have acted more moderately in Switzerland. At the same time, we observe a more disruptive action repertoire for the antinuclear and peace movements. This, however, holds especially for the United States and Switzerland, whereas Italian movements seem to be more homogeneous

Table 5.2. Forms of Action by Movement and by Country, 1975–1999

	United States	Italy	Switzerland
Ecology Movement			
Peaceful	92.9	87.1	96.6
Disruptive	7.1 (1.1)	12.9 (2.9)	3.4 (1.3)
Total	100%	100%	100%
N	946	754	683
Antinuclear Movement			
Peaceful	78.2	87.3	90.9
Disruptive	21.8 (2.0)	12.7 (3.6)	9.1 (4.1)
Total	100%	100%	100%
N	252	55	197
Peace Movement			
Peaceful	81.2	85.7	90.5
Disruptive	18.8 (1.4)	14.3 (5.0)	9.5 (5.4)
Total	100%	100%	100%
N	505	279	222
All Three Movements			
Peaceful	87.3	86.8	94.4
Disruptive	12.7 (1.3)	13.2 (3.5)	5.6 (2.6)
Total	100%	100%	100%
N	1,703	1,088	1,102

Note: Peaceful protests include demonstrative actions and signature collection campaigns (except for referenda). Disruptive protests include confrontational and violent actions. The percentage of violent actions is shown in parentheses.

in the forms of action they use. Thus, while the ecology movement was more radical in Italy, the antinuclear and peace movements were more radical in the United States.

Yet, the longitudinal approach followed in this book leads me to focus above all on how the use of the different forms of actions by ecology, antinuclear, and peace movements has changed over time, as well as whether the movements have radicalized their action repertoires since 1975. I do so by looking at the development of disruptive actions with respect to that of the total unconventional protests over the 1975–1999 period.[11] Figures 5.3, 5.4, and 5.5 do so, respectively, for the case of the United States, Italy, and Switzerland. In interpreting these figures, we must take into account the fact that they display the stacked annual sum of disruptive actions and nondisruptive actions; in other words, the figures do not display the relative share of one or the other. Thus, the upper line refers to all unconventional events, the upper area to peaceful protests, and the lower area to disruptive protests, the last of which we are most interested in here. The point is not to discuss the development of the total unconventional events (which is done in chapter 3) but the relationship between disruptive and peaceful forms of action.

Let us first look at the case of the United States (figures 5.3a, 5.3b, and 5.3c).

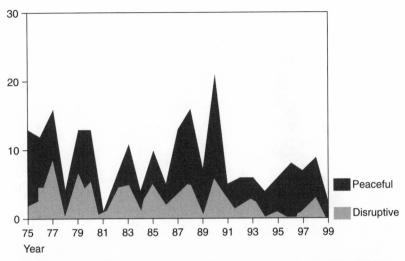

Figure 5.3a. Number of Unconventional Ecology Protests in the United States.

Since this is not my purpose here, I do not provide a detailed examination of the development year after year; rather, I concentrate on the overall trends. The general impression, in this respect, is that it is difficult to gauge a clear trend toward a radicalization—or, conversely, a moderation—of the action repertoires of the three movements, as the level of unconventional mobilization tends to either fluctuate over time (as in the case of the ecology movement) or become skewed with a large protest

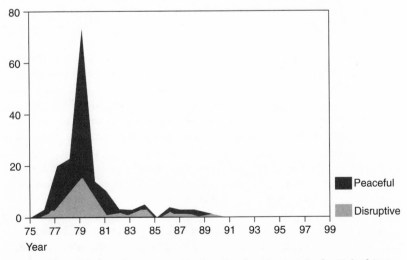

Figure 5.3b. Number of Unconventional Antinuclear Protests in the United States.

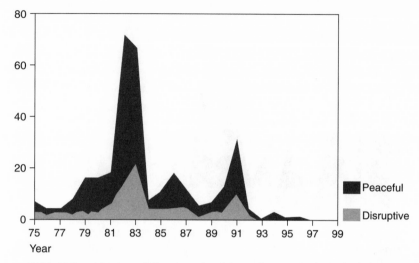

Figure 5.3c. Number of Unconventional Peace Protests in the United States.

wave and a low number of protests outside the wave (as in the case of the peace and, even more so, antinuclear movements). However, some significant patterns can be discerned. First, the U.S. ecology movement has progressively, though slowly, reduced the number of disruptive protests. If we compare this distribution with that of the total number of unconventional events and look at the width of the area concerning peaceful actions, which is the way all these figures should be read, the impression of a deradicalization of the movement gets reinforced. Especially in the two phases in which the movement increased its level of mobilization—in the 1980s and partly so in the late 1990s—the number of disruptive actions remained stable or even diminished.

Apart from certain specific instances, disruptive and peaceful protests tend to go hand in hand: when one increase or decreases, the other does so as well, although the extent of the change may not necessarily be the same. In other words, disruption seems to be part of a more general cycle of contention, whereby all forms of actions become first more frequent and then decline toward the end of the cycle. This can be seen quite well in the U.S. peace and antinuclear movements. Both display a large wave of contention, each composed of both disruptive and peaceful protests and each following a similar pattern—similar but not identical. In effect, these two examples also show another quite interesting pattern. In both cases, the protest wave usually starts with moderate forms and then is followed by radical forms. Afterward, at the end of the wave, peaceful actions decline, reflecting the demobilization of the movement; however, disruptive—sometimes violent—actions suddenly tend to increase, or at least decline at a slower pace. In the case of the antinuclear movement, this points to an actual radicalization of the movement in the 1980s, when disruptive actions were more frequent than peaceful ones. Overall, this holds in part for

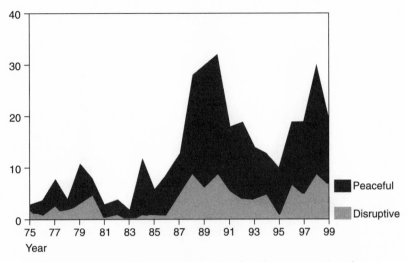

Figure 5.4a. Number of Unconventional Ecology Protests in Italy.

the peace movement. This pattern supports the view that the radicalization of social movements occurs toward the end of protest cycles and is due, among other things, to competition between movement organizations (della Porta and Tarrow 1986; Tarrow 1989, 1998).

Figures 5.4a, 5.4b, and 5.4c show the same distributions for the case of Italy.

Even less so than in the case of the United States, we cannot speak of a clear trend toward a radicalization of the movements. What we observe are rather parallel

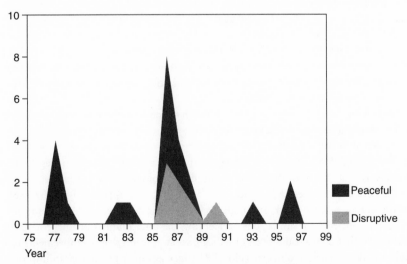

Figure 5.4b. Number of Unconventional Antinuclear Protests in Italy.

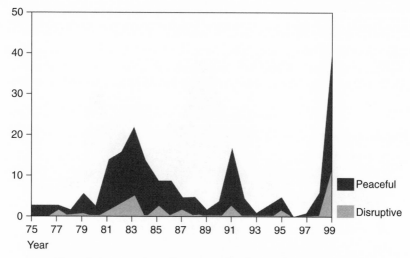

Figure 5.4c.   Number of Unconventional Peace Protests in Italy.

fluctuations of both disruptive and peaceful forms of actions. To be sure, radical ecology protests have become much more frequent since 1975, but peaceful protests have increased even more. Therefore, the share of disruptive actions over the total number of unconventional actions has become smaller in time, hence pointing to a moderation of the movement's action repertoire. The picture for the antinuclear movement is quite peculiar, with a short period in which disruptive actions make their appearance, namely, during the phase of mobilization around the antinuclear referenda of 1987. However, here is where the sampling problem evoked earlier might play a role, as the number of events per year is low, with the partial exception of the period surrounding 1987. Finally, peace protests point once again to what seems to be the main kind of relationship between disruptive and peaceful unconventional actions: a parallel development of both forms of action but at the same time a tendency to start a protest wave mainly with peaceful actions and end it with a higher share of disruptive ones, hence attesting to a radicalization specific to a phase of strong mobilization and limited in time.

Finally, figures 5.5a, 5.5b, and 5.5c deal with the radicalness of the action repertoire of the three movements in Switzerland.

Here, apart from the already noted lower share of disruptive protests, we find a similar, though less pronounced, pattern to those in the two other countries. Radical actions were absent from the mobilization of the ecology movement in the first part of the period considered, and, at least in the sample, they appear only in the 1980s. In this sense, we may speak of a radicalization of the movement. This trend, however, is paralleled by a similar one concerning the total number of unconventional actions. Rather than a real process of radicalization, it seems that the movements have radicalized at specific moments, as in 1991 (once again, at the end of an important protest wave), when disruptive actions became more frequent than usual. Similarly, for

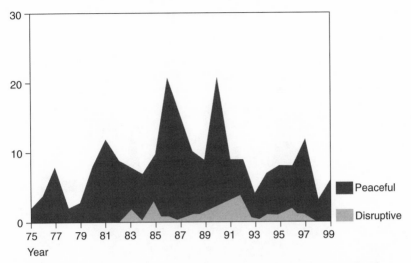

Figure 5.5a. Number of Unconventional Ecology Protests in Switzerland.

antinuclear and peace protests, we cannot conclude that the movements radicalized or became more moderate. They did radicalize on certain occasions, however—in 1983 and 1997, for the antinuclear movement; and in 1995, for the peace movement—but it is difficult to discern a clear pattern that would allow us to conclude that, during the period under study, the movements radicalized their action repertoire.

Turning now to the impact of disruption, table 5.3 presents, per country, the results of bivariate regressions between the indicator of radical mobilization for the

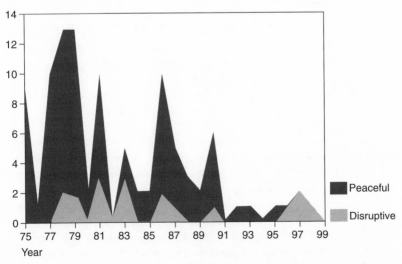

Figure 5.5b. Number of Unconventional Antinuclear Protests in Switzerland.

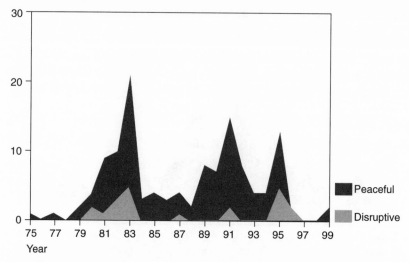

Figure 5.5c. Number of Unconventional Peace Protests in Switzerland.

three movements (the number of disruptive actions) and the indicators of policy change. Unfortunately, due to the sampling of protest event data, I cannot use a relative measure of radicalization, such as the percentage of radical actions over all unconventional actions. I must instead rely on the development over time of the number of disruptive actions.

We note only one general difference as compared to the direct effect of unconventional mobilization. It refers to the positive impact of radical actions by the ecology movement in Italy. While all unconventional actions carried by this movement are not found to affect changes in spending for environmental protection (see table 5.1), its disruptive actions are significantly related to environmental policy at the national level. The other two significant coefficients simply reflect the results concerning unconventional mobilization as a whole. In particular, the mobilization of the Italian antinuclear movement affects nuclear energy production in the desired direction, when taken as a whole and when the movement radicalizes. In contrast, the significant coefficient regarding defense spending still suggests a lack of policy impact resulting from the American peace movement.

Finally, the additional analyses conducted with radical mobilization measured as annual differences provide even less support to the hypothesis of a positive effect of disruption on public policy (see table B5.3, in appendix B). Taking differenced independent variables instead of absolute numbers, only radical mobilization by the Italian antinuclear movement seems associated with policy changes. In this case, however, we must keep in mind the particular distribution of nuclear energy production, which leads us to be wary about this finding. In general, disruption had only a limited impact on public policy. Were particularly moderate and conventional forms of action more successful? I address this question next.

Table 5.3. Effect of Radical Mobilization on Public Policy in Three Countries, 1975–1995

Dependent Variables	Spending for Environmental Protection (National) (t_1)	Spending for Environmental Protection (States) (t_1)	Nuclear Energy Production (t_1)	Number of Construction Permits (t_1)	Spending for Defense (t_1)
United States					
Radical mobilization (t_0)	−.27	−.35	−.29	.15	.44*
(D-W)	(1.95)	(1.96)	(1.96)	(2.06)	(1.89)
N	20	20	20	20	20
Italy					
Radical mobilization (t_0)	.42*	—	−.47**	—	.13
(D-W)	(1.88)	—	(2.00)	—	(2.00)
N	20	—	20	—	20
Switzerland					
Radical mobilization (t_0)	.21	.09	.33	—	−.03
(D-W)	(2.20)	(2.00)	(1.86)	—	(1.91)
N	20	20	20	—	20

Note: Standardized regression coefficients (bivariate) generated with a generalized least-squared method of estimation (Prais-Winsten) assuming a first-order autoregressive process. Durbin-Watson test for serial correlation and number of observations (series length) are shown within parentheses. The independent variables include a one-year lag. The dependent variables are expressed in terms of annual percentage change.
$*p < .10; **p < .05; ***p < .01.$

The Impact of Lobbying

Apart from the indicative overview of the mobilization provided in chapter 3, thus far I have measured movement action only through unconventional protest events, either peaceful or disruptive. Yet the strength of social movements, especially the kind of policy-oriented movements studied here, lies elsewhere as well, namely, in conventional action such as lobbying and in organizational growth. Thus, although I am most interested in the impact of overt mobilization and protest, I conducted additional analyses with indicators for the other two aspects. The latter aspect is treated in chapter 6. Here I would like to confront the effects of protest activities with those of more conventional forms of action.

Data on conventional mobilization is less easily retrieved than data on unconventional actions. When I collected data about protest actions from newspapers, I included conventional forms, such as lobbying or judicial actions, in addition to unconventional forms. However, as mentioned earlier and as I explain in more detail in appendix A, newspapers are less suitable a source to get reliable data on these forms of actions. Furthermore, most of the conventional actions found in newspapers are speech acts and verbal forms of action, which do not exactly correspond to what I refer to here as conventional actions; they have more to do with lobbying than with public statements. Therefore, I had to look somewhere else. In case of the United

States, political action committees (PACs) can be used as proxies for the conventional or lobbying activities of social movements.

PACs are organizations set up by private companies, interest groups, or public-interest organizations to provide financial support to candidates seeking public office. They solicit campaign contributions from private individuals and distribute these funds to political candidates, especially for election to the U.S. Congress. The formation of PACs became a widespread practice with the Federal Election Campaign Act of 1971. This law and its amendments of 1974 imposed restrictions on the amount of money organizations could contribute directly to a candidate, but at the same time it allowed them to make contributions via PACs, to be able to control campaign financing through the Federal Election Commission. The advantage from a researcher's point of view is that information on spending must be made available to the public.

Figures 5.6 and 5.7 show the development of spending (expressed in current and constant U.S. dollars) by movement-related PACs to sponsor election campaigns of candidates who are considered potential supporters of the movements' claims from 1975 to 1995 (that is, since the very beginning of publicly available information on this type of action).

To be sure, this is a crude measure of conventional or lobbying activity by social movements, but it can at least help us to get a little bit beyond an impressionistic picture of this kind of activity by the movements under study. In addition, these data have two other limitations for our present purpose. First, they are limited to the United States, as the other two countries either do not have a similar channel of influence or do not have such easily accessible information. Second, I can use data only for the ecology and peace movements, whereas the antinuclear movement was much less active in this respect.[12]

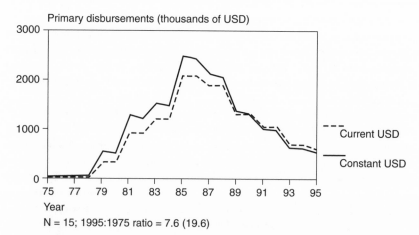

N = 15; 1995:1975 ratio = 7.6 (19.6)

Figure 5.6. Spending by Ecology Movement–Related PACs (USA).

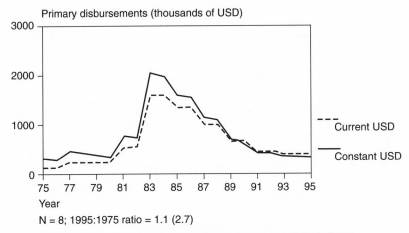

N = 8; 1995:1975 ratio = 1.1 (2.7)

Figure 5.7. Spending by Peace Movement–Related PACs (USA).

A first indication arising from these data is that PACs close to the ecology and peace movements have spent comparable amounts of money, as the scale is more or less the same. This contrasts with the amount of resources available to organizations, which is much higher for the ecology movement than for the peace movement (see chapter 6). If we consider these PACs as belonging to the movement (which is not entirely appropriate, however), this would suggest that the peace movement invests more than the ecology movement in this kind of activity, relative to the total amount of available resources. In fact, it is likely that the latter can invest more in direct lobbying activities, precisely due to the higher amount of money it has at its disposal, whereas the former must resort to private contributions raised through PACs during national election campaigns.

Yet, more interesting in our longitudinal perspective is the development of spending over time. Taken as a whole, spending by ecology PACs witnessed a more important growth than their peace counterparts. We can see this by comparing the 1995:1975 ratio shown in each figure's footnote: a growth by more than a factor of seven for ecology PACs overwhelms a stagnating development reflected in a ratio close to one (both based on constant terms). However, this way of looking at the distributions hides the significant fluctuations from one year to the next. In this regard, the two movements resemble each other more than they differ. Both ecology and peace PACs spent little money in the late 1970s. Then they suddenly rose between the 1970s and the 1980s, to peak between 1983 and 1984 (peace PACs) and between 1985 and 1986 (ecology PACs). What certainly provided the incentives for investing in this kind of activity was the threat of a Republican presidency and then an actual Republican president in office, who furthermore was particularly hostile to environmentalists and pacifists. After that, this strong investment in national election campaigns declined, and, in the case of peace movement PACs, it went down to the level of the 1970s.

A final remark that can be made about these figures is that they do not reflect the development of protest shown in chapter 3 (see figure 3.1).[13] In other words,

Table 5.4. Effect of Spending by Ecology and Peace PACs on Public Policy in the United States, 1975–1995

Dependent Variables	Spending for Environmental Protection (National) (t_1)	Spending for Environmental Protection (Local) (t_1)	Spending for Defense (t_1)
Spending by PACs (t_0)	−.20	−.43*	.25
(D-W)	(1.95)	(2.06)	(1.94)
N	20	20	20

Note: Standardized regression coefficients (bivariate) generated with a generalized least-squared method of estimation (Prais-Winsten) assuming a first-order autoregressive process. Durbin-Watson test for serial correlation and number of observations (series length) are shown within parentheses. The independent variables include a one-year lag. The dependent variables are expressed in terms of annual percentage change.
*$p < .10$; **$p < .05$; ***$p < .01$.

unconventional protest actions and lobbying (at least this crude measure of lobbying) do not necessarily go hand in hand. However, this is especially true for the ecology movement, whereas spending by PACs and protest display some affinities in the case of the peace movement. Specifically, both peaked in the early 1980s, during the large wave of peace protests that characterized that historical period, not only in the United States, but in other Western countries as well.

Given these distributions, the question remains: Is conventional mobilization, as measured through primary disbursements by movement-related PACs, effective in bringing about policy change? To assess the impact of conventional mobilization, I have conducted analyses using this measure in place of the number of protest events for the two movements for which data is available, namely, the ecology and peace movements. The results of these additional analyses, shown in table 5.4, are quite straightforward. No positive effect of the PACs related to the two movements can be observed.

There is a relation between spending by PACs related to the ecology movement and policy efforts for environmental protection, but the negative regression coefficient points to a lack of impact of the movement. However, we should note that the analyses conducted with differenced independent variables suggest a positive effect of ecology PACs on environmental policy at the local level (see table B5.4, in appendix B). Yet, as in the case of disruption, we can conclude that no consistent evidence is found that the conventional mobilization of the U.S. ecology and peace movements, as measured through spending by PACs, has had a strong impact on public policy.

Conclusion

In this chapter, I outlined the main ideas concerning the policy impact of ecology, antinuclear, and peace movements. These ideas can be summarized in two theoretical claims and three methodological features. The first theoretical claim is that social movements are more likely to have an impact on public policy when they get sustained support from political allies and public opinion. The mutual reinforcing of these two factors, the argument goes, makes the joint-effect model more apt to explain movement outcomes than an indirect-effect model and especially more than a direct-effect model. As a consequence, policy outcomes are most likely to occur when movements have at their disposal both institutional allies and public support. The second theoretical claim is that movement policy impact is more likely to occur when the types of issues they address are not affected by international constraints and do not threaten the core interests of the state. When movements address these kinds of issues, the need for a combination of political and public support is all the more urgent. As far as the three movements under study are concerned, this means that the ecology movement should be most successful, even in the absence of external support, followed by the antinuclear movement and then the peace movement.

The first methodological feature of the proposed approach is that a longitudinal approach is better suited to capture the dynamic nature of social movements and their outcomes. Time-series analysis is one promising way (though not the only one) to study the dynamics of movement outcomes.[14] As I suggested, movement outcomes are improved by the combination of political and public support; therefore, we need to incorporate into our analyses, as a second methodological feature, a number of interactive terms. Thus, interactive models should supplement additive models of movement outcomes. The third methodological feature is that, to make a stronger case for a causal relationship between protest and public policy, we need to include a chronological lag in our analyses (here, a one-year lag).

Beyond their technical aspects, the models adopted to explain the outcomes of social movements have important implications for democratic theory. In fact, underlying the two main lines of inquiry followed by previous work is the broader debate between pluralist and elitist views of politics and democracy (Schumaker 1975). Pluralists see protest groups as effective, and they see the political system as largely responsive to them, insofar as they do not stray too far from proper channels (Dahl 1961). The pluralist assumption of the permeability of the political system—in particular, the American political system—has been challenged theoretically as well as empirically by authors who see the political system as largely unresponsive to challengers (Bachrach and Baratz 1970; Bellush and David 1971; Edelmann 1964, 1977; Gamson 1990; Lowi 1969, 1971; McAdam 1982; Parenti 1970; Schattschneider 1960; Shorter and Tilly 1974). The theory of representative democracy shares this skepticism toward the responsiveness of power holders to minority groups to the extent that it views elites as responding to demands supported by a majority of citizens rather than to particular interests of minority groups, basically for electoral reasons (Burstein 1998a, 1998b; Krehbiel 1991; Lohmann 1993).

Thus, according to the theory of representative democracy, social movements and interest groups should not have a direct impact on public policy. The empirical analyses conducted in this chapter suggest indeed that the direct-effect model of social movement outcomes has only little—if any—explanatory power. If we exclude the case of the Italian antinuclear movement on the methodological ground mentioned earlier, only the Swiss ecology movement seems to have had some direct impact on policy. However, a positive relationship was also found for the ecology movement in Italy if we focus on disruptive actions. Similarly, spending by ecology PACs in the United States displays some effect, although in this case we have ambivalent results if we take absolute numbers or differences to measure the independent variable.

In the light of these findings, the criticisms of elitist and democratic theorists would seem to be correct, as we find little support for the direct-effect model of movement outcomes. It remains to be seen whether social movements are more successful when they take advantage of the presence of powerful institutional allies and a favorable public opinion. I address these two aspects in chapters 7 and 8. Before doing so, I would like to address the issue of movement organization, with the particular aim of ascertaining the extent to which the organizational strength and growth of the three movements studied can improve their chances of success.

Notes

This chapter draws extensively on ideas first expressed in an earlier paper (Giugni and Passy 1998).

1. Here I am clearly oversimplifying the theory of representative democracy for analytical purposes. In fact, authors in this theoretical perspective are not always as clear-cut as I assume to be in my brief account, and they often acknowledge the role of interest groups and social movements in blocking or facilitating short-run actions and decisions.

2. See Duyvendak (1995). These terms are often used in the extant literature to indicate the degree of visibility of an issue. In spite of their different meanings elsewhere, here I prefer to stick to these terms instead of using other labels, as I explicitly refer to their use in Kriesi and colleagues (1995).

3. To use McCarthy and Wolfson's (1992) terminology, the ecology movement in the United States is a "consensus movement."

4. Here I refer specifically to that branch of the solidarity movement that deals with issues not directly related to national politics (human rights, development aid to Third World countries, etc.).

5. Specifically, I produce standardized regression coefficients generated with the Prais-Winsten method, a generalized least-squares method for estimating a regression equation whose errors follow a first-order autoregressive process. A first-order autoregressive process is a model of a time series in which the current value of the series is a linear combination of previous values of the series, plus a random error. To check for the presence of serial correlation, I use the Durbin-Watson statistic, which is shown in brackets in all the tables that present the results of regression analysis among time series. See appendix A (in particular, for the values of acceptance or rejection of the Durbin-Watson statistic).

6. I used autocorrelation function (ACF) in ARIMA.

7. In interpreting the results of time-series analysis, I consider a 10 percent level of significance in addition to the more common 5 percent and 1 percent levels, as I am dealing with short time series. Furthermore, although current practice tends to prefer unstandardized regression coefficients when dealing with data with meaningful metrics, I use standardized coefficients because I am interested in the presence or absence of significant relationships, rather than the magnitude of effects. See appendix A.

8. In the case of environmental policy in Switzerland, the local level includes both national and local spending.

9. In the analyses of the impact of the three movements under study, I measure their mobilization through unconventional protest events only, hence excluding conventional forms of action. As I said in the introduction and as I explain in more detail in appendix A, the latter are more likely to display biased distributions and therefore be underrepresented in my sample. However, to explore all possible relationships between protest and public policy, and to see whether we obtain different results with the two measures, I conducted time-series analysis with movement mobilization measured through all protest events as well, that is, including conventional actions, with independent variables expressed in terms of absolute levels and differences. This was done with all the regressions that involve movement mobilization, or every time I made four types of analysis: one with unconventional actions as absolute levels (shown in the tables in the main text), one with unconventional actions as differences (shown in the tables in appendix B), one with all actions as absolute levels, and one with all actions as differences (results are not shown). In this case, the results of these additional analyses largely reflect those obtained with unconventional actions. Those referring to the number of protest events display the same significant coefficients (with slightly different values and levels of significance). Those referring to differences show three significant coefficients in the case of Switzerland: one for environmental spending at the local level, one for nuclear energy production (but the direction of change is opposed to the movement's aims), and one for defense spending. The latter is therefore the only new direct effect found overall with respect to the other three types of analyses.

10. Signature collection campaigns exclude those made for referenda, which are more institutionalized than petitions or other collections of signatures.

11. Calculating the percentage of disruptive actions over a total (which can be represented either by all actions or all unconventional actions) would be a more appropriate way to assess the degree of radicalization of the movements. However, since the data on protest events are sampled on the newspaper source, this cannot be done here. In effect, the sampling error might produce important differences in percentages when the total number of events over which the percentage is calculated is low. I therefore prefer to rely on the distribution over time of the number of disruptive actions and compare it to that of the total unconventional actions. See appendix A.

12. Data on PACs come from public files of the Federal Election Commission in Washington, D.C. I selected all PACs that I judged as being close to the movements (fifteen for the ecology movement, eight for the peace movement). Annual figures are the mean of two-year totals (that is, the duration of a legislature) in primary disbursements. Missing values for 1995 have been replaced with estimates based on linear interpolation. Spending by PACs related to the antinuclear movement appears only for the 1991–1992 period. While for this reason I cannot show data concerning this movement, this might indicate that it simply did not use this channel of influence. See appendix A.

13. The correlation coefficient between spending by ecology PACs and unconventional ecology protests equals .01. The correlation coefficient between spending by peace PACs and unconventional peace protests equals .36. Neither is statistically significant.

14. Event-history analysis, for example, is another time-sensitive method that is gaining increasing popularity among students of social movements (e.g., Myers 1997; Olzak 1989, 1992).

CHAPTER SIX

~~✑~~

Social Movement Organization

Chapter 3 shows that the mobilization of ecology, antinuclear, and peace movements in the last three decades has gone through ebbs and flows. This holds true not only in the United States, where the configuration of political power has been subject to change from one legislature to the next; but also in Italy and Switzerland, where political alignments have remained more stable over time. This fluctuating pattern of mobilization is most evident in the case of antinuclear and peace movements, while ecology protests display a more chronologically linear development. Yet, the overt protest activities carried out by social movements clearly have a discontinuous character. Protest actions are not equal to social movements. The latter possess at least two other crucial features: organization and culture. In other words, social movements are organized efforts based on a shared identity to reach a common goal mainly, though not exclusively, through noninstitutional means (Tarrow 1998; Tilly 1994). Protest is but one side of this more complex phenomenon. In addition, not all protest activities are carried out by social movements.

In this chapter, I address the organizational side of the three movements under study. In line with the principal aim of this book, I look at the role that movement organizations have in the dynamics of movement outcomes, but at the same time I pay attention to the organizational development of the three movements. Specifically, the research question I address is the following: Is there a relationship between the movements' organizational growth and their policy impact? In this regard, the hypothesis to be explored is that the greater the organizational strength of ecology, antinuclear, and peace movements, the stronger their impact on public policy. Furthermore, do we observe any differences in the relationship between movement organization and policy changes, both across countries and across movements? Before I address these questions, a brief excursus is in order regarding the literature that has underscored the importance of organization for social movements and, more broadly, contentious politics. The most important body of literature in this respect is that referring to resource mobilization theory.

Resource Mobilization Theory and the Role of Social Movement Organizations

In a pathbreaking article published in the *American Journal of Sociology*, John McCarthy and Mayer Zald (1977) laid out some of the central assumptions of resource mobilization theory. Two points are particularly important for the study of social movements in a macrosociological perspective (as opposed to a microsociological emphasis, on individual participation):

> First, study of the aggregation of resources (money and labor) is crucial to an understanding of social movement activity. Because resources are necessary for engagement in social conflict, they must be aggregated from collective purposes. Second, resource aggregation requires some minimal form of organization, and hence, implicitly or explicitly, we focus more directly upon social movement organizations than do those working within the traditional perspective. (McCarthy and Zald 1977, 44)

Their "partial theory" was clearly addressed against the collective behavior approach—what Tilly, Tilly, and Tilly (1975) call "breakdown theories," which stress the role of grievances and discontent, feelings of frustration and deprivation, social anomie, and generalized beliefs in explaining the rise of collective behavior (e.g., Gurr 1970; Kornhauser 1959; Smelser 1962; Turner and Killian 1957). "Solidarity theories," in contrast, emphasize the role of social networks, organization, resources, and opportunities (e.g., McAdam 1982; McCarthy and Zald 1977; Oberschall 1973; Tarrow 1998; Tilly 1978; Tilly, Tilly, and Tilly 1975).

Today, students of social movements and contentious politics have reached some degree of consensus as to the determinants of movement growth, decline, and change. They stress three broad sets of factors:

1. political opportunities that provide people with the incentives to act collectively;
2. cultural-framing processes by which people define and interpret situations and events; and
3. mobilizing structures by which groups seek to organize (McAdam, McCarthy, and Zald 1996; McAdam, Tarrow, and Tilly 2001).

As Tarrow (1998, 23) put it:

> Contentious politics is produced when political opportunities broaden, when they demonstrate the potential for alliances, and when they reveal the opponents' vulnerability. Contention crystallizes into a social movement when it taps embedded social networks and connective structures and produces collective action frames and supportive identities able to sustain contention with powerful opponents. By mounting familiar

forms of contention, movements become the focal points that transform external opportunities into resources. Repertoires of contention, social networks, and cultural frames lower the costs of bringing people into collective action, induce confidence that they are not alone, and give broader meaning to their claims. Together, these factors trigger the dynamic processes that have made social movements historically central to political and social change.

The role of organizations and, more broadly, mobilizing structures has been stressed most forcefully by proponents of resource mobilization theory, which relies on two basic tenets. First, proponents reject the underlying assumption of breakdown theories, where grievances and discontent are the main determinants of protest behavior. They underscore instead the crucial importance of social organization as a precondition for collective action. Second, they emphasize the availability and mobilization of resources for the emergence of collective action.

In spite of these core assumptions, resource mobilization theory includes a variegated ensemble of works, which can be subsumed under two different streams: one dealing mostly with the macrolevel of analysis and the ecology of organizational dynamics, the other stressing the importance of social networks as a crucial factor leading to individual participation in social movements. The first stream is perhaps best represented by the works carried out at the Center for Research of Social Organization at the University of Michigan, under the lead of Meyer Zald (e.g., McCarthy and Zald 1977; Zald and Ash 1966; Zald and McCarthy 1979, 1987). Gamson's well-known book (1990), which I refer to in chapter 2 as being one of the most influential studies of the outcomes of social movements to date, and which I discuss in more detail later, also follows this line of reasoning. The point of departure in this perspective is Olson's *Logic of Collective Action* (1965) and his theory of the "free rider," according to which collective action (at least in large groups) is unlikely in the absence of selective incentives, which produce collective action as a by-product of the search to fulfill individual interests. Since social movements deliver collective goods and since individuals are not likely to act to produce such goods, this perspective calls for an analysis of the selection of incentives, cost-reducing mechanisms or structures, and career benefits that lead to collective action (see also, Oberschall 1973). Thus, the crucial aspects of this approach include aggregating resources, creating the organization, obtaining external support, and evaluating the costs and benefits of action.[1]

Organizations are fundamental elements of contemporary social movements, in particular those examined in this book. However, a number of authors have contributed to resource mobilization theory without having too narrowly focused on formal organizations. This broader perspective is best exemplified by the work of Anthony Oberschall. His *Social Conflict and Social Movements* (1973) is among the earlier systematic attempts to formulate a theory of political mobilization based on the assumption that social organization and integration, rather than grievances and discontent, are most conducive to protest behavior. His book was addressed above all against Kornhauser's theory of mass society (1959) and certain modernization theories arguing that the dissolution of traditional social bonds and the lack of new forms of integration are the preconditions for collective action. For sustained mobilization, Oberschall points to the importance of organizational basis and of continuity in the leadership.

The version of resource mobilization theory that emphasizes the availability and allocation of resources, as well as the role played by social organization at the macrosociological level, has had the merit not only of having shifted our attention from "breakdown" to "solidarity" explanations of collective behavior but also of having brought together the study of collective action and organizational theory. This is also the perspective I adopt in this chapter in my attempt to assess the organizational strength and growth of the three movements under study, especially their impact on public policy. Before that, however, it is worth mentioning another important variant that has contributed to our knowledge of processes of political mobilization. I am alluding to the research tradition that has underscored the role of social networks as a precondition for collective action at the microsociological level. Here the notion of organization refers to the networks of interpersonal relationships of solidarity and identity, and that of resources reflects the importance of social capital. Indeed, one of the most consistent findings of previous research on social movements concerns the crucial role played by preexisting ties and mobilizing structures as facilitators for the emergence of collective action (e.g., Gould 1995; Fernandez and McAdam 1988, 1989; Kim and Bearman 1997; Kriesi 1988, 1993; McAdam 1986, 1988a, 1988b; McAdam and Paulsen 1993; McAdam, McCarthy, and Zald 1988; Rosenthal et al. 1985; Snow, Zurcher, and Ekland-Olson 1980).

This variant of resource mobilization theory pays a lot more attention to informal networks in the micromobilization process. In this regard, previous research has shown that people join collective action mainly through interpersonal ties, that is, informal networks (e.g., della Porta 1988; Gould 1995; McAdam 1988b; Snow, Zurcher, and Ekland-Olson 1980). Thus, while the research tradition related to organizational analysis has stressed the role of formal organizations, the social networks perspective has shown the importance of informal mobilizing structures. However, it is on the former aspect that I would like to focus in the next few pages.

Gamson's *Strategy of Social Protest* and Its Critics

When it comes to studying the consequences of social movements, William Gamson's *Strategy of Social Protest* ([1975] 1990) is the work that has most forcefully put forward the basic tenets of resource mobilization theory—in particular, the role of a strong organization for successful challenges. I mentioned this fundamental piece of work on several occasions, specifically in the literature review laid out in chapter 2. Given my focus on movement outcomes, however, this work and its subsequent reanalyses of data are worth dealing with in more detail. The authors of these subsequent studies are most interested in assessing either the role of a series of internal features of social movements for their outcomes or the relative importance of internal, protester-controlled variables as compared to external, situational variables.

Gamson's work is probably the first systematic attempt to study the success of social movements. The book is framed as a critique of the pluralist perspective regarding

American society (see, e.g., Dahl 1967). Through the analysis of the careers of fifty-three American challenging groups that have acted between 1800 and 1945, Gamson questions the permeability and openness of the American political system. Specifically, the author addresses several questions: "How can we account for the different experiences of a representative collection of American challenging groups? What is the characteristic response to groups of different types and what determines this response? What strategies work under what circumstances? What organizational characteristics influence the success of the challenge?" (Gamson 1990, 5). In fact, the last question emerges as the focus of the analysis, and of course, it is the one in which we are most interested here.

Gamson's study is based on a simple and straightforward typology of challengers' success, which is conceived of as a set of outcomes that fall into two basic clusters: the "acceptance of a challenger group by its antagonists as a valid spokesman for a legitimate set of interests" and the fact that "the group's beneficiary gains new advantages during the challenge and its aftermath" (Gamson 1990, 29). By combining these two dimensions, the author defines four possible outcomes of a challenge: full response, preemption, co-optation, and collapse. Unfortunately, this typology is not used systematically in the empirical analyses, which remain for the most part confined to the distinction between acceptance and new advantages. The author then tests the impact of a series of organizational variables on the success or failure of the sampled challenging groups. Although in one chapter he takes into account the effect of time as a historical context variable on the challenges' outcomes, he is most concerned with challenger-controlled variables (i.e., organizational variables).

The main findings of Gamson's study can be summarized in five points. First, groups with single-issue demands tended to be more successful than groups with multiple-issue demands. Second, the use of selective incentives was positively correlated with success. Third, the use of violence and, more generally, radical tactics was associated with success, while being the target of violence made it more difficult. Fourth—and most important for our present purpose, as it concerns the role of organizational variables—successful groups tended to be more bureaucratized and centralized and tended to escape factionalism. Finally, among the context variables, time did not matter much, but political crises seemed to have an effect on the challenging groups' outcomes. The two most important results are certainly those regarding the role of organizational variables and the use of violence. They are also those that have been most often discussed in the literature, as we saw in chapter 2.

Gamson's pathbreaking study raised a number of criticisms, mostly addressing methodological issues.[2] Webb and colleagues (1983, 318–25) have stressed four major areas of criticism:

1. the limits of Gamson's bivariate tabular analysis, which does not allow one to assess the relative impact of different explanatory variables and differentiate various kinds of relationships (Goldstone 1980a; Gurr 1980; Snyder and Kelly 1979; Zelditch 1978);

2. Gamson's static research design, as well as the lack of attention paid to time-related variables (Snyder and Kelly 1979; Gurr 1980);

3. Gamson's treatement of the outcomes of the challengers' actions (Goldstone 1980a; Gurr 1980; Snyder and Kelly 1979; Zelditch 1978), particularly his choice of indicators, the absence of a distinction between objective and subjective perceptions of success, and the problem of relating outcomes to the challengers' actions; and finally,

4. Gamson's choice of the units of analysis (Goldstone 1980a; Zelditch 1978), specifically with regard to the large proportion of trade unions in the sample and to the problem of identity.

Despite these objections, Gamson's study stimulated other authors to reanalyze his original data, for he had the clairvoyance to append his book with the complete dataset on the fifty-three challenging groups.[3] For example, Steedly and Foley (1979) repeated his analysis using more sophisticated techniques. Specifically, they tried to avoid the first of the four criticisms mentioned by employing multivariate statistical techniques, such as factor analysis, multidimensional scaling, multiple regression, and discriminant functional analysis. They obtained results supporting some of Gamson's findings: group success was related, in order of relative importance, to the nondisplacement nature of the goals, the number of alliances, the absence of factionalism, specific and limited goals, and the willingness to use sanctions. Furthermore, the authors developed predictive equations that allow for a generalization of findings.

Mirowsky and Ross (1981) undertook a similar task but with a slightly different purpose, namely, to find the locus of control over success. In other words, their study addresses the question of which among three sources of success is the most important: the protest group (beliefs, goals, organization), the third parties (social support, social control), or the situation (context, dynamic interaction). By means of factor-analysis and path-analysis techniques, the authors elaborated on Gamson's findings, especially those concerning the effect of violence, but basically agreed with him. In general, they found that, for a successful outcome, protester-controlled factors are more important than the support of third parties or the situation. Of these protester-controlled factors, the organization and, above all, the beliefs and goals are crucial for success.

The strongest threat to Gamson's results, however, came from Goldstone's reanalysis (1980a). On the basis of a series of methodological criticisms of Gamson's study, such as those mentioned here, Goldstone challenged its conclusions and central theoretical tenet. This author found that the organizational and tactical characteristics had no effect on group success. Instead, by means of a stochastic model, he was able to show that the timing of success is independent of the challengers' organization and tactics. Finally, he suggested that the resource mobilization model be replaced by a model that stresses the crucial role of broad, systemwide national crises for the success of social movements. Goldstone's study set in motion a debate with Gamson, which involved other authors as well (Foley and Steedly 1980; Gamson 1980; Goldstone 1980b; see also Gamson 1989). The debate was mostly about methodological issues but went "beyond the substantive arguments in *Strategy* to show contrasting approaches to general issues of sociological theory, methods, and practice" (Gamson 1990, 181).[4]

More recently, Frey, Dietz, and Kalof (1992) made an attempt to adjudicate between Gamson's and Goldstone's arguments. Using multivariate techniques, they tried to assess the relative importance of organizational and environmental variables for success in terms of new advantages. To do so, they created three different samples: a sample including Gamson's original data set, one with the changes suggested by Goldstone (1980a), and still another one with their own changes. Their findings point to the importance of not having displacement goals and group factionalism to obtain new advantages. Thus, Gamson's central argument, stressing internal variables and resource mobilization as determinants of group success, found further support. At the same time, on the basis of some of Goldstone's insights, the authors suggested a synthesis of the two perspectives by calling for a model that took into account strategy and structural constraints.

In addition to the empirical and methodological criticisms often based on reanalyses of his data, Gamson's study, as I mentioned in chapter 2, has raised a broader debate in the social movement literature about the role of organization in mounting successful challenges. This debate has mainly opposed Gamson himself to Frances Fox Piven and Richard Cloward. Whereas Gamson has shown the potential impact of organized challenges, Piven and Cloward (1979) have argued that movements have more chances to succeed when they avoid building a strong organization because the movements themselves can exploit their main resource: disruption (see, e.g., Gamson and Schmeidler 1984; Cloward and Piven 1984). In chapter 5, I address the question of which types of protests by ecology, antinuclear, and peace movements are more likely to influence public policy: disruptive/radical actions or moderate actions. Here I examine the impact of their organizational growth and internal resources (in terms of membership and financial resources).

Organizational Strength and Growth

Members and money are perhaps the two most important internal resources of social movements. Of course, other features are important, such as the size of the movement's staff and its degree of professionalization. These internal characteristics, however, depend on the amount of resources available. More generally, some authors have mentioned numbers (i.e., members or participants), radicalness, and novelty as important sources of movement strength (DeNardo 1985; Koopmans 1993). Likewise, Tilly (1994) has argued that the distinguishing feature of social movements lies in sustained challenges to authorities and their responses, whereby movements publicly display what he calls "WUNC," that is, worthiness, unity, numbers, and commitment. Thus, according to Tilly, the strength of movements depends on the following formula:

$$\text{strength} = \text{worthiness} \times \text{unity} \times \text{numbers} \times \text{commitment}.[5]$$

Let us focus on numbers, specifically on the members and amount of financial resources of the three movements under study. Table 6.1 shows average membership

Table 6.1. Average Membership and Financial Resources of Ecology, Antinuclear, and Peace Movement Organizations by Country and by Movement, 1995

	Members			Money		
	Abs.	Rel.	N	Abs.	Rel.	N
Country						
United States	198,257	754	28	14,713,881	55,929	42
(*Greenpeace/NWF*)[a]	(398,373)	(1,515)	(30)			
Italy	20,061	350	10	615,514	10,736	10
Switzerland	99,794	14,130	4	7,089,196	1,003,851	7
(*Greenpeace*)[a]	(127,294)	(18,025)	(4)			
U.S. Movements						
Ecology	341,800	1,299	15	28,829,400	109,604	20
(*Greenpeace/NWF*)[a]	(678,059)	(2,578)	(17)			
Antinuclear	23,840	90	5	999,286	3,799	7
Peace	38,125	145	8	2,293,333	8,719	15

Source: Various issues of the *Encyclopedia of Associations* (United States) and questionnaire sent to various social movement organizations (Italy and Switzerland).

Note: Figures for financial resources are expressed in USD. Missing data have been replaced with estimates based on linear interpolation. The lower section of the table refers to the United States only. The exchange rate as of January 1, 1995, has been used to convert Italian and Swiss currencies (Italy: 0.0006157/0.0006161; Switzerland: 0.76298/0.76348).

[a] Two ecology organizations for the United States (Greenpeace and the National Wildlife Federation) and one for Switzerland (Greenpeace) have been left out from the computation of membership (but not from financial resources) because they have supporters rather than actual members (figures including these two organizations are given within parentheses).

and financial resources of selected ecology, antinuclear, and peace movement organizations, both in absolute and relative terms (i.e., per million inhabitants). The table divides in two parts: the upper section compares the three countries aggregating all three movements; the lower section presents separate results for each movement in the United States.[6] The figures, expressed in U.S. dollars, indicate large differences across countries and across movements.

If we first look at membership in the three movements as a whole, we can see how U.S. organizations tend to be much larger, averaging about two hundred thousand members per organization; followed by the Swiss, with one hundred thousand; and, finally, the Italians, with twenty thousand. However, this refers to absolute numbers. If we take into account the size of the population, this "social movement sector," to use McCarthy and Zald's (1977) terminology, appears much stronger in Switzerland, while in Italy it remains the weakest. A similar pattern can be observed with regard to money. In absolute terms the United States ranks first, Switzerland second, and Italy a far third; yet, in relative terms the Swiss movements are clearly the richest, followed by the Americans, and lastly the Italians.

These results, however, should be read in the light of the number of organizations included in the sample. In the case of the United States, I found information on all three movements, but in Italy the reported figures concern only the ecology and peace movements; and in Switzerland, only the ecology movement. Especially in the last case, this tends to increase the average number of members and amount of money, for this movement is the richest in terms of internal resources, as we can see in the comparison among movements shown in the table's lower section. In addition, information was available for smaller organizations in the United States, which further underestimates the strength of the American organizations, once we look at the average amount of resources. Yet, with these qualifications in mind, we can conclude that

1. both in terms of membership and financial resources, organizations in Switzerland are richer than those in the United States and especially Italy; and
2. in the case of the United States, the ecology movement is by and large the most formalized and resourceful movement, followed by the peace movement and then the antinuclear movement.

This cross-country and cross-movement comparison, however, only gives us a static picture of the organizational strength of ecology, antinuclear, and peace movements. What we are most interested in, especially from the perspective adopted in this book, is the development of the resources available to the movements over time. Figures 6.1 to 6.5 give us longitudinal information on the organizational strength of the three movements.[7] To begin with, let us look at the case of the United States. Figures 6.1, 6.2, and 6.3 show the development of the number of members (expressed in thousands) and the amount of financial resources (expressed in billions of current and constant U.S. dollars) of the ecology, antinuclear, and peace movement organizations in the United States from 1975 to 1995.

In the light of these data, the organizational development of the three movements can be summarized in three points. First, the ecology movement has witnessed a steady growth of its membership, with a particularly strong rise in the first half of the 1990s. The 1995:1975 ratio shown in the figures' footnotes indicates that membership has increased about five times in twenty years. The movement's financial resources have also increased but at a slower pace, especially if we take inflation into account. Yet, if we look closer, we realize that the greatest gains were made in the 1990s, which evidently were a flourishing period for the U.S. ecology movement, if not in terms of mobilization (see chapter 3), certainly in terms of organizational resources.

Second, the internal resources of the antinuclear movement have remained rather stable, as the growth ratio attests. More precisely, the number of members has declined overall, while the financial resources have slightly increased. This holds as a general trend. If we look at the figures in more detail, we can see that the selected organizations for this movement went through a number of ebbs and flows. Membership in particular went up considerably between 1977 and 1978 and to a lesser extent between 1983 and 1984. However, it declined strongly from 1987 onward. By that time, the golden age of the antinuclear struggle was over. Money follows a similar pattern in the first years of the period, but the movement was able to stabilize its resources to some extent after 1985.

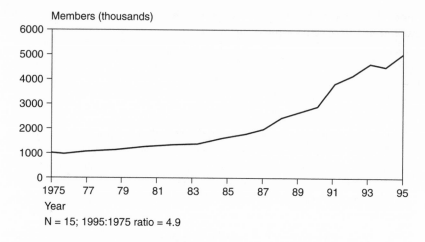

N = 15; 1995:1975 ratio = 4.9

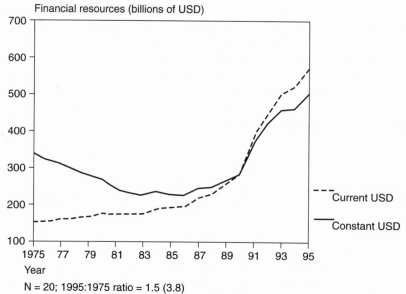

N = 20; 1995:1975 ratio = 1.5 (3.8)

Figure 6.1. Organizational Growth of the Ecology Movement (USA).

Third, as we can see in the much different values of the respective 1995:1975 ratios, the peace movement displays a peculiar development of its resources. First, its membership has witnessed the greatest increase among our three movements. However, the amount of financial resources has been halved over the twenty-year period considered here. Specifically, membership in the eight selected organizations went from less than fifty thousand to more than three hundred thousand. While this remains a raindrop as compared to the storm of the powerful ecology organizations, it represents a significant change, especially in the light of the strong

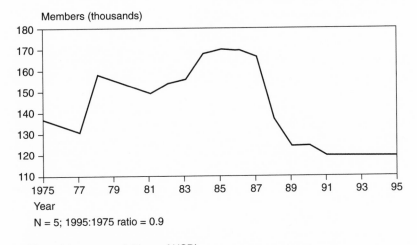

N = 5; 1995:1975 ratio = 0.9

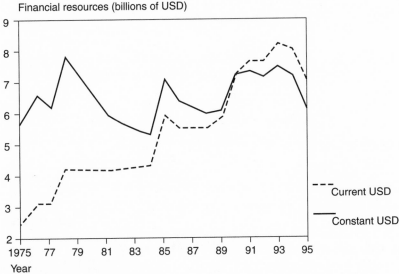

N =7; 1995:1975 ratio = 1.1 (2.8)

Figure 6.2. Organizational Growth of the Antinuclear Movement (USA).

demobilization undergone by the movement in the early 1980s. Indeed, here we have a clear indication that, while mobilizing structures are certainly a major determinant of mobilization, organizational development and protest do not necessarily go hand in hand.

Results for the other two countries are both less complete and less reliable because of the lower number of organizations included in the sample. Figure 6.4 shows the development of membership (in thousands) and financial resources (in billions of Italian lira) of ecology movement organizations in Italy. The distributions concerning

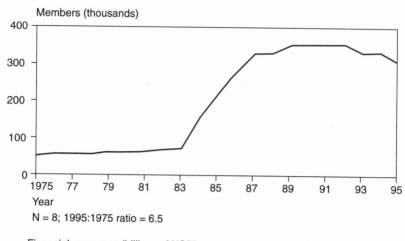

N = 8; 1995:1975 ratio = 6.5

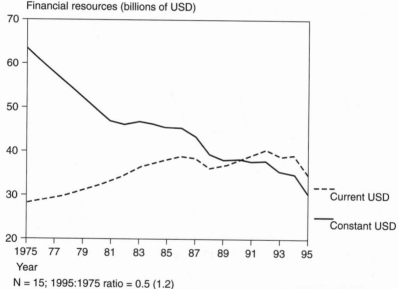

N = 15; 1995:1975 ratio = 0.5 (1.2)

Figure 6.3. Organizational Growth of the Peace Movement (USA).

this movement are to some extent similar to those observed in the United States, as both membership and financial resources have increased—the former at a particularly rapid pace, the latter more slowly and hesitantly.

Finally, we can have a look at the Swiss situation. Figure 6.5 shows the development of membership (in thousands) and financial resources (in billions of Swiss francs) of selected organizations of the ecology movement in Switzerland. Again, we observe an important growth of the movement. Unlike in the United States and Italy, however, here the increase of financial resources outweighs that of membership. The Swiss

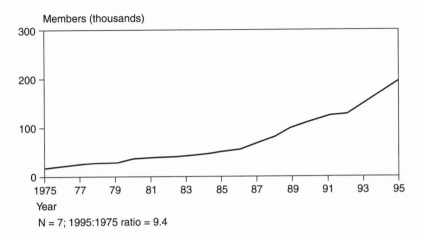

N = 7; 1995:1975 ratio = 9.4

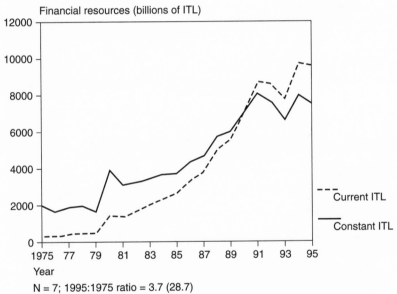

N = 7; 1995:1975 ratio = 3.7 (28.7)

Figure 6.4. Organizational Growth of the Ecology Movement (Italy).

ecology movement today is particularly rich, both in comparison with other countries and with previous periods in Switzerland.

In sum, our brief and far from exhaustive look at the organizational strength of ecology, antinuclear, and peace movements indicates important differences across movements and across countries. First, the ecology movement clearly is the most resourceful of the three movements, in terms of members and money. Antinuclear and peace movement organizations have fewer internal resources at their disposal, thus witnessing a lower degree of formalization and institutionalization. However,

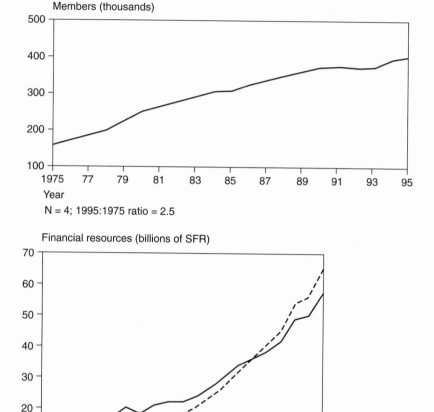

Figure 6.5. **Organizational Growth of the Ecology Movement (Switzerland).**

this "social movement sector" is much stronger in the United States and especially in Switzerland than in Italy. Furthermore, the Italian ecology and peace movements have developed later than those in the other two countries. At the same time, though, their organizational growth was more pronounced in Italy in recent years, perhaps partly due to their late development.

The crucial question for us at this point bears on the relationship between the movements' organizational strength and public policy. Specifically, are changes in state policies in the domains touched by the three movements linked to the movements' organizational development? The next section attempts to give an answer, though a tentative one, to this important question for the study of the impact of social movements.

Social Movement Organizations and Public Policy

As I mention earlier in this chapter and describe in more detail in chapter 2, there was an intense debate in the literature about the likelihood that strong organizational structure leads to a movement's success. Here I would like to briefly discuss this issue with respect to the three movements studied and see whether a relationship exists between their internal resources and any subsequent changes in public policy. More precisely and in line with the longitudinal approach adopted in this book, I would like to ascertain whether shifts in two major internal resources—members and money—of the ecology, antinuclear, and peace movements have affected changes in state policies concerning the issues they address.

Similar to the parallel made in the conclusion to part I, between the mobilization of the three movements and public policy, we can obtain a first picture of the relationship between organizational growth and public policy by comparing the development of policy, as shown in figures 4.1 to 4.12 (in chapter 4), with that of the movements' membership and financial resources, as depicted in figures 6.1 to 6.5. Let us again focus on the case of the United States, for which I have systematic information on the organizational development of all three movements.

We can safely conclude that no consistent pattern of covariation can be discerned. First, at least at the national level, state spending for the environment witnessed a strong decline in the early 1980s, after a growth in the late 1970s; for the ecology movement, the internal resources remained rather stable and even increased during the same period. However, the phase of stronger organizational growth, in the early 1990s, coincided with the renewal in state expenditures for environmental protection. The picture is even more complicated for the antinuclear movement, not least because different indicators—its organizational strength and the state policies in the nuclear energy domain—point to different directions. First, while nuclear energy production witnessed a steady increase between 1975 and 1995, the number of construction permits for new plants (see table 4.2, in chapter 4) dropped dramatically after the Three Mile Island accident in 1979. However, the movement's membership continued to increase until 1987, when it suddenly declined rapidly (long after the drop in construction permits); yet, its financial resources have remained rather stable, among ebbs and flows. Finally, the pattern for the peace movement confirms the apparent lack of a consistent relationship between movement organizational growth and policy change. If the growth of the membership of peace movement organizations from 1983 to 1987 was followed by a decrease in military spending after 1987 (hence pointing to a relationship between these two factors), this trend is contradicted by the continuing decline of the movement's financial resources,

Table 6.2. Effect of Movement Organizational Strength on Public Policy in Three Countries, 1975–1995

Dependent Variables	Spending for Environmental Protection (National) (t_1)	Spending for Environmental Protection (Local) (t_1)	Nuclear Energy Production (t_1)	Number of Construction Permits (t_1)	Spending for Defense (t_1)
United States					
Membership (t_0)	.04	−.29	.10	−.29	−.40*
(D-W)	(1.92)	(1.93)	(1.93)	(2.10)	(1.82)
N	20	20	20	20	20
Financial resources (t_0)	.26	.11	−.43*	.03	.10
(D-W)	(1.95)	(1.94)	(2.05)	(2.14)	(1.92)
N	20	20	20	20	20
Italy					
Membership (t_0)	.09	—	—	—	−.17
(D-W)	(1.95)	—	—	—	(1.97)
N	20	—	—	—	20
Financial resources (t_0)	.10	—	—	—	−.05
(D-W)	(1.95)	—	—	—	(1.96)
N	20	—	—	—	20
Switzerland					
Membership (t_0)	.42*	.00	—	—	—
(D-W)	(2.28)	(2.00)	—	—	—
N	20	20	—	—	—
Financial resources (t_0)	.37	−.08	—	—	—
(D-W)	(2.23)	(2.00)	—	—	—
N	20	20	—	—	—

Note: Standardized regression coefficients (bivariate) generated with a generalized least-squared method of estimation (Prais-Winsten) assuming a first-order autoregressive process. Durbin-Watson test for serial correlation and number of observations (series length) are shown within parentheses. The independent variables include a one-year lag. The dependent variables are expressed in terms of annual percentage change. Financial resources are measured in constant USD, ITL, and SFR (basis: 1990). Two ecology organizations in the United States (Greenpeace and the National Wildlife Federation) and one in Switzerland (Greenpeace) have been left out of the computation of membership (but not from financial resources) because they have supporters rather than actual members.
*$p < .10$; **$p < .05$; ***$p < .01$.

during times of both increasing and decreasing state expenditures for national defense purposes.

We can be more systematic in the attempt to ascertain the impact of social movement organization on public policy. I do so by regressing the indicators of state policies on the two measures of organizational growth using the same procedure as that in the analysis of the relationship between protest and public policy. Table 6.2 shows the results of this analysis, respectively for the United States, Italy, and Switzerland.[8]

The table's upper section refers to the case of the United States. Bearing in mind the limitations of bivariate analyses, the findings do not indicate a consistent impact of the internal organizational capacity of the movements on changes in state policies in the areas touched by these movements. While there is no effect of the ecology movement, two out of ten coefficients are statistically significant at the 10 percent threshold: one for the financial resources of the antinuclear movement and one for membership of the peace movement. In both cases, the negative sign of the coefficient indicates that the policy changes go in the direction of the movements' demands. Concerning the former, however, we should note that energy production is not the best indicator of state efforts in this domain, for production has continued to grow, in part due to a better and more rational use of the available resources, even though the American nuclear power industry clearly was in a bad shape after 1979 and even before that year. The number of construction permits provides a more reliable measure, but here the coefficient is not significant.

The table's middle section shows the results for the case of Italy, but it is limited to ecology and peace movements due to lack of data on the antinuclear movement. In addition, given the centralized character of the Italian state, I consider only spending for environmental protection by the national government. Here we do not have any indication of a positive effect of the two movements' organizational development on public policy. As in the case of the United States, my data for Italy do not support the thesis that strong organization increases the chances of success of social movements.

In contrast, this does seem to occur for the ecology movement in Switzerland. In this case, I can only look at the impact of the organizational strength of this movement, once again due to lack of information on the other movements. The results are shown in the lower section of table 6.2. Here, both the coefficient for the number of members and that for the amount of financial resources are statistically significant and in the right direction, that is, suggesting a positive effect of the movement's organizational growth. Does this mean that the Swiss ecology movement is more powerful than its American and Italian counterparts? This is difficult to say, and most of all difficult to say why it would be so. We do have to remember that these are simple bivariate analyses with no control for the effect of other important factors.

Before concluding this chapter and going back in the next chapters to the main focus of this book—the analysis of the relationship between protest and public policy—we can have a look at the results of regressions conducted with the independent variables measured as differences from one year to the next instead of absolute levels of membership and financial resources. If we measure the movements' organizational growth through differences, the significant relationships observed with absolute levels disappear. Results are shown in table B6.2, in appendix B. As we can see, only two coefficients are statistically significant, namely, those concerning the impact of membership and financial resources of the U.S. ecology movement on spending for environmental protection at the local level. Yet, the sign of the coefficients is negative, suggesting that an increase in the movements' internal resources is associated with a decline in spending. Thus, even in this case, we can hardly speak of a positive effect of the ecology movement. All the other coefficients are not significant.

Conclusion

Students of social movements have long debated the role of organization for the emergence and impact of protest. If the crucial impact of organizational variables on the emergence of movements is now a fait accompli, since resource mobilization theory has turned the study of contentious politics on its head, its importance for the outcomes and consequences of movements remains a debatable issue. Symbolized by the debate between Gamson and Piven–Cloward, we are still unclear as to whether a movement that builds a strong organizational structure and accumulates important internal resources is more likely than poor and loosely organized movements to be successful in its efforts to influence public policy.

Certainly, I will not attempt to give the definitive answer to this question here. This was not my aim in this chapter. My goal is much less ambitious: it is simply to ascertain whether the organizational development of the three movements under study and the changes in public policy in the areas they address are in some way related in terms of covariation, if not in terms of causality. That answer is rather negative. Some relationship seems to exist between organization and policy change in the case of the U.S. peace movement and the U.S. antinuclear movement (but only with the less-appropriate indicator of nuclear energy policy). In contrast, the organizational development of the Italian ecology and peace movements did not affect environmental and military spending by the state. Finally, the Swiss ecology movement displays a positive impact. Yet, for all the countries, the significant relationships disappear when we look at movement organization in relative instead of absolute terms, that is, in terms of annual differences. Altogether, internal resources are not consistently found to facilitate the impact of ecology, antinuclear, and peace movements on public policy.

Ascertaining the impact of social movement organization on policy was not the only goal of this chapter. Another equally important aim was to provide a picture of the organizational structure and development of ecology, antinuclear, and peace movements in the three countries. Unfortunately, due to lack of data, I can offer only an unbalanced comparison. Although I can account for the three movements in the United States, I can do so only for the ecology movement across the three countries. In spite of the partial character of this comparison, I am able to show that there exist important differences across movements and across countries. In particular, the ecology movement is the stronger of the three movements organizationally, while antinuclear and peace movements have a lower degree of formalization and institutionalization. At the same time, ecology movement organizations are stronger in the United States and even more so in Switzerland. Finally, organizational growth in Italy occurred later but more rapidly than in the other two countries. With this knowledge in mind, we can now go back to our main goal of testing the three interpretations of the policy impact of social movements.

Notes

1. In fact, while external support is often mentioned by resource mobilization theorists, this aspect is more thoroughly explored by proponents of the political process approach and especially by political opportunity theorists.

2. See Frey, Dietz, and Kalof (1992) for another overview of the criticisms addressed to Gamson's study. In a review essay, Zelditch (1978, 1517–19) made a particularly strong and detailed criticism of Gamson's study. He stressed in particular four main problems, both theoretical and methodological. First, he questioned the independence of the cases and pointed out that, for instance, a group's success may depend on the fate of other groups in the sample. The second problem has to do with the attribution of causality. The effectiveness of challenging groups depends not only on their internal characteristics or tactics but on external forces as well. Moreover, group-controlled variables and external factors may interact, leading to success or failure. Third, no distinction was made between the mobilization by challengers and that by members of the polity, hence producing a gap in the results, which has important theoretical implications with regard to legitimacy, a key concept in the book. Finally, like other critics, Zelditch pointed out the limits of the tabular method of analysis, particularly the weak variable control, the primitive measurement, and the small number of cases.

3. Most of the reanalyses have been included in the book's second edition (Frey, Dietz, and Kalof 1992; Goldstone 1980a; Mirowsky and Ross 1981; Steedly and Foley 1979). In addition, a study that did not reanalyze Gamson's data but built on his work was conducted by the Conflict Research Group of the European Consortium for Political Research (see Webb et al. 1983). This study shows, among other things, the usefulness of Gamson's work and, more generally, how further research on social movement outcomes can be built on previous works.

4. Emphasis in the original.

5. This implies that all four characteristics are necessary, since a value of zero in one of them would result in no strength at all.

6. The data shown in this table and in the figures in this chapter come from the *Encyclopedia of Associations* (United States) and from a questionnaire sent to selected organizations (Italy and Switzerland). The number of organizations included in the analyses varies across countries and across movements, depending among other things on the size of the country and the degree of formalization of the movement as well as, above all, the availability of information. This explains the higher number of organizations in the case of the United States, which has a population overwhelmingly higher than that of Italy and especially Switzerland; and in the case of the ecology movement, which is clearly the more formalized and professionalized movement. Furthermore, information on membership and financial resources of social movement organizations is much more easily accessible in the United States (where I could use an existing serial publication) than in the other two countries (where I had to send a questionnaire to individual organizations, whose response was not warranted). See appendix A for more details on the data collection concerning this aspect of the study.

7. Unfortunately, as I mentioned earlier, data on all three movements were available only in the case of the United States. In Italy, I was able to obtain information on ecology and, partly, peace organizations. In Switzerland, only data on the ecology movement were available. While this is in part due to the fact that the movements on which information is lacking are not very formalized and are poor in resources, it certainly prevents us from making a systematic cross-country comparison of all three movements. To have a basis for comparison across countries and

across movements, I nevertheless show the organizational development of the three movements in the United States (figures 6.1, 6.2, and 6.3) and of the ecology movement in Italy (figure 6.4) and in Switzerland (figure 6.5).

8. Once again, given the lack of information, the Italian and Swiss cases refer only to, respectively, the ecology and peace movements and the ecology movement.

CHAPTER SEVEN

~~~

Political Alliances

After having presented the three interpretations of the outcomes of social movements (direct, indirect, and joint-effect models), after having tested the first of these three models, and after having made an excursus on the organizational aspects of the movements under study, I would now like to discuss in more detail the two main external resources on which social movements can draw to increase their chances of success: *political alliances* and *public opinion*. This and the next chapter are devoted to these two aspects. In doing this, I test the indirect-effect model using the variant that looks at the roles of political alliances and public opinion. This chapter deals with political alliances as a first factor that might improve—or, conversely, deteriorate—the chances of success of social movements. The next chapter then deals with the role of public opinion.

The *structure of political alliances* is one element of the broader political opportunity structures for the mobilization of social movements. In the first part of the chapter, I discuss in some detail the literature on political opportunities, of course paying special attention to the role of allies among elite actors. Then I focus on the specific aspect of political alliances. To this purpose, I propose to distinguish between a formal and a substantive definition of elite support to social movements. The first refers to the configuration of power in the institutional system and hence looks at potential allies, while the second focuses on the actual behavior of elite allies.

The remainder of the chapter is devoted to the presentation and discussion of the empirical material collected on this aspect. In the process, it goes from the descriptive to the explanatory level. First, I examine the structure of political alliances for ecology, antinuclear, and peace movements in the three countries of the study, focusing in particular on potential and actual allies within the party arena. Next, I show the results of a time-series analysis in two stages. To begin, I consider the variant of the indirect-effect model of social movement outcomes that stresses the role of political alliances. This implies a separate analysis of the impact of political alliances on public policy. Then, I look at the joint-effect model, specifically its variant that treats political alliances as the most significant factor affecting the impact of social movements.

Political Opportunity Theory and the Role of Political Alliances

In spite of a return of the cultural dimension, first thanks to early proponents of the "framing" approach (e.g., Gamson 1992a, 1992b; Gamson, Fireman, and Rytina 1982; Snow and Benford 1992; Snow et al. 1986; see Benford and Snow 2000 for a review) and then through a number of more recent studies focusing on the role of culture and identity in social movements (e.g., Johnston and Klandermans 1995; Melucci 1996; Polletta 1997; see Polletta and Jasper 2001 for a review), much of the work done on social movements and contentious politics in the past few decades focuses on the concept of political opportunity structures. This concept was brought to the fore by the political process approach to social movements (e.g., Kriesi et al. 1995; McAdam 1982; McAdam, McCarthy, and Zald 1996; McAdam, Tarrow, and Tilly 2001; Tarrow 1998; Tilly 1978).

The political process approach maintains that processes of social change impinge indirectly on social protest, through a restructuring of existing power relations (McAdam 1982). In arguing so, it explicitly opposes classical theories of collective behavior, such as mass society (Kornhauser 1959); relative deprivation (Gurr 1970); and more generally collective behavior theories (Smelser 1962; Turner and Killian 1957), which stress a direct relationship between social change and protest. The fundamental tenets of the classical approaches—specifically, that structural social strains produce grievances that call for a response in the form of collective behavior—was first criticized by proponents of resource mobilization theory (e.g., Gamson 1990; McCarthy and Zald 1977; Oberschall 1973) who, as we saw in chapter 6, stress the role of organization and social networks.

Thus, while earlier explanations stress the role of grievances, discontent, deprivation, or social anomie for the emergence of collective action and the rise of protest, the political process approach looks at certain aspects of the political context of social movements that mediate structural conflicts given as latent political potentials. The concept of political opportunity structures has now become the main analytical tool to capture these aspects of the political context of movements. First introduced by Eisinger (1973) to study the relationship between the degree of institutional access of American cities and the 1960s riots, this concept was later elaborated by a number of authors who used it to study the impact of political–institutional factors on protest behavior (e.g., Brockett 1991; Costain 1992; Kitschelt 1986; Kriesi et al. 1992, 1995; Meyer 1990; Tarrow 1989, 1998; see also, McAdam, McCarthy, and Zald 1996).

Political opportunity structures can be defined in general terms as "*consistent—but not necessarily formal, permanent, or national—signals to social or political actors which either encourage or discourage them to use their internal resources to form social movements*" (Tarrow 1996, 54).[1] This broad definition indirectly refers to various aspects of the movements' context, which affects people's expectations for the success or failure of collective action and which either increases or decreases the social and political costs of mobilization; however, the numerous dimensions of political opportunity structures found in the extant literature can be summarized in a few main dimensions. McAdam (1996, 27) has proposed to distinguish among the following four aspects:

1. the relative openness or closure of the institutionalized political system;
2. the stability or instability of that broad set of elite alignments that typically undergird a polity;
3. the presence or absence of elite allies; and
4. the state's capacity and propensity for repression.

While some of these aspects are rather stable, such as the institutional structure of the state, others are more volatile and are subject to shifts over time, such as the configuration of power among elite actors. It is on these more volatile aspects that I focus in my study on the policy impact of social movements. Specifically, I look into the role of the third of the four aspects mentioned by McAdam: the presence or absence of elite allies. This is part of the more general configuration of power of a political system, which has been underscored in particular by the conceptualization of the political opportunity structures proposed by Tarrow (1989, 1998) and which Kriesi and colleagues (1995) have summarized under the term *alliance structures*.

Like Kriesi and colleagues (1995), who in their study of new social movements in Western European countries focus on two aspects that are of particular relevance for the type of movements they have studied—the configuration of power on the Left and the presence or absence of the Left in the government—I also restrict my attention to certain, more specific aspects of the alliance structures. Specifically, since ecology, antinuclear, and peace movements all belong to the family of the new social movements,[2] I look in particular at the role played by the parties on the Left as potential institutional allies. Later, I discuss in more detail the issue of what can be considered the "Left" and therefore the potential allies of ecology, antinuclear, and peace movements in the three countries of my study; furthermore, I elaborate on my empirical analysis of this aspect of the political opportunity structures. Here I would like to say a little more on the role played by these allies for the policy impact of social movements.

In Kriesi and colleagues' perspective (1995, ch. 3), the Social-Democratic Party is the main potential ally of the new social movements, as they share a similar constituency, whose core is formed by a sector of the new middle class (Kriesi 1989). However, the support the new social movements actually receive depends on the degree of pacification of the Left and its position with regard to and within the government. First, facilitation is higher when the Left is pacified, because in such a situation the Socialists do not have to subordinate their support to the struggle for the hegemony on the Left. Second, facilitation is more likely to be forthcoming when the Socialists are in the opposition, since they can profit from the challenges that the movements address to the government, and they can exploit their mobilization to build a large electoral basis.[3]

When we look at movement impact instead of mobilization capacity, however, this perspective must be modified. To have a substantial policy impact, social movements need allies who are responsive and who are in a position to be able to reform existing policies. Allies in the opposition represent an opportunity for the movement mobilization; however, when they are in government, they can bring the movements' demands into the political system and, especially if they have a strong position in the executive, they can meet those demands, provided they have the interest to do so. The same applies to the legislative arena, which is the place where laws are enacted. Other things being equal, the higher the share of seats held by the movements' allies in the parliament, the higher the chances that these allies will enact laws that reflect the movements' aims.

Thus, according to this view, to have a substantial impact on public policy, social movements need the support of powerful political allies who are able to take up the movements' claims in institutional arenas (Tarrow 1998). They need alliances with major parties who share the movements' goals and objectives. This theory implies an elitist view of democracy, according to which public policies stem from political elites and hence follow a top-down path. When the stimulus for change comes from below, it must be taken up by members of the polity—that is, political elites—to translate into policy changes and reform. This perspective is shared, implicitly or explicitly, by a number of authors who have argued that the impact of social movements on public policy depends on the presence of political allies within the institutional arenas who are willing to support the movements' claims and bring about policy changes that meet their demands. However, it is not so important here whether they do so for ideological or strategic reasons, as in Tarrow's (1993) example about the French student movement (see chapter 5). What counts is that there is no direct translation of protest into policy changes. If they are to succeed in influencing public policy, social movements must be backed by insiders. This is what comes out of works by Amenta, Carruthers, and Zylan (1992); Jenkins and Perrow (1977); Lipsky (1968); Schumaker (1975, 1978); Tarrow (1993, 1998); and many others. It is one variant of what I call the indirect-effect model of social movement outcomes.

The Structure of Political Alliances for Ecology, Antinuclear, and Peace Movements in the Three Countries

As I mentioned earlier, Kriesi and colleagues (1995) maintain that the Socialist-Democratic Party is the main potential institutional ally of the new social movements, including ecology, antinuclear, and peace movements, for they share a similar, new middle-class constituency. While this may apply to the countries studied by these authors (France, Germany, Switzerland, and the Netherlands), in the case of Italy the main ally of the new social movements is not represented by the Socialists but rather by the former Communist Party (della Porta 1996). It is this party that has most often supported the claims made by ecology, antinuclear, and peace movements. In addition, these movements are often supported by the smaller parties of the New Left, both in Italy and Switzerland. Here, however, I would like to focus on the most powerful institutional allies, in particular, the largest party of the Left. Yet, the meanings of "Left" and "Right" change according to the country at hand. This is all the more true when we compare Western European countries with other political contexts, such as that of the United States, which is characterized by a different history and a different cleavage structure. For example, to speak of the Left makes little sense in the American context, at least as far as the institutional arenas are concerned. In such a context, the major division relevant for my present purpose is not that between Left and Right—the former being closer to the constituencies and aims of the three movements studied—but rather that between liberals and conservative political forces, wherein the former certainly tend to be closer to ecology, antinuclear, and peace movements than the latter and hence more likely to support them. Thus, here I focus on the position of the Democratic Party in the United States, of the Communist Party in Italy, and the Socialist Party in Switzerland.

The Italian case requires some additional remarks. After long internal discussions, the Communist Party changed its name in 1992, becoming the Democratic Party of the Left. Shortly after this change, which was not simply cosmetic but also implied a shift to a more social–democratic stance, an internal scission led to the creation of the Party for Communist Refoundation. Thus, there are, after 1992, two legitimate descendants of the former Communist Party: a more social–democratic one, which later formed the main element of a center-left coalition that governed the country between 1996 and 2001; and one faithful to the value and political orientation of communism.[4]

These changes complicate the picture for Italy and may introduce a sort of bias, to the extent that the new Communist Party is the one that is closer to the three movements studied as well as to other movements, not only the labor movement, of course, but also the nonglobal groups and other groups of the civil society. As I said, however, to be able to substantially support the movements' claims and help them to reach their policy goals, a party must have a "critical mass" in the parliament, which is not the case for the Party of Communist Refoundation. The latter might contribute to the movements' mobilization, but its role for translating their claims into policy changes is less important. In any event, to have a more complete view of the potential support given to the three movements under study, I look both at the main party of the "Left" and at the position of the entire Left.[5] I consider in particular their position within the respective national parliaments as expressed through the proportion of seats held by these parties. The underlying assumption is that the stronger their position in the parliament (but also, especially in the United States, in the government), the higher the chances that they support the movements' claims.

Measuring the structure of political alliances through the formal configuration of power to a large extent rests on the idea that parties that are ideologically or socially closer to the movements will automatically support their claims. Yet, nothing assures us that this actually occurs, although we can be quite confident that this assumption has some foundation. A more direct way to operationalize this aspect would consist in looking at the actual behavior of elite actors vis-à-vis the demands made by the movements. Thus, in addition to the formal measure of political alliances, I also consider the presence of political allies in the public domain as a substantive measure of political alliances by looking at the number of public statements by elite actors on the issues addressed by ecology, antinuclear, and peace movements.[6] Of course, formal and substantive alliances may not necessarily correspond, as pro-movement statements may be made by actors other than the members of the Democratic Party. Unfortunately, this kind of data was gathered only in the case of the United States, which prevents me from using this measure for the cases of Italy and Switzerland.

To summarize, ecology, antinuclear, and peace movements have a structure of political alliances within the institutional arenas. The major party of the Left and, more generally, the whole leftist political family are the main potential allies of these movements. In the United States, whose political context is quite different from that of Western Europe, the Democratic Party can be considered a functional equivalent of the (former) Communist Party in Italy and the Socialist Party in Switzerland. To capture the importance of the alliance structure of the three movements, I look at the strength of these parties in the legislative arena. In addition, in the case of the United States, I look at the substantial support provided by elite actors in the public domain. With this simple framework in mind, we can now have a closer look at how the structure of political alliances of ecology, antinuclear, and peace movements has changed during the period under study in the three countries.

Changes in the Structure of Political Alliances

In addition to proposing a longitudinal and interactive approach to study and interpret the impact of social movements on public policy, one of the aims of this book is to provide an overview of the ecology, antinuclear, and peace movements as well as their contexts in the United States, Italy, and Switzerland. The important contextual aspects are political alliances and public opinion, which at the same time represent the two major resources on which movements can rely to improve their chances to bring about policy changes, at least according to the view put forward here. Therefore, in addition to showing the development of the movements' mobilization (chapter 3) and organization (chapter 6), including their respective effects on public policy (chapter 4) and public opinion (chapter 8), here I would like to do the same with regard to the structure of political alliances.

Yet, it is not only interesting to show the patterns of alliances and how they changed over time or to know what happened on this front in the three countries at hand; it is also an important step in the study of the policy impact of the movements. Knowing how the structure of political alliances has changed allows us to better interpret the findings of the time-series analysis preformed in the following. Therefore, I briefly discuss the development of the configuration of power within the institutional arenas—specifically, in the national parliament—in the three countries; and, in the case of the United States, I discuss changes in the presence of elite actors in the public domain on the issues addressed by the three movements.

Table 7.1. Distribution of Democratic Party's Seats in the U.S. Congress, 1975–1995 (percentages)

	House	Senate	Total
1975–1976	67	61	66
1977–1978	67	62	66
1979–1980	64	59	63
1981–1982	56	47	54
1983–1984	62	46	59
1985–1986	58	47	56
1987–1988	59	55	59
1989–1990	60	55	59
1991–1992	61	56	60
1993–1994	59	57	59
1995	47	48	47

Note: Number of Democratic seats over the total number of seats (435 in the House of Representatives, 100 in the Senate, 535 in the entire Congress). Figures are rounded by excess.

United States

Table 7.1 shows how the relevant power was configured for the alliance structure of ecology, antinuclear, and peace movements in the United States; how it operationalized through the share of seats of the Democratic Party in Congress; and how it has been modified between 1975 and 1995. To have as complete a picture as possible, I show separate distributions for the two branches of Congress—the House of Representatives and the Senate—as well as totals for both.

Assuming that the Democratic Party is closer to the three movements studied than the Republican Party, a statement that is only a gross approximation of reality, we can say that, broadly speaking, the situation looks relatively favorable to these movements. In the House, Democrats have held the majority during the whole period except in 1995, when the party suffered one of the most burning defeats in recent history. In the Senate, the party had the majority between 1975 and 1980, and again between 1987 and 1994. As a result, Democrats had been leading Congress during the entire 1975–1995 period except in 1995.

Of course, in addition to the configuration of power in the legislative branch, one must also look at the executive branch, especially in a political system such as the American, in which the president is so powerful. From this point of view, the situation is less positive, for between Carter's and Clinton's Democratic presidencies (respectively, 1976–1980, 1993–2000), there were Reagan's and Bush's less-movement-friendly Republican administrations (respectively, 1981–1988, 1989–1992), to which we should add Ford's replacement of President Nixon, in 1975.

On the whole, if we take into account the configuration of power in both the legislative and executive branches,[7] the structure of formal political alliances for ecology, antinuclear, and peace movements in the United States was more favorable in the

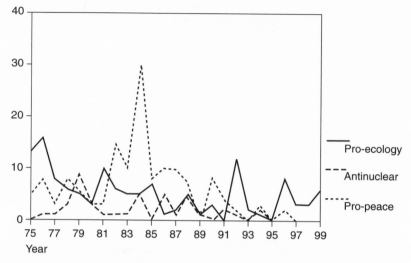

Figure 7.1. Pro-Movement Statements in the United States.

late 1970s, quite unfavorable up to the mid-1980s, relatively unfavorable in the late 1980s and early 1990s, and quite favorable in the mid-1990s (but not in 1995).

Yet, as I mentioned earlier, the formal configuration of power is only one side of the structure of elite support to social movements. To have the full picture, one should also look at the substantive measure of political alliances. To grasp this side of the alliance structure, figure 7.1 depicts the development of pro-ecology, antinuclear, and pro-peace statements publicly made by elite actors in the United States for the 1975–1999 period. Although measurement suffers from the potential bias due to the sampling method adopted in the data gathering, it nevertheless gives us a useful indicator of the actual support by elite actors to the three movements under study.

If we compare these distributions with those of the number of unconventional protest events carried by the three movements (see figures 3.1a, 3.1b, and 3.1c, in chapter 3), we can see that, generally speaking, movement mobilization and public support of elite actors for their cause follow similar developments, although the statistical correlation between the two distributions is not always strong and significant.[8] First, ecology protests and public statements reached their highest level in the mid-1970s, declined somewhat in the late 1970s, and then resumed in the early 1980s. Unlike the movement's mobilization, however, which displays an upward pattern during the years of the Republican administrations, elite statements have tended to slowly decline. They peaked again in 1992, during the presidential campaign in which the pro-environment Clinton–Gore ticket put a great deal of effort in stressing these kinds of issues; in addition, it went up in 1996 and 1999. Second, antinuclear statements by elite actors presented the same peak in 1979 as the movement's mobilization, but on a much lower scale. This was mainly a reaction to the accident at the Three Mile Island nuclear power plant, which provoked much concern among politicians but even more so among the population at large. After that year, antinuclear statements have followed a fluctuating pattern but always at lower levels. Third, the development of pro-peace elite statements quite aptly reflects that of the movement's mobilization. In both cases, we observe a large wave of public interventions in the early 1980s (in two times), a second but much lower peak in the mid-1980s, and a third larger increase in 1991. These three phases of public and political concern on peace-related issues deal, respectively, with the arms race (in particular, the nuclear weapons freeze proposal), the American intervention in Central America, and the Gulf War.

If we get a closer look at these distributions, we can note two interesting patterns. The first one refers to the timing of elite intervention in the public domain. The most intense public intervention by institutional actors often occurs in election years, especially in presidential election years. For example, pro-ecology statements peaked in 1976, 1992, and 1996, when two pro-environmental presidential candidates (Carter and Clinton) took the opportunity provided by the campaign to assert their position on these issues. This was most evident in the 1992 and 1996 elections, when the presidential ticket included Al Gore, a prominent environmentalist politician. Similarly, antinuclear statements, apart from the rise in 1979 related to the Three Mile Island accident, were more frequent in 1984 and 1988, but also in 1986, a midterm election year. Finally, the political use of certain issues by elites is perhaps most flagrant in the case of peace issues in the 1984 election. In that year, the nuclear issue was at the forefront of public debates, above all thanks to the activities carried out by the freeze movement during the preceding years. The 1984 presidential election was indeed conducted under the banner of arms control and disarmament issues. All the candidates included in their speeches statements about these themes, including (to a much lesser extent) nuclear energy.

Thus, during years of political campaigning, politicians are busy running across the country in search for votes at the primaries. Since a great many of the public statements reported in the figure were made by candidates at campaign meetings, it comes as no surprise that these events increase in election years, when candidates address salient public issues. However, public statements by elite actors do not increase simply as a result of purely strategic calculations by candidates during election years. They also rise when specific issues become salient, independent of contingent institutional opportunities such as elections.

This brings me to a second interesting pattern, which comes out of a comparison between the development of public statements by elite actors and that of the movements' mobilization. The distribution of public statements often follows that of protest actions, suggesting a causal path from the latter to the former. Again, this is most striking in the case of the peace movement. The peak of peace movement activities was reached in 1982. At that time, the Nuclear Weapons Freeze Campaign, launched in 1979 from within the movement ranks, was brought to the fore through impressive mobilizations and strong support by mainstream politicians (see chapter 3). The number of public statements by elite actors rose parallel to the movement's mobilization (we should not forget that midterm elections occurred in 1982). However, the most dramatic increase occurred in 1984, at a time when the movement's mobilization was already declining. This pattern suggests a complex relationship between social movements and institutional politics, and more specifically between movements and their institutional allies. In the case at hand, it is likely that the peace movement has brought the nuclear freeze issue to the fore, first through relentless work of consciousness raising, then through mass mobilizations. Soon the freeze issue was integrated into mainstream politics and became a matter for congressional debates (Meyer 1990). Then, when the movement had already abandoned the issue, at least in part and in terms of mass demonstrations, mainstream politicians took it up and made it a crucial theme in the 1984 presidential elections.

Italy

After having discussed in detail changes in the formal and substantive structure of political alliances in the United States, let us have a brief look at the configuration of power in the Italian and Swiss parliaments. As I said, for these two countries, I can only look at the formal side of alliances, as I did not gather information on the public statements by elite actors. For the case of Italy's parliament, between 1975 and 1995, table 7.2 shows the development of the share of seats held by the major leftist party (first the Communist Party; then its center-left descendant, the Democratic Party of the Left), respectively by the whole sector of the Left (including the Greens).

With regard to the configuration of power in the executive and legislative arenas, the period under study divides into two distinct phases separated by a fundamental change in Italian politics. The first phase covers nearly the whole period and is characterized by the presence of a proportional electoral system in which executive power was predominantly shared by a grand coalition of four or five parties from all sides of the political spectrum and in which the leadership of the government was mostly in the hands of the Christian Democrats, or (during the mid-1980s) the Socialists.[9] The

Table 7.2.   Distribution of Leftist Parties' Seats in the Italian Parliament, 1975–1995 (percentages)

	Left Parties			Communist Party		
	Chamber	Senate	Total	Chamber	Senate	Total
1975	42	44	43	28	25	27
1976–1978	47	49	48	35	31	34
1979–1982	47	38	44	31	30	30
1983–1986	48	49	49	28	28	28
1987–1991	50	49	50	25	26	25
1992–1993	45	42	44	17	20	18
1994–1995	33	38	35	27	26	26

Note: Number of leftist seats (left-hand side) and Communist seats (right-hand side) over the total number of seats (630 in the Chamber, 315 in the Senate, 945 in the entire Parliament). Figures are rounded by excess. Communist seats include the Partito Comunista Italiano (PCI) until 1991, the Partito Democratico della Sinistra (PDS) in 1992–1993, and Progressisti Federativo and Sinistra Democratica in 1994–1995.

second phase includes the years starting from 1993, when a degree of majority rule was introduced in the electoral system after a referendum asking for that was accepted the year before.

If we look at the development over time of the share of seats held by the Left (left-hand side of the table), we can see that the most favorable situation for the three movements studied occurred in the 1976–1978 period and then in the 1983–1991 period, when the Left controlled half of the parliament (or nearly so). The first period coincided with the heyday of the Communist Party, while the second period was characterized by a particularly strong Socialist Party, which moreover led the government for a large portion of that historical phase. However, the least favorable situation occurred in the last two years of the period, when the number of parliamentary seats of the Left fell to little more than one-third.

The picture is somewhat different if we take only the Communist Party (right-hand side of the table). Here the 1976–1978 period remains the most favorable, but the electoral strength of this party progressively declined, to reach its lowest level in years 1992–1993, just after the former Communist Party changed its name—and political orientation, now more social-democratic—to the Democratic Party of the Left and underwent a division with the creation of the Party for Communist Refoundation. It was only in the 1994–1995 period that the Democratic Party of the Left regained votes, so much so that it won the 1995 elections in a center-left coalition that ruled the country between 1996 and 2001.

A peculiarity of the Italian political system relevant to our present purpose is that the main party of the Left—first the Communist Party and then the Democratic Party of the Left—remained out of the governmental coalition in spite of the high share of votes it consistently gained in national elections. It finally entered the government for the first time in history as part of a center-left coalition in 1996, that is, after the end of the period I am focusing on here. In the perspective of Kriesi and colleagues' political opportunity theory (1995), this absence from the executive power should have provided our three movements with a strong political ally to help facilitate their mobilization. However, being outside the executive arena, the party could not meet the movements' demands (provided it shared them) by taking certain measures going in the direction of the movements' aims.

Switzerland

With direct democracy, federalism, and neutrality (Kriesi 1995b), stability is one of the main features of Swiss politics. Yet, in spite of this undeniable characteristic, the configuration of power relevant to the mobilization and outcomes of ecology, antinuclear, and peace movements has not always remained the same. Some shifts can be observed, especially in the electoral strength of the Socialist Party. For the case of Switzerland's parliament, between 1975 and 1995, table 7.3 shows the development of the share of seats held by the major leftist party (the Socialist Party) and by the whole sector of the Left (including the Greens).

The number of parliamentary seats held by the Left has indeed remained rather stable for the period being considered, ranging between 25 and 29 percent. The best

Table 7.3.   Distribution of Leftist Parties' Seats in the Swiss Parliament, 1975–1995 (percentages)

	Left Parties			Socialist Party		
	National Council	Council of States	Total	National Council	Council of States	Total
1975–1978	30	11	27	28	11	25
1979–1982	29	20	27	26	20	24
1983–1986	28	13	25	24	13	22
1987–1990	28	11	25	21	11	19
1991–1994	30	7	25	21	7	18
1995	34	11	29	27	11	24

Note: Number of leftist seats (left-hand side) and of Socialist seats (right-hand side) over the total number of seats (200 on the National Council, 46 in the Council of States, 246 in the entire Parliament). Figures are rounded by excess. Until 1978, the total seats in the Council of States equaled 44 because the Canton of Jura did not exist yet.

situation, in this respect, occurred in 1995. However, we should note the important difference between the two branches of the parliament. While the Left forms about one-third of the National Council, it hardly goes beyond one-tenth of the Council of States except in the years 1979 to 1982. This can be explained by the different nature of the two chambers, with the latter representing the cantons and being elected with the majority system, which does not favor the smaller parties. As a whole and beyond minor fluctuation from one legislature to the other, the Left has never had the majority in the Swiss parliament.

The same, of course, holds for the Socialist Party, the main party of the Left in Switzerland. Since this party represents the majority of the entire Left in this country, the development of its parliamentary seats to a large extent reflects that of the Left in general. Thus, its presence in the parliament was stronger in the first part of the period being considered and in 1995, while it weakened somewhat between 1987 and 1994.

Stability is most evident in the executive realm. Here, the Swiss political system is characterized by the so-called magic formula, which exists since 1959, according to which executive power is shared by a grand coalition including the four major parties.[10] Thus, the Socialists, which represent the Left in this coalition, are in a minority position within a largely bourgeois coalition. If this ambivalent position might prove favorable in some cases to the mobilization of the new social movements (Kriesi et al. 1995), then it is not fully instrumental for the movements' policy impact, although this situation is better than one in which their main potential ally is completely alien to the executive power.

Social Movements, Political Alliances, and Public Policy: Indirect Effects

After having outlined the changes in the structure of political alliances of ecology, antinuclear, and peace movements in each country, we can now address the question which is at the core of this book. We have seen in chapter 5 that the three movements had only a limited impact on public policy, leading to a rejection of the direct-effect model of social movement outcomes. It is now time to assess the explanatory power of the indirect-effect model, both in its political alliances and public opinion variants. Here I examine the former variant, while the latter is addressed in chapter 8. I do so with the help of the data described here concerning the formal configuration of power in the three countries and the public statements by political elites on environmental, nuclear energy, and peace issues in the United States.

This variant of the indirect-effect model posits that social movements influence the attitudes and behaviors of elite actors; then policy change occurs, owing to the impact of the latter on the decision-making process. Thus, the indirect-effect model implies a two-step procedure: first, it examines the relationship between protest and allies; then it looks at that between the alliance structure and public policy. For the sake of presentations, I look at this process the other way around—that is, first the effect of allies on policy, then the effect of protest on allies. Providing evidence bearing on the first step, table 7.4 shows the effect of the configuration of power on the five indicators of policies targeted by ecology, antinuclear, and peace movements in the three countries studied here.

In the case of the United States, I am using both the indicator of formal configuration of power and the indicator of substantial alliances (which consists of promovement statements). Environmental policy seems to be associated with the share of the Democratic Party in Congress, as both indicators (those at the national and the local level) display statistically significant coefficients with a positive sign. This is in line with the general stance of this party, which is more pro-environment than the Republican Party. Indeed, the overview provided in chapter 4 already shows that spending for environmental protection tends to increase under Democratic administrations (see table 4.1). Here we have confirmation through time-series analysis. In contrast, no positive effect can be observed in the areas of nuclear energy and national defense. The coefficient concerning the number of construction permits for new nuclear power plants is statistically significant but with a positive sign, indicating a relationship that goes opposite to the goals of the antinuclear movement.

The ecology movement is also the only one profiting from the presence of its potential institutional allies, this time not in the parliament but in the public domain. As we can see in the table, pro-ecology statements are positively associated with changes in spending for environmental protection at the local level (with a strong though nonsignificant coefficient for national-level spending). Of course, the presence of the party in Congress and its public statements on environmental issues are in part correlated, as it is likely that, at least to some extent, what party representatives say publicly is reflected in the policy position they take within the legislative arena.

The situation does not look favorable to the three movements in the cases of Italy and Switzerland. Since I did not collect data on the public statements by elite actors to measure the structure of political alliances in these two countries, I must rely on the formal indicator of power. Specifically, I regressed my indicators of policy change on two measures of configuration of power: by the percentage of seats held in parliament

Table 7.4. Effect of Configuration of Power on Public Policy in Three Countries, 1975–1995

Dependent Variables	Spending for Environmental Protection (National) (t_1)	Spending for Environmental Protection (Local) (t_1)	Nuclear Energy Production (t_1)	Number of Construction Permits (t_1)	Spending for Defense (t_1)
United States					
Percentage of Democratic seats in Congress (t_0)	.44*	.47**	.05	.67***	−.25
(D-W)	(1.96)	(2.13)	(1.92)	(1.99)	(1.99)
N	20	20	20	20	20
Pro-movement statements (t_0)	.37	.44*	−.24	.00	.09
(D-W)	(1.90)	(1.99)	(1.95)	(2.15)	(1.94)
N	20	20	20	20	20
Italy					
Percentage of leftist seats in parliament	−.23	—	−.20	—	−.09
(D-W)	(1.99)	—	(2.00)	—	(1.96)
N	20	—	20	—	20

Italy (cont.)

Percentage of (former) communist seats in parliament	−.05	—	.04	.03
(D-W)	(1.95)	—	(2.00)	(1.96)
N	20	—	20	20
Switzerland				
Percentage of leftist seats in parliament	−.40*	−.02	.22	.35
(D-W)	(2.28)	(2.00)	(1.95)	(1.92)
N	20	20	20	20
Percentage of socialist seats in parliament	−.38	.09	.33	.36
(D-W)	(2.29)	(2.00)	(1.99)	(1.89)
N	20	20	20	20

Note: Standardized regression coefficients (bivariate) generated with a generalized least-squared method of estimation (Prais–Winsten) assuming a first-order autoregressive process. Durbin–Watson test for serial correlation and number of observations (series length) are shown within parentheses. The independent variables include a one-year lag. The dependent variables are expressed in terms of annual percentage change.
*p < .10; **p < .05; ***p < .01.

Table 7.5. Effect of Unconventional Mobilization on Pro-movement Statements in the United States, 1975–1995

Dependent Variables	Pro-ecology Statements (t_1)	Antinuclear Statements (t_1)	Pro-peace Statements (t_1)
Unconventional mobilization (t_0)	.11	−.23	.45*
(D-W)	(2.19)	(2.09)	(2.21)
N	20	20	20

Note: Standardized regression coefficients (bivariate) generated with a generalized least-squared method of estimation (Prais-Winsten) assuming a first-order autoregressive process. Durbin-Watson test for serial correlation and number of observations (series length) are shown within parentheses. The independent variables include a one-year lag. The dependent variables are differenced.
*$p < .10$; **$p < .05$; ***$p < .01$.

by leftist parties; and by the principal potential ally of the three movements examined, namely, the Communist Party in Italy and the Socialist Party in Switzerland. None of the regression coefficients are found to be statistically significant, except for the one relating leftist seats' environmental spending at the national level in Switzerland. Yet, once again, the negative sign of the coefficient does not allow us to consider this an effect favorable to the ecology movement.

The impact of political alliances on public policy is even weaker when we look at differenced independent variables (see table B7.4, in appendix B). In this case, no coefficient overall is statistically significant. Thus, in general, the institutional allies of ecology, antinuclear, and peace movements did not significantly affect the policies targeted by these movements in the short run.

To assess the explanatory power of this variant of the indirect-effect model, we must make the second step and look at the impact of protest on political alliances. Table 7.5 does so for the case of the United States. I am forced to limit my analysis to this country since it would not be plausible to look at the impact of protest on the formal configuration of power; for it is hard to imagine that protest is so powerful as to modify the power balance in the parliamentary arena in the short or medium term. In contrast, it is much more plausible that they may affect the strategic stance and the policy position of elite actors in the public domain. I must therefore rely on our crude measure of the substantial configuration of power.

The results point to a lack of impact by the ecology and antinuclear movements, while a statistically significant coefficient can be observed in the case of the peace movement. Regarding the last, it should be stressed that national security and defense are salient issues that often become the object of a "framing struggle" among political elites. When a strong mobilization occurs on such issues, elites take them up in the public space, a phenomenon that becomes particularly intense during electoral campaigns. It is probably in this sense that this relationship has to be interpreted. For example, this was clearly the case in 1984, when the arms race issue was at the center of the debates during the presidential election that offered Reagan a second mandate. As I said earlier, peace issues in 1984 were at center stage in public debates, above all thanks to the activities carried out by the nuclear weapons freeze campaign during the preceding years. Elite actors took an active role in these debates, above all due to electoral reasons.

The analyses with differenced independent variables provide the same results, which are thus strengthened (see table B7.5, in appendix B). They suggest once again that only the peace movement was able to influence the public statements by political elites on issues pertaining to its policy areas, be it on purpose or as a by-product of its activities.[11]

If we now combine the two steps of the analysis to provide an overall assessment of the indirect-effect model of social movement outcomes, though limited to the case of the United States, we can conclude that the variant that stresses the intervening role of political alliances shows no consistent pattern. A larger presence of the main institutional ally of the ecology movement, both within the parliamentary arena and in the public domain, might increase the policy efforts aimed at protecting the environment; but there is no evidence that the movement's mobilization is instrumental in shaping the policy position of the Democratic Party on environmental matters. However, the peace movement influences in some way the position of the party on peace issues, but defense policy does not seem to be substantially affected by changes in the structure of political alliances. Finally, in the case of the antinuclear movement, neither of the two steps displays a significant effect that would suggest a policy impact of the movement. Do these factors—protest and political alliances— have a stronger effect when they mutually reinforce each other? This is what I examine next.

Social Movements, Political Alliances, and Public Policy: Joint Effects

Remember the subtle but substantial difference between the indirect-effect model and the joint-effect model of social movements outcomes? The former implies a two-stage process: first, movements influence the attitudes and behaviors of their potential political allies within the institutional arenas by engaging in protest activities; then the allies use their power to produce policy changes that meet the movements' aims and demands. The latter posits that these two factors—protest and political alliances— occur together, thus reinforcing each other. In a way, according to this variant of the model, both movements and elite actors may take advantage of the presence of their counterpart. The empirical question here is to what extent this has occurred in the case of ecology, antinuclear, and peace movements in the United States, Italy, and Switzerland between 1975 and 1995.

Table 7.6 shows, for each country, the results of time-series analysis of the relationship between the interactive terms combining protest and political alliances, as well as the five indicators of public policy. In the case of the United States, I created two interactive terms: one using the formal measure of configuration of power, the other using pro-movement statements. For the other two countries I took the formal configuration of power in the parliament.[12] Admittedly, this is a crude way to operationalize

Table 7.6. Joint Effect of Unconventional Mobilization and Political Alliances on Public Policy in Three Countries, 1975–1995

Dependent Variables	Spending for Environmental Protection (National) (t_1)	Spending for Environmental Protection (Local) (t_1)	Nuclear Energy Production (t_1)	Number of Construction Permits (t_1)	Spending for Defense (t_1)
United States					
Movement * allies 1 (t_0)	.04	−.17	−.32	−.07	.45*
(D-W)	(1.92)	(1.91)	(1.97)	(2.15)	(1.87)
N	20	20	20	20	20
Movement * allies 2 (t_0)	.48**	.37	−.29	−.14	.32
(D-W)	(1.93)	(2.04)	(1.99)	(2.16)	(1.90)
N	20	20	20	20	20
Italy					
Movement * allies (t_0)	.21	—	−.49**	—	.22
(D-W)	(1.92)	—	(2.02)	—	(2.02)
N	20	—	20	—	20
Switzerland					
Movement * allies (t_0)	.22	.45*	.52**	—	−.33
(D-W)	(2.13)	(1.97)	(1.91)	—	(1.90)
N	20	20	20	—	20

Note: Standardized regression coefficients (bivariate) generated with a generalized least-squared method of estimation (Prais-Winsten) assuming a first-order autoregressive process. Durbin-Watson test for serial correlation and number of observations (series length) are shown within parentheses. The independent variables include a one-year lag. The dependent variables are expressed in terms of annual percentage change. See appendix A for a full description of the interactive terms.
*$p < .10$; **$p < .05$; ***$p < .01$.

the joint effect, especially in the Italian and Swiss cases, but some interesting patterns can nevertheless be discerned.

The findings are less supportive of this first variant of the joint-effect model than expected. In the United States, we observe a statistically significant relationship between the first interactive term and the governmental spending for national defense. Once again, however, the positive sign of the coefficient counters the goals of the peace movement. There is also a significant relationship between the second interactive term and the spending for environmental protection at the national level. In this case, we can conclude that a joint effect has occurred, as the sign of the coefficient goes in the right direction. This is all the more true to the extent that neither ecology protests nor pro-ecology statements by elite actors display a direct impact on national environmental policy (see figure 5.1, in chapter 5; and figure 7.1).

In Italy, too, we observe one significant relationship, namely, for the antinuclear movement; and the negative sign of the coefficient attests to the presence of a joint effect. Yet, even without considering the problematic situation produced by the skewed distribution of the dependent variable that I mentioned earlier, here the joint effect occurs with a direct effect of the movement (see figure 5.1, in chapter 5). No joint effect, in contrast, occurs for the ecology and peace movements.

Finally, in Switzerland, the interactive terms concerning the ecology and antinuclear movements display significant coefficients; but, if we look at its sign, only the one for the ecology movement implies a joint effect on policy, specifically, on local environmental spending. Once again, however, if we confront this finding with the direct effect of ecology protests (see figure 5.1, in chapter 5), we can conclude that the position of institutional allies does not add to the movement's capability to have an impact on public policy.

The general conclusion that we can draw from these analyses—that the first variant of the joint-effect model of social movement outcomes has less explanatory power than expected—is strengthened when we look at the regressions with differenced independent variables (see table B7.6, in appendix B), as no statistically significant relationship can be observed in this case.[13] I explore the second variant of this model in the next chapter, the one positing that the policy impact of protest activities is boosted by the presence of a favorable public opinion. Before I address this issue, however, I would like to make some general conclusions about the role of political alliances for the impact of social movements on public policy.

Conclusion

Political opportunity structures have emerged in recent years as one of the main explanatory factors accounting for the emergence, mobilization, and outcomes of social movements. A growing number of studies have shown the significant impact of such aspects of the political environment of movements as the openness or closure of the institutionalized political system, the stability or instability of elite alignments, the presence or absence of elite allies, and the state's capacity and propensity for repression. In this chapter, I focus on the third of these four dimensions of political opportunities to inquire in a comparative perspective to what extent ecology, antinuclear, and peace movements were able to take advantage of the presence of political allies within the institutional arenas to reach their aims and to have their demands met. Accordingly, I first discuss scholarly work that examines the role of allies among elite actors. I then discuss all too cursorily the structure of political alliances for ecology, antinuclear, and peace movements in the three countries under study, focusing in particular on the formal configuration of power in parliament and, in the case of the United States, on the public statements made by elite actors on the issues addressed by the three movements. In line with the longitudinal approach of this book, I pay particular attention to changes over time in the structure of political alliances. Finally, I continue my exploration of the policy impact of the three movements by looking at the variants of the indirect-effect and joint-effect models, which stress the role of political alliances for social movement outcomes.

The results suggest that the presence of political allies within the institutional arenas may increase the chances of social movements' success, but not to the extent expected. First of all, no consistent evidence was found about the presence of an indirect effect of protest and political alliances. Unfortunately, in examining the indirect effect of the movements, I had to limit my analysis to the United States, due to lack of data. Therefore, nothing can be concluded about the other two countries. Second, a joint effect can be observed, but it is limited to the ecology movement and it is not found in Italy, that is, if we exclude the problematic finding concerning the Italian antinuclear movement. At this stage, however, it is too early to draw definitive conclusions on the explanatory power of the indirect-effect and joint-effect models, as compared to the direct-effect model. We still have to go further down the path that will lead us to a more general and consistent assessment of the policy impact of ecology, antinuclear, and peace movements. In particular, we must consider the role of the public opinion in this process.

Notes

1. Emphasis in the original.

2. Certain authors prefer to speak of a "left-libertarian" movement family (della Porta and Rucht 1995), instead of new social movements.

3. Kriesi and colleagues' theory (1995) is more complex than depicted here, as they also consider, among other things, the distinction between the old Left and the "New Left" (including the Green Party), as well as the potential support provided by the unions. For my present purpose, however, it suffices to focus on the two main aspects of their explanation.

4. To these two parties, we should add a third one—the Italian Communists—which emerged out of a second internal scission, this time within the Party for Communist Refoundation. This second division was related to different positions within the party about its role: whether to be a governmental or an oppositional party. Unlike the Party for Communist Refoundation, the Italian Communists thought they should take advantage of being in the government.

5. Of course, since there is a two-party system, the two aspects are merged in the case of the United States, where I therefore look only at the position of the Democratic Party.

6. Here I consider all conventional actions (i.e., juridical, political, and media-oriented actions) by institutional and elite actors as public statements. In practice, however, most events take the form of purely verbal acts (e.g., press conferences, interviews, public declarations, etc.). Since the data come from the same source, this measure of political alliances suffers from the same sampling problem as that of the conventional protest action by social movements. It should therefore be taken with some care. See appendix A.

7. Ideally, one would have to look at the judiciary arena as well, hence covering all three state powers (executive, legislative, and judiciary). The role of the judiciary power is particularly important in the United States, where it often acted as a real "ally" of social movements by formulating decisions that met the movements' aims. Here, however, I do not consider the judiciary in my definition of the alliance structure, mainly because I focus on political

alliances in the narrower sense, that is, on elite actors who participate directly in the political game.

8. The correlation coefficient (1975–1999) between unconventional protest events by the ecology movement and pro-ecology statements by elite actors equals .12 (n.s.), that between unconventional events by the antinuclear movement and antinuclear statements equals .73 ($p \leq .01$), and that between unconventional events by the peace movement and pro-peace statements by elite actors equals .38 (n.s., but $p \leq .10$).

9. These parties are the Christian-Democratic Party, the Socialist Party, the Social-Democratic Party, the Liberal Party, and the Republican Party.

10. These parties are the Free Democratic Party (two seats), the Christian-Democratic Party (two seats), the Socialist Party (two seats), and the Swiss People's Party (one seat). Following a recent major change in Swiss politics, starting from 2004, the Swiss People's Party will have two seats and the Christian-Democratic Party only one.

11. Similar to what I do in examining direct effects in chapter 5, in addition to the analyses with unconventional actions, I conduct the same analyses by taking all actions carried by the three movements, with independent variables expressed once as absolute numbers and once as annual differences. The results of these additional analyses largely reflect those discussed in the main text. Both with absolute and differenced independent variables, the only statistically significant coefficient is the one concerning the peace movement, but the positive sign contradicts the hypothesis of a policy impact of the movement.

12. Specifically, I use the percentage of parliamentary seats held by the Democratic Party in the United States and by leftist parties in Italy and Switzerland.

13. Here too, I conduct the same analyses using all actions carried by the three movements, instead of unconventional events only, both with independent variables expressed as absolute numbers and annual differences. The results suggest that only the ecology movement has really benefited from the presence of political allies within the institutional arenas, hence pointing in the same direction of the findings just discussed. The relationships are particularly strong with absolute numbers, as both the Italian and the Swiss ecology movements display a joint effect. The other coefficients parallel the findings just discussed. If we take differenced independent variables, once again, the joint effect is weaker, as only in Switzerland two of the three movements had a positive impact. Here, there is also a "deviant" case with respect to all the other analyses concerning the joint effect of protest and political alliances: national defense spending is negatively associated with the interactive terms for the Swiss peace movement.

CHAPTER EIGHT

Public Opinion

This chapter deals with public opinion as a second factor that might improve the chances of success of social movements. In other words, public opinion is considered here as a condition for the policy impact of ecology, antinuclear, and peace movements. The argument for this chapter is that when the public's preferences match the movements' aims, chances are higher that the latter are taken seriously by the political authorities and that, consequently, policy change will be forthcoming. This can be explained by the fact that, as democratic theory maintains, political elites respond to demands that are supported by a majority of the population—or, more precisely, by a majority of the potential voters—rather than to minority challenges. In this interpretation, the policy changes result from the politicians' fear of not being reelected if they fail to satisfy the majority demands.

The first question to be addressed, however, is what we mean by such terms as *public's preferences* and especially *public opinion*. These seem at first glance simple and intuitive notions, but they are far from being so; and the very definition of public opinion is likely to substantially affect our assessment of its role in the political and policy process. Therefore, I begin with a brief discussion about the nature of public opinion, before moving to theoretical issues.

On the empirical side, I first give a picture of trends in public opinion on the issues touched by the mobilization of the three movements under study. Specifically, I show the development of public opinion on environmental, nuclear energy, and national security matters, in particular in the United States but in part also in Italy and Switzerland. This continues the systematic overview of the developments of the main aspects that enter my analysis of the policy impact of social movements: protest (chapter 3), public policy (chapter 4), movement organization (chapter 6), political alliances (chapter 7), and now public opinion. In line with the longitudinal perspective adopted in the book, I focus on how public opinion has evolved over time during the 1975–1995 period, rather than provide a static snapshot.

At the same time, this overview represents the necessary descriptive stage for the more systematic analyses conducted in the last part of the chapter. These analyses follow the same logic as those in chapter 7 concerning the role of political alliances. First, I address the indirect effect of the three movements studied and discuss the impact of public opinion on public policy. Second, I apply the ideas of the joint-effect model on the variant that sees public opinion as the most relevant facilitating factor for social movement outcomes.

What Is Public Opinion?

If we argue that public opinion is a resource that social movements can use to better reach their goals, we must first agree on what we mean by this concept. Broadly speaking, public opinion refers to the expressed view of a given group about certain issues of common interest or concern. As such, it must be distinguished from attitudes and values. These three concepts try to capture certain individual characteristics that affect behavior and are located at increasing levels of embeddedness in one's personality. Values are the most rooted aspect and refer to relatively stable beliefs concerning broad societal issues. Attitudes are less stable but are still quite fundamental generalizations, predisposed to behave in a certain way in a given circumstance. Finally, opinions, the most volatile aspect, are the specific and overt manifestations of these underlying concepts.

Public opinion is determined by all three aspects, but in its observable expression it usually refers to the aggregate of individual attitudes or opinions at a given point. Therefore, in commonsense understanding and among social scientists, this concept is often conceived in a static perspective as something "given." However, such a view only deals with the end product, that is, the content of public opinion at one point in time. This has major limitations, for such a static approach does not allow us to study the process of opinion formation. While today there is a great focus on studies of the content of public opinion, social science has advanced less in understanding the dynamics of formation of opinion and its social construction. A more dynamic approach is better suited to inquire into the process by which the opinions and beliefs of the general public affect decision making or help social movements to reach their goals.

A good many works have discussed the components of public opinion and the determinants of its change over time (e.g., Zaller 1992), as well as its relation to policy making and agenda building (e.g., Jones 1994). It is not my aim to go into detail about this literature, but a few general remarks might help clarify my use of this notion. Generally speaking, public opinion covers two meanings. In the first and most straightforward, it indicates the aggregation of individual opinions, attitudes, and preferences that can be measured through survey research. In a second and more sophisticated meaning, it refers to a debate occurring in the public space and is not identical with the dominant views among the population given by opinion polls

(Gerhards and Neidhardt 1990). Following the lead of Habermas (1989), public opinion in this view implies a process of collective deliberation (Page and Shapiro 1993) that takes place in specific forums, above all the mass media. While American scholars have tended to follow the first meaning, European sociologists usually embrace the second. Here I follow the American tradition and refer to public opinion as the result of the process of opinion formation as it becomes visible in opinion polls, which are of special relevance for the study of public policy. Surveys are not only interesting for pollsters or social scientists; often, they are an instrument in the hand of decision makers to monitor the preferences of citizens with respect to several policy issues and choices, thus contributing to the formation of policy agendas.

In addition, in considering the potential impact of public opinion, I follow authors who believe that public opinion is real, rational, and measurable (Page and Shapiro 1992, 1993; Zaller 1992). Concerning the question of stability, there is no consensus among scholars, as several authors have pointed to the fundamental ambivalence and instability of public preferences (e.g., Converse 1964; Zaller 1992; Zaller and Feldman 1992). A relevant distinction in this respect is the one between preferences and attention. I agree with Jones (1994) that preferences are more stable than issue attention, which is more likely to be subject to abrupt shifts over time. Since I am interested in the evaluation that the general public gives of environmental, antinuclear, and peace issues, to determine to what extent these preferences help social movements to reach their policy goals, here I focus on preferences rather than issue attention, although in the case of the United States, I also have a glance at the latter aspect.

Thus, public opinion here is the expressed views of the general public on a more or less specific issue that is recognized as socially and politically relevant by the public and by decision makers. Such a view may concern the public's preferences (the direction, the pro or con of the issue at hand) or its attention (the saliency, how important the issue is to the public). Furthermore, although it is less stable than individual attitudes and even less so than values, public opinion displays a certain degree of stability, especially if one looks at preferences rather than issue attention. Thus, the preferences expressed through public opinion are not totally random and can to some extent be trusted as an indicator of what people think of a given issue and its shifts over time.

In sum, the analyses presented in this chapter assume the characteristics attributed to it by Page and Shapiro (1993; see also, 1992): public opinion is real; it is measurable through survey research; it forms coherent patterns that differentiate among alternative policies in reasonable ways that reflect citizens' values and beliefs; it is stable; when it changes, it does so in regular and understandable ways, following clear principles and patterns; and it nearly always changes in reasonable and sensible ways, in response to objective events and to changes that affect the costs and benefits of policy alternatives.

Public Opinion and Democracy

Just as students of social movements often argue about the role of organization or violence for movement success (see chapter 2), public policy researchers are often concerned with the role of public opinion on policy. At the same time, just as most scholars agree that a strong organization and the use of disruptive tactics are helpful internal resources for social movements, there is ample evidence suggesting that governments are responsive to shifts in public preferences.

The few existing studies that have examined the relationship of public opinion and national state policies found little, if any, evidence of a significant impact on policy change (e.g., Hamilton 1972). More recently, however, a growing number of studies pointed to a significant impact of public opinion on policy, arguing that political authorities are responsive to clear and visible shifts in the public opinion, especially when an issue is felt as important or salient by the public (e.g., Bartels 1991; Burstein 1998b; Burstein and Freudenburg 1978; Costain and Majstorovic 1994; Devine 1985; Erikson, McIver, and Wright 1993; Fording 1997; Goldberg 1990; Hartley and Russett 1992; Hays, Esler, and Hays 1996; Hibbs 1987; Hicks 1984; Hill and Hinton-Andersson 1995; Huberts 1989; Ignagni and Meernik 1994; Jackson and King 1989; Jacobs 1993; Jencks 1985; Jones 1994; Page and Shapiro 1983; Ringquist et al. 1997; Stimson, MacKuen, and Erikson 1995; see Burstein 1998a for a review).[1]

Thus, public preferences seem to play a crucial role in the democratic process. Four works deserve a special mention in this respect. The first two are among the best attempts so far to study the relationship between public opinion and public policy (see Burstein 1998a). Both are multiple-issue studies that attempt to reach broad conclusions about responsiveness in the United States, and both conclude that public opinion had a major effect in most instances. The first one is an article by Page and Shapiro (1983), for which the authors measured trends in public opinion concerning a broad range of issues. Focusing on various instances of policy change, they analyzed hundreds of surveys that sampled American opinion between 1935 and 1979. The advantage of their approach clearly lies in the quality and especially the width of their data, which allow for drawing general conclusions about the impact of public opinion on policy change. The second study is an article by Stimson, MacKuen, and Erikson (1995; see also, Stimson 1991), in which the authors look at public opinion and how it concerns policy liberalism and the U.S. government. While Page and Shapiro examine many specific issues separately, these authors prefer to focus on global measures of public opinion; nevertheless, they all reach the same conclusion: public opinion influences policy.

The other two studies that I would like to mention are of a particular kind, but they are nonetheless helpful to the purpose of assessing the role of public opinion for policy change. Burstein (1998a) as well as Burstein and Linton (2002) provide an unusual but interesting analysis aimed at assessing the impact of public opinion on policy, which provides at the same time two quite comprehensive reviews of the existing literature. In an attempt to ascertain the role of public opinion, they reviewed articles on the determinants of policy change that were published in major American scholarly journals. In both cases, the conclusion was that public opinion should be taken more seriously by sociologists and political scientists alike.

Paul Burstein is among those who in recent years has most thoroughly inquired into the role of public opinion for public policy in relation to the functioning of democratic institutions. Basing his conclusion on a systematic review of the aforementioned literature (among other resources), he has made a strong statement for including public opinion in the study of public policy. Burstein (1998a) argues that work on policy change has failed to take into account the role of public opinion. According to him, this is problematic, first, because the evidence strongly suggests that public opinion directly influences public policy and, second, because adding public opinion to the analysis of policy change may undermine the influence of other factors. In particular, when public opinion is taken into account, the direct impact of social movements and other political organizations—namely, parties and interest groups—may decline or even disappear (Burstein and Linton 2002).

One explanation is to be found in what he calls the theory of democratic representation (Burstein 1999). Briefly put, democratic governments are responsive to citizens' demands. As he points out: "Democratic governments often do what their citizens want, and they are especially likely to do so when an issue is important to the public and its wishes are clear" (Burstein 1998a, 15). However, responsiveness is forthcoming only under certain conditions. One major condition, in the perspective of the theory of representative democracy, is that a given demand reflect the preferences of a majority of the citizens. The rationale behind this view can be traced back to John Stuart Mill's utilitarianism and the logic of majority democracy: it is the idea that "only citizens themselves can be trusted to control government in their own interests" (Page and Shapiro 1993, 36). However, if the "represented" must ultimately control the policy process, the "representatives" must be informed about the interests and preferences of the former. Measuring public opinion is a way to come to know the interests and preferences of the citizens.[2]

According to the theory of representative democracy, democratic governments respond to the public basically for electoral reasons—that is, to retain political power; and, more specifically, to win reelection (Burstein 1999; Devine 1985; Hicks 1984; see also, Burk 1985). According to this interpretation, in the view of legislators, public opinion is a way to grasp the preferences of the majority of citizens. Clear-cut and significant shifts in public opinion may inform the legislators that the citizens' preferences are changing.

If this view is correct, then to hold power in a well-functioning democracy, political elites are responsive to majority demands rather than to special interests of minority groups such as social movements and interest groups (Krehbiel 1991; Lohmann 1993). As a result, social movements will not have a direct impact on public policy, only an indirect one, if any; for, if they respond to minority demands such as those carried by social movements, political elites risk defeat. In a way, it would be against their own interests to respond to those demands when the public's level of concern is high (Burstein and Linton 2002; Lohmann 1993).

Of course, critics of the public have stressed the dangers of the majority view of democracy, or a "tyranny of the majority," which so much worried Alexis de

Tocqueville more than 150 years ago. Critics of the public include, for example, classical studies, such as those by Almond (1950); Berelson, Lazarsfeld, and McPhee (1954); Campbell and colleagues (1960); Converse (1964); Lazarsfeld, Berelson, and Gaudet (1944); Lippmann (1922); and, more recently, Zaller (1992).[3] Generally speaking, these critics point to the artificial and unstable nature of public opinion and individual attitudes as well as to the difficulty in measuring them coherently and consistently. Zaller (1992), in particular, asked whether public opinion exists independently of the process of collecting data on it, that is, in the absence of a pollster.

Naturally, we should be wary of reifying public opinion and giving it certain qualities that it does not and cannot have, hence having an open ear to these critics. And regardless of the specific interpretation one gives to this in terms of representative democracy or other democratic theories, the important point for us here is that public opinion appears to be a crucial factor explaining policy change and that, in the absence of a favorable public opinion, social movements are unlikely to have an effect on public policy. In other words, if movements do have an impact, it is an indirect one.

Burstein (1999) stresses three ways in which social movements can have an indirect impact on public policy:

1. by changing the public's preferences, that is, by attracting public opinion to their cause;
2. by increasing public concern about the issues they address; and
3. by changing the legislator's perception of either the public's preferences or the saliency of the issue in the public space.

All three ways suggest an indirect effect of movements on policy, an effect obtained mainly by influencing public opinion in the first place. Thus, in this perspective and according to the theory of representative democracy, the policy impact of social movements is mediated by public opinion. In the following, I address this issue empirically for the case of ecology, antinuclear, and peace movements in the three countries of my study. Before I do so, however, I need to provide a better picture of the historical trends in public opinion in the three policy areas touched by these movements in each country.

Trends in Public Opinion on Environmental, Nuclear Energy, and National Security Matters

People aiming to take the pulse of the nation have at their disposal a number of resources provided by opinion polls. This is especially true in the case of the United States, but the use of opinion polls has become increasingly frequent in other countries, including Italy and Switzerland. Nevertheless, it is in the United States that information on this aspect is most widespread. The origin of public opinion research in the United States can be traced back to newspaper "straw votes," unofficial votes taken to assess the relative strengths of candidates and issues. The earliest recorded example dates back to 1824, and the first regular use of public opinion research by government occurs in 1939 (Sheatsley 2000). Today, large public opinion organizations such as Gallup, Harris Survey, and Roper conduct regular—sometimes monthly— surveys, hence offering a range of information on the preferences of American citizens.

Given this wealth of information, my attempt to provide an overview of trends in public opinion on environmental, nuclear energy, and peace issues between 1975 and 1995 is most successful for the American situation over those in the other two countries. Thus, for the case of the United States, I use indicators of opinion in terms of preferences; that is, I use different series of polls. I use five indicators of opinion for environmental matters, two for nuclear energy, and two for military affairs and national security issues. In addition, I use various indicators of opinion in terms of issue attention, namely, on the environment and especially on the military. In contrast, for Italy, I was not able to find any usable indicator of opinion on the environment, only a partial one on nuclear energy and one on the military. Finally, for Switzerland, I have at my disposal four independent measures of opinion on the environment, although I use only one on nuclear energy and a partial one on the military. Even in the case of the United States, however, some of the series are shorter than the period considered in my study; for example, some stop in 1990. This is due to the extremely difficult task to find consistent time series of public opinion, that is, series whose single observations over time can be systematically compared.[4]

United States

Figure 8.1 shows the development of American public opinion on the environment from 1975 to 1990. The five indicators displayed in the figure refer to the percentage of

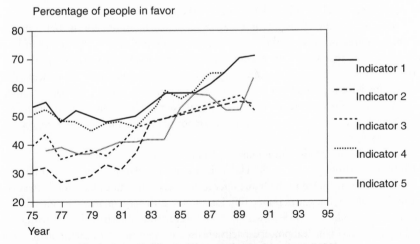

Figure 8.1. Public Opinion on the Environment (USA).

people in favor of the environment or environmental protection. The first interesting thing to note is that all five indicators point to the same direction, in spite of the fact that the wording of the question varies from one measure to the other, which therefore captures the slightly different aspects of preferences in favor of the environment.[5] This attests, first, to the validity of these polls to grasp trends in public opinion and, second, to the consistency of the Americans' preferences concerning the situation of the environment, regardless of the specific issue they were asked about. It also confirms Page and Shapiro's argument (1993) that public opinion forms coherent patterns that reflect people's values and beliefs.

The most important finding for my present purpose, however, concerns the substantive development of public opinion on this issue. As can be seen in the figure, American people have witnessed increasing concern in regard to environmental protection, and this holds for all five indicators. Such increasing concern can be observed, in particular, starting from the early 1980s, after a period in which it remained quite stable or even slightly declined. This regular upward trend can be seen especially in the third indicator, which is the one I use in the following time-series analysis.

It is interesting to compare the development over time of public opinion on the environment with that of the mobilization of the ecology movement, as shown in chapter 3 (figure 3.1a). Generally speaking, the two lines display similar trends, with a first phase in the late 1970s characterized by stability or decline and a second phase in the 1980s in which both mobilization and public concern increased.[6] In quite a speculative way, two possible interpretations of this parallel behavior can be advanced, although it is not possible here to decide in favor of one or the other. According to the first interpretation, shifts in public opinion precede the mobilization of the ecology movement. In this case, the latter might represent a sort of litmus test of the former, whereby a minority of more committed people act on behalf of a silent majority of concerned citizens, hence showing the power holders and other interested observers (for example, social scientists) that changes in the public concern about a given societal or political issue are taking place. However, a second interpretation is that shifts in public opinion occur after the movement starts to mobilize, which is more in line with the idea that social movements have a positive impact on public opinion. If this view is correct, protest acquires an important role in shaping or influencing the preferences of the general public. I try to ascertain in the following analyses whether this is empirically confirmed, at least in the case of the U.S. ecology movement. For the moment, I continue my description of trends in public opinion in the three areas of interest.

Figure 8.2 shows the development of public opinion on nuclear energy in the United States from 1975 to 1990. Unlike in the case of environmental protection, the two indicators included in the figure refer to two very different things. While the first one (indicator 1) measures public opinion on nuclear energy matters in general, the second one (indicator 2) deals with a more specific situation, namely, a situation in which increases in nuclear power capacity are used as a solution to an energy crisis.[7] As a result, the two indicators display two different and even opposing trends. Opposition

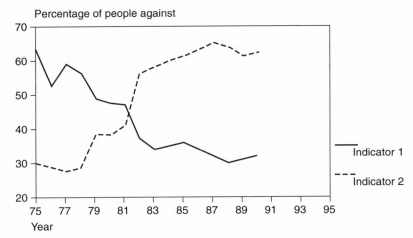

Figure 8.2. Public Opinion on Nuclear Energy (USA).

defined in general terms has strongly diminished in time, going from more than 60 percent in 1975 down to just over 30 percent in 1990. Opposition to the use of nuclear power to deal with the energy crisis, in contrast, went up from 30 percent to more than 60 percent during the same period.

Asking support or opposition to nuclear power in general, or as a means to solve energy crises, apparently alters the perception that people have of nuclear power and the degree of opposition to it. Although the aggregate-level data used here do not allow us to draw conclusions on the individual level of analysis, it is possible that one sees nuclear power as a "good" or "bad" solution to energy crises, without opposing it in general (and vice versa). In particular, it is likely that the existence of an energy crisis led people to have a more positive view of nuclear power as a way to get out of it. The fact that the United States in the late 1970s was touched by an important energy crisis could, at least in part, explain the low number of people opposed to nuclear power as a way to deal with energy crises, in spite of strong opposition in general.

Concerning military and national security issues, we observe yet another pattern. Figure 8.3 shows two indicators measuring the development of public opinion on the military, in the United States from 1975 to 1993 (indicator 1) and 1988 (indicator 2). Here, as in the case of environmental matters, the two indicators are quite similar and therefore are strongly correlated.[8] Both point to quite a volatile public concern about military issues, much more than about environmental and nuclear energy issues, which follow a more steady development over time.

If we compare it to the development of military spending by the U.S government, as shown in chapter 4 (figure 4.4), it appears that public opinion on this issue is related to actual spending. The percentage of American citizens who thought that their country was spending too much for military or national defense purposes declined rapidly in

Percentage of people against

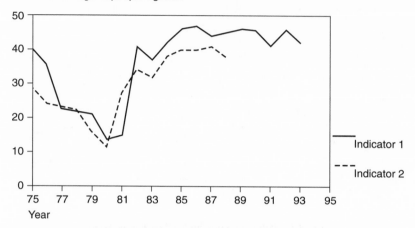

Figure 8.3. Public Opinion on the Military (USA).

the second half of the 1970s. This was a period in which government spending in this field was low (under Carter's administration and after the withdrawal of American troops from Vietnam). Then, public concern increased abruptly in 1982, shortly after Reagan started his strong commitment to military spending and after the Cold War took on new vigor with the arms race. Such public concern about military spending remained particularly high during the whole 1980s and even in the early 1990s, well after the Cold War was over and even while expenditures were diminishing. Thus, at least in this case, public opinion seems indeed to have changed in response to objective events that affected the costs and benefits of policy alternatives (Page and Shapiro 1993).

At the same time, however, the rising opposition against military spending paralleled the increase in the level of mobilization of the peace movement (see figure 3.1c, in chapter 3). This points to the existence of a close relationship between protest and public opinion, whereby a rise in the former went hand in hand with a rise in the latter, although opposition to military expenditures remained high even after the movement had demobilized. This dynamic of protest and public opinion can be observed in many instances and represents one of the most interesting and compelling aspects of the study of the policy impact of social movements.

As I mentioned earlier, public concern can be seen in the preferences of the citizens vis-à-vis a given issue or in the degree of attention given to that issue. The trends shown in the figures here, as well as in those concerning the other two countries, deal with shifts in preferences. To have a more complete picture of the position of the public on the issue areas at hand, for the case of the United States, I show available data on issue attention. To this purpose, we can use the standard "most important problem" question, which is regularly included in surveys conducted by the Gallup Organization.

Percentage of people who view this as a "major problem" (mean)

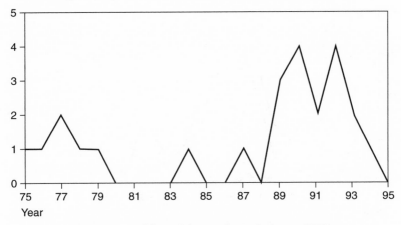

Figure 8.4.   Public Opinion on the Environment (USA).

Figure 8.4 looks at environmental matters.[9] Clearly, in spite of an undeniable increase in concern during the past three decades, the environment was never a very salient issue among American citizens. Other problems traditionally took a more central place in citizens' preoccupations—namely, jobs and employment, as well as crime and security. Thus, the proportion of people who thought that the state of the environment was the most important problem facing the country never went above 5 percent of the population.

A second characteristic of issue attention, as compared to preferences, is its higher volatility. The example of environmental matters clearly confirms this difference— as do military matters, which we will examine shortly. One's opinions and attitudes toward a given issue may remain the same or modify only slightly, while its saliency, and therefore the attention one pays to it, is subject to rapid change; for the priority one gives to a certain issue, and the extent to which he or she views it as a major problem, depend on the situation, not only with respect to that issue, but also with respect to other areas. This "competition" among issues is evident in our case, even within the restricted field formed by issues concerning ecology, antinuclear, and peace movements. In the view of Americans within the period under study, nuclear power was virtually nonexistent as a major problem,[10] but the environment provoked some concern in the late 1970s and especially in the late 1980s and early 1990s. As we see in figure 8.5, which shows issue attention to military matters, according to four indicators and a total measure,[11] the period of lowest priority given to environmental issues coincides with the years in which the saliency of military issues was very high, suggesting that the latter replaced the former in the preoccupations of American citizens.

However, we must be careful in drawing this comparison. While attention to environmental issues was always quite low, in spite of shifts from one period to the

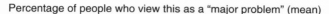

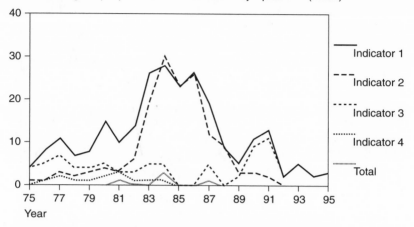

Figure 8.5. Public Opinion on the Military (USA).

other, military issues were always of concern to a much larger share of the population. In the years of the arms race under Reagan's administration, which was also the period when the U.S. peace movement was carrying the nuclear weapons freeze campaign, military issues were considered the major problem facing the country, by a sizable part of the citizens. This is largely, if not entirely, due to a sudden increase in public concern about peace and war issues in general, especially with respect to nuclear war and the arms race. A similar phenomenon occurred at the time of the Gulf War in the early 1990s. Could this be due to the fact that the American peace movement was mobilizing mostly around these issues at that particular time? Again, a definitive answer to this question cannot be given here, but I do try to ascertain in the following, by means of time-series analysis, whether the movement's mobilization was instrumental in bringing about a rise in public concern regarding military issues. Before doing so, let us have a look at trends in public opinion in the other two countries.

Italy

As I said, data on public opinion in Italy is more sporadic than in the United States. This prevents me from drawing a systematic parallel between the two countries. In spite of recent developments in this field, polling the public opinion is a younger and less-institutionalized enterprise in Italy. An unfortunate consequence of this for my present purpose is that no consistent measure of trends in public opinion on the environment was found for this country.

Figure 8.6 shows the development of public opinion on nuclear energy in Italy between 1978 and 1987.[12] However, this is the most interesting period, as the production of nuclear power virtually stopped after that year (see chapter 4). Although the wording is somewhat different, it is broadly comparable to the first indicator used in the case of the United States (see figure 8.2); that is, it refers to opposition to

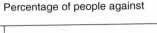

Percentage of people against

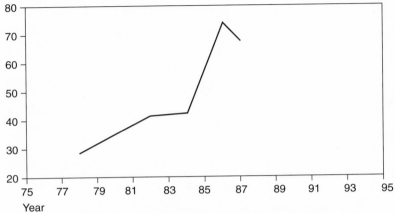

Figure 8.6. Public Opinion on Nuclear Energy (Italy).

nuclear power in general. Yet, we observe a trend completely different from that in the United States. Whereas in the latter country opposition had progressively declined, in the same period Italian citizens had been increasingly concerned about the use of this energy source. The rise of the number of people against nuclear power was predominant between 1984 and 1986, specifically, in a time when the political debate on this issue was becoming particularly intense, culminating with the 1987 antinuclear referendum. This shows once again the existence of a dynamics of mutual influence between protest and public opinion around certain issues that became the object of public debates.

The other available information on Italy deals with public opinion on the military, whose development is shown in figure 8.7. Here I have at my disposal a longer series, going from 1977 to 1995. Again, this indicator, which refers to military spending, is directly comparable to those used for the United States.[13]

Apparently, no distinct pattern can be discerned. Yet, if we compare this trend both to the actual situation on the front of military affairs and to the mobilization of the Italian peace movement, we can make sense at least of the first of the two peaks in opinion unfavorable to military spending. Within the period considered in this study, the first peak began to occur when NATO decided to deploy cruise missiles in five European countries, including Italy; the peak was ultimately reached when the Italian government accepted the missiles. At the same time, this was the period of stronger mobilization by the peace movement. We therefore review a situation similar to that of the United States, with an actual deterioration of the "problem," a strong mobilization of the movement, and an increasing public concern about the issue at hand—all this within the context of an intense public debate on that issue.

The second peak in public opinion unfavorable to military spending is more puzzling. At first glance we might think of it as a reaction to the involvement of Italian troops in the Gulf War, but if we look more closely, we see that the rise in

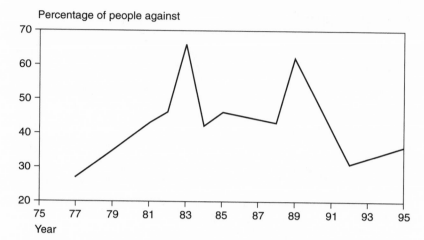

Percentage of people against

Figure 8.7. Public Opinion on the Military (Italy).

public opinion occurred in 1989, well before the whole issue became publicly salient. This rise could be related to the debate around conscientious objectors and the related decisions taken in 1989 by the Constitutional Court, which loosened certain rules in this field (see chapter 4). However, this debate certainly was much less important than the one concerning the arms race and the cruise missiles, which took place in the early 1980s; yet, opposition to military spending was nearly as strong in 1989 as it was at that time.

Switzerland

Finally, let us have a look at public opinion in Switzerland. In this case, although less exhaustive than in the United States, information on this aspect is more complete than that in Italy, thereby allowing us to draw a more systematic parallel with the former.

Figure 8.8 shows the development of the proportion of people in Switzerland who, in one way or another, were on the side of the environment. Here I was lucky enough to find three indicators that cover the entire period under study, as well as a fourth shorter and more specific measure.[14] The four indicators are much less correlated than those for the United States. In fact, although the general pattern is rather stable, some of them display quite opposing trends. Specifically, the number of people who judged the state of the environment as "unbearable" displays a weakly rising trend (indicator 1), whereas that of people who positively evaluated territory planning and landscape protection had been declining (indicator 3).

We can make sense of this divergence by thinking of the precise meaning of these two indicators. The first one refers to what one thought of the actual situation with regard to the environment. In this sense, the Swiss citizens had increased their concern about the state of the environment, although only to a limited extent. The second one refers to what one thought of the policy solution to the problem. Furthermore, it deals

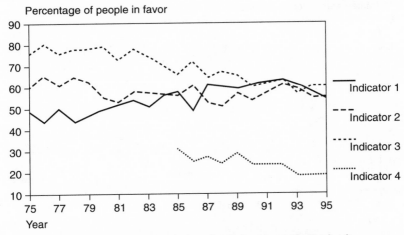

Figure 8.8. Public Opinion on the Environment (Switzerland).

only with a specific area of environmental protection, namely, territory planning and landscape protection, which was the area in which the Swiss government had made more efforts (see figure 4.9, in chapter 4). In a way, it is quite understandable that, the more one is concerned about the state of the environment, the more he or she evaluates policy efforts as being insufficient. The important point for our present purpose however, is that public concern about the environment in Switzerland had increased between 1975 and 1995, but only at a rather slow pace.

The same cannot be said of public opinion on nuclear energy, which is shown in figure 8.9 for the same period.[15] In this case, we observe two important rises of public concern about nuclear power. Both were preceded by an important mobilization of

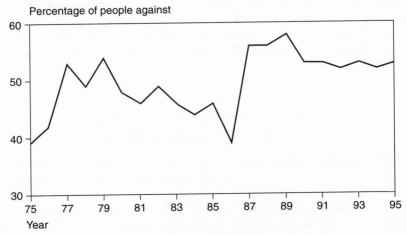

Figure 8.9. Public Opinion on Nuclear Energy (Switzerland).

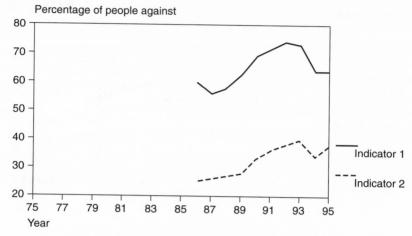

Figure 8.10.   Public Opinion on the Military (Switzerland).

the antinuclear movement (see chapter 3). The first one occurred between 1977 and 1979, when the movement remobilized strongly, after a short period of rest mainly due to internal divisions. The second one took place exactly ten years later, between 1987 and 1989, when discussions about the ten-year moratorium was underway. Thus, once again, public opinion seems to be part of a dynamics in which protest activities and public debates were important aspects.

Finally, figure 8.10 depicts the development of public opinion on the military in Switzerland, from 1986 to 1995. Although the two indicators at my disposal here are based on shorter series, they are nonetheless highly correlated and refer to the most recent period.[16] This lack of data for the earlier period is unfortunate because we cannot evaluate the relation between the strong mobilization of the peace movement in the early 1980s and the public concern on military issues at that time. What we can say is that public opinion displays a pattern similar to that of protest. Whether the former had influenced the latter is an issue I address in the next section.

Social Movements, Public Opinion, and Public Policy: Indirect Effects

I conclude this chapter with a systematic time-series analysis of the relationship among protest activities, public opinion, and public policy; and I do so in a way similar to what I did in chapter 7 for the political alliances. The main purpose is to assess the explanatory power of the second variant of the indirect-effect and the joint-effect models of social movement outcomes, those that stress the role—either in subsequent steps or simultaneously—of public opinion. I start with indirect effects.

Table 8.1. Effect of Public Opinion on Public Policy in Three Countries, 1975–1995

Dependent Variables	Spending for Environmental Protection (National) (t_1)	Spending for Environmental Protection (Local) (t_1)	Nuclear Energy Production (t_1)	Number of Construction Permits (t_1)	Spending for Defense (t_1)
United States					
Pro-movement opinion (t_0)	.34	−.29	−.09	.62**	−.33
(D-W)	(1.93)	(2.08)	(1.94)	(1.70)	(1.90)
N	16	16	16	16	19
Italy					
Pro-movement opinion (t_0)	—	—	—	—	−.31
(D-W)	—	—	—	—	(2.00)
N	—	—	—	—	18
Switzerland					
Pro-movement opinion (t_0)	.39	−.08	−.02	—	—
(D-W)	(2.29)	(2.00)	(1.87)	—	—
N	20	20	20	—	—

Note: Standardized regression coefficients (bivariate) generated with a generalized least-squared method of estimation (Prais-Winsten) assuming a first-order autoregressive process. Durbin-Watson test for serial correlation and number of observations (series length) are shown within parentheses. The independent variables include a one-year lag. The dependent variables are expressed in terms of annual percentage change.
$*p < .10; **p < .05; ***p < .01$.

This variant of the indirect-effect model posits that social movements first influence the attitudes of the general public; then, policy change occurs, owing to the impact of the latter on the responsiveness of policy makers. Again, to ascertain this model, we must proceed in two steps: first, we must look at the relationship between protest and public opinion; then we must address the one between opinion and public policy. Again, I first examine the latter step for practical reasons. Table 8.1 shows the effect of public opinion on the five indicators of policies targeted by ecology, antinuclear, and peace movements in the three countries.[17]

In all three countries, public opinion did not seem to have significantly affected public policy. The only statistically significant coefficient is the one relating antinuclear opinion to the number of construction permits for new nuclear plants in the United States. Yet, the positive sign points to the direction opposite that of the goals of the antinuclear movement, which means that the movement hardly took any advantage from the opinion of the public. Some of the other relationships display coefficients with rather high values, in particular, those concerning national environmental spending in the United States and Switzerland as well as those concerning defense spending in the United States and Italy; but they are not statistically significant.

If we do the same analyses using independent variables expressed in terms of annual differences instead of absolute levels, the situation is only marginally more favorable to the movements (see table B8.1, in appendix B). In this case, we observe a statistically significant relationship between pro-ecology statements and environmental spending by the national government in the United States. Overall, however, there is little evidence that public opinion strongly affects the responsiveness of the power holders.

The lack of impact of public opinion on public policy is quite surprising, especially in the light of previous work, which suggests that policy makers tend to be responsive to significant shifts in the attitudes of the general public (see Burstein 1998a). The distinction mentioned earlier, between preferences and saliency, might contribute to explaining this lack of effect when it comes to issues pertaining to environmental, nuclear energy, and peace issues. Here I measure public opinion in term of preferences. While previous work shows that public opinion often has an impact on policy, it also suggests that this is more likely to occur when the issues at hand are felt as important or salient by the public. Now, as we saw earlier (except in specific and short-lived historical phases), environmental, nuclear energy, and peace issues are usually not very salient, as compared to other social problems, such as unemployment or the state of the economy. The lack of impact might therefore be due to the lower saliency of these issues and to their resulting lower electoral importance in the eyes of the power holders, even if the public's preferences about these issues increase. In other words, if the public opinion is not particularly concerned about a given problem, policy makers are not likely to follow its preferences and will tend to focus on other issues to gain electoral consensus.

Table 8.2 shows the results of the analyses concerning the impact of protest on public opinion, which allows us, in combination with those just discussed, to assess the explanatory power of the indirect-effect model of this variant on the social movement outcomes. The results clearly indicate that the mobilization by ecology, antinuclear, and peace movements was not instrumental in producing changes in public policies concerning the issues addressed by these movements, at least if we look at unconventional mobilization.

Once again, taking differenced independent variables, instead of absolute levels, does not change the picture (see table B8.2, in appendix B). In this case, too, no statistically significant coefficient can be observed, although those concerning the ecology movement in the United States and Switzerland—as well as, in part, that concerning the peace movement in Italy—display high values.[18]

In sum, this two-stage time-series analysis provides very little support to this variant of the indirect-model of social movement outcomes. First, public opinion on environmental, nuclear energy, and peace issues seems to have a weaker impact on public policy than expected, at least if we measure it in terms of public preferences. However, the protest activities carried by ecology, antinuclear, and peace movements did not significantly affect shifts in public opinion. Thus, the variant of this model that stresses the intervening role of political alliances has little—if any—explanatory power. What remains is similar to what I did for the first variant in

Table 8.2. Effect of Unconventional Mobilization on Public Opinion in Three Countries, 1975–1995

Dependent Variables	Pro-ecology Opinion (t_1)	Antinuclear Opinion (t_1)	Pro-peace Opinion (t_1)
United States			
Unconventional mobilization (t_0)	.11	−.10	.16
(D-W)	(1.99)	(1.93)	(2.06)
N	15	15	18
Italy			
Unconventional mobilization (t_0)	—	—	−.23
(D-W)	—	—	(1.99)
N	—	—	18
Switzerland			
Unconventional mobilization (t_0)	.31	.22	—
(D-W)	(2.18)	(1.93)	—
N	20	20	—

Note: Standardized regression coefficients (bivariate) generated with a generalized least-squared method of estimation (Prais-Winsten) assuming a first-order autoregressive process. Durbin-Watson test for serial correlation and number of observations (series length) are shown within parentheses. The independent variables include a one-year lag. The dependent variables are expressed in terms of annual percentage change.
$^{*}p < .10; ^{**}p < .05; ^{***}p < .01.$

chapter 7, that is, to ascertain whether these factors—protest and public opinion—have a stronger effect when they mutually reinforce each other, an issue which I address next.

Social Movements, Public Opinion, and Public Policy: Joint Effects

The first variant of the joint-effect model of social movement outcomes posits that protest and political alliances mutually reinforce each other to influence public policy. The second variant follows the same logic but replaces political alliances with public opinion. Thus, according to this variant, the mobilization by ecology, antinuclear, and peace movements should be more successful when it is accompanied by public concern. Table 8.3 allows us to ascertain whether this is true by showing the joint effect of the interactive terms combining unconventional mobilization and the respective indicator of public opinion on public policy in the three countries.[19]

Only one statistically significant regression coefficient can be observed in the case of the United States. It refers to the joint effect of the mobilization of the antinuclear movement and the public's opposing nuclear energy. The negative sign of the coefficient suggests that these two factors indeed combine to influence nuclear energy production. If we confront this result with the absence of a direct effect of the

Table 8.3. Joint Effect of Unconventional Mobilization and Public Opinion on Public Policy in Three Countries, 1975–1995

Dependent Variables	Spending for Environmental Protection (National) (t_1)	Spending for Environmental Protection (Local) (t_1)	Nuclear Energy Production (t_1)	Number of Construction Permits (t_1)	Spending for Defense (t_1)
United States					
Movement* public (t_0)	.17	−.26	−.49*	−.10	.35
(D-W)	(1.93)	(1.95)	(2.12)	(1.99)	(1.89)
N	16	16	16	16	19
Italy					
Movement* public (t_0)	—	—	—	—	.17
(D-W)	—	—	—	—	(2.06)
N	—	—	—	—	18
Switzerland					
Movement* public (t_0)	.32	.49**	.51**	—	—
(D-W)	(2.14)	(1.99)	(1.91)	—	—
N	20	20	20	—	—

Note: Standardized regression coefficients (bivariate) generated with a generalized least-squared method of estimation (Prais-Winsten) assuming a first-order autoregressive process. Durbin-Watson test for serial correlation and number of observations (series length) are shown within parentheses. The independent variables include a one-year lag. The dependent variables are expressed in terms of annual percentage change. See appendix A for a description of the interactive terms.
*$p < .10$; **$p < .05$; ***$p < .01$.

movement (see figure 5.1, in chapter 5) and an impact of public opinion on policy (see figure 8.1), we can conclude that there is a joint effect of the antinuclear movement with the public's opposing nuclear power. The same cannot be said of the other two movements, as all the other coefficients are not significant.

Unfortunately, for the case of Italy, I can only look at the interactive term combining the mobilization of the peace movement and the public's opinion on military spending. As in the United States, this movement did not take advantage of shifts in public opinion to influence public policy.

Finally, in Switzerland, the ecology and antinuclear movements display a statistically significant impact on policy (however, I do not have data on the peace movement). Only in the case of the ecology movement, however, can we speak of a joint effect of the movement's mobilization and the public's pro-environment opinion. Specifically, the combination of these two factors is strongly correlated with spending for environmental protection at the local level; in addition, the coefficient referring to national spending displays a high value, although it is not statistically significant. Yet, as with political alliances, confronting this finding with the presence of a direct effect of ecology protests on policy (see figure 5.1, in chapter 5), leads us to conclude that public opinion only strengthens an impact that the movement was able to obtain autonomously.

Once again, I conduct the same analyses using differenced independent variables to check for the robustness of the findings and to ascertain whether absolute levels or differences matter more (see table B8.3, in appendix B). As in most of the other cases, the results do not change substantially, and they tend to be weaker with differences than with absolute levels. In particular, the joint effect concerning the U.S. antinuclear movement disappears, while the one concerning the Swiss ecology movement remains significant.[20]

In sum, the variant of the joint-effect model of social movement outcomes that stresses the combined role of protest and public opinion scores somewhat better than the corresponding indirect-effect model discussed earlier. Some evidence was found that the ecology and antinuclear protests can profit from the simultaneous presence of a favorable public opinion. In contrast, peace protests do not display a joint effect on policy. Yet, even for the latter two movements, the findings do not consistently hold across the three countries. Furthermore, the lack of information on certain measures of public opinion prevents me from providing a more general picture, which might have supported this explanation of the policy outcomes of social movements.

At this stage, one more move is missing in my attempt to assess the explanatory power of direct, indirect, and joint effects of social movements on public policy, which consists in seeing whether the joint action of all three factors—that is, protest actions, political alliances, and public opinion—is going to further improve the chances of success of the three movements under study. Before I do commence on this final task, however, I would like to make some concluding remarks about the discussion of the role of public opinion carried in this chapter.

Conclusion

Trying to determine the role of public opinion is a tricky endeavor both theoretically and methodologically. From a theoretical point of view, the concept of public opinion is difficult to define and may refer to different things. Most of the time, it takes one of two main definitions. First, it refers to the aggregate opinions, attitudes, and preferences of individuals, which can be measured by means of surveys and opinion polls. Second, it refers to the public space and the construction of a public debate, which, today, has in the mass media its principal carrier. Here I adopt the former definition to inquire into the role of public opinion as a facilitating factor for the policy impact of social movements. Even in this simpler version, however, this concept is not that easily grasped. In particular, from a methodological point of view, the picture might be very different whether we look at preferences or issue attention. Here I focus on preferences, mainly because they are less volatile over time and because the issues addressed by the three movements studied tend to have a lower saliency for the general public as compared to other social problems.

In this chapter, I first discuss existing work on the impact of public opinion on public policy. Many of the studies suggest that public preferences play a crucial role in the democratic process, as political authorities seem to be responsive to significant shifts in the public opinion, especially if the saliency of a given issue is strong. One possible interpretation of this lies in the theory of representative democracy and the idea that democratic governments are responsive to citizens' demands (Burstein 1999). That certain authors think that government representatives do so basically for electoral reasons is of relative importance for my present purpose. The important point of this interpretation in the perspective of the study of the consequences of social movements is that responsiveness is forthcoming to the extent that a given demand reflects the preferences of a majority of the citizens, and public opinion becomes important as a way for political elites to get a sense of the will of the majority of citizens.

Thus, according to democratic theory, social movements in a well-functioning democracy hardly have any chance to influence the decision-making process when their demands are not supported by a majority of citizens—or at least a sizable group. In terms of the different models of social movement outcomes proposed in chapter 5, protest does not have a direct impact on public policy, only an indirect one (if any). After having described the development of public opinion on issues pertaining to environmental protection, nuclear energy, and the military in the three countries under study, I confront this hypothesis with my longitudinal data. Specifically, I continue my time-series analysis of the relationship between protest and policy change by examining the indirect and joint effects of public opinion.

The results suggest that public opinion has a weaker impact on public policy than expected, but it seems to play a facilitating role for social movements to obtain a policy impact. This facilitating role, however, occurs above all with the mobilization of the movements in what I call the joint-effect model of social movement outcomes, whereas the indirect-effect model has received little support from the data. This explanation might have been stronger, but the lack of information on certain measures of public opinion makes its application impossible. In spite of this shortcoming, the variant of the indirect-effect and joint-effect models of social movement outcomes that stresses the role of public opinion—either following a two-step process or in simultaneous combination—score better than the direct-effect model. As in the case of political alliances, their explanatory power is weaker than expected. It is now time to make a more general assessment of the analyses proposed in chapters 5, 6, 7, and 8. That is the purpose of the conclusion to part II.

Notes

1. Reviewed by Burstein (1998a), these studies gauge the impact of public opinion on public policy, and they all point to a significant impact of public opinion. Even the only apparent exception (Wetstein 1996) partly supports this conclusion.

2. Of course, the theory of democratic representation is only one among several different—sometimes opposing—views concerning democracy in modern societies. For example, Marx Ferree and colleagues (2002) distinguish among four models of the public sphere in modern democracies, which can be seen as four different conceptions of democracy itself, as there is a close link among democratic theory and theories of the public sphere: representative liberal

theory (in practice, that discussed here), participatory liberal theory, discursive theory, and constructionist theory.

3. See Page and Shapiro (1993).

4. The data on public opinion shown in this chapter come from a variety of sources, such as published results of surveys and direct information on existing polls. For some of the indications, no information was available on certain years. In these cases, following a procedure similar to the one used for missing data on organizations, I introduce estimates based on linear interpolation. Therefore, the data shown in the figures in this chapter should not be taken as true values for each year but only as a way to approximate the trends in public opinion in the three issue areas of interest. See appendix A for a full list of the data sources and for remarks concerning methodology.

5. Here is the exact meaning of each indicator: percentage of people who are more on the side of protecting the environment (indicator 1); percentage of people who say that environmental protection laws and regulations have not gone far enough (indicator 2); percentage of people who say that U.S. spending on improving and protecting the environment is too little (indicator 3); percentage of people who would sacrifice economic growth to the benefit of environmental quality (indicator 4); percentage of people who say that we are spending too little to improve and protect the environment (indicator 5). Correlation coefficients among the five indicators are the following: .96 (1 and 2, $p \leq .01$), .86 (1 and 3, $p \leq .01$), .80 (1 and 4, $p \leq .01$), .87 (1 and 5, $p \leq .01$), .85 (2 and 3, $p \leq .01$), .84 (2 and 4, $p \leq .01$), .86 (2 and 5, $p \leq .01$), .82 (3 and 4, $p \leq .01$), .95 (3 and 5, $p \leq .01$), .83 (4 and 5, $p \leq .01$). Indicator 3 is the one used in the following time-series analysis. See appendix A.

6. This parallel development, however, is visible only in the long-term trend, whereas the two lines are less correlated as far as annual changes are concerned. In fact, the correlation coefficients between the mobilization of the ecology movement and this indicator of public opinion is not statistically significant (.33 with unconventional protest and .59 with all protest events).

7. Here is the exact meaning of each indicator: percentage of people who oppose the building of more nuclear power plants in the United States (indicator 1); percentage of people who oppose the building of more nuclear plants as a proposal for dealing with the energy crisis (indicator 2). The correlation coefficient between the two indicators is statistically significant ($p \leq .01$) and equals –.97. Indicator 1 is the one used in the following time-series analysis. See appendix A.

8. Here is the exact meaning of each indicator: percentage of people who say that spending for defense is too much (indicator 1); percentage of people who say that we are spending too much on the military, armaments, and defense (indicator 2). See appendix A. The correlation coefficient between the two indicators is statistically significant ($p \leq .01$) and equals .88. Indicator 1 is the one used in the following time-series analysis. See appendix A.

9. This indicator refers to the percentage of people who say that the environment/pollution is the most important problem facing the country today. See appendix A.

10. The proportion of people saying that nuclear power was the major problem facing the country was consistently under 1 percent of the population.

11. Here is the exact meaning of each indicator: percentage of people who say that military spending is the most important problem facing the country today (indicator 1); percentage of people who say that national defense/security is the most important problem facing the country today (indicator 2); percentage of people who say that peace/war/nuclear war is the most important problem facing the country today (indicator 3); percentage of people who say

that international problems/foreign policy is the most important problem facing the country today (indicator 4). The fifth line is a total measure that sums up all other indicators. Correlation coefficients among the five indicators are the following: .31 (1 and 2, n.s.), .53 (1 and 3, $p \leq .05$), .08 (1 and 4, n.s.), .48 (1 and 5, $p \leq .05$), −.02 (2 and 3, n.s.), .17 (2 and 4, n.s.), .19 (2 and 5, n.s.), −.28 (3 and 4, n.s.), .92 (3 and 5, $p \leq .01$), .01 (4 and 5, n.s.). See appendix A.

12. This indicator refers to the percentage of people who say that the risks implied by the development of nuclear plants are unacceptable. See appendix A.

13. This indicator refers to the percentage of people who say that spending for military should be diminished. See appendix A.

14. Here is the exact meaning of each indicator: percentage of people who say that today's stand on the environment is rather unbearable or absolutely unbearable (indicator 1); percentage of people who say that today's public tension about environmental protection is rather positive or absolutely positive (indicator 2); percentage of people who say that territory planning and landscape protection are rather positive or absolutely positive (indicator 3); percentage of people who say government attitude and measures with regard to emissions from motor vehicles are rather insufficient (indicator 4). Correlation coefficients among the four indicators are the following: −.60 (1 and 2, $p \leq .01$), −.84 (1 and 3, $p \leq .01$), .05 (1 and 4, n.s.), .47 (2 and 3, $p \leq .05$), −.06 (2 and 4, n.s.), .67 (3 and 4, $p \leq .05$). Indicator 1 is the one used in the following time-series analysis. See appendix A.

15. This indicator refers to the percentage of people who say that nuclear energy is rather negative or very negative. See appendix A.

16. Here is the exact meaning of each indicator: percentage of people who say that the costs of military are rather unbearable or absolutely unbearable (indicator 1); percentage of people who say that the role of the army, basically, is rather negative or very negative (indicator 2). The correlation coefficient between the two indicators is statistically significant ($p \leq .01$) and equals .85. See appendix A.

17. When more than one indicator of public opinion was available for a single movement, I chose the indicator that bears most directly on the corresponding dependent variable and that is directly comparable across the three issues areas. An alternative way is to index or factor-analyze the available indicators into a single summary measure. However, I opt for a single indicator for each movement to the extent *(a)* that this provides a more simple and straightforward measure of shifts in public opinion and *(b)* that indicators for the same issue area are often highly correlated among them. Specifically, to create the interactive terms, I use the following measures: indicator 3 (environment), indicator 1 (nuclear energy), and indicator 1 (national defense) in the United States; the available indicator on national defense in Italy; indicator 1 (environment) and the available indicator on nuclear energy in Switzerland. See appendix A (specifically, tables A.2a, A2.b, and A.2c).

18. Following the same procedure in chapters 5 and 7, in addition to the analyses with unconventional actions, I conduct the same analyses taking all actions carried by the three movements, with independent variables measured as absolute levels and as annual differences. In the former case, the results are the same as those found for unconventional actions; that is, there is an absence of significant relationships. In the latter case, however, the coefficients concerning the impact of the ecology movement on public opinion in the United States and Switzerland are statistically significant (respectively, with $p < .1$ and $p < .05$). Thus, if we include conventional actions in the measure of movement mobilization, ecology protests seem

to positively affect shifts in public opinion on environmental issues (but we should remember the caution in using these forms of action).

19. The indicators of public opinion are the same used to analyze indirect effects.

20. The additional analyses conducted with the measures of movement mobilization that include both conventional and unconventional actions differ little from those discussed in the main text. First, with independent variables expressed as absolute numbers, we observe a joint effect of the U.S. ecology movement, while that of the antinuclear movement disappears, although the value of the coefficient remains high. Furthermore, the joint effect of the Swiss ecology movement also disappears in spite of the high value of both coefficients. Second, with differenced independent variables, the only statistically significant coefficient that goes in the direction of the movements' goals remains the one concerning the impact of the Swiss ecology movement on spending for environmental protection at the local level. Thus, once again, the general conclusion does not change fundamentally whether we restrict our attention to unconventional actions or look at all forms of actions.

CONCLUSION TO PART II

In the first part of this book, I traced a historical comparison of long-term trends of protest and public policy. This comparison suggests that the development of the mobilization by ecology, antinuclear, and peace movements and that of environmental, nuclear energy, and national security policies appear at least in part to covary (see conclusion to part I). In the second part of the book, I provide a more systematic analysis of the relationship between protest and policy, looking at the same time at the role of political alliances and public opinion as facilitating factors for the policy impact of the three movements under study. The purpose of this short section is twofold. First, I examine whether a joint-effect model, including all explanatory factors (protest actions, political alliances, and public opinion), strengthens the impact of the three movements. Second, I provide an overall assessment of the analyses conducted in the book's second part.

Table II.1 shows the joint effect of the interactive terms, combining unconventional mobilization, political alliances, and public opinion on public policy in the three countries included in the study.[1] Two interactive terms are used for the United States, as political alliances are measured through both the formal and informal indicators, while a single interactive term is used for Italy and for Switzerland. In addition, the results concerning the two latter countries suffer from the same lack of data that prevents our evaluating certain effects, in particular, those that regard public opinion.

Like the previous analyses, these final ones do not yield results that hold consistently across countries and across movements (also due to the lack of data on certain aspects), but they do point to the expected direction. The strongest relationship, in the case of the United States, is the one concerning the joint effect of protest; political alliances, as measured through pro-ecology elite statements; and public opinion on environmental spending at the national level. In contrast, the coefficient concerning the local level is

Table II.1. Joint Effect of Unconventional Mobilization, Political Alliances, and Public Opinion on Public Policy in Three Countries, 1975–1995

Dependent Variables	Spending for Environmental Protection (National) (t_1)	Spending for Environmental Protection (Local) (t_1)	Nuclear Energy Production (t_1)	Number of Construction Permits (t_1)	Spending Defense for (t_1)
United States					
Movement * allies * public 1 (t_0)	.22	−.21	−.49*	−.09	.35
(D-W)	(1.93)	(1.95)	(2.11)	(1.99)	(1.89)
N	16	16	16	16	19
Movement * allies * public 2 (t_0)	.66***	.41	−.44*	−.17	.29
(D-W)	(2.02)	(2.10)	(2.16)	(2.00)	(1.89)
N	16	16	16	16	19
Italy					
Movement * allies * public (t_0)	—	—	—	—	.14
(D-W)	—	—	—	—	(2.05)
N	—	—	—	—	18
Switzerland					
Movement * allies * public (t_0)	.30	.48**	.52**	—	—
(D-W)	(2.14)	(1.98)	(1.91)	—	—
N	20	20	20	—	—

Note: Standardized regression coefficients (bivariate) generated with a generalized least-squared method of estimation (Prais-Winsten) assuming a first-order autoregressive process. Durbin-Watson test for serial correlation and number of observations (series length) are shown within parentheses. The independent variables include a one-year lag. The dependent variables are expressed in terms of annual percentage change. See appendix A for a description of the interactive terms.
*$p < .10$; **$p < .05$; ***$p < .01$.

not statistically significant, although it is relatively strong. A significant relationship can also be observed between the interactive terms for the antinuclear movement and nuclear energy production, this time with both the formal and informal indicators. Finally, as in most of the previous analyses, the peace movement does not seem to have had an impact on defense spending, even when supported by political allies and a favorable public opinion.

The only available measure for Italy confirms the lack of effect of the peace movement, as the coefficient referring to the relationship between the three-way interactive term and defense spending by the Italian government is not statistically significant. As I said, unfortunately, I do not have information on the other two movements.

Finally, the results concerning Switzerland reflect those seen previously. Specifically, among the two movements for which I could create a measure of joint effect, only the ecology movement seems to have been successful in bringing about policy changes in the desired direction. This, however, holds only for environmental spending at the local level. In contrast, the coefficient for the antinuclear movement is significant; but its sign is positive, which points to the lack of a real impact.

This time, the analyses, conducted with differenced independent variables instead of absolute measures, provide a substantially different picture (see table BII.1, in appendix B). In effect, none of the relationships examined displays a significant coefficient. Thus, at least in this case, the question of whether absolute levels or differences matter the most receives a clear-cut answer in favor of the former.[2]

We can now move to the final stage of our analysis by trying to put together the pieces presented in the second part of the book. I do so with the help of two summary tables. Table II.2 summarizes the results of time-series analysis conducted

Table II.2. Summary of Results of Time-Series Analysis (chapters 5, 7, 8, and conclusion to part II)

	Levels	Differences	Overall
Effect of Protest on Public Policy			
United States			
Ecology	no	no	no
Antinuclear	no	no	no
Peace	no	no	no
Italy			
Ecology	no	no	no
Antinuclear	yes	no	yes
Peace	no	no	no
Switzerland			
Ecology	(yes)	no	(yes)
Antinuclear	no	no	no
Peace	no	no	no
Effect of Configuration of Power on Public Policy			
United States			
Ecology	yes	no	yes
Antinuclear	no	no	no
Peace	no	no	no
Italy			
Ecology	no	no	no
Antinuclear	no	no	no
Peace	no	no	no
Switzerland			
Ecology	no	no	no
Antinuclear	no	no	no
Peace	no	no	no
Effect of Protest on Configuration of Power			
United States			
Ecology	no	no	no
Antinuclear	no	no	no
Peace	(yes)	yes	yes

(continued)

Table II.2. (Continued)

	Levels	Differences	Overall
Effect of Public Opinion on Public Policy			
United States			
Ecology	no	(yes)	(yes)
Antinuclear	no	no	no
Peace	no	no	no
Italy			
Peace	no	no	no
Switzerland			
Ecology	no	no	no
Antinuclear	no	no	no
Effect of Protest on Public Opinion			
United States			
Ecology	no	no	no
Antinuclear	no	no	no
Peace	no	no	no
Italy			
Peace	no	no	no
Switzerland			
Ecology	no	no	no
Antinuclear	no	no	no
Joint Effect of Protest and Political Alliances			
United States			
Ecology	yes	no	yes
Antinuclear	no	no	no
Peace	no	no	no
Italy			
Ecology	no	no	no
Antinuclear	yes	no	yes
Peace	no	no	no
Switzerland			
Ecology	(yes)	no	(yes)
Antinuclear	no	no	no
Peace	no	no	no
Joint Effect of Protest and Public Opinion			
United States			
Ecology	no	no	no
Antinuclear	(yes)	no	(yes)
Peace	no	no	no
Italy			
Peace	no	no	no
Switzerland			
Ecology	yes	(yes)	yes
Antinuclear	no	no	no

(continued)

Table II.2.   (Continued)

	Levels	Differences	Overall
Joint Effect of Protest, Political Alliances, and Public Opinion			
United States			
Ecology	yes	no	yes
Antinuclear	(yes)	no	(yes)
Peace	no	no	no
Italy			
Peace	no	no	no
Switzerland			
Ecology	yes	no	yes
Antinuclear	no	no	no

Note: The presence of effect is given by a significant regression coefficient with $p < .05$ or $p < .10$ (within parentheses). Protest is measured through unconventional actions. When there are two indicators for the same independent variable (e.g. configuration of power), an effect is present if at least one of them is significant. An effect concerning spending for environmental protection is present if the coefficient is significant either at the national or local level. Overall assessment: 0 yes = no; 1 or 2 yes = yes.

in chapters 5, 7, and 8, as well as in the conclusion to part II of the book (the findings concerning the organizational levels shown in chapter 6 are excluded from this general assessment).[3] The table divides in eight parts, each devoted to one of the specific types of effect examined in the preceding chapters. For each of these types of effects, I summarize the findings yielded by the analyses with independent variables expressed as absolute levels (first column) and annual differences (second column). In addition, I provide an overall assessment based on the first two counts (third column).[4]

The most evident result is the low number of positive scores, attesting to a general difficulty of the selected variables to have an impact on public policy. In terms of social movement outcomes, this suggests that ecology, antinuclear, and peace movements have not been very successful during the two decades examined in this study, at least as far as influencing spending for environmental protection, nuclear energy production, and military expenditures is concerned. This holds in general for all three countries and all three movements, although some variations can be observed in both respects.

If we next compare the first two columns across the eight types of effect, we can easily see that taking differences, instead of absolute levels, to measure the independent variables does not improve the chances of success of social movements. Quite on the contrary, except in the case of the impact of public opinion on policy, we observe a higher number of positive scores—that is, a greater amount of positive effects—in the column referring to levels than in the one concerning differences. Thus, as far as effects on public policy are concerned, it seems that the power holders are more likely to respond to changes in absolute levels from one year to the other—if any—than to differences, for example, in protest activities.

Finally, we can identify which kind of effect has occurred most often by looking at the third column in the table, which gives the overall assessment based on the scores shown in first two columns. Only two direct effects of protest can be observed, one for the Italian antinuclear movement, the other for the Swiss ecology movement (at the 10 percent significance level). The impact is not stronger with the two intervening variables. First, the configuration of power has played a positive role only in the case of environmental policy in the United States, while only the U.S. peace movement was instrumental in producing changes in the configuration of power (but we should remember that I did not test this relationship for the other two countries). Second, public opinion has had some impact on environmental policy in the United States, but I found no effect whatsoever of protest on public opinion.

Things are quite different if we look at the three parts of the table concerning the joint effects. In all three cases, the number of positive effects (based on the overall assessment) are significantly higher than with direct relationships. This confirms the hypothesis that interactions among protest activities, political alliances, and public opinion increase the likelihood that social movements bring about policy changes. Furthermore, the ecology movement displays the highest number of significant effects, followed by the antinuclear movement and then the peace movement, with the last having no joint effect at all. Again, this is in line with the hypothesis that these three movements act under different conditions for their policy impact, precisely in the order just mentioned.

What interests us the most in the perspective of this book is to compare the three models of social movement outcomes as well as to ascertain whether their impact varies across countries and across movements as a result of differences in political opportunity structures, respectively, in the viability of claims made by the three movements. Table II.3, which gives an overall assessment of direct, indirect, and joint effects of the three movements studied, allows us to do so. Each of the six parts of the table deals with one of the six models of social movement outcomes that I address in the preceding chapters: the direct-effect model, the two variants of the indirect-model, and the three variants of the joint-effect model. These models are evaluated by country and by movements. The yes/no scores are based on the third column in table II.2. In addition, an overall assessment of the strength of the impact is provided for each country across movements and for each movement across countries.[5]

Let us focus on the overall assessment of the strength of the impact (last row in each part of the table and fourth column). We can stress three points. First and most important, all three types of joint effect are stronger than either the direct or indirect effect. The indirect-effect model, in particular, was found not to be very powerful. In contrast, some limited direct impact can be observed, which goes counter to the hypothesis that the presence of political allies and a favorable public opinion improve the chances of success of social movements. However, according to the general idea put forward in this book, these two factors do facilitate the movements insofar as they intervene simultaneously with a rise in protest actions. The stronger explanatory power of the joint-effect model clearly supports this hypothesis.

Table II.3. Overall Assessment of Direct, Indirect, and Joint Effects of Social Movements

	United States	Italy	Switzerland	Overall
Direct Effect				
Ecology movement	no	no	(yes)	intermediate
Antinuclear movement	no	yes	no	intermediate
Peace movement	no	no	no	weak
Overall	weak	intermediate	intermediate	—
Indirect Effect (First Variant: Political Alliances)				
Ecology movement	no	—	—	weak
Antinuclear movement	no	—	—	weak
Peace movement	no	—	—	weak
Overall	weak	—	—	—
Indirect Effect (Second Variant: Public Opinion)				
Ecology movement	no	—	no	weak
Antinuclear movement	no	—	no	weak
Peace movement	no	no	—	weak
Overall	weak	weak	weak	—
Joint Effect (First Variant: Protest and Political Alliances)				
Ecology movement	yes	no	(yes)	strong
Antinuclear movement	no	yes	no	intermediate
Peace movement	no	no	no	weak
Overall	intermediate	intermediate	intermediate	—
Joint Effect (Second Variant: Protest and Public Opinion)				
Ecology movement	no	—	yes	intermediate
Antinuclear movement	(yes)	—	no	intermediate
Peace movement	no	no	—	weak
Overall	intermediate	weak	intermediate	—
Joint Effect (Third Variant: Protest, Political Alliances, and Public Opinion)				
Ecology movement	yes	—	yes	strong
Antinuclear movement	(yes)	—	no	intermediate
Peace movement	no	no	—	weak
Overall	strong	weak	intermediate	—

Note: Based on the third column of table II.2. Overall assessment: 0 yes = weak; 1 yes = intermediate; 2 or 3 yes = strong.

Second, comparing across movements, we observe a clear pattern of increasing influence as we move from one movement to the other. Specifically, as we saw earlier, the ecology movement is the most successful, followed by the antinuclear movement, and then the peace movement, which characterizes a lack of policy impact. The third variant of the joint-effect model of social movement outcomes (last row in the table) illustrates this pattern quite well.

Third, when comparing across countries, one finds it difficult to draw reliable conclusions. However, we do observe a difference consisting in a strong joint effect of the movements in the United States; an intermediate one in Switzerland; and a weak one in Italy, especially if we look at the third variant of the joint-effect model. In this case, the two federal countries with more open political opportunity structures seem to be more conducive to a policy impact of social movements than the more centralized country. However, this might simply be a result of the lack of data on public opinion available for the Italian case concerning the ecology and antinuclear movements. In fact, if we look at the first variant of the joint-effect model of social movement outcomes (fourth row in the table), we can see that no difference exists among the three countries, whereas Italy has a lower score on both the second and third variants.

In sum, the analyses presented in the second part of the book support the general hypothesis that the policy impact of social movements is facilitated by the presence of allies within the institutional arenas and a favorable public opinion. This facilitating action, however, occurs only if these two factors are accompanied by a sustained mobilization of the movements. The analyses also show that certain claims are more easy to meet than others due to the very nature of the policy areas and issues addressed, hence supporting the hypothesis about the varying viability of claims. Specifically, ecology movements are in a better position than antinuclear movements and especially peace movements to bring about policy changes. It is now time to conclude our journey through three decades of environmental, antinuclear, and peace protests by pointing out the limitations of my study, stressing some of its implications, and suggesting some avenues for further research. This is the task of the ninth and final chapter.

Notes

1. The indicators of political alliances and public opinion are the same used in previous chapters.

2. For these final analyses, I show the results obtained with the measures of movement mobilization that include all forms of action (conventional and unconventional). If independent variables are expressed in absolute terms, only the U.S. ecology movement has had a joint effect on public policy, both at the national and local levels (in the latter case, only with the informal measure of political alliances). If independent variables are measured as differences, the results remain basically the same as with unconventional actions only, namely, that none of the three movements displays an impact in the desired direction. Thus, when we take all forms of actions, instead of unconventional protests only, what changes is basically the disappearance of the impact of the U.S. antinuclear movement.

3. This summary table only refers to the analyses conducted with unconventional protest events. It thus excludes the additional analyses with all events (conventional and unconventional). However, it is the former that interest us the most. Furthermore, as we have seen, these additional analyses do not change the fundamental picture obtained with unconventional actions only.

4. The presence of an effect in this table is given by a regression coefficient significant at the 5 percent and 10 percent levels (shown within parentheses). Protest is measured through unconventional actions. When two indicators for the same independent variable are used in the analyses (e.g., for the configuration of power), I consider an effect to be present when at least

one of them is statistically significant. In the case of spending for environmental protection, I consider an effect to be present when the coefficient is significant, either at the national or local level. Scores for the overall assessment have been attributed as follows: "no," if no effect is observed on both counts (levels and differences); "yes," if an effect is observed on at least one of the two counts.

5. Scores for the overall assessment have been attributed as follows: "weak," if no effect is observed on the three counts (either across countries or across movements); "intermediate," if an effect is observed on one count; "strong," if an effect is observed on at least two counts.

CHAPTER NINE

Conclusion

The aims of this book were threefold. The first objective was to be descriptive: provide a picture of a quarter century of ecology, antinuclear, and peace movements in three Western countries, namely, the United States, Italy, and Switzerland. Given the importance and strong mobilization of these three movements in all three countries and elsewhere, it seemed to me that a comprehensive, though necessarily cursory, overview was in order. The second, more important goal was theoretical: to offer a model for explaining the policy consequences of social movements, that is, the impact of their protest activities on certain aspects of public policy. This proposal includes certain methodological suggestions, in particular, a longitudinal approach and a focus on interactive, or joint, effects. Third and related to this, is the explanatory goal of my study, insofar as I aimed to provide an illustration of how this model works through the example of ecology, antinuclear, and peace movements. In other words, I tried to explain variations in the policy impact of these three movements, both among them and across countries.

In an attempt to reach these three objectives, I adopted an approach based on protest event analysis. Thus, the empirical basis for my analysis was formed by a systematic reconstruction of the protest activities carried by the three movements under study, during a twenty-five-year period. Indicators for the other factors considered in my model were then added—most notably, those concerning the movements' organizational strength; the structure of political alliances; the state of public opinion in the areas addressed by the movements; and, of course, measures for the main dependent variable, public policy. All these variables were then transformed to be analyzed longitudinally. This empirical basis has provided the bone around which I tried to put some flesh for each of the main factors taken into account and their impact on public policy: protest, social movement organization, political alliances, and public opinion.

The findings of this book have already been summarized at the end of each chapter (concerning each aspect taken separately) and in the two partial conclusions (concerning the historical overview and time-series analysis). In particular, the conclusion to part II of the book provides a synthesis of the principal results of the whole analysis. Therefore, it would be redundant to repeat them here. In this concluding chapter, I briefly go back to some of their implications and point out the limitations of my study as well as suggest a number of avenues for further research on this topic.

Social Protest and Policy Change: Some Theoretical Implications

This book addresses the issue of the relation between social protest and policy change. Its central substantial question concerns the policy impact of ecology, antinuclear, and peace movements. Can we conclude that these movements were successful in the three countries and during the period considered? In the historical overview provided in the first part of the book, we observe to some extent the presence of patterns of covariation between the development of the mobilization of ecology, antinuclear, and peace movements in the three countries of the study, and that of environmental, nuclear energy, and national security policies (see conclusion to part I). The systematic analyses carried in the second part, however, have yielded only limited evidence that this covariation unveils an impact of protest on public policy, at least not a direct effect (see conclusion to part II). To be able to bring about policy change, protest needs two crucial external resources: political alliances and public opinion. More precisely, the policy impact of social movements—at least the three movements considered in this study—rests on a combination of at least four factors: their mobilization, the presence of elite allies ready to support their claims, a public opinion in favor of their claims, and the very nature of the policy issues they address. In other words, my analyses tend to support the joint-effect model of social movement outcomes, as opposed to the direct-effect and the indirect-effect models.

These results have implications for social movement theory and, more generally, for democratic theory. The implications for social movement theory are quite straightforward: my study confirms the role of political opportunity structures. Not only are the latter crucial for the emergence of protest and its unfolding over time, but they also play a role when it comes to explaining the consequences of social movements. Here I focus on one particular aspect of opportunity structures, namely, the structure of political alliances. Although I could fully address this issue only in the case of the United States, my analysis suggests that the presence of elite actors, and especially their overt support to the causes of movements in the public domain, increases the likelihood that things will move in the direction desired by movement participants. However, the presence and stance of the movements' potential allies do not automatically translate into policies that meet the movements' aims. For this to happen, the latter must mobilize and thus put some pressure on decision makers. It is here that we see the explanatory power of the joint-effect model of social movement outcomes.

Protest actions and the presence of powerful allies in the institutional arenas are both needed to bring about substantial policy changes.

From the point of view of social movement theory, my study confirms the importance of political opportunity structures—specifically, political alliances—not only to understand movement emergence but also to comprehend their outcomes. Yet, it does so by adding one qualification and two specifications. The qualification is that the type of issues raised by the movements matters. When the issue or policy area addressed by challengers is central to the core tasks of the state, protest is less likely to have an impact on public policy. The first specification refers to Kriesi and colleagues' argument (1995) that allies are an opportunity for social movements when they are in the opposition. When it comes to movement outcomes, allies have a greater impact when they are in the government and hence in a better position to formulate and implement public policies. The second, more general specification refers to the idea pointed out by authors such as Tarrow (1993, 1998) and Piven and Cloward (1979) that reform stems from particularly threatening cycles of protest or from periods of serious turmoil. Power holders respond to such protests to abate the protest and restore the public order. While I agree with this view, my study suggests that social movements can produce substantial policy change in the absence of a cycle of protest that threatens the public order. When movements can benefit from the presence of strong political alliances, even reformist movements (which only rarely resort to disruptive or violent actions) can have a substantial impact on public policy.

The implications of my study for democratic theory are underwritten by the role of public opinion. According to the theory of representative democracy (see Burstein 1998b, 1999), the power holders should not have any interest in responding to the claims made by social movements, because the latter are minority actors with little electoral weight. Public opinion, in contrast, usually represents the preferences of a majority of citizens. Therefore, shifts in public opinion should be followed by corresponding changes in public policy. The weak effect of public opinion found in my study might surprise analysts who study the public's role in policy change and theorists of representative democracy. The former have pointed out on several occasions that public opinion strongly influences public policy (see Burstein 1998a). The latter argue that democratic institutions and governments are largely responsive to the opinion held by the majority of citizens.

Thus, from the point of view of democratic theory, my study indicates that things are more complicated than the pluralist view and the theory of representative democracy suggest. For one thing, the fact that social movements have little—if any—direct effect on public policy counters the pluralist ideal of the possibility for minority groups to influence the power holders. At the same time, however, we find the shifts in public opinion to be less effective than democratic theorists may expect. At least in the areas of nuclear power and the military, if not in that of environmental protection, the decision makers in the three countries do not seem to have followed the will of the public. This might be due to the low public concern toward those issues, that is, the low salience of those issues; but it could as well be the result of a lower degree of responsiveness of power holders than those posited by the theory of representative democracy. My analysis suggests a third alternative: that democratic governments are most responsive to the combination of protest actions and public opinion. I would like to stress once again that here it is question of a combination, in the sense of a joint effect of these two factors, as I have rejected a model that sees social movements as having an indirect impact on policy via either political alliances or public opinion.

Finally, my study suggests that the impact of social movements on public policy depends on certain internal characteristics. This may not necessarily be their organizational features, which Gamson (1990) and many subsequent authors have stressed. In contrast, it appears that the chances of success of social movements rest on the very issues they raise. In other words, while political alliances and public opinion may constitute important external resources, their facilitating role varies according to what I call the viability of claims. The latter seems to play an important role regardless of country, as the three movements studied have all had varying impacts. Movements that address low-profile issues concerning domestic policy are more likely to be successful in their efforts to influence public policy, or issues that are considered relatively marginal for the interests of the state (low profile) and of which the state is more autonomous (domestic policy). This is the case of the ecology movement. In contrast, movements that address high-profile issues concerning foreign policy have little chances of success, that is, issues that belong to the core interests of the state (high profile) and for which the state is conditioned by its position in the system of international relations (foreign policy). This scenario is true even in the presence of external resources in the form of political allies and a favorable public opinion. The peace movement is a case in point. The antinuclear movement represents a sort of intermediary situation, as it addresses an often highly profiled domestic policy area.[1] These differences explain, at least in part, the varying impact of the three movements.

Limitations of the Study

In drawing the conclusions of my study, it is perhaps not useless to point out some of its limitations. I would like to stress three aspects in this regard. First the methodological approach that I have adopted to investigate the relationship between protest and policy change calls for some caution in assessing and interpreting the findings of the quantitative analyses shown in the second part of the book.[2] Time-series analysis is a promising and adequate method when one is interested in studying relationships between variables measured as developments over time; yet, one also has to be aware of the limitations of this method, in particular, the one owing to its rigidity with respect to the time unit used. In my analyses, the time unit is the year. This choice was dictated above all by the main explanandum: public policy. Since I chose to measure policy change through shifts in government spending for environmental protection or military purposes (or its equivalent in terms of nuclear energy production), the year as a unit of time seemed to be the most appropriate for this kind of analysis. Spending is decided yearly; therefore, this choice is the most appropriate. However, to some extent, the choice of the time unit is always arbitrary. Other periods could have been chosen as well, for example—and perhaps more appropriately—a two-year period. In fact, one could arguably maintain that policy makers react to protest activities and other changes in their social and political environment not after one year but after two years or even longer. Furthermore, it is likely that movement mobilization has "distributed lag effects" on public policy; that is, they may affect policy not only after one year but also after two, three, or even more years. All this must be taken into account when assessing the substantive findings of this book.

Second, while the comparative perspective allows us to see whether the hypothesis holds across countries (that social movements are more likely to have a policy impact), the limited number of countries certainly prevents us from drawing empirical generalizations from the analysis provided in the preceding chapters. The logic of comparison I adopted in this study resembles the one Skocpol and Somers (1980) have called "parallel demonstration of theory." Following this logic, more cases, representing other contexts, should be added to strengthen the demonstration. Similarly, the focus on certain movements allows us to look for variations among the three movements depending on the viability of their claims, but is not a strong basis for extending the findings to other types of movements, for example, to labor movements or—on the other side of the political spectrum—to extreme-right movements. Such impossibility to generalize the findings of my study beyond the cases at hand is made even more serious by the sizable amount of missing data in the time series, which makes the testing of certain hypotheses impossible for certain countries and movements.

Third, although I speak of public policy in general terms, it must be put clear once again that my analysis looks only at a particular form of state action, namely, those changes that can be seen in the increase in the amount of resources invested by the state in the areas touched by the movements' mobilization. This narrows the scope of the study and its results, in at least two respects. First, policy change obviously stems from a much wider range of phenomena than simply government spending, for example, the enactment of certain pieces of legislation. I address this aspect only marginally in the first part of the book, but I did not include measures of it in the quantitative analyses. Furthermore, my focus on public policy does not allow us to say anything about the substantive impact of these changes on the actual situation against which the three movements studied have mobilized. More broadly speaking, public policy only contributes in part to understanding the processes of social and political change, which in the final analysis is why we study social movements and their relations with the political institutions and with their larger social environment.

Second, social movements probably have effects well beyond policy changes. As Tilly (1999) has once underscored, their impact is far from being limited to the explicit demands made by movement participants. Furthermore, political effects are far from being the only outcomes of their challenges, and they are probably not even the most important ones. This is all the more true concerning policy outcomes, which are only one part of a broader category of their political effects. Protest can produce political changes in at least three ways: by altering the power relations between challengers and authorities; by forcing policy change; and by provoking broader and usually more durable systemic changes, both on the structural and the cultural level.[3] In other words, social movements—including the three movements addressed in this study—produce a range of consequences in the social and cultural realms. I try to at least in part grasp the latter aspect in the chapter devoted to public opinion, but it is clear that the main focus of the book is elsewhere, namely, in the relationship between protest and policy change, with public opinion intervening as an external resource to be used by social movements in their efforts to influence public policy.

Suggestions for Further Research

The suggestions for further research that I would make to conclude our journey through a quarter century of ecology, antinuclear, and peace protests follow straightforwardly from the limitations just mentioned. The first suggestion is that one should study the relation between protest and public policy through a comparative and historical research design. Comparing across movements as well as across countries undoubtedly strengthens the explanatory power of the proposed models. Most of all, the importance of a comparative perspective underlies two basic tools of social science and scientific research: first, controls that allow us to reject rival hypotheses and theories; and, second, empirical generalizations that allow us to extend the results of our own research beyond the particular case at hand. Concerning the time dimension, as the political process approach to social movements has made clear, contentious politics is a process that must be studied in its dynamic aspects as it unfolds over time. This is all the more true when we address the issue of the consequences of the protest activities carried by social movements, which implies dynamics of action–reaction between movements, their potential allies, the general public, and decision makers.

The second suggestion for further research is intimately related to the first, and it consists in extending the empirical basis of the analysis in space and time. While the dataset used in this study is quite rich, covering three countries and three movements over nearly three decades, it obviously is limited in space, content, and time. First, I think it would be worth the effort to push this kind of analysis further by including more countries and other movements. Second, other historical periods could be explored, and above all the length of the time series to be studied could be extended to cover longer historical periods.

A third suggestion concerns the kinds of analyses carried in the second part of the book. Time-series analysis presents certain rigidities that weaken its power and applicability.[4] The most important is that it utilizes fixed and often arbitrary units of time (e.g., the year, the quarter, the month, etc.). This can be problematic insofar as the relationships under investigation show their effects in shorter or longer periods. In the latter case, taking into account distributed lag effects can help to solve or at least reduce the problem. If the effects are to be felt in a period shorter than the selected time unit, however, they will not be shown in the analysis. It is very likely, for example, that some consequences of social movements can be observed within weeks or even days after their mobilization occurred. These effects clearly are lost in the kind of analysis discussed in the previous chapters. Event history analysis would be an alternative time-sensitive method that could be applied with success to the kind of theoretical issues addressed in this book.[5] This is a set of techniques for the study of the timing of various kinds of events, which might take the form of state transitions or event recurrences. Unlike time-series analysis, event history analysis does not impose any restrictions regarding the time unit to be considered, which is a considerable advantage compared to the former method.

The fourth and final suggestion concerns the focus of the research in another, yet complementary direction. I am referring to giving more "substance" to the rather abstract and formal approach proposed here. It is true that in the first part of the book I try to sketch a historical account of the three movements and the three policy areas addressed by them in each country. Yet, this was intended only to provide a background knowledge of the development of protest and relevant public policy during the period considered, and the quantitative analyses carried out in the second part are purged of any specific content of the relationship between protest and policy. In other words, time-series analysis tends to direct the focus toward quantity rather than quality. Furthermore, as I said, time-series analysis tells a story of covariation rather than causality, at least in the perspective followed here. A more qualitative approach that complements the quantitative approach adopted here would help to fill this "substance" gap and move the analysis toward the processes and mechanisms that account for the translation of protest activities into policy change. Considering the role of political alliances, public opinion, and the characteristics of the issues addressed by the movements is one step in this direction. Supplementing the quantitative analyses (such as the one proposed in the second part of this book) with a more qualitative approach is another, necessary step to be made.

In the end, the kind of analysis offered in this book is only one preliminary step in a much larger endeavor that will bring us closer to an understanding of the relationship between social protest and policy change, or, more generally speaking, to the processes through which social movements can produce social and political change by engaging in protest activities. As Tilly has suggested (1999, 270), this implies a six-step approach:

1. to formulate clear theories of the causal processes by which social movements produce their effects;
2. to limit investigations to the effects made plausible by those theories;
3. to work upstream by identifying instances of the effects, then seeing whether the hypothesized causal chain was actually operating;
4. to work downstream by identifying instances of the causal chain in operation, then seeing whether and how its hypothesized effects occurred;
5. to work midstream by examining whether the internal links of the causal chain operated as the theory requires; and
6. to rule out, to the extent possible, competing explanations of the effects.

Here I address at best the first two steps. I encourage other researchers interested in the consequences of social movements and protest to improve on my analysis and especially to go further in the six-step approach suggested by Tilly; then we will probably know a bit more about the role that popular contention has for social and political change.

Notes

1. In fact, we have to remember that the high-profile or low-profile character of a given issue of policy area can vary from one country to the other, hence further complicating the picture and especially the task of disentangling the policy impact of social movements.

2. See appendix A.

3. This threefold distinction corresponds roughly to Kitschelt's distinction (1986) between procedural, substantial, and structural impacts of social movements. See chapter 2 for other typologies found in the existing literature.

4. See appendix A.

5. See Strang (1994) for a brief introduction to event history methods. See Allison (1984) for a more comprehensive overview.

APPENDIX A

Data, Measurements, and Methods

This appendix is intended to provide more detailed information about the data, measurements, and methods used throughout this book. Specifically, I discuss three issues:

1. the sources and kind of data that provide the empirical material, as well as the operationalization of the variables used in the analyses;
2. the method adopted for time-series analysis; and
3. the reliability and robustness of protest event data.

Data and Measurements

The data analyzed in this book consist of yearly time series measuring social movement mobilization and organization; the structure of political alliances; trends in public opinion; and public policy in the United States, Italy, and Switzerland. Tables A.1a, A.1b, and A.1c describe the variables used in the empirical analyses for each country. Next I describe the data sources for each group of variables: social movement mobilization, social movement organizations, political alliances, public opinion, and public policy. In addition, I discuss the construction of interactive terms and the problem of missing data in the time series.

Social Movement Mobilization

Following a methodology that proved useful in previous studies of social movements (e.g., Kriesi et al. 1995; McAdam 1982; Rucht, Koopmans, and Neidhart 1998;

Table A.1a. Description of Variables Used in the Regression Analyses (United States)

	N	Min	Max	Mean	Standard Deviation
Social Movement Mobilization					
Number of protest events by the ecology movement	21	20.00	64.00	35.29	13.81
Number of protest events by the antinuclear movement	21	.00	87.00	11.67	19.17
Number of protest events by the peace movement	21	.00	124.00	23.76	29.37
Number of unconventional protest events by the ecology movement	21	1.00	21.00	9.14	5.15
Number of unconventional protest events by the antinuclear movement	21	.00	73.00	7.95	16.31
Number of unconventional protest events by the peace movement	21	.00	71.00	15.33	19.12
Number of radical protest events by the ecology movement	21	.00	9.00	3.00	2.49
Number of radical protest events by the antinuclear movement	21	.00	16.00	2.62	4.14
Number of radical protest events by the peace movement	21	.00	22.00	4.52	5.13
Spending by ecology PACs	21	61,575.45	2,469,333.10	1,045,634.40	766,866.92
Spending by peace PACs	21	291,516.69	2,052,665.80	775,145.87	569,244.05

Social Movement Organization

Number of members of selected ecology organizations	21	1,009,800.00	5,127,000.00	2,305,639.00	13,737,999.51
Financial resources of selected ecology organizations	21	223,000,000.00	502,000,000.00	306,000,000.00	86,951,491.68
Number of members of selected antinuclear organizations	21	119,200.00	170,474.00	142,192.19	19,126.92
Financial resources of selected antinuclear organizations	21	5,297,537.00	7,807,545.00	6,504,819.80	730,105.52
Number of members of selected peace organizations	21	46,800.00	353,500.00	199,679.19	135,024.95
Financial resources of selected peace organizations	21	29,920,615.00	63,638,252.00	45,190,571.00	8,940,916.37

Political Alliances

Percentage of Democratic seats in Congress	21	47.00	66.00	59.48	4.68
Number of pro-ecology statements by political elites	21	.00	16.00	5.29	4.45
Number of antinuclear statements by political elites	21	.00	9.00	1.95	2.33
Number of pro-peace statements by political elites	21	.00	30.00	6.81	6.61

(continued)

Table A.1a. (Continued)

	N	Min	Max	Mean	Standard Deviation
Public Opinion					
Percentage of people who say spending for the environment is too little	16	48.00	71.00	56.25	7.38
Percentage of people who oppose building of more nuclear plants	16	30.00	63.00	42.18	11.08
Percentage of people who say spending for defense is too much	19	14.00	47.00	36.50	11.32
Public Policy					
Total budget of the Environmental Protection Agency over total central government expenditures	21	.40	1.07	.61	.22
Spending by the states for environmental protection over total states' expenditures	21	1.78	7.78	4.68	1.98
Nuclear energy production over total electricity production	21	9.00	22.49	15.91	4.66
Number of construction permits for nuclear plants	21	6.00	90.00	39.71	32.40
Defense outlays over total central government expenditures	21	17.92	28.08	23.97	2.85

Note: Descriptive statistics referring to variables expressed in absolute terms. All variables concerning money are expressed in constant USD (basis: 1990).

Table A.1b. Description of Variables Used in the Regression Analyses (Italy)

	N	Min	Max	Mean	Standard Deviation
Social Movement Mobilization					
Number of protest events by the ecology movement	21	10.00	55.00	28.00	13.70
Number of protest events by the antinuclear movement	21	.00	16.00	2.38	3.93
Number of protest events by the peace movement	21	1.00	44.00	10.90	9.97
Number of unconventional protest events by the ecology movement	21	.00	32.00	11.95	8.96
Number of unconventional protest events by the antinuclear movement	21	.00	8.00	1.10	2.00
Number of unconventional protest events by the peace movement	21	1.00	22.00	7.14	5.88
Number of radical protest events by the ecology movement	21	.00	9.00	3.29	2.70
Number of radical protest events by the antinuclear movement	21	.00	3.00	.33	.80
Number of radical protest events by the peace movement	21	.00	6.00	1.29	1.55
Social Movement Organization					
Number of members of selected ecology organizations	21	20,781.00	198,107.00	75,898.62	53,810.90

(continued)

Table A.1b. (Continued)

	N	Min	Max	Mean	Standard Deviation
Financial resources of selected ecology organizations	21	1,680,000,000.00	8,110,000,000.00	4,590,000,000.00	2,231,455,429.40
Number of members of selected peace organizations	21	.00	3,675.00	1,075.33	1,386.25
Financial resources of selected peace organizations	21	.00	307,000,000.00	73,207,496.00	103,360,989.27
Political Alliances					
Percentage of leftist seats in parliament	21	35.00	50.00	46.05	4.49
Percentage of (former) communist seats in parliament	21	18.00	34.00	27.33	4.29
Public Opinion					
Percentage of people who say spending for military should be diminished	19	27.00	66.00	41.92	10.05
Public Policy					
Central government spending for environmental protection over total central government expenditures	21	1.12	4.76	1.91	.88
Nuclear energy production over total electricity production	21	.00	4.60	1.54	1.58
Central government spending for national defense over total central government expenditures	21	19.39	23.03	21.25	1.09

Note: Descriptive statistics referring to variables expressed in absolute terms. All variables concerning money are expressed in constant ITL (basis: 1990).

Table A.1c. Description of Variables Used in the Regression Analyses (Switzerland)

	N	Min	Max	Mean	Standard Deviation
Social Movement Mobilization					
Number of protest events by the ecology movement	21	12.00	54.00	27.62	12.24
Number of protest events by the antinuclear movement	21	.00	23.00	8.86	7.05
Number of protest events by the peace movement	21	.00	33.00	9.81	7.52
Number of unconventional protest events by the ecology movement	21	2.00	21.00	8.90	5.21
Number of unconventional protest events by the antinuclear movement	21	.00	13.00	4.57	4.45
Number of unconventional protest events by the peace movement	21	.00	21.00	5.86	5.39
Number of radical protest events by the ecology movement	21	.00	4.00	.95	1.32
Number of radical protest events by the antinuclear movement	21	.00	3.00	.67	1.06
Number of radical protest events by the peace movement	21	.00	5.00	.90	1.61
Social Movement Organization					
Number of members of selected ecology organizations	21	160,412.00	399,176.00	298,996.57	75,171.14
Financial resources of selected ecology organizations	21	14,418,270.00	57,237,459.00	27,833,138.00	12,862,889.84

(continued)

Table A.1c. (Continued)

	N	Min	Max	Mean	Standard Deviation
Political Alliances					
Percentage of leftist seats in parliament	21	25.00	29.00	25.95	1.20
Percentage of socialist seats in parliament	21	18.00	25.00	21.71	2.78
Public Opinion					
Percentage of people who say today's stand on the environment is unbearable	21	44.00	63.00	54.38	6.01
Percentage of people who say nuclear energy is negative	21	39.00	58.00	49.57	5.46
Public Policy					
Central government spending for environmental protection over total central government expenditures	21	.47	2.15	.93	.50
Spending by the confederation, cantons, and communes for environmental protection over total expenditures by the confederation, cantons, and communes	21	3.07	4.72	3.87	.49
Nuclear energy production over total electricity production	21	17.30	42.60	32.67	8.33
Central government spending for national defense over total central government expenditures	21	14.17	22.04	19.12	2.34

Note: Descriptive statistics referring to variables expressed in absolute terms. All variables concerning money are expressed in constant SFR (basis: 1990).

Tarrow 1989; Tilly, Tilly, and Tilly 1975), data on protest events carried by ecology, antinuclear, and peace movements were collected by content-analyzing three major newspapers, one in each country. Basic characteristics were coded for each event, such as its place and time, form, goal, and number of participants. From the original, event-based file, the data were aggregated into yearly counts of the protest events carried by each of the three movements and stored into a new file specifically organized for time-series analysis. This gives us a first and most straightforward indicator of the level of mobilization by social movements. A second indicator is the yearly sum of participants, which can be obtained by aggregating the number of participants to each event over the year.

The analyses, both descriptive and explanatory, presented in this book rely on the first indicator of the mobilization of the three movements, that is, the number of protest events. I opt for this indicator because it is less volatile than the number of participants, for if we exclude one or few events from the dataset, the distribution is not affected in the same way that it would be affected if we looked at the number of participants. Indeed, while excluding one event over several hundreds does not change the whole distribution, excluding a large demonstration attended by thousands of people would significantly modify the picture. This is all the more important insofar as the data used here stem from a sampling strategy. However, my goal in this book is not to ascertain whether a movement has mobilized more people than another movement but rather to see how protest has developed over time. Therefore, the number of events provides a useful indicator of mobilization.

Some of the analyses were performed on the number of events and the number of participants. Apart from some exceptions, the results did not change substantially, which confirms my choice of looking at protest events. In these analyses I use the natural logarithm of the number of participants to reduce the variation due to out-layers. It should be noted that, depending on the form of action, this variable displays a relatively high number of missing data. These are replaced with estimates based on the annual median for each form of action.

Of course, any assessment of the development of the mobilization of a given movement over time to a large extent depends on the very definition of protest events and the forms of action included in it. A *protest event* can be defined as an action by a social movement that attempts to influence the political decisions and/or sensitize the public opinion. Thus defined, it includes unconventional actions, which are most typical of social movements and which may take the form of demonstrative, confrontational, or violent actions; but it also includes more conventional actions, such as judicial actions, institutional activities, or (more generally) public statements and other media-oriented actions. Furthermore, demonstrative actions include signature-collection campaigns (in particular, petitions). Collection of signatures for popular referenda, however, are considered conventional actions because of their institutional anchoring. This is particularly true for the case of Switzerland, where it is indeed important.

From the point of view of the data retrieval, I collected conventional and unconventional actions. In chapter 3, the description of the development of the mobilization of the three movements in the three countries is based on both types. However, to study the relationships between protest and public policy by means of regression analysis in the subsequent chapters, I focus on unconventional protest actions only. These are not only the most typical actions carried by social movements. As I discuss in more detail later, the sample of protest events I use in the empirical analyses is much less reliable for conventional actions than for unconventional ones. In addition, previous studies have focused on unconventional actions as an indicator of social movement mobilization (e.g., Kriesi et al. 1995; Tarrow 1989; Tilly, Tilly, and Tilly 1975), not least because scholars tend to identify social movements with their use of noninstitutional protest actions. Finally, in this book I am more interested in assessing the policy impact of the protest activities carried out by ecology, antinuclear, and peace movements rather than the effect of each of these movements as a whole. In any case, this would be impossible, for certain kinds of actions, such as lobbying activities, are not visible in newspapers; hence, they would be outside the reach of my data-gathering net.

Yet, having at least some grasp of the impact of more conventional channels of mobilization might help us to understand the effect of movements when they act outside these channels. Therefore, although in this book I am most interested in the impact of overt mobilization and protest, that is, of unconventional actions, I conduct additional analyses with an indicator of conventional mobilization by the U.S. ecology and peace movements. To capture this aspect of movement activities, I use a proxy for lobbying activities: the amount of money spent by movement-related political action committees (PACs) to sponsor election campaigns by candidates who are considered as potential supporters of the movements' claims. Data on PACs come from public files of the Federal Election Commission, in Washington, D.C. I selected PACs that I judged as being close to the movements (fifteen for the ecology movement, eight for the peace movement). Yearly figures are the mean of two-year totals (the duration of a legislature) in primary disbursements.

Social Movement Organizations

Chapter 6 shows data on the organizational strength and growth of the three movements studied. Information on these aspects comes from a systematic search conducted in parallel with the retrieval of data on the movements' mobilization. This search was facilitated in the United States by the *Encyclopedia of Associations*, a serial publication that was used to gather data on membership and financial resources of ecology, antinuclear, and peace movement organizations. Given the lack of such a data source in the other two countries, I sent a questionnaire to the major organizations of the three movements asking, among other things, for information on the development of the number of members and the amount of financial resources of each organization.

In all three countries, missing information was completed with the help of additional sources, where possible. Nevertheless, the number of organizations for which data were available varies across the three countries as well as according to the aspect at hand (members or money). In the end, I was able to obtain usable data on 44 organizations for membership and on 59 organizations for financial resources: for membership, 30 for the United States, 10 for Italy, and 4 for Switzerland; for money, 42 for the United States, 10 for Italy, and 7 for Switzerland. Concerning members, they are distributed across countries and movements as follows: 17 ecology, 5 antinuclear, and 8 peace movement organizations in the United States; 7 ecology and 3 peace movement organizations in Italy; 4 ecology movement organizations in Switzerland. Concerning money, the distribution is as follows: 20 ecology, 7 antinuclear, and 15 peace movement organizations in the United States; 7 ecology and 3 peace movement organizations in Italy; 7 ecology movement organizations in Switzerland.

Political Alliances

Political opportunity theorists have shown that the configuration of power relations among institutional actors and the structure of political alliances influence the mobilization and impact of social movements (della Porta and Rucht 1995; Kriesi et al. 1995; Tarrow 1998). My argument regarding the role of political alliances is general and applies to all types of allies. However, as a way to operationalize this variable, I focus on parties. This choice seems appropriate in the light of the fact that parties are the most powerful actors when it comes to decide the course of public policy. Therefore, I measure this variable by looking at the formal configuration of power in the institutional arenas. The parties of the Left are the main potential allies of these movements and, more generally, of the new social movements (Kriesi et al. 1995). Accordingly, I measure this aspect with the proportion of parliamentary seats held by the parties of the Left in the respective national parliaments. For the United States, I took the Democratic Party as an equivalent of the European Left, assuming that in the American two-party system, the party that is closer to this role within the institutional arenas is the Democratic Party. Thus, the first indicator of political alliances is the proportion of seats held in both branches of the parliament by the Democratic Party in the United States and by the parties of the Left in Italy and Switzerland.

An additional variable was used in the case of the United States. I operationalize political alliances in the case of the United States by means of a crude indicator of the substantial support given by institutional and elite actors to the three movements, or at least to the issues they address. These data come from the same newspaper source used to gather the protest events carried by the movements. I collected conventional actions (mostly public statements) by political elites dealing with the issues raised by the three movements. More precisely, three types of events have been collected to the extent that they were addressing the movements' goals: conventional actions by legislators, conventional actions by political elites who are running for elections, and conventional actions by executive and administrative officials insofar as they were addressed to higher-level officials (for example, local governments to state administrations). The indicator of political alliance—or support by institutional elites—is thus given by the number of pro-environment, antinuclear power, and pro-peace public statements by these elite actors (most of the time, party members or electoral candidates).

Public Opinion

Creating time-series data on public opinion spanning several years is difficult and sometimes impossible, simply due to a lack of available data. This task is made easier for data in the United States by the presence of long-standing opinion poll institutes. Even so, the series concerning this aspect are often shorter than the twenty-one-year period covered by the study and include missing data that are replaced with estimated figures based on linear interpolation.

For the measures of changes in public opinion entered into the time-series analysis, I use one indicator for each type of issue—that is, one series for each movement. In the United States:

for environmental issues, the percentage of people who think that spending on improving and protecting the environment is too little (National Opinion Research Center poll reported in Dunlap 1992);

for nuclear energy issues, the percentage of people who oppose the building of more nuclear plants (Harris poll reported in Rosa and Dunlap 1994);

for peace issues, the percentage of people saying that spending for defense is too much (reported in Stanley and Niemi 1995).

In Switzerland (no indicators used for peace issues):

for environmental issues, the percentage of people who say that today's stand of the environment is rather unbearable or absolutely unbearable (Demoscope, Berichtsband 1995);

for nuclear energy issues, the percentage of people who say that nuclear energy is rather negative or very negative (Demoscope, Berichtsband 1995).

In Italy (no indicators used for environmental and antinuclear issues):

for peace issues, the percentage of people who say that spending for military should be diminished.

As in all other variables, data were aggregated on a yearly basis. When several measures of the same aspect were given for different months of a single year (as is most often the case), I took the mean between those measures. Furthermore, since in some cases I found several indicators of public opinion about the issues dealt with by the three movements, I could have indexed or factor-analyzed them to produce a single summary measure. However, I preferred to use a single indicator for each movement because this provides a more simple and straightforward measure of shifts in public opinion, and similar indicators are often highly correlated among them. For example, the five available indicators of public opinion about the environment in the United States are strongly correlated (coefficients range between .80 and .96). Therefore, I selected the measure that bears most directly on the corresponding dependent variable, which is directly comparable to the measures of public opinion about nuclear power and peace issues.

All these indicators of public opinion refer to shifts in preferences. In the case of the United States (where this kind of data was available), I created a number of indicators based on two measures of issue salience to test for the possibility *(a)* that the impact of public opinion depends on the degree of attention or concern of the public toward a given issue (Jones 1994), and *(b)* that decision makers would react to the salience of an issue rather than to the public's preferences. The first measure consists of the mean of the figures from all available surveys in each year. The second measure takes only the highest figure in each year. The resulting variables refer to six areas that correspond to the various items in the polls (environment and pollution; nuclear power; peace, war, and nuclear; international problems and foreign policy; national defense and security; military spending); also included is an aggregate measure for the four peace items. Data for these variables were provided by the Gallup Organization, through its "most important problem" questions.

Public Policy

Public policy is the dependent variable in this study of movement impact. In spite of the problems that have been evoked for using expenditure data (Burstein and Freundenburg 1978; Hofferbert 1974), I follow the lead of earlier work (e.g., Dye 1966; Hofferbert and Sharkansky 1971; Jacob and Vines 1971) and measure public policy in the environmental protection and national defense domains through government spending. Alternatively, I could have focused on legislative activity or production. Burstein and Freudenburg (1978), for example, have looked at roll call votes received by bills and amendments related to the Vietnam War and voted by the U.S. Senate between 1963 and 1974. More recently, Costain and Majstorovic (1994) employed a coded measure of the percentage of bills that focused on gender and were passed by the U.S. Congress. Yet, bills introduced in Congress, roll calls, amendments, congressional hearings, and so forth capture legislative activity and debates rather than state action, which is the main focus of this book. Laws enacted would be a more accurate alternative, but here I prefer to use spending because in this measure the value of a unit change is equally distributed over time. In contrast, laws are often qualitatively different from one another: some laws imply a fundamental transformation in a given policy area, while others are merely cosmetic changes and hence have much less important implications. Since all observation units in time-series analysis are treated as equally important, looking at spending is more appropriate than counting laws. A similar reasoning applies to the nuclear energy domain. In this case, however, nuclear power production replaces spending as an indicator of public policy.

Environmental policy, especially in federal states, is largely implemented at the local and regional levels; therefore, for the United States and Switzerland, I consider both national spending and that by the states/cantons. This was not made for the case of Italy because it is more a centralized state and, also, because of lack of information on the local and regional levels.

Thus, the variables used to measure changes in public policy in the domains touched by the mobilization of the three movements studied are based on government outputs (expenditures or production). In the United States:

the total annual budget of the Environmental Protection Agency (as a percentage of total central government expenditures) and spending by the states for environmental protection (as a percentage of total states' expenditures);

nuclear energy production (as a percentage of total electricity production) and the number of construction permits for nuclear power plants;

federal outlays for national defense (as a percentage of total central government expenditures).

In Italy:

central government spending for environmental protection (as a percentage of total central government expenditures);

nuclear energy production (as a percentage of total electricity production);

central government spending for national defense (as a percentage of total central government expenditures).

In Switzerland:

central government spending for environmental protection (as a percentage of total central government expenditures) and spending by the confederation, the cantons, and the communes for environmental protection (as a percentage of total expenditures by the confederation, cantons, and communes);

nuclear energy production (as a percentage of total electricity production);

central government spending for national defense (as a percentage of total central government expenditures).

These data were retrieved from various sources. Data for the United States come from the Budget of the United States Government (Historical Tables 1998), for environmental policy; the Annual Energy Review (Energy Information Administration), for nuclear energy policy; and Stanley and Niemi (1995), for national defense policy. Data for Italy come from Istat, for environmental policy; Eurostat (basic statistics of the European Community), and Eurostat (basic statistics of the European Union), for nuclear energy policy; and OECD (National Accounts, Volume II, 1986, 1997), for national defense policy. All data for Switzerland come from the Swiss Statistical Yearbook (various issues).

While environmental spending is a straightforward indicator of the policy changes sought by the ecology movement, our use of measures of nuclear policy and defense spending requires some clarifications. First, it might be argued that nuclear energy production is not a measure of public policy in the case of the United States, because it does not represent government action. To be sure, in the United States, orders and construction are mainly in the hands of utilities. However, there are indications that the state is far from being absent from this game. First, the federal government has invested large amounts of money to help the private sector to develop and commercialize the light water nuclear reactor, the basis of American nuclear energy systems (Campbell 1988). The public sector, though not directly involved in exploiting the commercial advantages of nuclear power, engaged intensively in its promotion. Second, governmental regulation is fundamental for the development of private industry, even in a country with a light bureaucratic apparatus and a traditionally discreet form of state intervention. Third, political processes influenced choices in nuclear policy, and the state was part of such processes. Even in the United States, decisions made outside the state by utilities, manufacturers, and banks were shaped decisively by public policies (Jasper 1990).

However, defense spending is admittedly less direct an indicator of the policy changes sought by the peace movement than the indicators we use for ecology and antinuclear movements. Most peace movement mobilization during the period under study has focused on the arms race or on specific military interventions, such as those in the Gulf War, which are only indirectly related to the size of defense spending. Yet, building a nuclear arsenal and intervening in a conflict presuppose large state appropriations that fall into the military budget, to which the increases in spending attest during the most intense period of the arms race in the early 1980s and after the Gulf War.

Interactive Terms

My principal argument is that social movements have the greatest impact on public policy when they are supported by powerful political allies and when they face a favorable public opinion. For my analyses, I introduce a number of two-way and three-way interactive terms. They are meant to capture the joint effect of protest and one or both of the two external resources, political alliances and public opinion.

Fifteen interactive terms were created in the case of the United States:

six variables, two for each movement, combine protest and two indicators of political alliances—that is, as measured through (a) the number of protest events and (b) the number of Democratic seats in Congress and pro-movement statements;

three variables, one for each movement, measure the joint effect of protest and one indicator of public opinion;

six variables, two for each movement, look at the joint effect of protest, political alliances, and public opinion, using the same indicators as in the two-way interactive terms.

Since, for the other two countries, I have only one indicator referring to the configuration of power, the number of interactive terms is lower. Furthermore, only three interactive terms could be made useful in the case of Italy: those combining protest and the indicator of political alliances. Finally, nine interactive terms were used in the case of Switzerland: three for protest and political alliances; three for protest and public opinion; and three for all factors together. Tables A.2a, A.2b, A.2c give the complete list of interactive terms for each country.

It is important to note that, contrary to the standard procedure followed in these cases and in order to avoid multicollinearity, I did not include the original variables in the regressions with interactive terms. Therefore, tables 7.6, 8.3, and II.1 (as well as tables 7.6a, 8.3a, and II.1a in appendix B) only show regression coefficients between the interactive terms as independent variables and the respective indicators of public policy as dependent variables.

A Note on Missing Data

Producing consistent time series data on many aspects that cover a long period is an extremely difficult task. Almost inevitably, the time series will have some blind spots. The series used in this book are no exception to this unwritten rule. First, when information on a given aspect was unavailable for the whole period or for a part of the period that was too long to be used in time-series analysis, the corresponding variable was simply not created. This problem concerns especially Italy and Switzerland. For the case of the United States, all of the data in the empirical analyses are more comprehensive due to better availability and accessibility of information.

A second, less problematic but still troublesome problem is when information is lacking for one or a few of the years of the time series. This occurred with data on the organizational resources of movements, PACs, and public opinion. This kind of missing data was treated in a simple and straightforward way, by means of linear interpolation. Concretely, missing values for the movements' organizational resources and public opinion have been replaced with estimates using one of three agencies:

1. estimates based on the mean of the first and last actual values, when available;
2. estimates based on a linear continuation of actual values, that is, by adding or subtracting the same difference between the last two values, thus keeping the same increase or decrease; or
3. estimates made by repeating the last available value, when more plausible, for example, when the value for the first year of the series would be lower than zero.

Table A.2a.   Description of Interactive Terms (United States)

Ecology Movement

Movement * allies 1:	number of unconventional protest events by the ecology movement * percentage of seats of the Democratic Party in Congress
Movement * allies 2:	number of unconventional protest events by the ecology movement * number of pro-ecology statements by political elites
Movement * public:	number of unconventional protest events by the ecology movement * percentage of people who say spending for the environment is too little
Movement * allies * public 1:	number of unconventional protest events by the ecology movement * percentage of seats of the Democratic Party in Congress * percentage of people who say spending for the environment is too little
Movement * allies * public 2:	number of unconventional protest events by the ecology movement * number of pro-ecology statements by political elites * percentage of people who say spending for the environment is too little

Antinuclear Movement

Movement * allies 1:	number of unconventional protest events by the antinuclear movement * percentage of seats of the Democratic Party in Congress
Movement * allies 2:	number of unconventional protest events by the antinuclear movement * number of antinuclear statements by political elites
Movement * public:	number of unconventional protest events by the antinuclear movement * percentage of people who oppose building of more nuclear plants
Movement * allies * public 1:	number of unconventional protest events by the antinuclear movement * percentage of seats of the Democratic Party in Congress * percentage of people who oppose building of more nuclear plants
Movement * allies * public 2:	number of unconventional protest events by the antinuclear movement * number of antinuclear statements by political elites * percentage of people who oppose building of more nuclear plants

Peace Movement

Movement * allies 1:	number of unconventional protest events by the peace movement * percentage of seats of the Democratic Party in Congress
Movement * allies 2:	number of unconventional protest events by the peace movement * number of pro-peace statements by political elites
Movement * public:	number of unconventional protest events by the peace movement * percentage of people who say spending for defense is too much

(*continued*)

Table A.2a. (Continued)

Movement * allies * public 1:	number of unconventional protest events by the peace movement * percentage of seats of the Democratic Party in Congress * percentage of people who say spending for defense is too much
Movement * allies * public 2:	number of unconventional protest events by the peace movement * number of pro-peace statements by political elites * percentage of people who say spending for defense is too much

Table A.2b. Description of Interactive Terms (Italy)

Ecology Movement

Movement * allies:	number of unconventional protest events by the ecology movement * percentage of seats of leftist parties in parliament
Movement * public:	(no indicator available)
Movement * allies * public:	(no indicator available)

Antinuclear Movement

Movement * allies:	number of unconventional protest events by the antinuclear movement * percentage of seats of leftist parties in parliament
Movement * public:	(no indicator available)
Movement * allies * public:	(no indicator available)

Peace Movement

Movement * allies:	number of unconventional protest events by the peace movement * percentage of seats of leftist parties in parliament
Movement * public:	number of unconventional protest events by the peace movement * percentage of people who say spending for military should be diminished
Movement * allies * public:	number of unconventional protest events by the peace movement * percentage of seats of leftist parties in parliament * percentage of people who say spending for military should be diminished

Time-Series Analysis

Time-series analysis techniques are used in this book to study the relationship between social movements, political alliances, public opinion, and public policy. Time-series analysis is a longitudinal method that is particularly suited to capturing the dynamic nature of social and political phenomena. This approach allows us to incorporate time into the explanation of the effects of protest activities on public policy.

Table A.2c. Description of Interactive Terms (Switzerland)

Ecology Movement

Movement * allies: number of unconventional protest events by the ecology movement * percentage of seats by leftist parties in parliament

Movement * public: number of unconventional protest events by the ecology movement * percentage of people who say today's stand of the environment is unbearable

Movement * allies * public: number of unconventional protest events by the ecology movement * percentage of seats by leftist parties in parliament * percentage of people who say today's stand on the environment is unbearable

Antinuclear Movement

Movement * allies: number of unconventional protest events by the antinuclear movement * percentage of seats by leftist parties in parliament

Movement * public: number of unconventional protest events by the antinuclear movement * percentage of people who say nuclear energy is negative

Movement * allies * public: number of unconventional protest events by the antinuclear movement * percentage of seats by leftist parties in parliament * percentage of people who say nuclear energy is negative

Peace Movement

Movement * allies: number of unconventional protest events by the peace movement * percentage of seats by leftist parties in parliament

Movement * public: (no indicator available)

Movement * allies * public: (no indicator available)

There are several more or less sophisticated ways to conduct time-series analysis to explore relationships between variables of interest. Perhaps the two most widely used methods are the regression approach and the Box-Jenkins approach (or so-called ARIMA models approach), the latter of which is often used in univariate analyses, such as in forecasting. Here I use the regression approach, which is simply based on the search of covariation between variables expressed as developments over time. The results are presented, as in cross-sectional regression, in the form of regression coefficients representing the strength of relationships between one or more independent variables and a dependent variable of interest. However, unlike cross-sectional analysis, coefficients here capture the strength of a relationship as it evolves over time.

All the dependent variables used in the empirical analyses are expressed as percentage changes; that is, I look at rates of change in public policy. The only exception to this rule is represented by the indicators of substantial political alliance (pro-movement statements), for these data come from the same sampled source of event data used to gather information on protest actions. Since these data are sampled (see the following), there could be important changes in percentages due to the sampling error; therefore, the data would not reflect the real distributions of events (pro-movement statements, in this case).

Using rates of change, rather than absolute levels, to measure the dependent variables (e.g., public policy) is a also a way to technically reduce the chances that the error terms of the regressions display significant serial correlation. This indeed is a major problem in time-series analysis, especially with expenditure variables that present a strong trend. The presence of serial correlation can yield spurious relationships due to the effect of the observation at time t_0 on the observation at time t_1 on the same variable. Differencing the dependent variable is the simplest and most straightforward solution to this problem (Janoski and Isaac 1994). Using percentage changes is a similar procedure to reach the same aim.

The independent variables (e.g., movement mobilization) are expressed in absolute terms. However, I also made analyses with differenced independent variables, that is, with variables expressed as differences from one period to the next. This is done to ascertain the extent to which social actors (in this case, policy makers) react not so much to the levels reached by a given component in the social environment but more so to the changes occurring in that component. In other words, one might argue that people are more sensible to variations from a previous situation than to the "amounts" observable at a given time. This holds both for ordinary citizens and for political elites. For example, power holders would respond (positively or negatively) to an increase from a previous period in the protest actions carried by a social movement rather than to the level of mobilization that it displays at a given moment. Therefore, all the analyses presented in chapters 5, 7, and 8, as well as in the conclusion to part II, are conducted with variables measured as differences. The results of these additional analyses are shown in the tables included in appendix B.

I certainly do not mean that absolute levels are unimportant. In addition to the analyses shown, in many cases I tested relationships between levels to compare these two aspects and control the results obtained using differences. The results of these additional analyses concerning levels were not shown, to keep my discussion as simple as possible. However, I assume that variations in time are more conducive to a reaction by social actors than absolute levels are. The use of differences in the empirical analyses is more in line with the idea of people responding to what they perceive as a significant change from a preceding situation.

All the findings from time-series analysis presented in this book consist of standardized coefficients indicating the strength of relationships between lagged variables, that is, independent variables measured at time t_0 and dependent variables measured at time t_1, with a one-year lag. Although I have dealt with the classical problem of serial correlation in time-series analysis by differencing variables, for each coefficient I also show the Durbin-Watson statistic for autocorrelation. The Durbin-Watson statistic, which is used to test for the presence of first-order autocorrelation (both positive and negative) in the residuals (or error terms) of a regression equation, has a range between zero and four. In the case of a series with nineteen observations (such as most of those used here) and with one independent variable in the equation (i.e., for bivariate regressions), the null hypothesis that there is no significant correlation in the residuals can be accepted (at the level of significance of 5 percent) when the regression coefficient ranges between 1.40 and 2.60 (i.e., 4.00–1.40).

I opted for lagged relationships because they allow us to make a stronger case for causal effects. Coefficients were generated with the Prais-Winsten method, a generalized least-squares method for estimating a regression equation whose errors follow a first-order autoregressive process. Specifically, I use the AREG procedure in SPSS. The Prais-Winsten method assumes a first-order autoregressive process among the error terms, that is, a model of a time series in which the current value of the series is a linear combination of previous values of the series, plus a random error. Autocorrelation function (ACF) in ARIMA shows that most of the variables used in our analyses follow an autoregressive process of order 1, which leads us to opt for a specification of time series with a one-year lag. Protest event data do not allow for shorter lags (especially those regarding antinuclear and peace protests) due to the small number of events. However, we think that the use of a one-year lag is a reasonable choice to study policy change with the dependent variable that we are using. This holds true especially in the case of government spending, as budgets are adopted in one fiscal year for the following year; thus, it usually takes a year before the administration can have an impact on budgets and hence policy. As I am dealing with relatively short time series, I consider a 10 percent level of significance in addition to the standard 5 percent and 1 percent levels. Although current practice often looks at unstandardized regression coefficients when dealing with data with meaningful metrics, I use standardized coefficients because I am interested in the presence or absence of significant relationships, rather than the magnitude of effects.

Protest Event Data

My use of protest event data to measure the level of mobilization of the three movements studied requires a number of methodological remarks. Specifically, I discuss three aspects:

1. the use of newspapers as a source for the collection of protest events,
2. the choice of a sampling strategy, and
3. a comparison of my sample with continuous time data.

Data Sources

The problem of sources in protest event analysis has captured much attention from scholars in both recent and less-recent years (e.g., Barranco and Wisler 1999; Danzger 1975; Snyder and Kelly 1977; Franzosi 1987; Kriesi et al. 1995, app.; Mueller 1997; Oliver and Myers 1999; Oliver and Maney 2000; Olzak 1989; Rucht and

Ohlemacher 1992; McCarthy, McPhail, and Smith 1996; see various articles in Rucht, Koopmans, and Neidhart 1998). Previous work seems to point to newspapers as the best choice among the limited number of possible sources (for example, police archives) for quantitative data on protest development (Koopmans 1998).

The principal advantage of newspapers for the study of social movement mobilization—as compared to other quantitative sources, such as official statistics, yearbooks, or archives—is perhaps that they provide a continuous and easily accessible source that includes a broad range of protest actions. In addition, newspapers are relatively reliable when it comes to factual information such as timing, locality, number of participants, form of action, stated goal, and so forth. For this kind of information, both selection and description biases are limited, although they cannot be completely avoided (see the following).

For all these reasons, and also because of previous positive experiences I had with this kind of source (see Kriesi et al. 1995), I opted for three major newspapers as the sources for protest event data. Specifically, I content-analyzed the *New York Times*, for the case of the United States; the *Corriere della Sera*, for the case of Italy; and the *New Zürcher Zeitung*, for the case of Switzerland for the 1975–1999 period. I chose these three newspapers because all three are nationwide papers that have provided the basis for previous important studies (see, e.g., Jenkins and Perrow 1977; McAdam 1982; Olzak 1992, for the United States; Tarrow 1989, for Italy; Kriesi et al. 1995, for Switzerland).

Although I tried to limit changing coders for a single country, the protest event data were collected by different coders. Specifically, the data on the United States were collected by myself (1975–1995) and by a second coder (1996–1999); the data on Italy were all coded by the same coder, except for the last four months of 1999; the data on Switzerland were coded by myself (1975–1989), by a second coder (1990–1995), and by a third coder (1996–1999). The data on Switzerland for the 1975–1989 period come from the Kriesi and colleagues' research (1995). Altogether, six coders have been involved in the data retrieval. They were all instructed as to the rules concerning the definition of the protest event, the sampling strategy, and the kinds of events to be included in the sample. To end up with a homogeneous and reliable dataset, I checked all the data and dropped or corrected those events that were coded wrong.

Sampling Strategy

The newspapers were consulted following a sampling procedure similar to that used by Kriesi and colleagues (1995). For the cases of the United States and Italy, all Sunday and Monday editions were consulted; however, since the Swiss newspaper did not have a Sunday edition, only the Monday edition was used.

The basic reason behind my decision to sample the Sunday and Monday issues is a pragmatic one: to cover a period spanning a quarter of a century for three movements in three countries would need a much greater amount of resources than were available for this data collection. An alternative choice would be to trace events from the newspaper's index, such as the *New York Times Index*. However, this strategy is likely to provide biased and incomplete data, as the index often does not allow one to infer the goal of the action but only the general theme. Furthermore, events of interest are often found in the body of the article without being mentioned in the title on which the index is based. Olzak (1992) has adopted a mixed strategy, tracing events in the index and then going back to the article. This might avoid part of the description bias but not all the selective biases. In addition, by doing so, the advantage of looking at the index is largely lost, as this is nearly as time-consuming as going directly to the articles.

The rationale for taking the Sunday and Monday editions is also that they cover events that occurred during the weekend. Public demonstrations in particular, the most frequent form of protest, tend to concentrate in weekend days. For example, Barranco and Wisler (1999) found that about half of the public demonstrations in Swiss cities took place either on Saturday or Sunday. Similarly, in tests conducted by Koopmans (1995), the Monday issue in Germany included more than a third of the total events (there was no Sunday issue in that case). My own comparison with continuous time data for the case of the United States provides similar results (see the following).

In any case, to be more encompassing, especially with regard to more conventional or more radical actions (which are less likely to take place on weekend days), I decided to code all actions that were referenced in the Sunday or Monday issues, whether they had occurred in the preceding week or would occur in the following week. This also ensured that most, if not all, of the major events would be included in the sample, a condition that is particularly important during phases of strong mobilization. Of course, since nonweekend events are still likely to be underrepresented in the sample, one cannot infer the actual distribution of events. However, in my analyses, I do not look at absolute levels; I am more interested in trends and differences. In other words, it is not a problem when the proportion of demonstrations is different in the weekend issues than in the weekday issues. What is important is that this bias is systematic; that is, there must be no reason to assume that the propensity of demonstrations to occur during the weekend has changed over time. As the bias is systematic, it is not likely to affect trends and differences.

Sampling, however, has its drawbacks. Apart from the underrepresentation of certain types of events, an issue which I discuss in more detail later, a major one is that the number of cases can sometimes be quite low, not because the actual number of events was low, but because of sampling. This can become problematic especially when one is looking at percentages instead of absolute numbers. For example, in the analysis in chapter 5 of the possible radicalization of the movements and of the relationship between action repertoires and public policy, I could not use the percentage of disruptive or radical events to measure the radicalness of the movements, even though it would have been a more accurate way to address this aspect. The sampling procedure followed in the collection of protest event data implies that there may be a sampling error. While I cannot measure this error because the sample is not probabilistic, this fact must be taken into account. As a result, while taking the percentage would be more accurate, it would not provide a robust indicator of radicalization. In effect, a difference of one event over a total of, say, five events would mean a difference of 20 percent ($1/5 = .20$). Thus, if the one event difference is due to a sampling error (e.g., a single event was overlooked by the coder), this reflects a quite important difference in the distribution in the sample, which might lead to wrong conclusions. The lower the number of cases over which percentages are computed, the worse this situation becomes; conversely, the higher this number, the less and less important this situation becomes. In the analyses mentioned here, I therefore use the number of disruptive actions, which is a less valid but more reliable measure of radicalization.

Comparison with Continuous Time Data

Even if the bias is systematic, when underrepresentation of certain types of events becomes too strong, sampling weekend issues of the newspaper becomes an inadequate strategy; furthermore, trends and differences become difficult to discern because numbers become too low to claim any sort of representativeness. I suspect that this is true for conventional events. There are valid reasons to assume that the weekend is an unlikely time for these kinds of events to occur. A comparison of data sampled on the weekend issue with continuous time data, even on a short period, would help us to ascertain whether this is actually the case and would give us a more accurate picture of the potential bias inherent in using a sampling strategy based on the weekend issue of the newspaper for measuring conventional mobilization. Therefore, I collected additional data on the same source used for the case of the United States (the *New York Times*) for a four-month period. I content-analyzed every issue of the newspaper from January 1 to April 30, 1980, using the same coding scheme adopted for the 1975–1999 sample. This period was chosen because it was one that had witnessed an important mobilization of all the three movements under study. It was quite short, but it nevertheless allowed us to confront the representativeness of conventional and unconventional events and thus, to some extent, assess the validity and reliability of the data used in my empirical analyses.

If we first compare the distribution of weekday and weekend events according to their conventional or unconventional form of action (table A.3), we see that, over

Table A.3. Distribution of Weekday and Weekend Events by Form of Action (United States, January–April 1980)

	Conventional	Unconventional	Total
Weekday	82.7	56.8	71.9
Weekend	17.3	43.2	28.1
Total	100%	100%	100%
N	52	37	89

Table A.4. Distribution of Conventional and Unconventional Events by Newspaper Issue (United States, January–April 1980)

	Weekday	Weekend	Total
Conventional	67.2	36.0	58.4
Unconventional	32.8	64.0	41.6
Total	100%	100%	100%
N	64	25	89

a total of eighty-nine events retrieved in the four months, sixty-four (71.9 percent) were found on weekday issues, and twenty-five (28.1 percent) were found on weekend issues (i.e., on a Sunday or Monday issue, as in the samples used in the aforementioned analyses).

Most important, however, conventional and unconventional events have different shares in weekday and weekend issues. While the two forms of actions are nearly homogeneously distributed across newspaper issues, conventional protests are much less frequent during the weekend. Thus, my suspicion that the latter are underrepresented in the sample is correct. In contrast, this table shows that sampling the weekend issues of the newspaper yields a sufficient number of unconventional protest events relative to the total events retrieved in the paper.

We can also look at the inverse relationship between newspaper issues and forms of actions. If we compare the distribution of conventional and unconventional events according to the newspaper issue (table A.4), we see that weekday and weekend issues do not present the same proportion of conventional and unconventional events. During the week, about two-thirds of conventional events and one-third of unconventional events have occurred; however, the reverse distribution is observed during the weekend. Therefore, conventional and unconventional protests have very different weights, depending from which newspaper issue they are retrieved. The same is not true, for example, when we distinguish between moderate actions and radical actions (i.e., confrontational, illegal, and violent; table A.5). These two forms of action follow very similar distributions in both weekday and weekend issues. Therefore, unlike the case for conventional events, we need not exclude one or the other from the analyses.

Table A.5. Distribution of Moderate and Radical Events by Newspaper Issue (United States, January–April 1980)

	Weekday	Weekend	Total
Moderate	87.5	88.0	87.6
Radical	12.5	12.0	12.4
Total	100%	100%	100%
N	64	25	89

In sum, conventional events are likely to be underrepresented in a sample that is produced by looking only at the newspaper issues that report events that occurred during the weekend. For this reason, I have excluded them from most of the analyses presented in this book. In contrast, unconventional events are more equally distributed across weekday and weekend issues; therefore, they represent a valid and reliable empirical basis for the study of protest and its outcomes.

APPENDIX B

≈

Results of Time-Series Analysis with Differenced Independent Variables

This appendix shows results of time-series analysis with differenced independent variables—that is, with explanatory factors expressed in terms of annual differences instead of absolute levels. Specifically, the following tables correspond, respectively, to tables 5.1, 5.3, and 5.4 (chapter 5); table 6.2 (chapter 6); tables 7.4, 7.5, and 7.6 (chapter 7); tables 8.1, 8.2, and 8.3 (chapter 8); and table II.1 (conclusion to part II).

Table B5.1. Effect of Unconventional Mobilization on Public Policy in Three Countries, 1975–1995 (differenced independent variables)

Dependent Variables	Spending for Environmental Protection (National) (t_1)	Spending for Environmental Protection (Local) (t_1)	Nuclear Energy Production (t_1)	Number of Construction Permits (t_1)	Spending for Defense (t_1)
United States					
Unconventional mobilization (t_0)	−0.7	−.23	−.20	−.14	.24
(D-W)	(1.54)	(1.69)	(1.48)	(1.99)	(1.93)
N	19	19	19	19	19
Italy					
Unconventional mobilization (t_0)	.11	—	−.28	—	−.01
(D-W)	(1.93)	—	(1.99)	—	(2.01)
N	19	—	19	—	19

(*continued*)

259

Table B5.1.   (Continued)

Dependent Variables	Spending for Environmental Protection (National) (t_1)	Spending for Environmental Protection (Local) (t_1)	Nuclear Energy Production (t_1)	Number of Construction Permits (t_1)	Spending for Defense (t_1)
Switzerland					
Unconventional mobilization (t_0)	.14	.39	.33	—	−.29
(D-W)	(1.92)	(2.02)	(1.53)	—	(1.88)
N	19	19	19	—	19

Note: Standardized regression coefficients (bivariate) generated with a generalized least-squared method of estimation (Prais-Winsten) assuming a first-order autoregressive process. Durbin-Watson test for serial correlation and number of observations (series length) are shown within parentheses. The independent variables are expressed as differences from the previous year and include a one-year lag. The dependent variables are expressed in terms of annual percentage change.
$^*p < .10; ^{**}p < .05; ^{***}p < .01.$

Table B5.3.   Effect of Radical Mobilization on Public Policy in Three Countries, 1975–1995 (differenced independent variables)

Dependent Variables	Spending for Environmental Protection (National) (t_1)	Spending for Environmental Protection (Local) (t_1)	Nuclear Energy Production (t_1)	Number of Construction Permits (t_1)	Spending for Defense (t_1)
United States					
Radical mobilization (t_0)	−0.9	−.21	−.24	.28	.29
(D-W)	(1.54)	(1.68)	(1.47)	(1.94)	(1.91)
N	19	19	19	19	19
Italy					
Radical mobilization (t_0)	.36	—	−.43*	—	−.17
(D-W)	(1.82)	—	(1.99)	—	(1.97)
N	—	—	19	—	19
Switzerland					
Radical mobilization (t_0)	.14	−.01	.22	—	−.15
(D-W)	(1.97)	(2.00)	(1.48)	—	(1.91)
N	19	19	19	—	19

Note: Standardized regression coefficients (bivariate) generated with a generalized least-squared method of estimation (Prais-Winsten) assuming a first-order autoregressive process. Durbin-Watson test for serial correlation and number of observations (series length) are shown within parentheses. The independent variables are expressed as differences from the previous year and include a one-year lag. The dependent variables are expressed in terms of annual percentage change.
$^*p < .10; ^{**}p < .05; ^{***}p < .01.$

Table B5.4. Effect of Spending by Ecology and Peace PACs on Public Policy in the United States, 1975–1995 (differenced independent variables)

Dependent Variables	Spending for Environmental Protection (National) (t_1)	Spending for Environmental Protection (Local) (t_1)	Spending for Defense (t_1)
Spending by PACs (t_0)	.00	.42*	.12
(D-W)	(1.54)	(1.65)	(1.94)
N	20	20	20

Note: Standardized regression coefficients (bivariate) generated with a generalized least-squared method of estimation (Prais-Winsten) assuming a first-order autoregressive process. Durbin-Watson test for serial correlation and number of observations (series length) are shown within parentheses. The independent variables are expressed as differences from the previous year and include a one-year lag. The dependent variables are expressed in terms of annual percentage change.
*$p < .10$; **$p < .05$; ***$p < .01$.

Table B6.2. Effect of Movement Organizational Strength on Public Policy in Three Countries, 1975–1995 (differenced independent variables)

Dependent Variables	Spending for Environmental Protection (National) (t_1)	Spending for Environmental Protection (Local) (t_1)	Nuclear Energy Production (t_1)	Number of Construction Permits (t_1)	Spending for Defense (t_1)
United States					
Membership (t_0)	−.06	−.51**	−.10	.15	.06
(D-W)	(1.56)	(1.90)	(1.50)	(2.00)	(1.97)
N	19	19	19	19	19
Financial resources (t_0)	.08	−.46*	.02	.02	−.24
(D-W)	(1.51)	(1.79)	(1.49)	(2.03)	(1.91)
N	19	19	19	19	19
Italy					
Membership (t_0)	.35	—	—	—	.07
(D-W)	(1.97)	—	—	—	(1.99)
N	19	—	—	—	19
Financial resources (t_0)	.38	—	—	—	.06
(D-W)	(1.97)	—	—	—	(2.00)
N	19	—	—	—	19

(continued)

Table B6.2. (Continued)

Dependent Variables	Spending for Environmental Protection (National) (t_1)	Spending for Environmental Protection (Local) (t_1)	Nuclear Energy Production (t_1)	Number of Construction Permits (t_1)	Spending for Defense (t_1)
Switzerland					
Membership (t_0)	−.13	.07	—	—	—
(D-W)	(1.99)	(2.00)	—	—	—
N	19	19	—	—	—
Financial resources (t_0)	.26	−.13	—	—	—
(D-W)	(2.04)	(2.02)	—	—	—
N	19	19	—	—	—

Note: Standardized regression coefficients (bivariate) generated with a generalized least-squared method of estimation (Prais-Winsten) assuming a first-order autoregressive process. Durbin-Watson test for serial correlation and number of observations (series length) are shown within parentheses. The independent variables are expressed as differences from the previous year and include a one-year lag. The dependent variables are expressed in terms of annual percentage change. Financial resources are measured in constant USD, ITL, and SFR (basis: 1990). Two ecology organizations in the United States (Greenpeace and the National Wildlife Federation) and one in Switzerland (Greenpeace) have been left out from the computation of membership (but not from financial resources) because they have supporters rather than actual members.
$*p < .10; **p < .05; ***p < .01$.

Table B7.4. Effect of Configuration of Power on Public Policy in Three Countries, 1975–1995 (differenced independent variables)

Dependent Variables	Spending for Environmental Protection (National) (t_1)	Spending for Environmental Protection (Local) (t_1)	Nuclear Energy Production (t_1)	Number of Construction Permits (t_1)	Spending for Defense (t_1)
United States					
Percentage of Democratic seats in Congress (t_0)	.05	−.39	.07	.25	−.15
(D-W)	(1.54)	(1.63)	(1.48)	(2.03)	(1.97)
N	19	19	19	19	19
Pro-movement statements (t_0)	.31	.22	−.24	.12	−.20
(D-W)	(1.60)	(1.72)	(1.45)	(2.01)	(1.98)
N	19	19	19	19	19

(*continued*)

Table B7.4. (Continued)

Dependent Variables	Spending for Environmental Protection (National) (t_1)	Spending for Environmental Protection (Local) (t_1)	Nuclear Energy Production (t_1)	Number of Construction Permits (t_1)	Spending for Defense (t_1)
Italy					
Percentage of leftist seats in parliament	−.15	—	.03	—	.08
(D-W)	(2.00)	—	(2.00)	—	(2.00)
N	19	—	19	—	19
Percentage of communist seats in parliament	.20	—	−.01	—	−.05
(D-W)	(1.93)	—	(2.00)	—	(2.02)
N	19	—	19	—	19
Switzerland					
Percentage of leftist seats in parliament	−.22	−.03	−.35	—	.07
(D-W)	(1.95)	(2.00)	(1.48)	—	(1.91)
N	19	19	19	—	19
Percentage of socialist seats in parliament	−.03	−.22	−.15	—	.28
(D-W)	(1.96)	(1.99)	(1.56)	—	(1.89)
N	19	19	19	—	19

Note: Standardized regression coefficients (bivariate) generated with a generalized least-squared method of estimation (Prais-Winsten) assuming a first-order autoregressive process. Durbin-Watson test for serial correlation and number of observations (series length) are shown within parentheses. The independent variables are expressed as differences from the previous year and include a one-year lag. The dependent variables are expressed in terms of annual percentage change.
$*p < .10; **p < .05; ***p < .01.$

Table B7.5. Effect of Unconventional Mobilization on Pro-movement Statements in the United States, 1975–1995 (differenced independent variables)

Dependent Variables	Pro-Ecology Statements (t_1)	Antinuclear Statements (t_1)	Pro-Peace Statements (t_1)
Unconventional mobilization (t_0)	−.23	.22	.56**
(D-W)	(2.02)	(2.32)	(2.50)
N	19	19	19

Note: Standardized regression coefficients (bivariate) generated with a generalized least-squared method of estimation (Prais-Winsten) assuming a first-order autoregressive process. Durbin-Watson test for serial correlation and number of observations (series length) are shown within parentheses. The independent variables are expressed as differences from the previous year and include a one-year lag. The dependent variables are differenced.
$*p < .10; **p < .05; ***p < .01.$

Table B7.6. Joint Effect of Unconventional Mobilization and Political Alliances on Public Policy in Three Countries, 1975–1995 (differenced independent variables)

Dependent Variables	Spending for Environmental Protection (National) (t_1)	Spending for Environmental Protection (Local) (t_1)	Nuclear Energy Production (t_1)	Number of Construction Permits (t_1)	Spending for Defense (t_1)
United States					
Movement * allies 1 (t_0)	−.08	−.25	−.20	−.13	.24
(D-W)	(1.54)	(1.69)	(1.48)	(1.99)	(1.92)
N	19	19	19	19	19
Movement * allies 2 (t_0)	.10	−.20	−.26	−.17	.05
(D-W)	(1.56)	(1.71)	(1.50)	(2.00)	(1.97)
N	19	19	19	19	19
Italy					
Movement * allies (t_0)	.13	—	−.28	—	−.02
(D-W)	(1.92)	—	(1.99)	—	(2.01)
N	19	—	19	—	19
Switzerland					
Movement * allies (t_0)	.12	.39	.33	—	−.29
(D-W)	(1.92)	(2.02)	(1.53)	—	(1.88)
N	19	19	19	—	19

Note: Standardized regression coefficients (bivariate) generated with a generalized least-squared method of estimation (Prais-Winsten) assuming a first-order autoregressive process. Durbin-Watson test for serial correlation and number of observations (series length) are shown within parentheses. The independent variables are expressed as differences from the previous year and include a one-year lag. The dependent variables are expressed in terms of annual percentage change.
*$p < .10$; **$p < .05$; ***$p < .01$.

Table B8.1. Effect of Public Opinion on Public Policy in Three Countries, 1975–1995 (differenced independent variables)

Dependent Variables	Spending for Environmental Protection (National) (t_1)	Spending for Environmental Protection (Local) (t_1)	Nuclear Energy Production (t_1)	Number of Construction Permits (t_1)	Spending for Defense (t_1)
United States					
Pro-movement opinion (t_0)	.46*	−.15	−.07	−.07	.10
(D-W)	(1.45)	(1.84)	(1.52)	(1.86)	(1.95)
N	15	15	15	15	18

(continued)

Table B8.1. (Continued)

Dependent Variables	Spending for Environmental Protection (National) (t_1)	Spending for Environmental Protection (Local) (t_1)	Nuclear Energy Production (t_1)	Number of Construction Permits (t_1)	Spending for Defense (t_1)
Italy					
Pro-movement opinion (t_0)	—	—	—	—	−.25
(D-W)	—	—	—	—	(1.82)
N	—	—	—	—	17
Switzerland					
Pro-movement opinion (t_0)	.01	.10	−.11	—	—
(D-W)	(1.96)	(1.99)	(1.51)	—	—
N	19	19	19	—	—

Note: Standardized regression coefficients (bivariate) generated with a generalized least-squared method of estimation (Prais-Winsten) assuming a first-order autoregressive process. Durbin-Watson test for serial correlation and number of observations (series length) are shown within parentheses. The independent variables are expressed as differences from the previous year and include a one-year lag. The dependent variables are expressed in terms of annual percentage change.
*$p < .10$; **$p < .05$; ***$p < .01$.

Table B8.2. Effect of Unconventional Mobilization on Public Opinion in Three Countries, 1975–1995 (differenced independent variables)

Dependent Variables	Pro-Ecology Statements (t_1)	Antinuclear Statements (t_1)	Pro-Peace Statements (t_1)
United States			
Unconventional mobilization (t_0)	.27	−.03	−.02
(D-W)	(1.50)	(1.60)	(1.95)
N	14	14	17
Italy			
Unconventional mobilization (t_0)	—	—	−.20
(D-W)	—	—	(1.98)
N	—	—	18
Switzerland			
Unconventional mobilization (t_0)	.33	.28	—
(D-W)	(2.19)	(1.61)	—
N	19	19	—

Note: Standardized regression coefficients (bivariate) generated with a generalized least-squared method of estimation (Prais-Winsten) assuming a first-order autoregressive process. Durbin-Watson test for serial correlation and number of observations (series length) are shown within parentheses. The independent variables are expressed as differences from the previous year and include a one-year lag. The dependent variables are expressed in terms of annual percentage change.
*$p < .10$; **$p < .05$; ***$p < .01$.

Table B8.3. Joint Effect of Unconventional Mobilization and Public Opinion on Public Policy in Three Countries, 1975–1995 (differenced independent variables)

Dependent Variables	Spending for Environmental Protection (National) (t_1)	Spending for Environmental Protection (Local) (t_1)	Nuclear Energy Production (t_1)	Number of Construction Permits (t_1)	Spending for Defense (t_1)
United States					
Movement ∗ public (t_0)	.04	−.35	−.20	−.16	.23
(D-W)	(1.48)	(1.75)	(1.49)	(1.82)	(1.92)
N	15	15	15	15	18
Italy					
Movement ∗ public (t_0)	—	—	—	—	−.03
(D-W)	—	—	—	—	(1.89)
N	—	—	—	—	—
Switzerland					
Movement ∗ public (t_0)	.22	.45*	.29	—	—
(D-W)	(1.90)	(1.99)	(1.54)	—	—
N	19	19	19	—	—

Note: Standardized regression coefficients (bivariate) generated with a generalized least-squared method of estimation (Prais-Winsten) assuming a first-order autoregressive process. Durbin-Watson test for serial correlation and number of observations (series length) are shown within parentheses. The independent variables are expressed as differences from the previous year and include a one-year lag. The dependent variables are expressed in terms of annual percentage change. See appendix A for a description of the interactive terms.
*$p < .10$; **$p < .05$; ***$p < .01$.

Table BII.1. Joint Effect of Unconventional Mobilization, Political Alliances, and Public Opinion on Public Policy in Three Countries, 1975–1995 (differenced independent variables)

Dependent Variables	Spending for Environmental Protection (National) (t_1)	Spending for Environmental Protection (Local) (t_1)	Nuclear Energy Production (t_1)	Number of Construction Permits (t_1)	Spending for Defense (t_1)
United States					
Movement ∗ allies ∗ public 1 (t_0)	.03	−.36	−.20	−.15	.24
(D-W)	(1.48)	(1.75)	(1.49)	(1.82)	(1.91)
N	15	15	15	15	18
Movement ∗ allies ∗ public 2 (t_0)	.19	−.16	−.28	−.20	.04
(D-W)	(1.54)	(1.75)	(1.51)	(1.82)	(1.94)
N	15	15	15	15	18

(*continued*)

Table BII.1. (Continued)

Dependent Variables	Spending for Environmental Protection (National) (t_1)	Spending for Environmental Protection (Local) (t_1)	Nuclear Energy Production (t_1)	Number of Construction Permits (t_1)	Spending for Defense (t_1)
Italy					
Movement * allies * public (t_0)	—	—	—	—	−.04
(D-W)	—	—	—	—	(1.89)
N	—	—	—	—	17
Switzerland					
Movement * allies * public (t_0)	.20	.12	.30	—	—
(D-W)	(1.97)	(1.99)	(1.54)	—	—
N	19	19	19	—	—

Note: Standardized regression coefficients (bivariate) generated with a generalized least-squared method of estimation (Prais-Winsten) assuming a first-order autoregressive process. Durbin-Watson test for serial correlation and number of observations (series length) are shown within parentheses. The independent variables are expressed as differences from the previous year and include a one-year lag. The dependent variables are expressed in terms of annual percentage change.

$*p < .10; **p < .05; ***p < .01.$

References

Abramowitz, S. I., and A. J. Nassi. 1981. "Keeping the Faith: Psychological Correlates of Activism Persistence into Middle Adulthood." *Journal of Youth and Adolescence* 10: 507–23.

Albritton, Robert B. 1979. "Social Amelioration through Mass Insurgency? A Reexamination of the Piven and Cloward Thesis." *American Political Science Review* 73: 1003–11.

Allison, Paul D. 1984. *Event History Analysis: Regression for Longitudinal Event Data*. Beverly Hills, Calif.: Sage.

Almond, Gabriel A. 1950. *The American People and Foreign Policy*. New York: Praeger.

Amenta, Edwin, Bruce G. Carruthers, and Yvonne Zylan. 1992. "A Hero for the Aged? The Townsend Movement, the Political Mediation Model, and U.S. Old-Age Policy, 1934–1950." *American Journal of Sociology* 98: 308–39.

Astin, Alexander W., Helen S. Astin, Alan E. Bayer, and Ann D. Bisconti. 1975. *The Power of Protest*. San Francisco: Jossey-Bass.

Bachrach, Peter, and Morton S. Baratz. 1970. *Power and Poverty*. Oxford: Oxford University Press.

Banaszak, Lee Ann. 1996. *Why Movements Succeed or Fail*. Princeton, N.J.: Princeton University Press.

Barkan, Steven E. 1984. "Legal Control of the Southern Civil Rights Movement." *American Sociological Review* 49: 552–65.

Barnett, Harold C. 1994. *Toxic Debts and the Superfund Dilemma*. Chapel Hill: University of North Carolina Press.

Barranco, José, and Dominique Wisler. 1999. "Validity and Systematicity of Newspaper Data in Event Analysis." *European Sociological Review* 15: 301–22.

Bartels, Larry M. 1991. "Constituency Opinion and Congressional Policy Making: The Reagan Defense Buildup." *American Political Science Review* 85: 457–74.

Bassand, Michel, Thérèse Burnier, Pierre Meyer, Robert Stüssi, and Léopold Veuve. 1986. *Politique des routes nationales*. Lausanne: Presses Polytechniques Romandes.

Battistelli, Fabrizio, Pierluigi Crescenzi, Antonietta Graziani, Angelo Montebovi, Giulia Ombuen, Serafina Scaparra, and Carlo Presciuttini. 1990. *I movimenti pacifisti e antinucleari in Italia, 1980–1988*. Gaeta: Rivista Militare.

Beck, Ulrich. 1986. *Risikogesellschaft*. Frankfurt: Shurkamp.

Bedford, Henry F. 1990. *Seabrook Station*. Amherst: Massachusetts University Press.

Bein, Thomas, and Rudolf Epple. 1984. "Die Friedensbewegung in der Schweiz." In *Kriegsursachen*, edited by R. Steinweg, 446–83. Frankfurt: Suhrkamp.

Bellucci, Paolo. 1994. *Politica militare e sistema politico*. Gaeta: Rivista Militare.

Bellush, Jewell, and Stephen M. David, eds. 1971. *Race and Politics in New York City*. New York: Praeger.

Benford, Robert D., and David A. Snow. 2000. "Framing Processes and Social Movements: An Overview and Assessment." *Annual Review of Sociology* 26: 611–40.

Benninghoff, Martin, Peter Knoepfel, Serge Terribilini, and Frédéric Varone. 1999. "Aménagement du territoire, politiques infrastructurelles (transports, énergie) et de l'environnement." In *Handbuch der Schweizer Politik*, edited by Ulrich Klöti, Peter Knoepfel, Hanspeter Kriesi, Wolf Linder, and Yannis Papadopoulos, 767–806. Zurich: NZZ Verlag.

Berelson, Bernard R., Paul F. Lazarsfeld, and William N. McPhee. 1954. *Voting*. Chicago: University of Chicago Press.

Berkowitz, William R. 1974. "Socioeconomic Indicator Changes in Ghetto Riot Tracts." *Urban Affairs Quarterly* 10: 69–94.

Betz, Michael. 1974. "Riots and Welfare: Are They Related? *Social Problems* 21: 345–55.

Biorcio, Roberto, and Giovanni Lodi, eds. 1988. *La sfida verde*. Padova: Liviana.

Brand, Karl-Werner. 1982. *Neue soziale Bewegungen*. Opladen: Westdeutscher Verlag.

Brassel, Ruedi, and Jakob Tanner. 1986. "Zur Geschichte der Friedensbewegung in der Schweiz." In *Handbuch Frieden Schweiz*. Basel: Forum für praxisbezogene Friedensforschung.

Brill, Harry. 1971. *Why Organizers Fail*. Berkeley: University of California Press.

Brockett, Charles D. 1991. "The Structure of Political Opportunities and Peasant Mobilization in Central America." *Comparative Politics* 23: 253–74.

Brown, Michael. 1979. *Laying Waste*. New York: Pantheon.

Burk, James. 1985. "The Origins of Federal Securities Regulation." *Social Forces* 63: 1010–29.

Burnier, Thérèse. 1985. *La démocratie du rouleau compresseur*. Lausanne: Editions d'en Bas.

Burns, Grant. 1992. *The Nuclear Present*. Metuchen, N.J.: Scarecrow Press.

Burstein, Paul. 1979a. "Public Opinion, Demonstrations, and the Passage of Anti-Discrimination Legislation." *Public Opinion Quarterly* 43: 157–72.

———. 1979b. "Equal Employment Opportunity Legislation and the Incomes of Women and Nonwhites." *American Sociological Review* 44: 367–91.

———. 1979c. "Senate Voting on the Vietnam War, 1964–1973." *Journal of Political and Military Sociology* 7: 271–82.

———. 1985. *Discrimination, Jobs, and Politics*. Chicago: University of Chicago Press.

———. 1991. "Legal Mobilization as a Social Movement Tactic: The Struggle for Equal Employment Opportunity." *American Journal of Sociology* 96: 1201–25.

———. 1998a. "Bringing the Public Back In: Should Sociologists Consider the Impact of Public Opinion on Public Policy." *Social Forces* 77: 27–62.

———. 1998b. *Discrimination, Jobs, and Politics*. 2nd ed. Chicago: University of Chicago Press.

———. 1999. "Social Movements and Public Policy." In *How Social Movements Matter*, edited by Marco Giugni, Doug McAdam, and Charles Tilly, 3–21. Minneapolis: University of Minnesota Press.

Burstein, Paul, Rachel L. Einwohner, and Jocelyn A. Hollander. 1995. "The Success of Political Movements: A Bargaining Perspective." In *The Politics of Social Protest*, edited by J. Craig Jenkins and Bert Klandermans, 275–95. Minneapolis: University of Minnesota Press.

Burstein, Paul, and William Freundenburg. 1978. "Changing Public Policy: The Impact of Public Opinion, Anti-War Demonstrations and War Costs on Senate Voting on Vietnam War Motions." *American Journal of Sociology* 84: 99–122.

Burstein, Paul, and April Linton. 2002. "The Impact of Political Parties, Interest Groups, and Social Movement Organizations on Public Policy: Some Recent Evidence and Theoretical Concerns." *Social Forces* 81: 380–408.

Button, James W. 1978. *Black Violence*. Princeton, N.J.: Princeton University Press.

———. 1989. *Blacks and Social Change*. Princeton, N.J.: Princeton University Press.

Caligaris, Luigi. 1990. "La politica militare." In *Le politiche pubbliche in Italia*, edited by Bruno Dente, 65–82. Bologna: Il Mulino.

Campbell, Angus, Philip E. Converse, Warren E. Miller, and Donald E. Stokes. 1960. *The American Voter*. New York: Wiley.

Campbell, John L. 1988. *Collapse of an Industry*. Ithaca, N.Y.: Cornell University Press.

Carson, Rachel. 1962. *Silent Spring*. Boston: Houghton Mifflin.

Caulfield, Henry P. 1989. "The Conservation and Environmental Movements: An Historical Analysis." In *Environmental Politics and Policy*, edited by James P. Lester, 13–56. Durham, N.C.: Duke University Press.

Chatfield, Charles. 1992. *The American Peace Movement*. New York: Twayne Publishers.

Clemens, Elisabeth S. 1993. "Organizational Repertoires and Institutional Change: Women's Groups and the Transformation of U.S. Politics, 1890–1920." *American Journal of Sociolology* 98: 755–98.

———. 1998. "To Move Mountains: Collective Action and the Possibility of Institutional Change." In *From Contention to Democracy*, edited by Marco Giugni, Doug McAdam, and Charles Tilly, 109–23. Lanham, Md.: Rowman & Littlefield.

Cloward, Richard A., and Frances Fox Piven. 1984. "Disruption and Organization: A Rejoinder." *Theory and Society* 13: 587–99.

Cobb, Roger W., and Charles D. Elder. 1972. *Participation in American Politics*. Baltimore, Md.: Johns Hopkins University Press.

Cohn, Samuel. 1993. *When Strikes Make Sense—and Why*. New York: Plenum Press.

Colby, David. 1975. "The Effects of Riots on Public Policy: Exploratory Note." *International Journal of Group Tensions* 5: 156–62.

———. 1982. "A Test of the Relative Efficacy of Political Tactics." *American Journal of Political Science* 26: 741–53.

Converse, Phillip. 1964. "The Nature of Belief Systems in Mass Publics." In *Ideology and Discontent*, edited by David Apter. New York: Free Press.

Costain, Anne N. 1992. *Inviting Women's Rebellion*. Baltimore, Md.: Johns Hopkins University Press.

Costain, Anne N., and Steven Majstorovic. 1994. "Congress, Social Movements and Public Opinion: Multiple Origins of Women's Rights Legislation." *Political Research Quarterly* 47: 111–35.

Cudry, G. 1988. *Kaiseraugst: Le défi*. Lausanne: Editions d'en Bas.

Dahl, Robert. 1961. *Who Governs?* New Haven, Conn.: Yale University Press.

———. 1967. *Pluralist Democracy in the United States*, Chicago: Rand-McNally.

Danzger, M. Herbert. 1975. "Validating Conflict Data." *American Sociological Review* 40: 570–84.

DeBenedetti, Charles. 1980. *The Peace Reform in American History*. Bloomington: Indiana University Press.

DeBenedetti, Charles, and Charles Chatfield. 1990. *An American Ordeal*. Syracuse, N.Y.: Syracuse University Press.

della Porta, Donatella. 1988. "Recruitment Processes in Clandestine Political Organizations: Italian Left-Wing Terrorism." In *International Social Movement Research*, edited by Bert Klandermans, Hanspeter Kriesi, and Sidney Tarrow, vol. 1, *From Structure to Action*, 155–72. Greenwich, Conn.: JAI Press.

———. 1995. *Social Movements, Political Violence, and the State*. Cambridge: Cambridge University Press.

———. 1996. *Movimenti collettivi e sistema politico in Italia, 1960–1995*. Bari: Laterza.

———. 1999. "Protest, Protesters, and Protest Policing: Public Discourses in Italy and Germany from the 1960s to the 1980s." In *How Social Movements Matter*, edited by Marco Giugni, Doug McAdam, and Charles Tilly, 66–96. Minneapolis: University of Minnesota Press.

della Porta, Donatella, and Dieter Rucht. 1995. "Left-Libertarian Movements in Context: A Comparison of Italy and West Germany, 1965–1990." In *The Politics of Social Protest*, edited by J. Craig Jenkins and Bert Klandermans, 229–73. Minneapolis: University of Minnesota Press.

della Porta, Donatella, and Sidney Tarrow. 1986. "Unwanted Children: Political Violence and the Cycle of Protest in Italy, 1966–1973." *European Journal of Political Research* 14: 607–32.

De Meo, M., and F. Giovannini, eds. 1985. *L'onda verde*. Roma: Alfamedia.

Demerath, N.J., Gerald Marwell, and Michael Aiken. 1971. *Dynamics of Idealism*. San Francisco: Jossey-Bass.

DeNardo, James. 1985. *Power in Numbers. The Political Strategy of Protest and Rebellion*. Princeton, N.J.: Princeton University Press.

Deng, Fang. 1997. "Information Gaps and Unintended Outcomes of Social Movements: The 1989 Chinese Student Movement." *American Journal of Sociology* 102: 1085–112.

Devine, Joel E. 1985. "State and State Expenditure: Determinants of Social Investment and Social Consumption in the Postwar United States." *American Sociological Review* 50: 150–65.

Diani, Mario. 1988. *Isole nell'arcipelago. Il movimento ecologista in Italia*. Bologna: Il Mulino.

———. 1989. "Italy: The 'Liste Verdi'." In *New Politics in Western Europe*, edited by Ferdinand Müller-Rommel, 113–22. Boulder, Colo.: Westview.

———. 1990. "The Italian Ecology Movement: From Radicalism to Moderation." In *Green Politics One*, edited by Wolfgang Rüdig, 153–76. Edinburgh: Edinburgh University Press.

———. 1994. "The Conflict over Nuclear Energy in Italy." In *States and Anti-Nuclear Movements*, edited by Helena Flam, 201–31. Edinburgh: Edinburgh University Press.

———. 1995. *Green Networks*. Edinburgh: Edinburgh University Press.

———. 1997. "Social Movements and Social Capital: A Network Perspective on Movement Outcomes." *Mobilization* 2: 129–47.

Donati, Paolo R. 1995. "Mobilitazione delle risorse e trasformazione organizzativa: Il caso dell'ecologia politica in Italia." *Quaderni di Scienza Politica* 2: 167–99.

Dunlap, Riley E. 1989. "Public Opinion and Environmental Policy." In *Environmental Politics and Policy*, edited by James P. Lester, 87–134. Durham, N.C.: Duke University Press.

———. 1992. "Trends in Public Opinion toward Environmental Issues: 1965–1990." In *American Environmentalism*, edited by Riley E. Dunlap and Angela G. Mertig, 89–116. New York: Taylor and Francis.

Dunlap, Riley E., and Richard P. Gale. 1972. "Politics and Ecology: A Political Profile of Student Eco-activists." *Youth and Society* 3: 379–97.

Dunlap, Riley E., and Angela G. Mertig. 1992. *American Environmentalism*. New York: Taylor and Francis.

Duyvendak, Jan Willem. 1995. *The Power of Politics*. Boulder, Colo.: Westview Press.

Duyvendak, Jan Willem, and Ruud Koopmans. 1995. "The Political Construction of the Nuclear Energy Issue and Its Impact on the Mobilization of the Anti-Nuclear Movements in Western Europe." *Social Problems* 42: 201–18.

Dye, Thomas. 1966. *Politics, Economics, and the Public*. Chicago: Rand McNally.

Ebbin, Steven, and Raphael Kasper. 1974. *Citizen Groups and the Nuclear Power Controversy*. Cambridge, Mass.: MIT Press.

Edelman, Murray. 1964. *The Symbolic Uses of Politics*. Urbana: University of Illinois Press.

———. 1977. *Political Language*. New York: Academic Press.

Eisinger, Peter K. 1973. "The Conditions of Protest Behavior in American Cities." *American Political Science Review* 67: 11–28.

Epple, Rudolf. 1988. *Friedensbewegung und Direkte Demokratie in der Schweiz*. Frankfurt: Haag und Herchen.

Epstein, Barbara. 1991. *Political Protest and Cultural Revolution*. Berkeley: University of California Press.

Epstein, Samuel S., Lester O. Brown, and Carl Pope. 1982. *Hazardous Waste in America*. San Francisco: Sierra Club Books.

Erikson, Robert S., John P. McIver, and Gerald C. Wright Jr. 1993. *Statehouse Democracy*. Cambridge University Press.

Etzioni, Amitai. 1970. *Demonstration Democracy*. New York: Gordon and Breach.

Farro, Antimo. 1991. *La lente verde*. Milano: FrancoAngeli.

Feagin, Joe R., and Harlan Hahn. 1973. *Ghetto Revolts*. New York: Macmillan.

Fendrich, James M. 1974. "Activists Ten Years Later: A Test of Generational Unit Continuity." *Journal of Social Issues* 30: 95–118.

———. 1977. "Keeping the Faith or Pursuing the Good Life: A Study of the Consequences of Participation in the Civil Rights Movement." *American Sociological Review* 42: 144–57.

Fendrich, James M., and E. M. Krauss. 1978. "Student Activism and Adult Left-Wing Politics: A Causal Model of Political Socialization for Black, White and Japanese Students of the 1960s Generation." *Research in Social Movements, Conflict and Change* 1: 231–56.

Fendrich, James M., and Kenneth L. Lovoy. 1988. "Back to the Future: Adult Political Behavior of Former Political Activists." *American Sociological Review* 53: 780–84.

Fendrich, James M., and A. T. Tarleau. 1973. "Marching to a Different Drummer: Occupational and Political Correlates of Former Student Activists." *Social Forces* 52: 245–53.

Fernandez, Roberto M., and Doug McAdam. 1988. "Social Networks and Social Movements: Multiorganizational Fields and Recruitment to Mississippi Freedom Summer." *Sociological Forum* 3: 357–38.

———. 1989. "Multiorganizational Fields and Recruitment to Social Movements." In *Organizing for Change*, edited by Bert Klandermans, 315–44. Greenwich, Conn.: JAI Press.

Fiore, Crescenzo, ed. 1991. *L'arcipelago verde*. Firenze: Vallecchi.

Foley, John W., and Homer R. Steedly. 1980. "*The Strategy of Social Protest:* A Comment on a Growing Industry." *American Journal of Sociology* 85: 1426–28.

Fording, Richard C. 1997. "The Conditional Effect of Violence as a Political Tactic: Mass Insurgency, Welfare Generosity, and Electoral Context in the American States." *American Journal of Political Science* 41: 1–29.

Fowler, Linda L., and Ronald G. Shaiko. 1987. "The Grass Roots Connection: Environmental Activists and Senate Roll Calls." *American Journal of Political Science* 31: 484–510.

Fowlkes, M. R., and P. Y. Miller. 1982. *Love Canal*. Washington, D.C.: Federal Emergency Management Agency.

Franzosi, Roberto. 1987. "The Press as a Source of Socio-Historical Data: Issues in the Methodology of Data Collection from Newspapers." *Historical Methods* 20: 5–16.

———. 1994. *The Puzzle of Strikes*. Cambridge: Cambridge University Press.

Freudenberg, Nicholas. 1984. *Not in Our Backyards!* New York: Monthly Review Press.

Freudenberg, Nicholas, and Carol Steinsapir. 1992. "Not in Our Backyards: The Grassroots Environmental Movement." In *American Environmentalism*, edited by Riley E. Dunlap and Angela G. Mertig, 27–37. New York: Taylor and Francis.

Freudenburg, William, and Eugene A. Rosa, eds. 1984. *Public Reactions to Nuclear Power*. Boulder, Colo.: Westview Press.

Frey, R. Scott, Thomas Dietz, and Linda Kalof. 1992. "Characteristics of Successful American Protest Groups: Another Look at Gamson's *Strategy of Social Protest*." *American Journal of Sociology* 98: 368–87.

Gabriel, Jürg M., and Sandra Hedinger. 1999. "Aussen- und Sicherheitspolitik." In *Handbuch der Schweizer Politik*, edited by Ulrich Klöti, Peter Knoepfel, Hanspeter Kriesi, Wolf Linder, and Yannis Papadopoulos, 693–723. Zurich: NZZ Verlag.

Gamson, William A. 1980. "Understanding the Careers of Challenging Groups: A Commentary on Goldstone." *American Journal of Sociology* 85: 1043–60.

———. 1989. "Reflections on the *Strategy of Social Protest*." *Sociological Forum* 4: 455–67.

———. [1975] 1990. *The Strategy of Social Protest*. 2nd ed. Belmont, Calif.: Wadsworth Publishing.

———. 1992a. "The Social Psychology of Collective Action." In *Frontiers of Social Movement Theory*, edited by Aldon D. Morris and Carol McClurg Mueller, 53–76. New Haven, Conn.: Yale University Press.

———. 1992b. *Talking Politics*. New York: Cambridge University Press.

———. 1998. "Social Movements and Cultural Change." In *From Contention to Democracy*, edited by Marco Giugni, Doug McAdam, and Charles Tilly, 57–77. Lanham, Md.: Rowman & Littlefield.

Gamson, William A., Bruce Fireman, and Steven Rytina. 1982. *Encounters with Unjust Authority*. Homewood, Ill.: Dorsey Press.

Gamson, William A., and Emilie Schmeidler. 1984. "Organizing the Poor." *Theory and Society* 13: 567–85.

Gamson, William A., and Gadi Wolfsfeld. 1993. "Movements and Media as Interacting Systems." *Annals of the American Academy of Political and Social Science*. 528: 114–25.

Garfinkle, A. M. 1984. *The Politics of the Nuclear Freeze.* Philadelphia: Foreign Policy Research Institute.

Gelb, Joyce. 1989. *Feminism and Politics.* Berkeley: University of California Press.

Gelb, Joyce, and Marian Lief Palley. 1987. *Women and Public Policies.* 2nd ed. Princeton, N.J.: Princeton University Press.

Gerhards, Jürgen, and Friedhelm Neidhardt. 1990. "Strukturen und Funktionen moderner Öffentlichkeit: Fragestellung und Ansätze." FS III 90–101. Berlin: Wissenschaftzzentrum für Sozialforschung.

Gibbs, Lois M. 1982. *Love Canal.* Albany: State University of New York Press.

Giugni, Marco. 1994. "The Outcomes of Social Movements: A Review of the Literature." Working Paper 197. Center for Studies of Social Change, New School for Social Research, New York.

———. 1995. *Entre stratégie et opportunité.* Zurich: Seismo.

———. 1998. "Was if Worth the Effort? The Outcomes and Consequences of Social Movements." *Annual Review of Sociology* 24: 371–93.

———. 2001. "L'impact des mouvements écologistes, antinucléaires et pacifistes sur les politiques publiques: Le cas des Etats-Unis, de l'Italie et de la Suisse, 1975–1995." *Revue Française de Sociologie* 42: 641–68.

Giugni, Marco, Doug McAdam, and Charles Tilly, eds. 1999. *How Social Movements Matter.* Minneapolis: University of Minnesota Press.

Giugni, Marco, and Florence Passy. 1997. *Histoires de mobilisation politique en Suisse.* Paris: L'Harmattan.

———. 1998. "Social Movements and Policy Change: Direct, Mediated, or Joint Effect?" *American Sociological Association Section on Collective Behavior and Social Movements.* Working Paper Series. Vol. 1, no. 4.

Goldberg, David Howard. 1990. *Foreign Policy and Ethnic Interest Groups.* Westport, Conn.: Greenwood Press.

Goldstone, Jack A. 1980a. "The Weakness of Organization: A New Look at Gamson's *The Strategy of Social Protest." American Journal of Sociology* 85: 1017–42.

———. 1980b. "Mobilization and Organization: Reply to Foley and Steedly and to Gamson." *American Journal of Sociology* 85: 1428–32.

Gould, Roger V. 1993. "Collective Action and Network Structure." *American Sociological Review* 58: 182–96.

———. 1995. *Insurgent Identities.* Chicago: University of Chicago Press.

Gurr, Ted R. 1970. *Why Men Rebel.* Princeton, N.J.: Princeton University Press.

———. 1980. "On the Outcomes of Violent Conflict." In *Handbook of Political Conflict, Theory and Research,* edited by Ted R. Gurr, 238–94. New York: Free Press.

Gusfield, Joseph R. 1981. *The Culture of Public Problems.* Chicago: University of Chicago Press.

Habermas, Jürgen. 1989. *The Structural Transformation of the Public Sphere.* Cambridge, Mass.: MIT Press.

Hahn, Harlan. 1970. "Civic Responses to Riots: A Reappraisal of Kerner Commission Data." *Public Opinion Quarterly* 34: 101–7.

Halstead, Fred. 1978. *Out Now!* New York: Pathfinder Press.

Hamilton, Richard F. 1972. *Class and Politics in the United States.* New York: Wiley.

Handler, Joel. 1978. *Social Movements and the Legal System.* New York: Academic Press.

Hardin, Russel. 1982. *Collective Action.* Baltimore: Johns Hopkins University Press.

Hartley, Thomas, and Bruce Russett. 1992. "Public Opinion and the Common Defense: Who Governs Military Spending in the United States?" *American Political Science Review* 86: 905–15.

Hays, Samuel P. 1987. *Beauty, Health, and Permanence*. Cambridge: Cambridge University Press.

Hays, Scott P., Michael Esler, and Carol E. Hays. 1996. "Environmental Commitment among the States: Integrating Alternative Approaches to State Environmental Policy." *Publius: The Journal of Federalism* 26: 41–58.

Heineman, Kenneth. J. 1993. *Campus Wars*. New York: New York University Press.

Hibbs, Douglas A. 1987. *The American Political Economy*. Cambridge, Mass.: Harvard University Press.

Hicks, Alexander. 1984. "Elections, Keynes, Bureaucracy, and Class: Explaining U.S. Budget Deficits, 1961–1978." *American Sociological Review* 49: 165–81.

Hicks, Alexander, and Duane H. Swank. 1983. "Civil Disorder, Relief Mobilization, and AFDC Caseloads: A Reexamination of the Piven and Cloward Thesis." *American Journal of Political Science* 27: 695–716.

Hill, Kim Quaile, and Angela Hinton-Andersson. 1995. "Pathways of Representation: A Causal Analysis of Public Opinion-Policy Linkages." *American Journal of Political Science* 39: 924–35.

Hofferbert, Richard. 1974. *The Study of Public Policy*. Indianapolis: Bobbs-Merrill.

Hofferbert, Richard, and Ira Sharkansky. 1971. *State and Urban Politics*. Boston: Little, Brown.

Howlett, Charles F., and Glen Zeitzer. 1985. *The American Peace Movement*. Washington, D.C.: American Historical Association.

Huberts, Leo W. 1989. "The Influence of Social Movements on Government Policy." In *Organizing for Change*, edited by Bert Klandermans, 395–426. Greenwich, Conn.: JAI Press.

Ignagni, Joseph, and James Meernik. 1994. "Explaining Congressional Attempts to Reverse Supreme Court Decisions." *Political Research Quarterly* 47: 353–71.

Ilari, Virgilio. 1994. *Storia militare della prima repubblica, 1943–1993*. Ancona, Italy: Nuove Ricerche.

Isaac, Larry, and William R. Kelly. 1981. "Racial Insurgency, the State, and Welfare Expansion: Local and National Level Evidence from the Postwar United States." *American Journal of Sociology* 86: 1348–86.

Jackson, John E., and David C. King. 1989. "Public Goods, Private Interests, and Representation." *American Political Science Review* 83: 1143–64.

Jacob, Herbert, and Kenneth Vines. 1971. *Politics in the American States*. Boston: Little, Brown.

Jacobs, Lawrence R. 1993. *The Health of Nations*. Ithaca, N.Y.: Cornell University Press.

Jänicke, Martin, and Helmut Weidner, eds. 1997. *National Environmental Policies*. Berlin: Springer.

Janoski, Thomas, and Larry W. Isaac. 1994. "Introduction to Time-Series Analysis." In *The Comparative Political Economy of the Welfare State*, edited by Thomas Janoski and Alexander M. Hicks, 31–53. Cambridge: Cambridge University Press.

Jasper, James M. 1990. *Nuclear Politics*. Princeton, N.J.: Princeton University Press.

Jasper, James M., and Jane Poulsen. 1993. "Fighting Back: Vulnerabilities, Blunders, and Countermobilization by the Targets in Three Animal Rights Campaigns." *Sociological Forum* 8: 639–57.

Jencks, Christopher. 1985. "Methodological Problems in Studying 'Military Keynesianism'." *American Journal of Sociology* 91: 373–79.

Jenkins J. Craig. 1981. "Sociopolitical Movements." In *The Handbook of Political Behavior*, vol. 4, edited by S. L. Long, 81–153. New York: Plenum Press.

Jenkins, J. Craig, and Barbara Brents. 1989. "Social Protest, Hegemonic Competition, and Social Reform: A Political Struggle Interpretation of the Origins of the American Welfare State." *American Sociological Review* 54: 891–909.

Jenkins, J. Craig, and Charles Perrow. 1977. "The Insurgency of the Powerless: Farm Workers' Movements (1946–1972)." *American Sociological Review* 42: 249–68.

Jennings, Edward T. 1979. "Civil Turmoil and the Growth of Welfare Rolls: A Comparative State Policy Analysis." *Policy Studies Journal* 7: 739–45.

———. 1980. "Urban Riots and Welfare Policy Change: A Test of the Piven-Cloward Theory." In *Why Policies Succeed or Fail*, edited by Helen M. Ingram and Dean E. Mann, 59–82. Beverly Hills, Calif.: Sage.

———. 1983. "Racial Insurgency, the State, and Welfare Expansion: A Critical Comment and Reanalysis." *American Journal of Sociology* 88: 1220–36.

Jennings, M. Kent. 1987. "Residues of a Movement: The Aging of the American Protest Generation." *American Political Science Review* 81: 367–82.

Jennings, M. Kent, and Richard G. Niemi. 1981. *Generations and Politics*. Princeton, N.J.: Princeton University Press.

Johnston, Hank, and Bert Klandermans, eds. 1995. *Social Movements and Culture*. Minneapolis: University of Minnesota Press.

Jones, Bryan. 1994. *Reconceiving Decision-Making in Democratic Politics*. Chicago: University of Chicago Press.

Joppke, Christian. 1993. *Mobilizing against Nuclear Energy*. Berkeley: University of California Press.

Katz, Milton S. 1986. *A History of SANE, 1957–1985*. New York: Greenwood Press.

Kelly, William R., and David Snyder. 1980. "Racial Violence and Socioeconomic Changes among Blacks in the United States." *Social Forces* 58: 739–60.

Kerbo, Harold R., and Richard A. Shaffer. 1992. "Lower Class Insurgency and the Political Process: The Response of the U.S. Unemployed, 1890–1940." *Social Problems* 39: 139–54.

Kim, Hyojoung, and Peter S. Bearman. 1997. "The Structure and Dynamics of Movement Participation." *American Sociological Review* 62: 70–93.

Kitschelt, Herbert. 1986. "Political Opportunity Structures and Political Protest: Anti-Nuclear Movements in Four Democracies." *British Journal of Political Science* 16: 57–85.

Klandermans, Bert. 1997. *The Social Psychology of Protest*. Oxford: Blackwell.

Kleidman, Robert. 1993. *Organizing for Peace*. Syracuse, N.Y.: Syracuse University Press.

Kline, Benjamin. 2000. *First along the River*. 2nd ed. San Francisco: Acada Books.

Knoepfel, Peter. 1990. "A Survey on Current Environmental Law in Switzerland." *Cahiers de l'IDHEAP* 65. Institut de Hautes Etudes en Administration Publique, Lausanne.

Koopmans, Ruud. 1993. "The Dynamics of Protest Waves: West Germany, 1965 to 1989." *American Sociological Review* 58: 637–58.

———. 1995. *Democracy from Below*. Boulder, Colo.: Westview Press.

———. 1998. "The Use of Protest Event Data in Comparative Research: Cross-National Comparability, Sampling Methods and Robustness." In *Acts of Dissent*, edited by Dieter Rucht, Ruud Koopmans, and Friedhelm Neidhardt, 90–110. Berlin: Sigma.

Kornhauser, William. 1959. *The Politics of Mass Society*. New York: Free Press.

Kowalewski, David, and Paul D. Schumaker. 1981. "Protest Outcomes in the Soviet Union." *Sociological Quarterly* 22: 57–68.

Kraft, Michael E., and Norman J. Vig. 1994. "Environmental Policy from the 1970s: Continuity and Change." In *Environmental Policy in the 1990s*, 2nd ed., edited by Norman J. Vig and Michael E. Kraft, 3–29. Washington, D.C.: CQ Press.

Krehbiel, Keith. 1991. *Information and Legislative Organization*. Ann Arbor: University of Michigan Press.

Kriesi, Hanspeter. 1982. *AKW-Gegner in der Schweiz*. Diessenhofen: Rüegger.

———. 1988. "The Interdependence of Structure and Action: Some Reflections on the State of the Art." In *International Social Movement Research*, edited by Bert Klandermans, Hanspeter Kriesi, and Sidney Tarrow, vol. 1, *From Structure to Action*, 349–68. Greenwich, Conn.: JAI Press.

———. 1989. "New Social Movements and the New Class in the Netherlands." *American Journal of Sociology* 94: 1078–116.

———. 1993. *Political Mobilization and Social Change*. Aldershot, U.K.: Avebury.

———. 1995a. "The Political Opportunity Structure of New Social Movements: Its Impact on Their Mobilization." In *The Politics of Social Protest*, edited by J. Craig Jenkins and Bert Klandermans, 167–98. Minneapolis: University of Minnesota Press.

———. 1995b. *Le système politique suisse*. Paris: Economica.

Kriesi, Hanspeter, Ruud Koopmans, Jan Willem Duyvendak, and Marco G. Giugni. 1992. "New Social Movements and Political Opportunities in Western Europe." *European Journal of Political Research* 22: 219–44.

———. 1995. *New Social Movements in Western Europe*. Minneapolis: University of Minnesota Press.

Kriesi, Hanspeter, René Levy, Gilbert Ganguillet, and Heinz Zwicky, eds. 1981. *Politische Aktivierung in der Schweiz, 1945–1978*. Diessenhofen: Rüegger.

Kriesi, Hanspeter, and Dominique Wisler. 1999. "The Impact of Social Movements on Political Institutions: A Comparison of the Introduction of Direct Legislation in Switzerland and the United States." In *How Social Movements Matter*, edited by Marco Giugni, Doug McAdam, and Charles Tilly, 42–65. Minneapolis: University of Minnesota Press.

Ladner, Andreas. 1989. "Switzerland: The 'Green' and 'Alternative Parties'." In *New Politics in Western Europe*, edited by Ferdinand Müller-Rommel, 155–65. Boulder, Colo.: Westview.

Lawson, Steven F. 1976. *Black Ballots*. New York: Columbia University Press.

Lazarsfeld, Paul F., Bernard Berelson, and Hazel Gaudet. 1944. *The People's Choice*. New York: Columbia University Press.

Levine, Adeline G. 1982. *Love Canal*. Lexington, Mass.: Lexington Books.

Levitan, Sar A., William B. Johnston, and Robert Taggart. 1975. *Still a Dream*. Cambridge, Mass.: Harvard University Press.

Lewanski, Rodolfo. 1990. "La politica ambientale." In *Le politiche pubbliche in Italia*, edited by Bruno Dente, 281–314. Bologna: Il Mulino.

Lippmann, Walter. 1922. *Public Opinion*. New York: Macmillan.

Lipsky, Michael. 1968. "Protest as a Political Resource." *American Political Science Review* 62: 1144–58.

———. 1970. *Protest in City Politics*. Chicago: Rand McNally.

Lipsky, Michael, and Margaret Levi. 1972. "Community Organization as a Political Resource." In *People and Politics in Urban Society*, edited by Harlan Hahn. Beverly Hills, Calif.: Sage.

Lipsky, Michael, and David J. Olson. 1977. *Commission Politics*. New Brunswick, N.J.: Transaction Books.

Lodi, Giovanni. 1984. *Uniti e diversi*. Milano: Unicopli.

Lofland, John. 1993. *Polite Protesters*. Syracuse, N.Y.: Syracuse University Press.

Lohmann, Susanne. 1993. "A Signaling Model of Informative and Manipulative Political Action." *American Political Science Review* 87: 319–33.

Lowi, Theodor J. 1969. *The End of Liberalism*. New York: Norton.

———. 1971. *The Politics of Disorder*. New York: Basic Books.

MacDougall, John, Stephen D. Minicucci, and Doug Myers. 1995. "The House of Representatives' Vote on the Gulf War, 1991: Measuring Peace Movement Impact." *Research in Social Movements, Conflict and Change* 18: 255–84.

Marwell, Gerald, Michael Aiken, and N. J. Demerath. 1987. "The Persistence of Political Attitudes among 1960s Civil Rights Activists." *Public Opinion Quarterly* 51: 359–75.

Marx, Gary T., and James L. Wood. 1975. "Strands of Theory and Research in Collective Behavior." *Annual Review of Sociology* 1: 363–428.

Marx Ferree, Myra, William A. Gamson, Jürgen Gerhards, and Dieter Rucht. 2002. "Four Models of the Public Sphere in Modern Democracies." *Theory and Society* 31: 289–324.

Mazmanian, Daniel, and David Morell. 1992. *Beyond Superfailure*. Boulder, Colo.: Westview.

McAdam, Doug. 1982. *Political Process and the Development of Black Insurgency, 1930–1970*. Chicago: University of Chicago Press.

———. 1983. "Tactical Innovation and the Pace of Insurgency." *American Sociological Review* 48: 735–54.

———. 1986. "Recruitment to High-Risk Activism: The Case of Freedom Summer." *American Journal of Sociology* 92: 64–90.

———. 1988a. *Freedom Summer*. Oxford: Oxford University Press.

———. 1988b. "Micromobilization Contexts and Recruitment to Activism." *International Social Movement Research* 1: 125–54.

———. 1989. "The Biographical Consequences of Activism." *American Sociological Review* 54: 744–60.

———. 1995a. "'Initiator' and 'Spin-off' Movements: Diffusion Processes in Protest Cycles." In *Repertoires and Cycles of Collective Action*, edited by Marc Traugott, 217–39. Durham, N.C.: Duke University Press.

———. 1995b. "Revisiting the 'Insurgency Project': Events Research and Contemporary Movement Theory." Workshop on "Protest Event Analysis: Methodology, Applications, Problems." Berlin (Germany), June 12–14.

———. 1996. "Conceptual Origins, Current Problems, Future Directions." In *Comparative Perspectives on Social Movements*, edited by Doug McAdam, John D. McCarthy, and Mayer N. Zald, 23–40. Cambridge: Cambridge University Press.

———. 1999. "The Biographical Impact of Activism." In *How Social Movements Matter*, edited by Marco Giugni, Doug McAdam, and Charles Tilly, 117–49. Minneapolis: University of Minnesota Press.

McAdam, Doug, John D. McCarthy, and Mayer N. Zald. 1988. "Social Movements." In *Handbook of Sociology*, edited by Neil J. Smelser, 695–737. Beverly Hills, Calif.: Sage.

———, eds. 1996. *Comparative Perspectives on Social Movements*. Cambridge: Cambridge University Press.

McAdam, Doug, and Ronnelle Paulsen. 1993. "Specifying the Relationship between Social Ties and Activism." *American Journal of Sociology* 98: 735–54.

McAdam, Doug, and Dieter Rucht. 1993. "The Cross-National Diffusion of Movement Ideas." *Annals of the American Academy of Political and Social Science* 528: 56–74.

McAdam, Doug, Sidney Tarrow, and Charles Tilly. 2001. *Dynamics of Contention*. Cambridge: Cambridge University Press.

McCarthy, John D., Clark McPhail, and Jackie Smith. 1996. "Images of Protest: Dimensions of Selection Bias in Media Coverage of Washington Demonstrations, 1982, 1991." *American Sociological Review* 61: 478–99.

McCarthy, John D., and Mark Wolfson. 1992. "Consensus Movements, Conflict Movements, and the Cooptation of Civic and State Infrastructures." In *Frontiers in Social Movement Theory*, edited by Aldon D. Morris and Carol McClurg Mueller, 273–98. New Haven, Conn.: Yale University Press.

McCarthy, John D., and Mayer N. Zald. 1977. "Resource Mobilization and Social Movements: A Partial Theory." *American Journal of Sociology* 82: 1212–41.

McCrae, Frances B., and Gerald E. Markle. 1989. *Minutes to Midnight*. Newbury Park, Calif.: Sage.

Melucci, Alberto. 1989. *Nomads of the Present*. Philadelphia: Temple University Press.

———. 1996. *Challenging Codes*. Cambridge: Cambridge University Press.

Metz, Steven. 1986. "The Anti-Apartheid Movement and Populist Instinct in American Politics." *Political Science Quarterly* 101: 379–95.

Meyer, David S. 1990. A *Winter of Discontent*. New York: Praeger.

———. 1993. "Political Process and Protest Movement Cycles: American Peace Movements in the Nuclear Age." *Political Research Quarterly* 46: 451–79.

———. 1999. "How the Cold War Was Really Won: The Effects of the Antinuclear Movements of the 1980s." In *How Social Movements Matter*, edited by Marco Giugni, Doug McAdam, and Charles Tilly, 182–203. Minneapolis: University of Minnesota Press.

Meyer, David S., and Nancy Whittier. 1994. "Social Movement Spillover." *Social Problems* 41: 277–98.

Meyer, Philip, and Michael Maidenberg. 1970. "The Berkeley Rebels Five Years Later: Has Age Mellowed the Pioneer Radicals?" *Public Opinion Quarterly* 24: 477–78.

Midttun, Atle, and Dieter Rucht. 1994. "Comparing Policy Outcomes of Conflicts over Nuclear Power: Description and Explanation." In *States and Anti-Nuclear Movements*, edited by Helena Flam, 383–415. Edinburgh: Edinburgh University Press.

Milbrath, Lester. 1970. "The Impact of Lobbying on Governmental Decisions." In *Policy Analysis in Political Science*, edited by Ira Sharkansky, 360–81. Chicago: Markham Publishing Company.

Minsch, J., A. Eberle, B. Meier, and U. Schneidewind. 1996. *Mut zum Umbau*. Basel, Switzerland: Birkhäuser.

Mirowsky, John, and Catherine Ross. 1981. "Protest Group Success: The Impact of Group Characteristics, Social Control, and Context." *Sociological Focus* 14: 177–92.

Moore, Kelly. 1999. "Political Protest and Institutional Change: The Anti-Vietnam War Movement and American Science." In *How Social Movements Matter*, edited by Marco Giugni, Doug McAdam, and Charles Tilly, 97–115. Minneapolis: University of Minnesota Press.

Mueller, Carol McClurg. 1978. "Riot Violence and Protest Outcomes." *Journal of Political and Military Sociology* 6: 49–63.

———. 1997. "International Press Coverage of East German Protest Events, 1989." *American Sociological Review* 62: 820–32.

Myers, Daniel J. 1997. "Racial Rioting in the 1960s: An Event History Analysis of Local Conditions." *American Sociological Review* 62: 94–112.

Nelkin, Dorothy. 1971. *Nuclear Power and Its Critics*. Ithaca, N.Y.: Cornell University Press.

Nichols, Elisabeth. 1987. "U.S. Nuclear Power and the Success of the American Anti-Nuclear Movement." *Berkeley Journal of Sociology* 32: 167–92.

Oberschall, Anthony. 1973. *Social Conflict and Social Movements*. Englewood Cliffs, N.J.: Prentice-Hall.

———. 1996. "Opportunities and Framing in the Eastern European Revolts of 1989." In *Comparative Perspectives on Social Movements*, edited by Doug McAdam, John D. McCarthy, and Mayer N. Zald, 93–121. Cambridge: Cambridge University Press.

O'Keefe, M., and P. D. Schumaker. 1983. "Protest Effectiveness in Southeast Asia." *American Behavioral Scientist* 26: 375–94.

Oliver, Pamela E., and Gregory M. Maney. 2000. "Political Processes and Local Newspaper Coverage of Protest Events: From Selection Bias to Triadic Interactions." *American Journal of Sociology* 106: 463–505.

Oliver, Pamela E., and Daniel J. Myers. 1999. "How Events Enter the Public Sphere: Conflict, Location and Sponsorship in Local Newspaper Coverage of Public Events." *American Journal of Sociology* 105: 38–87.

Olson, Mancur. 1965. *The Logic of Collective Action*. Harvard, Mass.: Harvard University Press.

Olzak, Susan. 1989. "Analysis of Events in the Study of Collective Action." *Annual Review of Sociology* 15: 119–41.

———. 1992. *The Dynamics of Ethnic Competition and Conflict*. Stanford, Calif.: Stanford University Press.

Opp, Karl-Dieter. 1989. *The Rationality of Political Protest*. Boulder, Colo.: Westview Press.

Orfield, Gary. 1975. *Congressional Power*. New York: Harcourt Brace Jovanovich.

Page, Benjamin I., and Robert Y. Shapiro. 1983. "Effects of Public Opinion on Policy." *American Political Science Review* 77: 175–90.

———. 1992. *The Rational Public*. Chicago: University of Chicago Press.

———. 1993. "The Rational Public and Democracy." In *Reconsidering the Democratic Public*, edited by George E. Marcus and Russell L. Hanson, 35–64. University Park, Pa.: Pennsylvania State University Press.

Parenti, Michael. 1970. "Power and Pluralism: A View from the Bottom." *Journal of Politics* 32: 501–30.

Peace, Roger C. 1991. *A Just and Lasting Peace*. Chicago: Noble Press.

Perrot, Michelle. 1987. *Workers on Strike*. Leamington Spa, U.K.: Berg.

Peterson, Paul E. 1994. "The President's Dominance in Foreign Policy Making." *Political Science Quarterly* 109: 215–34.

Piven, Frances Fox, and Richard A. Cloward. 1979. *Poor People's Movements*. New York: Vintage Books.

———. 1993. *Regulating the Poor*. 2nd ed. New York: Vintage Books.

Polletta, Francesca. 1997. "Culture and Its Discontents: Recent Theorizing on Culture and Protest." *Sociological Inquiry* 67: 431–50.

Polletta, Francesca, and James M. Jasper. 2001. "Collective Identity and Social Movements." *Annual Review of Sociology* 27: 283–305.

Price, Jerome. 1990. *The Antinuclear Movement*. Revised ed. Boston: Twayne Publishers.

Raschke, Joachim. 1985. *Soziale Bewegungen*. Frankfurt: Campus.

Ringquist, Evan J., Kim Quaile Hill, Jan E. Leighley, and Angela Hinton-Andersson. 1997. "Lower-Class Mobilization and Policy Linkage in the U.S. States: A Correction." *American Journal of Political Science* 41: 339–44.

Rochon, Thomas R. 1988. *Mobilizing for Peace*. Princeton, N.J.: Princeton University Press.

Rochon, Thomas R., and Daniel A. Mazmanian. 1993. "Social Movements and the Policy Process." *Annals of the American Academy of Political and Social Science* 528: 75–87.

Rolph, Elizabeth S. 1979. *Nuclear Power and the Public Safety*. Lexington, Mass.: Lexington Books.

Rosa, Eugene A., and Riley E. Dunlap. 1994. "Nuclear Power: Three Decades of Public Opinion." *Public Opinion Quarterly* 58: 295–325.

Rosenbaum, Walter A. 1995. *Environmental Politics and Policy*. 3rd ed. Washington, D.C.: CQ Press.

Rosenthal, Naomi, Meryl Fingrutd, Michele Ethier, Roberta Karant, and David McDonald. 1985. "Social Movements and Network Analysis: A Case Study of Nineteenth Century Women's Reform in New York State." *American Journal of Sociology* 90: 1022–55.

Rucht, Dieter. 1989. "Environmental Movement Organizations in West Germany and France: Structure and Interorganizational Relations." In *Organizing for Change*, edited by Bert Klandermans, 61–94. Greenwich, Conn.: JAI Press.

———. 1992. "Studying the Effects of Social Movements: Conceptualization and Problems." Paper for the ECPR Joint Session. Limerick (Ireland), March 30–April 4.

———. 1994. *Modernisierung und neue soziale Bewegungen*. Frankfurt: Campus.

Rucht, Dieter, Ruud Koopmans, and Friedhelm Neidhart, eds. 1998. *Acts of Dissent*. Berlin: Sigma.

Rucht, Dieter, and Thomas Ohlemacher. 1992. "Protest Event Data: Collection, Uses and Perspectives." In *Studying Collective Action*, edited by Ron Eyerman and Mario Diani, 76–106. Beverly Hills, Calif.: Sage.

Rüdig, Wolfgang. 1990. *Anti-Nuclear Movements*. Harlow, U.K.: Longman.

Ruzza, Carlo. 1997. "Institutional Actors and the Italian Peace Movement: Specializing and Branching Out." *Theory and Society* 26: 87–127.

Sabatier, Paul. 1975. "Social Movements and Regulatory Agencies." *Policy Sciences* 6: 301–42.

Sale, Kirkpatrick. 1973. *SDS*. New York: Random House.

———. 1993. *The Green Revolution*. New York: Hill and Wang.

Sandler, Todd. 1992. *Collective Action*. Ann Arbor: University of Michigan Press.

Schattschneider, Elmer E. 1960. *The Semi-Sovereign People*. New York: Holt, Rinehart and Winston.

Schramm, Sanford F., and J. Patrick Turbott. 1983. "Civil Disorder and the Welfare Explosion: A Two-Step Process." *American Sociological Review* 48: 408–14.

Schroeren, M. 1977. *Zum Beispiel Kaiseraugst*. Zurich: Schweizerischer Friedensrat.

Schumaker, Paul D. 1975. "Policy Responsiveness to Protest-Group Demands." *Journal of Politics* 37: 488–521.

———. 1978. "The Scope of Political Conflict and the Effectiveness of Constraints in Contemporary Urban Protest." *Sociological Quarterly* 19: 168–84.

Sears, David O., and John B. McConahay. 1973. *The Politics of Violence*. Boston: Houghton Mifflin.

Shabecoff, Philip. 1993. *A Fierce Green Fire*. New York: Hill and Wang.

Sharp, Elaine B., and Steven Maynard-Moody. 1991. "Theories of the Local Welfare Role." *American Journal of Political Science* 35: 934–50.

Sheatsley, Paul B. 2000. "Public Opinion." In *The American Presidency*. Grolier Multimedia Encyclopedia. At http://gi.grolier.com/presidents/ea/side/pubop.html.

Shorter, Edward, and Charles Tilly. 1971. "Le déclin de la grève violente en France de 1890 à 1935." *Le Mouvement Social* 79: 95–118.

———. 1974. *Strikes in France, 1830–1968*. London: Cambridge University Press.

Skocpol, Theda, and Margaret Somers. 1980. "The Uses of Comparative History in Macrosocial Inquiry." *Comparative Studies in Society and History* 22: 174–197.

Small, Melvin. 1988. *Johnson, Nixon, and the Doves*. New Brunswick, N.J.: Rutgers University Press.

Smelser, Neil J. 1962. *Theory of Collective Behavior*. New York: Free Press.

Smith, Christian. 1996. *Resisting Reagan*. Chicago: University of Chicago Press.

Snow, David A., and Robert D. Benford. 1992. "Master Frames and Cycles of Protest." In *Frontiers of Social Movement Theory*, edited by Aldon D. Morris and Carol McClurg Mueller, 133–55. New Haven, Conn.: Yale University Press.

Snow, David A., E. Burke Rochford Jr., Steven K. Worden, and Robert D. Benford. 1986. "Frame Alignment Processes, Micromobilization, and Movement Participation." *American Sociological Review* 51: 464–81.

Snow, David A., Louis A. Zurcher, and Sheldon Ekland-Olson. 1980. "Social Networks and Social Movements: A Microstructural Approach to Differential Recruitment." *American Sociological Review* 45: 787–801.

Snyder, David, and William R. Kelly. 1976. "Industrial Violence in Italy, 1878–1903." *American Journal of Sociology* 82: 131–62.

———. 1977. "Conflict Intensity, Media Sensitivity and the Validity of Newspaper Data." *American Sociological Review* 42: 105–23.

———. 1979. "Strategies for Investigating Violence and Social Change: Illustrations from Analyses of Racial Disorders and Implications for Mobilization Research." In *The Dynamics of Social Movements*, edited by Mayer N. Zald and John D. McCarthy, 212–37. Cambridge, Mass.: Winthrop.

Solo, Pam. 1988. *From Protest to Policy*. Cambridge, Mass.: Ballinger.

Staggenborg, Susan. 1988. "The Consequences of Professionalization and Formalization in the Pro-Choice Movement." *American Sociological Review* 53: 585–605.

Stanley, Harold W., and Richard G. Niemi. 1995. *Vital Statistics on American Politics*. 5th ed. Washington, D.C.: CQ Press.

Steedly, Homer R., and John W. Foley. 1979. "The Success of Protest Groups: Multivariate Analyses." *Social Science Research* 8: 1–15.

Stever, Donald W. 1980. *Seabrook and the Nuclear Regulatory Commission*. Hanover, N.H.: University Press of New England.

Stimson, James A. 1991. *Public Opinion in America*. Boulder, Colo.: Westview.

Stimson, James A., Michael B. MacKuen, and Robert S. Erikson. 1995. "Dynamic Representation." *American Political Science Review* 89: 543–65.

Strang, David. 1994. "Introduction to Event History Methods." In *The Comparative Political Economy of the Welfare State*, edited by Thomas Janoski and Alexander Hicks, 245–53. Cambridge: Cambridge University Press.

Strang, David, and Sarah A. Soule. 1998. "Diffusion in Organizations and Social Movements: From Hybrid Corn to Poison Pills." *Annual Review of Sociology* 24: 265–90.

Szasz, Andrew. 1994. *EcoPopulism*. Minneapolis: University of Minnesota Press.

Taft, Philip, and Philip Ross. 1969. "American Labor Violence: Its Causes, Character, and Outcome." In *Violence in America*, edited by Hugh D. Graham and Ted R. Gurr, 281–395. New York: Bantam Books.

Tanner, Jakob. 1986. *The Contentious French*. Cambridge, Mass.: Harvard University Press.

———. 1988. "Le pacifisme Suisse après 1945." *Relations Internationales* 53: 69–82.

———. 1989. *Democracy and Disorder*. Oxford: Clarendon Press.

———. 1993. "Social Protest and Policy Reform: May 1968 and the *Loi d'Orientation* in France." *Comparative Political Studies* 25: 579–607.

———. 1996. "Social Movements in Contentious Politics: A Review Article." *American Political Science Review* 90: 874–83.

———. 1998. *Power in Movement*. 2nd ed. Cambridge: Cambridge University Press.

Tarrow, Sidney. 1989. *Democracy and Disorder: Protest and Politics in Italy, 1965–1975*. Oxford: Clarendon Press.

———. 1993. "Social Protest and Policy Reform: May 1968 and the Loi d'Orientation in France." *Comparative Political Studies* 25: 579–607.

———. 1996. "Social Movements in Contentious Politics: A Review Article." *American Political Science Review* 90: 874–83.

———. 1998. *Power in Movement: Social Movements and Contentious Politics*. 2nd ed. Cambridge: Cambridge University Press.

Tilly, Charles. 1978. *From Mobilization to Revolution*. Reading, Mass.: Addison-Wesley.

———. 1984. "Social Movements and National Politics." In *Statemaking and Social Movements*, edited by Charles Bright and Susan Harding, 297–317. Ann Arbor: University of Michigan Press.

———. 1986. *The Contentious French*. Cambridge, Mass.: Harvard University Press.

———. 1994. "Social Movements as Historically Specific Clusters of Political Performances." *Berkeley Journal of Sociology* 38: 1–30.

———. 1995. *Popular Contention in Great Britain, 1758–1834*. Cambridge, Mass.: Harvard University Press.

———. 1996. "Invisible Elbow." *Sociological Forum* 11: 589–601.

———. 1999. "From Interactions to Outcomes in Social Movements." In *How Social Movements Matter*, edited by Marco Giugni, Doug McAdam, and Charles Tilly, 253–70. Minneapolis: University of Minnesota Press.

Tilly, Charles, Louise Tilly, and Richard Tilly. 1975. *The Rebellious Century, 1830–1930*. Cambridge, Mass.: Harvard University Press.

Tomain, Joseph P. 1987. *Nuclear Power Transformation*. Bloomington: Indiana University Press.

Touraine, Alain. 1978. *La voix et le regard*. Paris: Seuil.

———. 1984. *Le retour de l'acteur*. Paris: Fayard.

Trattner, Walter I., ed. 1983. *Social Welfare or Social Control*. Knoxville: University of Tennessee Press.

Turk, Herman, and Lynne G. Zucker. 1984. "Majority and Organized Opposition: On Effects of Social Movements." *Research in Social Movements, Conflict and Change* 7: 249–69.

Turner, Ralph H., and Lewis M. Killian. 1957. *Collective Behavior*. Englewood Cliffs, N.J.: Prentice-Hall.

Valocchi, Steve. 1990. "The Unemployed Workers Movement of the 1930s: A Reexamination of the Piven and Cloward Thesis." *Social Problems* 37: 191–205.

Waller, Douglas C. 1987. *Congress and the Nuclear Freeze*. Amherst: University of Massachusetts Press.

Walsh, Edward J. 1988. *Democracy in the Shadows*. New York: Greenwood Press.

Wälti, Sonia. 1993. "Neue Problemlösungsstrategien in der nuklearen Entsorgung." *Schweizerisches Jahrbuch für Politische Wissenschaft* 33: 205–24.

———. 1995. "Dealing with Centralized Implementation in Federal Systems: The Example of Nuclear Waste Disposal in Switzerland." Paper for the Annual Meeting of the American Political Science Association. Chicago, August 31–September 3.

Webb, Keith, Ekkart Zimmermann, Michael Marsh, Anne-Marie Aish, Christina Mironesco, Christopher Mitchell, Leonardo Morlino, and James Walston. 1983. "Etiology and Outcomes of Protest: New European Perspectives." *American Behavioral Scientist* 26: 311–31.

Weissberg, Robert. 1976. *Public Opinion and American Democracy*. Englewood Cliffs, N.J.: Prentice-Hall.

Welch, Susan. 1975. "The Impact of Urban Riots on Urban Expenditures." *American Journal of Political Science* 29: 741–60.

Wetstein, Matthew E. 1996. *Abortion Rates in the United States*. Albany: State University of New York Press.

Whalen, Jack, and Richard Flacks. 1980. "The Isla Vista 'Bank Burners' Ten Years Later: Notes on the Fate of Student Activists." *Sociological Focus* 13: 215–36.

Wittner, Lawrence S. 1984. *Rebels against War*. Philadelphia: Temple University Press.

Yandle, Bruce. 1989. *The Political Limits of Environmental Regulation*. New York: Quorum Books.

Zald, Mayer N., and Roberta Ash. 1966. "Social Movement Organizations: Growth, Decay and Change." *Social Forces* 44: 327–41.

Zald, Mayer N., and John D. McCarthy, eds. 1979. *The Dynamics of Social Movements*. Cambridge, Mass.: Winthrop Publishers.

———. 1987. *Social Movements in an Organizational Society*. New Brunswick, N.J.: Transaction Books.

Zaller, John. 1992. *The Nature and Origins of Mass Opinion*. Cambridge: Cambridge University Press.

Zaller, John, and Stanley Feldman. 1992. "A Simple Theory of Survey Response: Answering Questions versus Revealing Preferences." *American Journal of Political Science* 36: 579–616.

Zelditch, M. 1978. "Review Essay: Outsiders' Politics." *American Journal of Sociology* 83: 1514–20.

Zwicky, Heinrich. 1993. "Umweltaktivierung in den 80-er Jahren." *Schweizerisches Jahrbuch für Politische Wissenschaft* 33: 185–204.

Index

About the Author

Marco Giugni is a researcher and a teacher at the Department of Political Science at the University of Geneva. His work has dealt with social movements and political opportunity structures, with a particular focus on the consequences of protest activities. Publications include several authored or edited books on social movements, including *New Social Movements in Western Europe* (1995), *Histoires de mobilisation politique en Suisse* (1997), *From Contention to Democracy* (1998), *How Social Movements Matter* (1999), *Political Altruism?* (2001), and *Sphères d'exclusion* (2003), as well as articles in major French-, English-, and Italian-language journals. His current research focuses on political claims making in the fields of immigration, unemployment, and social exclusion.